THE MODERN WORLD:
1848 TO THE PRESENT

IDEAS AND INSTITUTIONS IN WESTERN CIVILIZATION

Norman F. Cantor, *General Editor*

The Modern World:

1848 TO THE PRESENT

Edited by

HANS KOHN
College of the City of New York

The Macmillan Company, New York
Collier-Macmillan Ltd., London

Second Printing, 1963

Library of Congress catalog card number: 63–8431

The Macmillan Company, New York
Collier-Macmillan Canada, Ltd., Galt, Ontario
Divisions of The Crowell-Collier Publishing Company

Printed in the United States of America

Design by R. A. Kaseler

PREFACE:

History is a multicausal complex process in which many factors, often accidents, play decisive roles. History involves most diversified, yet often connected, aspects of change in the political and social institutions, in the technology of production and the economic order, and in the moral and intellectual climate. The present selection of readings deals with the latter category of changes as they influenced the most recent period of European history, from 1848 to the present day.

History is, of course, not determined only by the trend of ideas through the centuries, nor does it express itself mainly in that trend. Yet religion has profoundly influenced human attitudes throughout most of recorded history, as have the various manifestations of civilization, letters, and art in all higher forms of culture. Since 1848 the thoughts of Marx, an economist, of Darwin, a natural scientist, and of Freud, a psychologist, have powerfully shaped man's understanding of history and life—and thereby shaped history itself.

The reasons why ideas have assumed a greater role in contemporary history may be found in general education and literacy—a phenomenon unique to contemporary civilization—in improved means of communication, in the unprecedented geographic, social, and intellectual mobility of the people, in their sense of active participation in historical decisions, and in their easier abandonment of age-old traditions and ways of life. In such revolutionary periods an understanding of the intellectual and moral climate of a period gains in importance. Europe, after 1848, after 1918, and after 1945, had little in common with the quiet, rural Europe of 1815 with its great distances and its conservative social hierarchy, which did not differ substantially from those of the Middle Ages.

In 1848 four great trends began to determine European history: nationalism, socialism, secularism, and a faith in science. In March, 1848, nationalism swept and shook the whole of Central Europe; in June of the same year the Parisian workers fought, for the first time, a republican government—which itself had grown out of a revolutionary attempt to overthrow the ancient regime—in a bitter battle for socialism; the widely read and discussed books of Feuerbach, Comte, Darwin, and Huxley laid the groundwork for the shift from a theological to a humanist and scientific world outlook. Ernest Renan's book *L'Avenir de la science* ("The Future of Science"), which the former student for the Catholic priesthood wrote in 1848, but which was not published until 1890, bore witness to this shift. There Renan declared, "It is here on earth, not in a fantastic heaven, that the life of the spirit will be realized." Science gave man new hope and confidence. "Man," Renan wrote, "has ceased to regard evil as ordained by fate." A decade after the publication of the book, discoveries in physics and biology, in which creative imagination and systematic experiment played equal roles, began to reveal secrets of the universe and of life. The new industrial revolution which followed surpassed by far the old one. Unlike the old one, it was no longer confined to a few North Atlantic countries. Like nationalism, socialism, and secularism, the new scientific and technological revolution has become world-wide.

There are no unilinear developments in history. The complexities and profound differentiations in the intellectual and moral trends of any age must not be underrated. Old habits and traditions survive everywhere. It is impossible to reflect the variety and contradictory multiplicity of cultural trends in one handy volume. Nevertheless, it is hoped that, with the necessary reservations, the student might find here some of the most significant trends of contemporary Europe in the words of some of their representative thinkers.

ACKNOWLEDGMENTS: The editor wishes to express his gratitude to the following publishers and individuals for copyright permission to quote selections from the works designated:

George Allen & Unwin Ltd.: Hobhouse, *The Metaphysical Theory of the State.*

George Allen & Unwin: Nietzsche, *Ecce Homo,* translated by Anthony Ludovici.

Mrs. George Bambridge, Macmillan Company of Canada Ltd., Methuen Co. Ltd., and Doubleday & Company Inc. for permission to reprint Rudyard Kipling's "Recessional" and "The White Man's Burden."

Constable & Co., Ltd.: Treitschke, *Politics,* translated by Mrs. Blanche Dugdale.

C. W. Daniels Company: Gassett, *The Modern Theme,* translated by James Cleugh.

Faber & Faber: Breton, *What is Surrealism,* translated by David Gascoyne.

Harper & Row: Barth, K., *The Word of God and the Word of Man,* translated by Douglas Horton.

William Heinemann Ltd. and the Macmillan Company: Dostoevsky, *The Possessed,* translated by Constance Garnett.

Hodder and Stoughton Ltd. and J. C. Smuts: Smuts: *League of Nations; A Practical Suggestion.*

Houghton Mifflin Company: Hitler, *Mein Kampf,* translated by Ralph Manheim.

Alfred A. Knopf, Inc., and George Allen & Unwin Ltd.: Spengler, *Decline of the West,* Vol. II, *Man and Technics, The Hour of Decision.*

Liveright Publishing Company and The Hogarth Press: *A General Selection from the Works of Sigmund Freud,* Rickman, J., ed.

The Macmillan Company and Cambridge University Press: Whitehead, *Science and the Modern World.*

W. W. Norton & Company and George Allen & Unwin Ltd.: Russell, *Scientific Outlook.*

Oxford University Press: Toynbee, *A Study of History*, Vol. XII, *Reconsiderations*.

Routledge & Kegan Paul Ltd.: Bryce, *Handbook of Home Rule*.

Rutgers University Press: Solovev, *Against the Slavophiles*, Kohn, H., ed., *The Mind of Modern Russia*.

Vintage Books, Hamish Hamilton, and Librairie Gallimard: Camus, *The Myth of Sisyphus*.

Contents

X / CONTENTS

I

1848—1871

THE revolutions of 1848, which established the Second Republic in France and aroused hopes for the victory of liberal constitutionalism and nationalism in Central Europe, ended in disappointment. The June, 1848, uprising of the workers in Paris revealed the growing antagonism between the urban proletariat and the middle classes. This antagonism helped Louis Napoleon to replace the Second Republic by the Second Empire. In Central Europe everywhere the old aristocratic absolutist regimes were restored. A wave of pessimism followed upon the idealistic optimism which had characterized the years before the "Spring of the Peoples" of March, 1848.

The development in Britain was different. In the 1830's and 1840's Britain seemed destined for a revolutionary social upheaval (Chartist movement, Irish potato famine). But the great international fair of 1851 in London's Hyde Park opened an era of growing prosperity and social peace which lasted until the 1880's. During that period Britain was the industrial workshop of the world and the pivotal center of the Pax Britannica.

During the same period, the industrial revolution gained on the European continent. Railroads, the telegraph, steamships brought on an acceleration of the formerly slow rural life in Europe. But the industrial workers lived in poverty and suffered from the lack of organization. The emancipation of the serfs in Russia (1861) did not improve the general social conditions in the country, although it was a time when the penetration of Western ideas produced a desire for fundamental changes.

The social tensions on the European continent were increased by the new interpretation of nature and history as being a permanent struggle in which the strong overcome the weak. The emphasis on class war in the writings of Karl Marx, and on the survival of the fittest in the works of Charles Darwin, helped to create a temper which accepted success as a yardstick and force as a legitimate means to a desirable end. This mood was spreading when Count Cavour and Count Bismarck succeeded, where the popular movements of 1848 had failed, in the unification of Italy and Germany through a "realistic" power policy supported by military might and diplomatic cunning. Bismarck's success weakened the forces of liberalism in Central and Eastern Europe and inaugurated an era of armament races, unknown in Europe since the end of the Napole-

3

onic wars. Count Arthur de Gobineau's "Essay on the Inequality of the Human Races" (1853–55) contributed to the rising spirit of conflict. Through the German composer Richard Wagner, this racial theory exercized a great influence on Germany.

The quarter of a century between 1848 and 1871 witnessed the progressive secularization of public and private life. Darwin's theories undermined the faith in the literal truth of the Book of Genesis; man and society, no longer theology, began to occupy the center of attention. Books such as Ludwig Büchner's *Energy and Matter* (1855) were characteristic of the spread of opposition to the romantic idealism and the theological interpretation of the previous period. Himself a physician, Büchner wished to prove the physical substance of man and nature. At the same time, his work was inspired by a deep love for mankind.

In the artistic and literary fields, which often are of great importance for a diagnosis of the intellectual trends of a period, a similar reaction against the prevailing idealism of the generations of the 1820's and 1830's predominated. It found its expression in the paintings of the impressionists, of whom Edouard Manet (1832–1883) can be regarded as the first master. In literature Charles Baudelaire and Gustave Flaubert initiated new movements in poetry and the novel. Their chief works, *The Flowers of Evil* and *Madame Bovary*, appeared in the same year (1857) and aroused as much opposition by their "realism" as the paintings of the impressionists. They reflected the contemporary pessimism about the nature of man and the banality of life. The new trend in music was marked by the work of Richard Wagner, whose fundamental attitude, as revealed in his chief work *The Ring of the Nibelung*, was equally pessimistic, but whose stagecraft and orchestral power conformed to the loudness and confidence of the industrial bourgeois age of 1871–1914.

1. MARX AND ENGELS:
THE COMMUNIST MANIFESTO

Early in 1848 a little-noticed pamphlet was published which, by the middle of the twentieth century, was exercising a worldwide influence. It was written by two German exiles on behalf of the small Communist League formed by a few German workers in Belgium and England. The pamphlet appeared in the late winter of 1848, almost simultaneously with the outbreak of the revolution, with which, however, it had no connection. The two authors were close life-long friends, Karl Marx (1818–1883) and Friedrich Engels (1820–1895), both born in western Germany, the former the son of a lawyer, the other of a well-to-do industrialist. Both spent most of their lives in England, Marx as a student in the British Museum, Engels as a manufacturer.

Marx and Engels started on the one hand from the industrial revolution and the struggle of the middle class against the aristocracy, which they witnessed, and on the other from Hegel's historical determinism. But whereas Hegel saw in history the unfolding of the human spirit, Marx found historical development rooted in the material conditions of life. Marx and Engels were not only social philosophers and economists, but also revolutionaries. Marx founded in 1864 the International Working Men's Association, which did not become very important and disintegrated after 1872. Only after Marx's death, in 1889, was a second International established, which by this time consisted of several important Social Democratic parties, of which the German party was the best organized.

This party adopted at a meeting in 1875 in the small Thuringian town of Gotha a program which Marx criticized. In his *Critique* he wrote: "Between capitalist and communist society lies the period of the revolutionary transformation of the one into the other. There corresponds to this also a political transformation in which the state can be nothing but the revolutionary dictatorship of the proletariat." At the same time Engels declared, "It is pure nonsense to talk of a free people's state; so long as the proletariat continues to use the state, it does not use it in the interests of freedom but in order to hold down its adversaries, and as soon as it becomes possible to speak of freedom, the state as such ceases to exist."[1]

A spectre is haunting Europe—the spectre of Communism. All the powers of old Europe have entered into a holy alliance to ex-

---

[1] *A Handbook of Marxism*, being a collection of extracts from the writings of Marx, Engels, and the greatest of their followers (New York: International Publishers, 1935), pp. 21–59

orcise this spectre: Pope and Tsar, Metternich and Guizot, French Radicals and German police-spies.[2]

Where is the party in opposition that has not been decried as communistic by its opponents in power? Where is the Opposition that has not hurled back the branding reproach of Communism, against the more advanced opposition parties, as well as against its reactionary adversaries? . . .

The history of all hitherto existing society is the history of class struggles.

Freeman and slave, patrician and plebeian, lord and serf, guild-master and journey-man, in a word, oppressor and oppressed, stood in constant opposition to one another, carried on an uninterrupted, now hidden, now open fight, a fight that each time ended, either in a revolutionary reconstitution of society at large, or the common ruin of the contending classes. . . .

The modern bourgeois society that has sprouted from the ruins of feudal society has not done away with class antagonism. It has but established new classes, new conditions of oppression, new forms of struggle in place of the old ones.

Our epoch, the epoch of the bourgeoisie, possesses, however, this distinctive feature: it has simplified the class antagonism. Society as a whole is more and more splitting up into two great hostile camps, into two great classes directly facing each other—bourgeoisie and proletariat. . . .

We see, therefore, how the modern bourgeoisie is itself the product of a long course of development, of a series of revolutions in the modes of production and of exchange. . . .

The bourgeoisie, historically, has played a most revolutionary part. . . .

The bourgeoisie has been the first to show what man's activity can bring about. It has accomplished wonders far surpassing Egyptian pyramids, Roman aqueducts, and Gothic cathedrals; it has conducted expeditions that put in the shade all former Exoduses of nations and crusades.

The bourgeoisie cannot exist without constantly revolutionising the instruments of production, and thereby the relations of production, and with them the whole relations of society. . . .

The need of a constantly expanding market for its products chases the bourgeoisie over the whole surface of the globe. It must nestle everywhere, settle everywhere, establish connections everywhere.

[2] Prince Klemens Metternich (1773–1859), Austrian minister of foreign affairs (1809–1848) and chancellor, and Tsar Nicholas I (1796–1855), who became Tsar in 1825, were the main supporters of the Holy Alliance. François Guizot (1787–1874), French historian and a moderate liberal, was prime minister of France from 1840 to 1848.

The bourgeoisie has through its exploitation of the world market given a cosmopolitan character to production and consumption in every country. To the great chagrin of reactionaries, it has drawn from under the feet of industry the national ground on which it stood. All old-established national industries have been destroyed or are daily being destroyed. They are dislodged by new industries, whose introduction becomes a life and death question for all civilized nations, by industries that no longer work up indigenous raw material, but raw material drawn from the remotest zones; industries whose products are consumed, not only at home, but in every quarter of the globe. In place of the old wants, satisfied by the production of the country, we find new wants, requiring for their satisfaction the products of distant lands and climes. In place of the old local and national seclusion and self-sufficiency, we have intercourse in every direction, universal interdependence of nations. And as in material, so also in intellectual production. The intellectual creations of individual nations become common property. National one-sidedness and narrow-mindedness become more and more impossible, and from the numerous national and local literatures there arises a world literature.

The bourgeoisie, by the rapid improvement of all instruments of production, by the immensely facilitated means of communication, draws all, even the most barbarian, nations into civilization. The cheap prices of its commodities are the heavy artillery with which it batters down all Chinese walls, with which it forces the barbarians' intensely obstinate hatred of foreigners to capitulate. It compels all nations, on pain of extinction, to adopt the bourgeois mode of production; it compels them to introduce what it calls civilization into their midst, i.e., to become bourgeois themselves. In one word, it creates a world after its own image. . . .

The bourgeoisie, during its rule of scarce one hundred years, has created more massive and more colossal productive forces than have all preceding generations together. Subjection of nature's forces to man, machinery, application of chemistry to industry and agriculture, steam-navigation, railways, electric telegraphs, clearing of whole continents for cultivation, canalization of rivers, whole populations conjured out of the ground—what earlier century had even a presentiment that such productive forces slumbered in the lap of social labour?

We see then; the means of production and of exchange, on whose foundation the bourgeoisie built itself up, were generated in feudal society. At a certain stage in the development of these means of production and of exchange, the conditions under which feudal society produced and exchanged, the feudal organization of agriculture and manufacturing industry, in one word, the feudal relations of property became no longer compatible with the already developed productive forces; they became so many fetters. They had to be burst asunder; they were burst asunder.

Into their place stepped free competition, accompanied by a social and political constitution adapted to it, and by the economical and political sway of the bourgeoisie class.

A similar movement is going on before our own eyes. Modern bourgeois society with its relations of production, of exchange and of property, a society that has conjured up such gigantic means of production and of exchange, is like the sorcerer who is no longer able to control the powers of the nether world whom he has called up by his spells. For many a decade past the history of industry and commerce is but the history of the revolt of modern productive forces against modern conditions of production, against the property relations that are the conditions for the existence of the bourgeoisie and of its rule. It is enough to mention the commercial crises that by their periodical return put the existence of the entire bourgeois society on its trial, each time more threateningly. In these crises a great part not only of the existing products, but also of the previously created productive forces, are periodically destroyed. In these crises there breaks out an epidemic that, in all earlier epochs, would have seemed an absurdity—the epidemic of over-production. Society suddenly finds itself put back into a state of momentary barbarism; it appears as if a famine, a universal war of devastation had cut off the supply of every means of subsistence; industry and commerce seem to be destroyed. And why? Because there is too much civilization, too much means of subsistence, too much industry, too much commerce. The productive forces at the disposal of society no longer tend to further the development of the conditions of bourgeois property; on the contrary, they have become too powerful for these conditions, by which they are fettered, and so soon as they overcome these fetters, they bring disorder into the whole of bourgeois society, endanger the existence of bourgeois property. The conditions of bourgeois society are too narrow to comprise the wealth created by them. And how does the bourgeoisie get over these crises? On the one hand by enforced destruction of a mass of productive forces; on the other, by the conquest of new markets, and by the more thorough exploitation of the old ones. That is to say, by paving the way for more extensive and more destructive crises, and by diminishing the means whereby crises are prevented.

The weapons with which the bourgeoisie felled feudalism to the ground are now turned against the bourgeoisie itself.

But not only has the bourgeoisie forged the weapons that bring death to itself; it has also called into existence the men who are to wield those weapons—the modern working class—the prole-tarians. . . .

But with the development of industry the proletariat not only in-creases in number; it becomes concentrated in greater masses, its strength grows, and it feels that strength more. The various interests and conditions of life within the ranks of the proletariat are more and more equalised, in proportion as machinery obliterates all dis-tinctions of labour, and nearly everywhere reduces wages to the same low level. . . . Thereupon the workers begin to form com-binations (trades unions) against the bourgeoisie; they club together in order to keep up the rate of wages; they found permanent as-sociations in order to make provision beforehand for these occasional revolts. Here and there the contest breaks out into riots.

Now and then the workers are victorious, but only for a time. The real fruit of their battles lies, not in the immediate result, but in the ever-expanding union of the workers. . . .

Finally, in times when the class struggle nears the decisive hour, the process of dissolution going on within the ruling class, in fact within the whole range of old society, assumes such a violent, glaring character that a small section of the ruling class cuts itself adrift and joins the revolutionary class, the class that holds the future in its hands. Just as, therefore, at an earlier period, a section of the nobility went over to the bourgeoisie, so now a portion of the bourgeoisie goes over to the proletariat, and, in particular, a portion of the bourgeois ideologists, who have raised themselves to the level of comprehending theoretically the historical movement as a whole.

Of all the classes that stand face to face with the bourgeoisie today, the proletariat alone is a really revolutionary class. The other classes decay and finally disappear in the face of modern industry; the proletariat is its special and essential product. . . .

All previous historical movements were movements of minorities, or in the interest of minorities. The proletarian movement is the self-conscious, independent movement of the immense majority, in the interest of the immense majority. The proletariat, the lowest stratum of our present society, cannot stir, cannot raise itself up, without the whole superincumbent strata of official society being sprung into the air.

Though not in substance, yet in form, the struggle of the prole-tariat with the bourgeoisie is at first a national struggle. The prole-tariat of each country must, of course, first of all settle matters with its own bourgeoisie.

In depicting the most general phases of the development of the proletariat, we traced the more or less veiled civil war, raging within existing society, up to the point where that war breaks out into an open revolution, and where the violent overthrow of the bourgeoisie lays the foundation for the sway of the proletariat. . . .

The modern labourer, instead of rising with the progress of industry, sinks deeper and deeper below the conditions of existence of his own class. He becomes a pauper, and pauperism develops more rapidly than population and wealth. And here it becomes evident that the bourgeoisie is unfit any longer to be the ruling class in society and to impose its conditions of existence upon society as an overriding law. It is unfit to rule because it is incompetent to assure an existence to its slave within his slavery, but it cannot help letting him sink into such a state, that it has to feed him, instead of being fed by him. Society can no longer live under this bourgeoisie; in other words, its existence is no longer compatible with society.

The essential condition for the existence and for the sway of the bourgeois class is the formation and augmentation of capital; the condition for capital is wage-labour. Wage-labour rests exclusively on competition between the labourers. The advance of industry, whose involuntary promoter is the bourgeoisie, replaces the isolation of the labourers, due to competition, by their revolutionary combination, due to association. The development of modern industry, therefore, cuts from under its feet the very foundation on which the bourgeoisie produces and appropriates products. What the bourgeoisie therefore produces, above all, are its own grave-diggers. Its fall and the victory of the proletariat are equally inevitable. . . .

. . . Thanks to the economic and political development of France since 1789, for fifty years the position in Paris has been such that no Revolution could break out there without assuming a proletarian character, that is to say, without the proletariat, which had bought victory with its blood, advancing its own demands after victory had been won. These demands were more or less unclear and even confused, corresponding to the state of evolution reached by the workers of Paris at the particular period, but the ultimate purpose of them all was the abolition of the class antagonism between capitalists and workers. It is true that no one could say how this was to be brought about. But the demand itself, however indefinite it still was in its formulation, contained a threat to the existing order of society; the workers who put it forward were still armed, and therefore the disarming of the workers was the first commandment for whatever bourgeois group was at the helm of the State. Hence, after every revolution won by the workers, a new struggle, ending with the defeat of the workers. . . .

The Communists turn their attention chiefly to Germany, because that country is on the eve of a bourgeois revolution that is bound to be carried out under more advanced conditions of European civilisation and with a much more developed proletariat than that of England was in the seventeenth, and of France in the eighteenth century, and because the bourgeois revolution in Germany will be but the prelude to an immediately following proletarian revolution.

In short, the Communists everywhere support every revolutionary movement against the existing social and political order of things.

In all these movements they bring to the front, as the leading question in each, the property question, no matter what its degree of development at the time.

Finally, they labour everywhere for the union and agreement of the democratic parties of all countries.

The Communists disdain to conceal their views and aims. They openly declare that their ends can be attained only by the forcible overthrow of all existing social conditions. Let the ruling classes tremble at a Communist revolution. The proletarians have nothing to lose but their chains. They have a world to win. Working men of all countries, unite!

2. KARL MARX: *DAS KAPITAL*

Karl Marx never finished his main work, *Capital, A Critique of Political Economy*. The first volume appeared in German in 1867; the two remaining volumes, edited by Friedrich Engels, were published only after the death of Marx, in 1885 and in 1894. Additional material, intended by Marx to complete the work, was published after Engels' death by Karl Kautsky in German in three volumes under the title *Theories of Surplus Value*. The first volume was made accessible in English only in 1886 in a translation by Samuel Moore and Edward Aveling, published by Swan Sonnenschein, Lowrey & Company in London. All three volumes were published only once in English by Charles H. Kerr & Company in Chicago (1909–1932).

The ultimate aim of this gigantic work was defined by Marx himself in his introduction: "to lay bare the economic law of modern society." Perhaps the best classic statement can be found in his *Critique of Political Economy* (1859), out of which the massive argument of *Das Kapital* grew:

In the social production which men carry on, they enter into definite relations that are indispensable and independent of their will; these relations of production correspond to a definite stage of development of their material powers of production. The sum total of these productive relations constitutes the economic structure of society—the real foundation on which rise legal and political superstructures, and to which correspond definite forms of social consciousness. The mode of production in material life determines the general character of the social, political and spiritual processes of life. It is not the consciousness of men that determines their existence, but on the contrary their social existence that determines their consciousness.

At a certain stage of their development, the material forces of production in society come into conflict with the existing relations of production, or—what is but a legal expression for the same thing—with the property relations within which they had been at work before. From forms of development of the productive forces these relations turn into their fetters. Then comes the period of social revolution. With the change of the economic foundation the whole vast superstructure is sooner or later entirely transformed. But in considering such transformations the distinction should always be made between the material transformation of the economic conditions of production, which can be determined with the precision of natural science, and the legal, political, religious, esthetic or philosophic—in short, the ideological forms in which men become conscious of the conflict and fight it out.

The following excerpt is taken from Volume I of *Das Kapital*, Chapter XXXII, "Historical Tendency of Capitalist Accumulation."[3]

What does the primitive accumulation of capital, i.e., its historical genesis, resolve itself into? In so far as it is not immediate transformation of slaves and serfs into wage labourers, and therefore a mere change of form, it only means the expropriation of the immediate producers, i.e., the dissolution of private property based on the labour of its owner. Private property, as the antithesis to social, collective property, exists only where the means of labour and the external conditions of labour belong to private individuals. But according as these private individuals are labourers or not labourers, private property has a different character. The numberless shades, that it at first sight presents, correspond to the intermediate stages lying between these two extremes. The private property of the labourer in his means of production is the foundation of petty in-

[3] *A Handbook of Marxism* (New York: International Publishers, 1935), pp. 401–404

dustry, whether agricultural, manufacturing or both; petty industry, again, is an essential condition for the development of social production and of the free individuality of the labourer himself. Of course, this petty mode of production exists also under slavery, serfdom, and other states of dependence. But it flourishes, it lets loose its whole energy, it attains its adequate classical form only where the labourer is the private owner of his own means of labour set in action by himself: the peasant of the land which he cultivates, the artisan of the tool which he handles as a virtuoso. This mode of production pre-supposes parcelling of the soil, and scattering of the other means of production. As it excludes the concentration of these means of production, so also it excludes co-operation, division of labour within each separate process of production, the control over, and the productive application of the forces of Nature by society, and the free development of the social productive powers. It is compatible only with a system of production, and a society, moving within narrow and more or less primitive bounds. To perpetuate it would be, as Pecqueur rightly says, "to decree universal mediocrity." At a certain stage of development it brings forth the material agencies for its own dissolution. From that moment new forces and new passions spring up in the bosom of society; but the old social organisation fetters them and keeps them down. It must be annihilated; it is annihilated. Its annihilation, the transformation of the individualised and scattered means of production into socially concentrated ones, of the pigmy property of the many into the huge property of the few, the expropriation of the great mass of the people from the soil, from the means of subsistence, and from the means of labour, this fearful and painful expropriation of the mass of the people forms the prelude to the history of capital. It comprises a series of forcible methods, of which we have passed in review only those that have been epoch-making as methods of the primitive accumulation of capital. The expropriation of the immediate producers was accomplished with merciless vandalism, and under the stimulus of passions the most infamous, the most sordid, the pettiest, the most meanly odious. Self-earned private property, that is based, so to say, on the fusing together of the isolated, independent labouring-individual with the conditions of his labour, is supplanted by capitalistic private property, which rests on exploitation of the nominally free labour of others, i.e., on wages-labour.

As soon as this process of transformation has sufficiently decomposed the old society from top to bottom, as soon as the labourers are turned into proletarians, their means of labour into capital, as soon as the capitalist mode of production stands on its own feet, then the further socialisation of labour and further transformation of the land and other means of production into socially exploited and, therefore, common means of production, as well as the further expropriation of private proprietors, takes a new form. That which is now to be expropriated is no longer the labourer working for himself, but the capitalist exploiting many labourers. This expropriation is accomplished by the action of the immanent laws of capitalistic production itself, by the centralisation of capital. One capitalist always kills many. Hand in hand with this centralisation, or this expropriation of many capitalists by few, develop, on an ever extending scale, the co-operative form of the labour-process, the conscious technical application of science, the methodical cultivation of the soil, the transformation of the instruments of labour into instruments of labour only usable in common, the economising of all means of production by their use as the means of production of combined, socialised labour, the entanglement of all peoples in the net of the world-market, and this, the international character of the capitalistic regime. Along with the constantly diminishing number of the magnates of capital, who usurp and monopolise all advantages of this process of transformation, grows the mass of misery, oppression, slavery, degradation, exploitation; but with this too grows the revolt of the working-class, a class always increasing in numbers, and disciplined, united, organised by the very mechanism of the process of capitalist production itself. The monopoly of capital becomes a fetter upon the mode of production, which has sprung up and flourished along with, and under it. Centralisation of the means of production and socialisation of labour at last reach a point where they become incompatible with their capitalist integument. This integument is burst asunder. The knell of capitalist private property sounds. The expropriators are expropriated.

The capitalist mode of appropriation, the result of the capitalist mode of production, produces capitalist private property. This is the first negation of individual private property, as founded on the labour of the proprietor. But capitalist production begets, with the inexorability of a law of Nature, its own negation. It is the negation of negation. This does not re-establish private property for the producer, but gives him individual property based on the acquisitions of the capitalist era: i.e., on co-operation and the possession in common of the land and of the means of production.

The transformation of scattered private property, arising from individual labour, into capitalist private property is, naturally, a process, incomparably more protracted, violent, and difficult, than the transformation of capitalistic private property, already practically resting on socialised production, into socialised property. In the former case, we had the expropriation of the mass of the people by a few usurpers; in the latter, we have the expropriation of a few usurpers by the mass of the people.

3. MAZZINI: *TO THE ITALIANS*

Karl Marx laid the foundations of modern socialism. The foremost spokesman of nationalism in the middle of the nineteenth century was an Italian, Giuseppe Mazzini (1805–1872). He, too, lived most of his mature life as an exile in London. In 1831 he started the movement which he named Young Italy and which became the model of many similar movements. In Mazzini's mind Young Italy and Young Europe remained closely connected. But as a typical nationalist he did not doubt that among all peoples the Italians were predestined to lead mankind on the road of civilization and that Rome was the historical center of the universe. The Rome of the free and united Italian people, he was convinced, would live up to its mission.

Mazzini shared and propagated the generous belief in the moral faculties of the nationally aroused common people, and hoped for a world of peaceful, cooperating peoples organized on the basis of free self-determination. "The Europe of the peoples will be one," he wrote in 1849, "avoiding alike the anarchy of absolute independence and the centralization of conquest."

Mazzini's life was dedicated to the awakening of a unified republican Italian nation. But he had no part in its actual unification, which was achieved largely through the aid of France, which he distrusted, through the Sardinian monarchy, which he abhorred, and through unscrupulous diplomacy, which he detested. He returned to unified Italy as an exile in his own land. Early in 1871 he founded a newspaper, *La Roma del Popolo* (Rome of the People), in which the following appeal *To the Italians* appeared. It faithfully reflects the hopes of the nationalism which Mazzini represented from 1848, when he stood at the head of the short-lived Roman Republic, until his death.[4]

[4] From *Essays* by Joseph Mazzini, most of them translated for the first time by Thomas Okey. Edited with an introduction by Bolton King (London, 1894)

The first number . . . bears in front the title, La Roma del Popolo; at foot, the names of men who whatever may be their intellectual worth, have never, despite delusions and baits of worldly success, despite suffering, exile, imprisonment, denied the ideal of their hearts. It should not, therefore, be necessary to lay a *programme* before our readers. Everybody knows who we are. Our programme, the *Republican Unity of Italy,* dates back more than a third of a century. We have been silent concerning it at times when the people had strayed in opposite directions, and it needed experience and disillusion to confirm its truth; we have never abdicated it. And today, more than ever convinced by the experience of the last ten years, we raise again in Rome the flag we planted there forty years ago. Our publication is the cry of the Italian conscience, to uphold that formula of the national life which historical tradition and the instincts of our people have pointed out, to condemn all that spirit of conventionality or falsehood that betrays it with a kiss, or deliberately denies it. . . .

The title that we have chosen betokens the mission of Rome in the world, and the historical evolution that calls upon her to spread for the third time among the nations a gospel of civilisation, a gospel of that moral unity which has vanished for the present in the slow death-agony of the ancient faith. "This Unity all pray for"—I wrote as long ago as 1844—"can come, Italians, whatever men may do, from your country alone, and you can only write it on the flag, which is destined to shine on high above those two milliary columns, that mark the course of thirty centuries and more in the world's life—the Capitol and the Vatican. Rome of the Caesars gave the Unity of civilisation that Force imposed upon Europe. Rome of the Popes gave a Unity of civilization that Authority imposed on a great part of the human race. Rome of the People will give, when you Italians are nobler than you are now, a Unity of civilisation accepted by the free consent of the nations for Humanity." And this faith, that sustained our life through bitterest trials, is still ours. The materialists who misgovern us see in Rome no more than a fraction of Italian earth, peopled by a certain number of inhabitants capable of paying taxes and furnishing armed levies: we look on Rome as the sanctuary of the Nations, the Sacred City of Italy, the Historic Centre, whence by providential mission came Italy's message to Men, the message that makes for unity, and our *initiative* in the world. . . .

From Rome must come, must permeate Humanity, that message that the common thought of all Italy has shaped, the message that two earlier worlds have baptized and consecrated. Without a common faith, without conception of an *ideal* that shall bind the nations together, and show to each its special function for the common good, without unity of standard for its whole moral, political, economic life, the world today is at the mercy of caprice, of dynastic and popular ambition and egotism. The *initiative*, which France has lost since 1815 lives no longer, visible and accepted, in any people. England deliberately abdicated it when she introduced, under the name of *non-intervention*, a policy of local *interests*. Germany threatens to sterilise all her vast power of *thought*, by surrendering the *action* that should be collective, and the formation of her unity, to a military monarchy hostile to liberty. The Slav populations who have so great a part in the future reserved for them, dismembered and without centre of national life, still hesitate between the rule of a Czar fatal to them all, and the old difficulty of local antagonisms. And, faced by such a void, we—who are ready to hail and applaud the *initiative* wherever it may arise—we cherish as the ideal of our heart the sacred hope that it may arise on the ruins of the Papacy and of every similar lie, from the third Rome, from the Rome of the People. Reborn at the cradle of an Age, Italy and Rome are called to inaugurate it, if only they know their destinies, and the moral force they have behind them.

Unity at home, and a new development of civilisation abroad— these two terms include the whole programme of our publication. . . .

The Europe of today is, on the whole, we believe, in this second stage, seeking, like the Israelites in the desert, a promised land still unknown,—seeking a new *principle*, a new order of things, since the old one is exhausted. He who watches Europe under the light of the great historical tradition, at once recurs to the memory of those times that eighteen centuries ago announced the slow breaking-up of Paganism, and the inevitable rise of Christianity. The absence of an *initiative* of any general and harmonious civilisation in the world, the moral anarchy that is its consequence—the wars promoted by the interests of dynasties or some few individuals—the neutrality founded on the indifference of egotism—the treaties of peace based on foolish theories of an *equilibrium* which is impossible so long as it takes into count material facts only—the question of nationality, which today is dominant over all others, and, as eighteen centuries ago, points to a new European birth—the emancipation of the working classes which has become, as in those times was the emancipation of the *slave*, the universal subject of a powerful agitation—the awakening of the Slav races, as in those days of the Teutonic races, to a life that now is assured them—the materialism —the exaggerated rejection of old beliefs—the aspirations after new beliefs dawning everywhere—the insensate attempts at an impossible reconciliation between the old and the new—everything points to the near advent of an order of things, founded on *principles* radically different from those that preceded the development of the present Age that now is visibly exhausted. A new conception of Life, and of the divine Law that governs it, throbs in every manifestation of the two faculties of *thought* and *action*, that make up the unity of human nature. Monarchy can neither strangle it nor make it its handmaid.

Monarchy had its day and mission. It came to fight and destroy *feudalism*, which was a system of territorial dismemberment, that hindered all possibility of unity in countries destined to form *nations*. . . .

Today, the feudal organisation has disappeared for ever, and with it the function that gave life to the monarchical idea. A new conception, based on the Divine Law of Progress, takes the place of the conception that was based on the doctrines of the Fall and the *Atonement*, and hence perishes the Papacy, the authority that ordained the *monarch* for his function.

The world is seeking, not the *material* solidarity which is now assured, and which is only the outward form of the nations, but the vivifying spirit that shall guide their life towards its end; the *moral* unity that can only be based on the *association* of men and nations equal and free. Monarchy, based upon the doctrine of inequality, on the *privilege* of an individual or of a family, can never give that unity. The flag that leads towards that destined future means Progress, and dynastic interests mean *stagnation*. . . .

In the ideal that Europe is seeking, and will realise, the Government will be the *mind* of a Nation, the people its *arm*, and the educated and free individual its prophet of *future progress*. The first will point out the path that leads to the *ideal* which at present is the only thing that makes a Nation. The second will direct the forces of the country towards it. The third will protest in the name of a new and further ideal, against intolerance, and every tendency to deny the possibility of unlimited progress. . . .

The first condition of this life is the solemn declaration, made with the unanimous and free consent of our greatest in wisdom and virtue, that Italy, feeling the times to be ripe, rises with one spontaneous impulse, in the name of the Duty and Right inherent in a people, to constitute itself a Nation of free and equal brothers, and demand that rank which by right belongs to it among the Nations that are already formed. The next condition is the declaration of the body of religious, moral, and political *principles* in which the Italian people believes at the present day, of the common ideal to which it is striving, of the *special* mission that distinguishes it from other peoples and to which it intends to consecrate itself for its own benefits and for the benefit of Humanity. And the final condition is to determine the methods to be employed, and the men to whom the country should delegate the function of developing the national conception of life, and the application of its practical consequences to the manifold branches of social activity. . . .

Our party is faithful to the ideal of our country's Traditions, but ready to harmonise them with the Traditions of Humanity and the inspirations of conscience; it is tolerant and moral, and it must therefore now confute, without attacking or misconstruing motives. We need not fear that we are forging weapons for the enemy, if we declare the religions of the world to be successive expressions of a series of ages that have educated the human race; if we recognise the religious faculty as eternal in the human soul, eternal, too, the bond between heaven and earth. We can admire in Gregory VII,[5] the gigantic energy of will, the sublime moral effort that could not be realised with the instrument that Christianity could lend, and, at the same time, in the name of the progress we have made, declare the Papacy to be for ever dead. We can recognise the Mission which Aristocracy and Monarchy had for other peoples in the past, and yet proclaim, for all of us, the duty and the right to outstrip those worn-out forms. We may, without denying the reverence due to Authority—for that is the real object of all our efforts—claim the task of attacking every Authority that is not based on two conditions—the free and enlightened consent of the governed, and the power of directing the national life and making it fruitful.

We believe in God.

In a providential Law given by Him to life.

In a Law, not of *Atonement,* not of the *Fall,* and *Redemption* by the *grace* of past or present mediators between God and *man,* but of Progress, unlimited Progress, founded on, and measured by, our works.

In the *Unity* of Life, misunderstood, as we believe, by the Philosophy of the last two centuries.

In the *Unity* of the Law through both the manifestations of Life, *collective* and *individual.*

In the immortality of the *Ego,* which is nothing but the application of the Law of Progress, revealed beyond doubt now and for ever by Historical Tradition, by Science, by the aspirations of the soul, to the Life that is manifested in the individual.

In Liberty, by which alone exists responsibility, the consciousness and price of *progress.*

[5] Saint Gregory VII, pope from 1073–1085, tried to establish supremacy of the pope within the Church and of the Church over the state.

In the successive and increasing *association* of all human faculties and powers, as the sole normal means of *progress*, at once collective and individual.

In the *Unity* of the human race, and in the moral *equality* of all the children of God, without distinction of sex, colour, or condition, to be forfeited by *crime* alone.

And hence we believe in the holy, inexorable, dominating idea of Duty, the sole standard of Life. *Duty* that embraces in each one, according to the sphere in which he moves and the means that he possesses, Family, Fatherland, Humanity. Family the altar of the Fatherland; Fatherland the sanctuary of Humanity; Humanity a part of the Universe, and a temple built to God, who created the Universe, that it might draw near to Him. *Duty*, that bids us promote the progress of others that our own may be effected, and of ourselves that it may profit that of others. *Duty*, without which no *right* exists, that creates the virtue of self-sacrifice, in truth the only pure virtue, holy and mighty in power, the noblest jewel that crowns and hallows the human soul.

And finally, we believe, not in the doctrines of the present day, but in a great religious manifestation founded upon these principles, that sooner or later will arise from the initiative of a people of freemen and believers—perhaps from Rome if Rome knows her mission—and which, while it includes that chapter of Truth that former religions won, will reveal yet another chapter and will open the road to future progress, destroying in their germ all privilege and intolerance of caste. . . .

We believe that to make politics an *art*, and sever them from morality, as the royal statesmen and diplomatists desire, is a sin before God and destructive to the peoples. The *end* of politics is the application of the moral Law to the civil constitution of a Nation in its double activity, domestic and foreign. The *end* of economics is the application of the same Law to the organisation of Labour in its double aspect, production and distribution. All that *makes* for that *end* is Good and must be promoted; all that contradicts it or gives it no help must be opposed till it succumb. People and Government must proceed united, like thought and action in individuals, towards the accomplishment of that mission. And what is true for one Nation is true as between Nations. Nations are the individuals of Humanity. The internal national organization is the instrument with which the Nation accomplishes its mission in the world. Nationalities are sacred, and providentially constituted to represent, within Humanity, the division or distribution of labour for the advantage of the peoples, as the division and distribution of labour within the limits of the state should be organised for the greatest benefit of all the citizens. If they do not look to that *end* they are useless and fall. If they persist in evil, which is egotism, they perish: nor do they rise again unless they make Atonement and return to Good.

But to staunch the two sources of our worst wounds,—the dissension between the Government and the governed, and the selfishness that dominates individuals,—we must constitute a Government that represents the mind, the tendencies, the duties of the Nation, and we must determine the National ideal, the origin and standard of our duties. . . .

Sovereignty exists neither in the *"I"* nor the *"We"; it exists in God, the source of Life; in the Progress that defines life; in the Moral Law that defines Duty.

In other terms, Sovereignty is in the Ideal.

We are all called to do its work.

The knowledge of the *ideal* is given to us—so far as it is understood by the age in which we live—by our intelligence when it is inspired by the love of Good, and proceeds from the Tradition of Humanity to question its own *conscience*, and reconciles these two sole criteria of Truth.

But the knowledge of the *ideal* needs an *interpreter* who may forthwith indicate the means that may best attain to it, and direct its application to the various branches of activity. And as this *interpreter* must embrace within itself the *"I"* and the *"We,"* Authority and Liberty, State and Individual; and as, moreover, it must be *progressive,* it cannot be a man or any order of men selected by chance, or by the prerogative of a privilege unprogressive by its very nature, or birth, or riches, or aught else. Given the principles contained in the contract of faith and brotherhood, this interpreter can only be the People, the Nation.

God and the People: these are the only two terms that survive the analysis of the elements which the Schools have given as the foundation of the social communion. . . .

The Italian Mission is therefore:—

The Unity of the Nation, in its *material* aspect, by the reconquest of the Trentino, of Istria and of Nice; in its *moral* aspect, by National Education, accompanied by the free and protected Instruction of every heterodox doctrine.

Unity of defence, or the *Nation armed.* . . .

Communal liberty to be decreed so far as regards the special progress of the various localities.

Suppression of all offices intended at the present day to represent an undue influence of the Government over the different local districts. . . .

Universal Suffrage as the beginning of political education.

Legislation tending to advance the intellectual and economical progress of those classes that need it most; and the nation to encourage industrial, agricultural, and labour associations, founded on certain general conditions, and of proven morality and capacity.

Special attention to be given to the uncultivated lands of Italy, to the vast unhealthy zones, to neglected communal property, and to the creation on them of a new class of small proprietors. . . .

International policy to be governed by the moral *principle* that rules the Nation.

Alliances to be based on uniformity of tendencies and objects.

Especial favour to be shown to every movement that may fraternise Italy with the elements of future or growing Nationalities, with the Greek, Roumanian, or Slav populations, who are destined to solve the problem of Eastern Europe.

4. LORD ACTON: *ON NATIONALITY*

The potential dangers which the development of nationalism might bring forth for the cause of individual liberty and of international peace were rarely seen in Mazzini's time, but an English political thinker and historian foresaw them clearly in an essay which he wrote in 1862. In it he objected to the idea that political boundaries should be determined by racial, ethnic, or religious factors and that a state should necessarily represent racial or ethnic uniformity. He stressed the value of tolerance and of diversity in equality as being more in accord with true liberty.

John Emerich Edward Dalberg Acton (1834–1902) was well equipped for such a point of view, both by his background and by his political attitude. He fused a broad cosmopolitan understanding of history with an ardent liberalism. Born of a noble English family which had lived for several generations in France and Italy, he was related through his mother to the German aristocracy. As a Catholic he rejected ultramontanism. His ambition was to write The History of Liberty. Though he was appointed Regius Professor of Modern History at Cambridge in 1895 and though his lectures there, which were published only after his death, exercized a wide influence, he never wrote the work on which his heart was set. His essay on nationalism remains relevant even today to an understanding of the complex nature of this movement.[6]

Whenever great intellectual cultivation has been combined with that suffering which is inseparable from extensive changes in the condition of the people, men of speculative or imaginative genius have sought in the contemplation of an ideal society a remedy, or at least a consolation, for evils which they were practically unable to remove. . . . The eighteenth century acquiesced in this oblivion of corporate rights on the Continent, for the absolutists cared only for the State, and the liberals only for the individual. . . .

The old despotic policy which made [in the eighteenth century] the Poles its prey had two adversaries,—the spirit of English liberty, and the doctrines of that revolution which destroyed the French monarchy with its own weapons; and these two contradicted in contrary ways the theory that nations have no collective rights. At the present day, the theory of nationality is not only the most powerful auxiliary of revolution, but its substance in the movements of the last three years. This, however, is a recent alliance, unknown to the first French Revolution. The modern theory of nationality arose partly as a legitimate consequence, partly as a reaction against it. As the system which overlooked national division was opposed by liberalism in two forms, the French and the English, so the system which insists upon them proceeds from two distinct sources, and exhibits the character either of 1688 or 1789.

Napoleon [I] called a new power into existence by attacking nationality in Russia, by delivering it in Italy, by governing in defiance of it in Germany and Spain. The sovereigns of these countries were deposed or degraded; and a system of administration was introduced which was French in its origin, its spirit, and its instruments. The people resisted the change. The movement against it was popular and spontaneous, because the rulers were absent or helpless; and it was national, because it was directed against foreign institutions. In Tyrol, in Spain, and afterwards in Prussia, the people did not receive the impulse from the government, but undertook of their own accord to cast out the armies and the ideas of revolutionized France. Men were made conscious of the national element of the revolution by its conquests, not in its rise. The three things which the Empire most openly oppressed— religion, national independence, and political liberty—united in a

[6] "Nationality," *The Home and Foreign Review*, vol. I, no. 1 (July, 1862), pp. 1–25, reprinted in *The History of Freedom and Other Essays*, ed. by J. N. Figgis and R. V. Laurence (London, 1907), pp. 270–300

short-lived league to animate the great uprising by which Napoleon fell. . . .

At first, in 1813, the people rose against their conquerors, in defence of their legitimate rulers. They refused to be governed by usurpers. In the period between 1825 and 1831, they resolved that they would not be misgoverned by strangers. The French administration was often better than that which it displaced, but there were prior claimants for the authority exercised by the French, and at first the national contest was a contest for legitimacy. In the second period this element was wanting. No dispossessed princes led the Greeks, the Belgians, or the Poles. The Turks, the Dutch, and the Russians, were attacked, not as usurpers, but as oppressors —because they misgoverned, not because they were of a different race. Then began a time when the text simply was, that nations would not be governed by foreigners. Power legitimately obtained, and exercised with moderation, was declared invalid. . . . Now nationality became a paramount claim, which was to assert itself alone, which might put forward as pretexts the rights of rulers, the liberties of the people, the safety of religion, but which, if no such union could be formed, was to prevail at the expense of every cause for which nations make sacrifices. . . . It was appealed to in the name of the most contradictory principles of government, and served all parties in succession, because it was one in which all could unite. Beginning by a protest against the dominion of race over race, its mildest and least-developed form, it grew into a condemnation of every State that included different races, and finally became the complete and consistent theory, that the State and the nation must be co-extensive.

The outward historical progress of this idea from an indefinite aspiration to be the keystone of a political system, may be traced in the life of the man who gave to it the element in which its strength resides—Giuseppe Mazzini. He found Carbonarism[7] impotent against the measures of the governments, and resolved to give new life to the liberal movement by transferring it to the ground of nationality. Exile is the nursery of nationality, as oppression is the school of liberalism; and Mazzini conceived the idea of Young Italy when he was a refugee at Marseilles. In the same way, the Polish exiles are the champions of every national movement; for to them all political rights are absorbed in the idea of independence, which, however they may differ with each other, is the one aspiration common to them all.

In pursuing the outward and visible growth of the national theory we are prepared for an examination of its political character and

---

[7] A secret nationalist Italian movement, responsible for the Italian uprisings between 1820 and 1831

value. The absolutism which has created it denies equally that absolute right of national unity which is a product of democracy, and that claim of national liberty which belongs to the theory of freedom. These two views of nationality, corresponding to the French and to the English systems, are connected in name only, and are in reality the opposite extremes of political thought. In one case, nationality is founded on the perpetual supremacy of the collective will, of which the unity of the nation is the necessary condition, to which every other influence must differ, and against which no obligation enjoys authority, and all resistance is tyrannical. The nation is here an ideal unit founded on the race, in defiance of the modifying action of external causes, of tradition, and of existing rights. It overrules the rights and wishes of the inhabitants, absorbing their divergent interests in a fictitious unity; sacrifices their several inclinations and duties to the higher claim of nationality, and crushes all natural rights and all established liberties for the purpose of vindicating itself.

Connected with this theory in nothing except in the common enmity of the absolute state, is the theory which represents nationality as an essential, but not a supreme element in determining the forms of the State. It is distinguished from the other, because it tends to diversity and not to uniformity, to harmony and not to unity; because it aims not at an arbitrary change, but at careful respect for the existing conditions of political life, and because it obeys the laws and results of history, not the aspirations of an ideal future. While the theory of unity makes the nation a source of despotism and revolution, the theory of liberty regards it as the bulwark of self-government, and the foremost limit to the excessive power of the State. . . .

The presence of different nations under the same sovereignty is similar in its effect to the independence of the Church in the State. It provides against the servility which flourishes under the shadow of a single authority, by balancing interests, multiplying associations, and giving to the subject the restraint and support of a combined opinion. . . . Liberty provokes diversity, and diversity preserves liberty by supplying the means of organization. This diversity in the same State is a firm barrier against the intrusion of the government beyond the political sphere which is common to all into the social department which escapes legislation and is ruled by spontaneous laws. . . . That intolerance of social freedom which is natural to absolutism is sure to find a corrective in the national diversities, which no other force could so efficiently provide. The co-existence of several nations under the same State is a test, as well as the best security of its freedom. It is also one of the chief instruments of civilisation; and, as such, it is in the natural and providential order, and indicates a state of greater advancement than the national unity which is the ideal of modern liberalism.

If we take the establishment of liberty for the realisation of moral duties to be the end of civil society, we must conclude that those states are substantially the most perfect which, like the British and Austrian Empires, include various distinct nationalities without oppressing them. Those in which no mixture of races has occurred are imperfect; and those in which its effects have disappeared are decrepit. A State which is incompetent to satisfy different races condemns itself; a State which labours to neutralise, to absorb, or to expel them, destroys its own vitality; a State which does not include them is destitute of the chief basis of self-government. The theory of nationality, therefore, is a retrograde step in history.

Nationality is more advanced than socialism, because it is a more arbitrary system. The social theory endeavors to provide for the existence of the individual beneath the terrible burdens which modern society heaps upon labour. It is not merely a development of the notion of equality, but a refuge from real misery and starvation. However false the solution, it was a reasonable demand that the poor should be saved from destruction; and if the freedom of the State was sacrificed to the safety of the individual, the more immediate object was, at least in theory, attained. But nationality does not aim either at liberty or prosperity, both of which it sacrifices to the imperative necessity of making the nation the mould and measure of the State. Its course will be marked with material as well as moral ruin, in order that a new invention may prevail over the works of God and the interests of mankind.

5. CHARLES DARWIN:
THE ORIGIN OF SPECIES

Darwin's *The Origin of Species by Means of Natural Selection, or the Preservation of Favored Races in the Struggle for Life,* which appeared in 1859, was one of the books the general thesis of which altered the main currents of human thought. Before Darwin, the general public believed that species were immutable productions and had been separately created by God at the time when He created the universe. In the eighteenth century nature was regarded as the reign of benign harmony and peace, the shelter of man from the rough battles of life. Now Darwin's work applied to biology not only the idea of evolution by gradual and continuous changes, which had been widely accepted in early nineteenth-century geology and historical writing; it also accustomed the public to rapidly accepted popular slogans like "struggle for life," "favored races," and "survival of the fittest." The image of Nature changed from benevolent to "red in tooth and claw" (Alfred Tennyson, 1809–1892); struggle was accepted as an inevitable element of growth and development, success as a confirmation of the legitimacy of deeds and events; evolution spelled inevitable progress. "There is warrant for the belief," wrote Herbert Spencer (1820–1903), one of the most influential English philosophers of the Victorian age, "that Evolution can end only in the establishment of the greatest perfection and the most complete happiness."

Charles Darwin (1809–1882) was educated for the ministry, but became a naturalist. His voyage to southern lands on H.M.S. *Beagle* (1831–1836) gave him an opportunity to study plants, animals, and geology in many lands. His main work aroused bitter controversy, as it contradicted the story in Genesis; he was supported above all by Thomas Huxley (1825–1895), an English biologist and paleontologist. "The conception of the constancy of the order of nature has become the dominant idea of modern thought," wrote Huxley in his *Essays*. "Whatever may be man's speculative doctrines, it is quite certain that every intelligent person guides his life and risks his fortune upon the belief that the order of nature is constant, and that the chain of natural causation is never broken." Already in his *The Origin of Species* Darwin insisted on including man in his theory: "Light will be thrown on the origin of man and his history." But only in 1871 did he publish his *The Descent of Man.* And elsewhere he wrote that "science and her methods gave me a resting place independent of authority and tradition." This became the fundamental faith of modern Western man.

The Origin appeared in its sixth, much-revised edition in 1872. It consists of fifteen chapters, the last being "Recapitulation and Conclusion." The following excerpts are from this last chapter.[8]

[8] Charles Darwin, *The Origin of Species,* a reprint of the sixth edition (London: The World's Classics, 1951)

That many and serious objections may be advanced against the theory of descent with modification through variation and natural selection, I do not deny. I have endeavoured to give to them their full force. Nothing at first can appear more difficult to believe than that the more complex organs and instincts have been perfected, not by means superior to, though analogous with, human reason, but by the accumulation of innumerable slight variations, each good for the individual possessor. Nevertheless, this difficulty, though appearing to our imagination insuperably great, cannot be considered real if we admit the following propositions, namely, that all parts of the organisation and instincts offer, at least, individual differences—that there is a struggle for existence leading to the preservation of profitable deviations of structure or instinct—and, lastly, that gradations in the state of perfection of each organ may have existed, each good of its kind. The truth of these propositions cannot, I think, be disputed. . . .

Variability is not actually caused by man; he only unintentionally exposes organic beings to new conditions of life, and then nature acts on the organisation and causes it to vary. But man can and does select the variations given to him by nature, and thus accumulates them in any desired manner. He thus adapts animals and plants for his own benefit or pleasure. He may do this methodically, or he may do it unconsciously by preserving the individuals most useful or pleasing to him without any intention of altering the breed. It is certain that he can largely influence the character of a breed by selecting, in each successive generation, individual differences so slight as to be inappreciable except by an educated eye. This unconscious process of selection has been the great agency in the formation of the most distinct and useful domestic breeds. That many breeds produced by man have to a large extent the character of natural species, is shown by the inextricable doubts whether many of them are varieties or aboriginally distinct species.

There is no reason why the principles which have acted so efficiently under domestication should not have acted under nature. In the survival of favoured individuals and races, during the constantly-recurrent Struggle for Existence, we see a powerful and ever-acting form of Selection. The struggle for existence inevitably follows from the high geometrical ratio of increase which is common to all organic beings. This high rate of increase is proved by calculation,—by the rapid increase of many animals and plants during a succession of peculiar seasons, and when naturalised in new countries. More individuals are born than can possibly survive. A grain in the balance may determine which individuals shall live and which shall die,—which variety or species shall increase in number, and which shall decrease, or finally become extinct. As the individuals of the same species come in all respects into the closest competition with each other, the struggle will generally be most severe between them; it will be almost equally severe between the varieties of the same species, and next in severity between the species of the same genus. On the other hand the struggle will often be severe between beings remote in the scale of nature. The slightest advantage in certain individuals, at any age or during any season, over those with which they come into competition, or better adaptation in however slight a degree to the surrounding physical conditions, will, in the long run, turn the balance. . . .

As geology plainly proclaims that each land has undergone great physical changes, we might have expected to find that organic beings have varied under nature, in the same way as they have varied under domestication. And if there has been any variability under nature, it would be an unaccountable fact if natural selection had not come into play. It has often been asserted, but the assertion is incapable of proof, that the amount of variation under nature is a strictly limited quantity. Man, though acting on external characters alone and often capriciously, can produce within a short period a great result by adding up mere individual differences in his domestic productions; and every one admits that species present individual differences. But, besides such differences, all naturalists admit that natural varieties exist, which are considered sufficiently distinct to be worthy of record in systematic works. No one has drawn any clear distinction between individual differences and slight varieties; or between more plainly marked varieties and sub-species, and species. On separate continents, and on different parts of the same continent when divided by barriers of any kind, and on outlying islands, what a multitude of forms exist which some experienced naturalists rank as varieties, others as geographical races or sub-species, and others as distinct, though closely allied species!

If, then, animals and plants do vary, let it be ever so slightly or slowly, why should not variations or individual differences, which are in any way beneficial, be preserved and accumulated through natural selection, or the survival of the fittest? If man can by patience select variations useful to him, why, under changing and complex conditions of life, should not variations useful to nature's living products often arise, and be preserved or selected? What limit can be put to this power, acting during long ages and rigidly scrutinising the whole constitution, structure, and habits of each creature,—favouring the good and rejecting the bad? I can see no limit to this power, in slowly and beautifully adapting each form to the most complex relations of life. The theory of natural selection, even if we look no farther than this, seems to be in the highest degree probable. I have already recapitulated, as fairly as I could, the opposed difficulties and objections; now let us turn to the special facts and arguments in favour of the theory. . . .

As natural selection acts solely by accumulating slight, successive, favourable variations, it can produce no great or sudden modifications; it can act only by short and slow steps. Hence, the canon of "Natura non facit saltum," which every fresh addition to our knowledge tends to confirm, is on this theory intelligible. We can see why throughout nature the same general end is gained by an almost indefinite diversity of means, for every peculiarity when once acquired is long inherited, and structures already modified in many different ways have to be adapted for the same general purpose. We can, in short, see why nature is prodigal in variety, though niggard in innovation. But why this should be a law of nature if each species has been independently created no man can explain.

If we admit that the geological record is imperfect to an extreme degree, then the facts, which the record does give, strongly support the theory of descent with modification. New species have come on the stage slowly and at successive intervals; and the amount of change, after equal intervals of time, is widely different in different groups. The extinction of species and of whole groups of species which has played so conspicuous a part in the history of the organic world, almost inevitably follows from the principle of natural selection; for old forms are supplanted by new and improved forms. Neither single species nor groups of species reappear when the chain of ordinary generation is once broken. The gradual diffusion of dominant forms, with the slow modification of their descendants, causes the forms of life, after long intervals of time, to appear as if they had changed simultaneously throughout the world. The fact of the fossil remains of each formation being in some degree intermediate in character between the fossils in the formations above and below, is simply explained by their intermediate position in the chain of descent. The grand fact that all extinct beings can be classed with all recent beings, naturally follows from the living and the extinct being the offspring of common parents. As species have generally diverged in character during their long course of descent and modification, we can understand why it is that the more ancient forms, or early progenitors of each group, so often occupy a position in some degree intermediate between existing groups. Recent forms are generally looked upon as being, on the whole, higher in the scale of organisation than ancient forms; and they must be higher, in so far as the later and more improved forms have conquered the older and less improved forms in the struggle for life; they have also generally had their organs more specialised for different functions. This fact is perfectly compatible with numerous beings still retaining simple and but little improved structures, fitted for simple conditions of life; it is likewise compatible with some forms having retrograded in organisation, by having become at each stage of descent better fitted for new and degraded habits of life. Lastly, the wonderful law of the long endurance of allied forms on the same continent,—of marsupials in Australia, of edentata in America, and other such cases,—is intelligible, for within the same country the existing and the extinct will be closely allied by descent. . . .

The fact, as we have seen, that all past and present organic beings can be arranged within a few great classes, in groups subordinate to groups, and with the extinct groups often falling in between the recent groups, is intelligible on the theory of natural selection with its contingencies of extinction and divergence of character. On these same principles we see how it is, that the mutual affinities of the forms within each class are so complex and çircuitous. We see why certain characters are far more serviceable than others for classification;—why adaptive characters, though of paramount importance to the beings, are of hardly any importance in classification; why characters derived from rudimentary parts, though of no service to the beings, are often of high classificatory value; and why embryological characters are often the most valuable of all. The real affinities of all organic beings, in contradistinction to their adaptive resemblances, are due to inheritance or community of descent. The Natural System is a genealogical arrangement, with the acquired grades of difference, marked by the terms, varieties, species, genera, families, &c.; and we have to discover the lines of descent by the most permanent characters whatever they may be and of however slight vital importance.

Why, it may be asked, until recently did nearly all the most eminent living naturalists and geologists disbelieve in the mutability of species? It cannot be asserted that organic beings in a state of nature are subject to no variation; it cannot be proved that the amount of variation in the course of long ages is a limited quality; no clear distinction has been, or can be, drawn between species and well-marked varieties. It cannot be maintained that species when intercrossed are invariably sterile, and varieties invariably fertile; or that sterility is a special endowment and sign of creation. The belief that species were immutable productions was almost unavoidable as long as the history of the world was thought to be of short duration; and now that we have acquired some idea of the lapse of time, we are too apt to assume, without proof, that the geological record is so perfect that it would have afforded us plain evidence of the mutation of species, if they had undergone mutation.

But the chief cause of our natural unwillingness to admit that one species has given birth to clear and distinct species, is that we are always slow in admitting great changes of which we do not see the steps. The difficulty is the same as that felt by so many geologists, when Lyell first insisted that long lines of inland cliffs had been formed, and great valleys excavated, by the agencies which we see still at work. The mind cannot possibly grasp the full meaning of the term of even a million years; it cannot add up and perceive the full effects of many slight variations, accumulated during an almost infinite number of generations.

Although I am fully convinced of the truth of the views given in this volume under the form of an abstract, I by no means expect to convince experienced naturalists whose minds are stocked with a multitude of facts all viewed, during a long course of years, from a point of view directly opposite to mine. It is so easy to hide our ignorance under such expressions as the "plan of creation," "unity of design," &c., and to think that we give an explanation when we only re-state a fact. Anyone whose disposition leads him to attach more weight to unexplained difficulties than to the explanation of a certain number of facts will certainly reject the theory. A few naturalists, endowed with much flexibility of mind, and who have already begun to doubt the immutability of species, may be influenced by this volume; but I look with confidence to the future,— to young and rising naturalists, who will be able to view both sides of the question with impartiality. Whoever is led to believe that species are mutable will do good service by conscientiously expressing his conviction; for thus only can the load of prejudice by which this subject is overwhelmed be removed. . . .

Analogy would lead me one step farther, namely, to the belief that all animals and plants are descended from some one prototype. But analogy may be a deceitful guide. Nevertheless all living things have much in common, in their chemical composition, their cellular structure, their laws of growth, and their liability to injurious influences. We see this even in so trifling a fact as that the same poison often similarly affects plants and animals; or that the poison secreted by the gall-fly produces monstrous growths on the wild rose or oak-tree. With all organic beings excepting perhaps some of the very lowest, sexual production seems to be essentially similar. With all, as far as is at present known the germinal vesicle is the same; so that all organisms start from a common origin. If we look even to the two main divisions—namely, to the animal and vegetable kingdoms—certain low forms are so far intermediate in character that naturalists have disputed to which kingdom they should be referred. As Professor Asa Gray has remarked, "the spores and other reproductive bodies of many of the lower algæ may claim to have first a characteristically animal, and then an unequivocally vegetable existence." Therefore, on the principle of natural selection with divergence of character, it does not seem incredible that, from such low and intermediate form, both animals and plants may have been developed; and, if we admit this, we must likewise admit that all the organic beings which have ever lived on this earth may be descended from some one primordial form. But this inference is chiefly grounded on analogy and it is immaterial whether or not it be accepted. No doubt it is possible, as Mr. G. H. Lewes has urged, that at the first commencement of life many different forms were evolved; but if so we may conclude that only a very few have left modified descendants. For, as I have recently remarked in regard to the members of each great kingdom, such as the Vertebrata Articulata &c., we have distinct evidence in their embryological homologous and rudimentary structure that within each kingdom all the members are descended from a single progenitor. . . .

The other and more general departments of natural history will rise greatly in interest. The terms used by naturalists, of affinity, relationship, community of type, paternity, morphology, adaptive characters, rudimentary and aborted organs, &c., will cease to be metaphorical, and will have a plain signification. When we no longer look at an organic being as a savage looks at a ship, as something wholly beyond his comprehension; when we regard every production of nature as one which has had a long history; when we contemplate every complex structure and instinct as the summing up of many contrivances, each useful to the possessor, in the same way as any great mechanical invention is the summing up of the labour, the experience, the reason, and even the blunders of numerous workmen; when we thus view each organic being, how far more interesting—I speak from experience—does the study of natural history become!

A grand and almost untrodden field of inquiry will be opened, on the causes and laws of variation, on correlation, on the effects of use and disuse, on the direct action of external conditions, and so forth. The study of domestic productions will rise immensely in value. A new variety raised by man will be a more important and interesting subject for study than one more species added to the infinitude of already recorded species. Our classifications will come to be, as far as they can be so made, genealogies; and will then truly give what may be called the plan of creation. The rules for classifying will no doubt become simpler when we have a definite object in view. We possess no pedigrees or armorial bearings; and we have to discover and trace the many diverging lines of descent in our natural genealogies, by characters of any kind which have long been inherited. Rudimentary organs will speak infallibly with respect to the nature of long-lost structures. Species and groups of species which are called aberrant, and which may fancifully be called living fossils, will aid us in forming a picture of the ancient forms of life. Embryology will often reveal to us the structure, in some degree obscured, of the prototype of each great class. . . .

When I view all beings not as special creations, but as the lineal descendants of some few beings which lived long before the first bed of the Cambrian system was deposited, they seem to me to become ennobled. Judging from the past, we may safely infer that not one living species will transmit its unaltered likeness to a distant futurity. And of the species now living very few will transmit progeny of any kind to a far distant futurity; for the manner in which all organic beings are grouped, shows that the greater number of species in each genus, and all the species in many genera, have left no descendants, but have become utterly extinct. We can so far take a prophetic glance into futurity as to foretell that it will be the common and widely spread species, belonging to the larger and dominant groups within each class, which will ultimately prevail and procreate new and dominant species. As all the living forms of life are the lineal descendants of those which lived long before the Cambrian epoch, we may feel certain that the ordinary succession by generations has never once been broken, and that no cataclysm has desolated the whole world. Hence we may look with some confidence to a secure future of great length. And as natural selection works solely by and for the good of each being, all corporeal and mental endowments will tend to progress towards perfection.

It is interesting to contemplate a tangled bank, clothed with many plants of many kinds, with birds singing on the bushes, with various insects flitting about, and with worms crawling through the damp earth, and to reflect that these elaborately constructed forms, so different from each other and dependent upon each other in so complex a manner, have all been produced by laws acting around us. These laws, taken in the largest sense, being Growth, with Reproduction; Inheritance which is almost implied by reproduction; Variability from the indirect and direct action of the conditions of life, and from use and disuse; a Ratio of Increase so high as to lead to a Struggle for Life, and as a consequence to Natural Selection, entailing Divergence of Character and the Extinction of less-improved forms. Thus, from the war of nature, from famine and death, the most exalted object which we are capable of conceiving, namely, the production of the higher animals, directly follows. There is grandeur in this view of life, with its several powers, having been originally breathed by the Creator into a few forms or into one; and that, whilst this planet has gone cycling on according to the fixed law of gravity, from so simple a beginning endless forms most beautiful and most wonderful have been, and are being evolved.

6. JOHN STUART MILL: *ON LIBERTY*

John Stuart Mill (1806–1873) was the leading representative thinker of English nineteenth-century liberalism. He broadened the utilitarian tradition of Jeremy Bentham (1748–1832) and of his father, James Mill (1773–1836), Bentham's foremost disciple, by humanizing it through infusing, partly under French influence, partly under his wife's, esthetic, idealistic and socialistic elements. It was also due to the influence of his wife, Harriet Taylor, née Hardy (1807–1858), whom he married in 1851, that Mill became one of the first advocates of women's suffrage. When he was a member of the House of Commons (1865–1868), he moved a bill giving women equal rights, and published in 1869 his plea against "The Subjection of Women." He dedicated his essay "On Liberty" to the memory of his wife, "who was the inspirer, and in part the author, of all that is best in my writings."

The book appeared in 1859, the year Darwin published his *The Origin of Species* and Marx his *Critique of Political Economy*. Darwin tried to discover the laws governing natural history, Marx those governing modern society; Mazzini's concern was the freedom of nations; Mill's concern, the liberty of the individual. He introduced his argument with a quotation from *Sphere and Duties of Government* (written 1792) by Wilhelm von Humboldt, a German statesman, philosopher, and philologist (1767–1835), a friend of the great German classical poets, Goethe and Schiller: "The grand, leading principle, towards which every argument unfolded in these pages directly converges, is the absolute and essential importance of human development in its richest diversity."

To the student of European intellectual history in the nineteenth century Mill's *Autobiography,* published after his death in 1873, will be of the greatest interest. Introducing it to the general reader in 1924, Harold J. Laski, then professor at the London School of Economics and Political Science, gave what appears to be a just estimate of Mill's importance: "In the fifty years that have passed since Mill's death no teacher has arisen whose influence upon the mind of his generation has been so beneficent or so far-reaching. . . . Accessibility to new ideas, indignation against injustice, catholicity of temper, and an infinite patience—these were the qualities that made him the mirror of all that was best in his age. . . . He was a democrat, but no one was more critical of the evils of democracy. He was an individualist, but no one was more hostile to the excesses of *laissez-faire.* . . . The thing for which Mill was concerned was that the citizen should be given the full chance to be himself at his best. That, at bottom, is the meaning alike of his emphasis upon the importance of diversity and upon the fact that there are reserves within the human mind into which organization cannot, and ought not, to enter."

On Liberty consists of five chapters: "Introduction"; "Of the Liberty Of Thought and Discussion"; "Of Individuality," as one of the "Elements of Well-Being"; "Of the Limits of the Authority of Society over the Individual"; "Applications." The following excerpts are taken from all of these, with the exception of the fourth.[9]

The object of this Essay is to assert one very simple principle, as entitled to govern absolutely the dealings of society with the individual in the way of compulsion and control, whether the means used be physical force in the form of legal penalties, or the moral coercion of public opinion. That principle is, that the sole end for which mankind are warranted, individually or collectively, in interfering with the liberty of action of any of their number, is self-protection. That the only purpose for which power can be rightfully exercised over any member of a civilized community, against his will, is to prevent harm to others. His own good, either physical or moral, is not a sufficient warrant. He cannot rightfully be compelled to do or forbear because it will be better for him to do so, because

[9] John Stuart Mill, *On Liberty, Representative Government, The Subjection of Women* (London: The World's Classics, 1912), pp. 5–141

it will make him happier, because, in the opinions of others, to do so would be wise, or even right. These are good reasons for remonstrating with him, not for compelling him, or visiting him with any evil in case he do otherwise. To justify that, the conduct from which it is desired to deter him must be calculated to produce evil to some one else. The only part of the conduct of any one, for which he is amenable to society, is that which concerns others. In the part which merely concerns himself, his independence is, of right, absolute. Over himself, over his own body and mind, the individual is sovereign. . . .

This, then, is the appropriate region of human liberty. It comprises, first, the inward domain of consciousness; demanding liberty of conscience in the most comprehensive sense; liberty of thought and feeling; absolute freedom of opinion and sentiment on all subjects, practical or speculative, scientific, moral, or theological. The liberty of expressing and publishing opinions may seem to fall under a different principle, since it belongs to that part of the conduct of an individual which concerns other people; but, being almost of as much importance as the liberty of thought itself, and resting in great part on the same reasons, is practically inseparable from it. Secondly, the principle requires liberty of tastes and pursuits; of framing the plan of our life to suit our own character; of doing as we like, subject to such consequences as may follow: without impediment from our fellow-creatures, so long as what we do does not harm them, even though they should think our conduct foolish, perverse, or wrong. Thirdly, from this liberty of each individual, follows the liberty, within the same limits, of combination among individuals; freedom to unite, for any purpose not involving harm to others: the persons combining being supposed to be of full age, and not forced or deceived.

No society in which these liberties are not on the whole respected, is free, whatever may be its form of government; and none is completely free in which they do not exist absolute and unqualified. The only freedom which deserves the name, is that of pursuing our own good in our own way, so long as we do not attempt to deprive others of theirs, or impede their efforts to obtain it. Each is the proper guardian of his own health, whether bodily, *or* mental and spiritual. Mankind are greater gainers by suffering each other to live as seems good to themselves, than by compelling each to live as seems good to the rest. . . .

Apart from the peculiar tenets of individual thinkers, there is also in the world at large an increasing inclination to stretch unduly the powers of society over the individual, both by the force of opinion and even by that of legislation; and as the tendency of all the changes taking place in the world is to strengthen society, and diminish the power of the individual, this encroachment is not one of the evils which tend spontaneously to disappear, but, on the contrary, to grow more and more formidable. The disposition of mankind, whether as rulers or as fellow-citizens, to impose their own opinions and inclinations as a rule of conduct on others, is so energetically supported by some of the best and by some of the worst feelings incident to human nature, that it is hardly ever kept under restraint by anything but want of power; and as the power is not declining, but growing, unless a strong barrier of moral conviction can be raised against the mischief, we must expect, in the present circumstances of the world, to see it increase. . . .

We have now recognized the necessity to the mental well-being of mankind (on which all their other well-being depends) of freedom of opinion, and freedom of the expression of opinion, on four distinct grounds; which we will now briefly recapitulate.

First, if any opinion is compelled to silence, that opinion may, for aught we can certainly know, be true. To deny this is to assume our own infallibility.

Secondly, though the silenced opinion be an error, it may and very commonly does, contain a portion of the truth; and since the general or prevailing opinion on any subject is rarely or never the whole truth, it is only by the collision of adverse opinions that the remainder of the truth has any chance of being supplied.

Thirdly, even if the received opinion be not only true, but the whole truth; unless it is suffered to be, and actually is, vigorously and earnestly contested, it will, by most of those who receive it, be held in the manner of a prejudice, with little comprehension or feeling of its rational grounds. And not only this, but, fourthly, the meaning of the doctrine itself will be in danger of being lost, or enfeebled, and deprived of its vital effect on the character and conduct: the dogma becoming a mere formal profession, inefficacious for good, but cumbering the ground, and preventing the growth of any real and heartfelt conviction, from reason or personal experience. . . .

He who lets the world, or his own portion of it, choose his plan of life for him, has no need of any other faculty than the ape-like one of imitation. He who chooses his plan for himself, employs all his faculties. He must use observation to see, reasoning and judgment to foresee, activity to gather materials for decision, discrimination to decide, and when he has decided, firmness and self-control to hold to his deliberate decision. And these qualities he requires and exercises exactly in proportion as the part of his conduct which he determines according to his own judgment and feelings is a large one. It is possible that he might be guided in some good path, and kept out of harm's way, without any of these things. But what will be his comparative worth as a human being? It really is of importance, not only what men do, but also what manner of men they are that do it. Among the works of man, which human life is rightly employed in perfecting and beautifying, the first in importance surely is man himself. Supposing it were possible to get houses built, corn grown, battles fought, causes tried, and even churches erected and prayers said, by machinery—by automatons in human form—it would be a considerable loss to exchange for these automatons even the men and women who at present inhabit the more civilised parts of the world, and who assuredly are but starved specimens of what nature can and will produce. Human nature is not a machine to be built after a model, and set to do exactly the work prescribed for it, but a tree, which requires to grow and develop itself on all sides, according to the tendency of the inward forces which make it a living thing. . . .

But society has now fairly got the better of individuality; and the danger which threatens human nature is not the excess, but the deficiency, of personal impulses and preferences. Things are vastly changed since the passions of those who were strong by station or by personal endowment were in a state of habitual rebellion against laws and ordinances, and required to be rigorously chained up to enable the persons within their reach to enjoy any particle of security. In our times, from the highest class of society down to the lowest, every one lives as under the eye of a hostile and dreaded censorship. Not only in what concerns others, but in what concerns only themselves, the individual or the family do not ask themselves—what do I prefer? or, what would suit my character and disposition? or, what would allow the best and highest in me to have fair play, and enable it to grow and thrive? They ask themselves, what is suitable to my position? what is usually done by persons of my station and pecuniary circumstances? or (worse still) what is usually done by persons of a station and circumstances superior to mine? I do not mean that they choose what is customary in preference to what suits their own inclination. It does not occur to them to have any inclination, except for what is customary. Thus the mind itself is bowed to the yoke: even in what people do for pleasure, conformity is the first thing thought of; they live in crowds; they exercise choice only among things commonly done: peculiarity of taste, eccentricity of conduct, are shunned equally with crimes: until by dint of not following their own nature they have no nature to follow: their human capacities are withered and starved: they become incapable of any strong wishes or native pleasures, and are generally without either opinions or feelings of home growth, or properly their own. Now is this, or is it not, the desirable condition of human nature? . . .

In sober truth, whatever homage may be professed, or even paid, to real or supposed mental superiority, the general tendency of things throughout the world is to render mediocrity the ascendant power among mankind. In ancient history, in the Middle Ages, and in a diminishing degree through the long transition from feudality to the present time, the individual was a power in himself; and if he had either great talents or a high social position, he was a considerable power. At present individuals are lost in the crowd. In politics it is almost a triviality to say that public opinion now rules the world. The only power deserving the name is that of masses, and of governments while they make themselves the organ of the tendencies and instincts of masses. This is as true in the moral and social relations of private life as in public transactions. Those whose opinions go by the name of public opinion are not always the same sort of public: in America they are the whole white population; in England, chiefly the middle class. But they are always a mass, that is to say, collective mediocrity. . . . The initiation of all wise or noble things comes and must come from individuals; generally at first from some one individual. The honour and glory of the average man is that he is capable of following that initiative; that he can respond internally to wise and noble things, and be led to them with his eyes open. I am not countenancing the sort of "hero-worship" which applauds the strong man of genius for forcibly seizing on the government of the world and making it do his bidding in spite of itself. All he can claim is, freedom to point out the way. The power of compelling others into it is not only inconsistent with the freedom and development of all the rest, but corrupting to the strong man himself. . . .

What has made the European family of nations an improving, instead of a stationary portion of mankind? Not any superior excellence in them, which, when it exists, exists as the effect, not as the cause; but their remarkable diversity of character and culture. Individuals, classes, nations, have been extremely unlike one another: they have struck out a great variety of paths, each leading to something valuable; and although at every period those who travelled in different paths have been intolerant of one another, and each would have thought it an excellent thing if all the rest could have been compelled to travel his road, their attempts to thwart each other's development have rarely had any permanent success, and each has in time endured to receive the good which the others have offered. Europe is, in my judgment, wholly indebted to this plurality of paths for its progressive and many-sided development. But it already begins to possess this benefit in a considerably less degree. It is decidedly advancing towards the Chinese ideal of making all people alike. M. de Tocqueville, in his last important work, remarks how much more the Frenchmen of the present day resemble one another than did those even of the last generation. The same remark might be made of Englishmen in a far greater degree. In a passage already quoted from Wilhelm von Humboldt, he points out two things as necessary conditions of human development, because necessary to render people unlike one another; namely, freedom, and variety of situations. The second of these two conditions is in this country every day diminishing. The circumstances which surround different classes and individuals, and shape their characters, are daily becoming more assimilated. Formerly, different ranks, different neighborhoods, different trades and professions, lived in what might be called different worlds; at present to a great degree in the same. Comparatively speaking, they now read the same things, listen to the same things, see the same things, go to the same places, have their hopes and fears directed to the same objects, have the same rights and liberties, and the same means of asserting them. Great as are the differences of position which remain, they are nothing to those which have ceased. And the assimilation is still proceeding. All the political changes of the age promote it, since they all tend to raise the low and to lower the high. Every extension of education promotes it, because education brings people under common influences, and gives them access to the general stock of facts and sentiments. Improvement in the means of communication promotes it, by bringing the inhabitants of distant places into personal contact, and keeping up a rapid flow of changes of residence between one place and another. The increase of commerce and manufactures promotes it, by diffusing more widely the advantages of easy circumstances, and opening all objects of ambition, even the highest, to general competition, whereby the desire of rising becomes no longer the character of a particular class, but of all classes. A more powerful agency than even all these, in bringing about a general similarity among mankind, is the complete establishment, in this and other free countries, of the ascendancy of public opinion in the State. As the various social eminences which enabled persons entrenched on them to disregard the opinion of the multitude gradually become levelled; as the very idea of resisting the will of the public, when it is positively known that they have a will, disappears more and more from the minds of practical politicians; there ceases to be any social support for nonconformity —any substantive power in society which, itself opposed to the ascendancy of numbers, is interested in taking under its protection opinions and tendencies at variance with those of the public.

The combination of all these causes forms so great a mass of influences hostile to Individuality, that it is not easy to see how it can stand its ground. It will do so with increasing difficulty, unless the intelligent part of the public can be made to feel its value—to see that it is good there should be differences, even though not for the better, even though, as it may appear to them, some should be for the worse. If the claims of Individuality are ever to be asserted, the time is now, while much is still wanting to complete the enforced assimilation. It is only in the earlier stages that any stand can be successfully made against the encroachment. The demand that all other people shall resemble ourselves grows by what it feeds on. If resistance waits till life is reduced *nearly* to one uniform type, all deviations from that type will come to be considered impious, immoral, even monstrous and contrary to nature. Mankind speedily become unable to conceive diversity, when they have been for some time unaccustomed to see it. . . .

The fact itself, of causing the existence of a human being, is one of the most responsible actions in the range of human life. To undertake this responsibility—to bestow a life which may be either a curse or a blessing—unless the being on whom it is to be bestowed will have at least the ordinary chances of a desirable existence, is a crime against that being. And in a country either over-peopled, or threatened with being so, to produce children, beyond a very small number, with the effect of reducing the reward of labour by their competition, is a serious offense against all who live by the remuneration of their labour. The laws which, in many countries on the Continent, forbid marriage unless the parties can show that they have the means of supporting a family, do not exceed the legitimate powers of the State: and whether such laws be expedient or not (a question mainly dependent on local circumstances and feelings), they are not objectionable as violations of liberty. Such laws are interferences of the State to prohibit a mischievous act—an act injurious to others, which ought to be a subject of reprobation, and social stigma, even when it is not deemed expedient to superadd legal punishment. Yet the current ideas of liberty, which bend so easily to real infringements of the freedom of the individual in things which concern only himself, would repel the attempt to put any restraint upon his inclinations when the consequence of their indulgence is a life or lives of wretchedness and depravity to the offspring, . . .

The objections to government interference, when it is not such as to involve infringement of liberty, may be of three kinds.

The first is, when the thing to be done is likely to be better done by individuals than by the government. Speaking generally, there is no one so fit to conduct any business, or to determine how or by whom it shall be conducted, as those who are personally interested in it. . . .

The second objection is more nearly allied to our subject. In many cases, though individuals may not do the particular thing so well, on the average, as the officers of government, it is nevertheless desirable that it should be done by them, rather than by the government, as a means to their own mental education—a mode of strengthening their active faculties, exercising their judgment, and giving them a familiar knowledge of the subjects with which they are thus left to deal. . . .

The third and most cogent reason for restricting the interference of government is the great evil of adding unnecessarily to its power. Every function superadded to those already exercised by the government causes its influence over hopes and fears to be more widely diffused, and converts, more and more, the active and ambitious part of the public into hangers-on of the government, or of some party which aims at becoming the government. If the roads, the railways, the banks, the insurance offices, the great joint-stock companies, the universities, and the public charities, were all of them branches of the government; if, in addition, the municipal corporations and local boards, with all that now devolves on them, became departments of the central administration; if the employes of all these different enterprises were appointed and paid by the government, and looked to the government for every rise in life; not all the freedom of the press and popular constitution of the legislature would make this or any other country free otherwise than in name. And the evil would be greater, the more efficiently and scientifically the administrative machinery was constructed—the more skilful the arrangements for obtaining the best qualified hands and heads with which to work it. . . .

A government cannot have too much of the kind of activity which does not impede, but aids and stimulates, individual exertion and development. The mischief begins, when, instead of calling forth the activity and powers of individuals and bodies, it substitutes its own activity for theirs; when, instead of informing, advising, and, upon occasion, denouncing, it makes them work in fetters, or bids them stand aside and does their work instead of them. The worth of a State, in the long run, is the worth of the individuals composing it; and a State which postpones the interests of *their* mental expansion and elevation to a little more of administrative skill, or of that semblance of it which practice gives, in the details of business;

a State which dwarfs its men, in order that they may be more docile instruments in its hands even for beneficial purposes—will find that with small men no great thing can really be accomplished; and that the perfection of machinery to which it has sacrificed everything will in the end avail it nothing, for want of the vital power which, in order that the machine might work more smoothly, it has preferred to banish.

7. WALTER BAGEHOT:
THE AGE OF DISCUSSION

Bagehot belonged to a generation twenty years younger than Mill. His book *Physics and Politics, or Thoughts on the Application of Natural Selection and Inheritance to Political Society* appeared in 1867, nine years after Mill's *On Liberty*. It shows clearly in its title the growing influence of Darwin and natural science on social thought. It is the chief literary document of the liberal temper, as distinct from the radical temper, in the mid-Victorian period.

Walter Bagehot (1826–1877) was the editor of the famous London weekly *The Economist*, himself an economist and political scientist. In his attempt to explain the evolution of societies and civilizations and the foundations of progress in human history, he stressed division of power and intellectual freedom as the main factors in the growth of national strength and prosperity. He called a government based on these principles "government by discussion." Even today his defense of limited government and freedom of discussion and competition represents one of the best-reasoned pleas for the superiority of the free form of society over autocracy or totalitarianism.

Physics and Politics consists of six chapters. The following excerpts are taken from the fifth chapter, entitled "The Age of Discussion."[10]

The greatest living contrast is between the old Eastern and customary civilizations and the new Western and changeable civilizations. A year or two ago an inquiry was made of our most intelligent

[10] Walter Bagehot, *Physics and Politics*, Introduction by Hans Kohn (Boston: Beacon Press, 1956), pp. 114–148

officers in the East, not as to whether the English government were really doing good in the East, but as to whether the natives of India themselves thought we were doing good. In a majority of cases, the officers who were the best authority answered thus: "No doubt you are giving the Indians many great benefits: you give them continued peace, free trade, the right to live as they like, subject to the laws; in these points and others they are far better off than they ever were; but still they cannot make you out. What puzzles them is your constant disposition to change or, as you call it, improvement. Their own life in every detail being regulated by ancient usage, they cannot comprehend a policy which is always bringing something new; they do not a bit believe that the desire to make them comfortable and happy is the root of it; they believe, on the contrary, that you are aiming at something which they do not understand—that you mean to 'take away their religion'; in a word, that the end and object of all these continual changes is to make Indians not what they are and what they like to be, but something new and different from what they are, and what they would not like to be." In the East, in a word, we are attempting to put new wine into old bottles—to pour what we can of a civilization whose spirit is progress into the form of a civilization whose spirit is fixity, and whether we shall succeed or not is perhaps the most interesting question in an age abounding almost beyond example in questions of political interest.

Historical inquiries show that the feeling of the Hindus is the old feeling, and that the feeling of the Englishman is a modern feeling. . . . No doubt most civilizations stuck where they first were; no doubt we see now why stagnation is the rule of the world, and why progress is the very rare exception; but we do not learn what it is which has caused progress in these few cases, or the absence of what it is which has denied it in all others.

To this question history gives a very clear and very remarkable answer. It is that the change from the age of status to the age of choice was first made in states where the government was to a great and a growing extent a government by discussion, and where the subjects of that discussion were in some degree abstract or, as we should say, matters of principle. It was in the small republics of Greece and Italy that the chain of custom was first broken. "Liberty said, Let there be light, and, like a sunrise on the sea, Athens arose," says Shelley, and his historical philosophy is in this case far more correct than is usual with him. A free state—a state with liberty—means a state, call it republic or call it monarchy, in which the sovereign power is divided between many persons, and in which there is a discussion among those persons. Of these the Greek republics were the first in history, if not in time, and Athens was the greatest of those republics. . . .

But a government by discussion, if it can be borne, at once breaks down the yoke of fixed custom. The idea of the two is inconsistent. As far as it goes, the mere putting up of a subject to discussion, with the object of being guided by that discussion, is a clear admission that that subject is in no degree settled by established rule, and that men are free to choose in it. It is an admission too that there is no sacred authority—no one transcendent and divinely appointed man whom in that matter the community is bound to obey. And if a single subject or group of subjects be once admitted to discussion, ere long the habit of discussion comes to be established, the sacred charm of use and wont to be dissolved. "Democracy," it has been said in modern times, "is like the grave; it takes, but it does not give." The same is true of "discussion." Once effectually submit a subject to that ordeal, and you can never withdraw it again; you can never again clothe it with mystery, or fence it by consecration; it remains forever open to free choice and exposed to profane deliberation. . . .

Tolerance too is learned in discussion and, as history shows, is only so learned. In all customary societies bigotry is the ruling principle. In rude places to this day, anyone who says anything new is looked on with suspicion, and is persecuted by opinion if not injured by penalty. One of the greatest pains to human nature is the pain of a new idea. It is, as common people say, so "upsetting"; it makes you think that, after all, your favorite notions may be wrong, your firmest beliefs ill-founded; it is certain that till now there was no place allotted in your mind to the new and startling inhabitant, and now that it has conquered an entrance you do not at once see which of your old ideas it will or will not turn out, with which of them it can be reconciled, and with which it is at essential enmity. Naturally, therefore, common men hate a new idea, and are disposed more or less to ill-treat the original man who brings it. Even nations with long habits of discussion are intolerant enough. In England, where there is on the whole probably a freer discussion of a greater number of subjects than ever was before in the world, we know how much power bigotry retains. But discussion, to be successful, requires tolerance. It fails wherever, as in a French political assembly, any one who hears anything which he dislikes tries to howl it down. If we know that a nation is capable of enduring continuous discussion, we know that it is capable of practicing with equanimity continuous tolerance. . . .

The next question, therefore, is: Why did discussions in some cases relate to prolific ideas, and why did discussions in other cases relate only to isolated transactions? The reply which history suggests is very clear and very remarkable. Some races of men at our earliest knowledge of them have already acquired the basis of a free constitution; they have already the rudiments of a complex polity—a monarch, a senate, and a general meeting of citizens. The Greeks were one of those races, and it happened, as was natural, that there was in process of time a struggle, the earliest that we know of, between the aristocratic party, originally represented by the senate, and the popular party, represented by the "general meeting." This is plainly a question of principle, and its being so has led to its history being written more than two thousand years afterwards in a very remarkable manner. Some seventy years ago an English country gentleman named Mitford,[11] who, like so many of his age, had been terrified into aristocratic opinions by the first French Revolution, suddenly found that the history of the Peloponnesian War was the reflex of his own time. He took up his Thucydides, and there he saw, as in a mirror, the progress and the struggles of his age. It required some freshness of mind to see this; at least, it had been hidden for many centuries. All the modern histories of Greece before Mitford had but the vaguest idea of it; and, not being a man of supreme originality, he would doubtless have had very little idea of it either, except that the analogy of what he saw helped him by a telling object lesson to the understanding of what he read. Just as in every country of Europe in 1793 there were two factions, one of the old-world aristocracy, and the other of the incoming democracy, just so there was in every city of ancient Greece, in the year 400 B.C., one party of the many and another of the few. This Mr. Mitford perceived and being a strong aristocrat, he wrote a "history," which is little except a party pamphlet, and which, it must be said, is even now readable on that very account. The vigor of passion with which it was written puts life into the words, and retains the attention of the reader. And that is not all. Mr. Grote,[12] the great scholar whom we have had lately to mourn, also recognizing the identity between the struggles of Athens and Sparta and the struggles of our modern world, and taking violently the contrary side to that of Mitford, being as great a democrat as Mitford was an aristocrat, wrote a reply, far above Mitford's history in power and learning, but being in its main characteristic almost identical—being above all things a book of vigorous political passion, written for persons who care for politics and not, as almost all histories of antiquity are and must be, the book of a man who cares for scholar-

[11] William Mitford (1744–1827), author of *History of Greece* in five volumes (1784–1810)

[12] George Grote (1794–1871), author of *History of Greece* in eight volumes (1846–1856)

ship more than for anything else, written mainly, if not exclusively, for scholars. And the effect of fundamental political discussion was the same in ancient as in modern times. The whole customary ways of thought were at once shaken by it, and shaken not only in the closets of philosophers but in the common thought and daily business of ordinary men. The "liberation of humanity," as Goethe used to call it—the deliverance of men from the yoke of inherited usage, and of rigid unquestionable law—was begun in Greece, and had many of its greatest effects, good and evil, on Greece. It is just because of the analogy between the controversies of that time and those of our times that some one has said, "Classical history is a part of modern history; it is medieval history only which is ancient."

If there had been no discussion of principle in Greece, probably she would still have produced works of art. Homer contains no such discussion. . . . In Herodotus you have the beginning of the age of discussion. He belongs in his essence to the age which is going out. He refers with reverence to established ordinance and fixed religion. Still, in his travels through Greece, he must have heard endless political arguments; and accordingly you can find in his book many incipient traces of abstract political disquisition. The discourses on democracy, aristocracy, and monarchy, which he puts into the mouth of the Persian conspirators when the monarchy was vacant, have justly been called absurd, as speeches supposed to have been spoken by those persons. No Asian ever thought of such things. You might as well imagine Saul or David speaking them as those to whom Herodotus attributes them. They are Greek speeches, full of free Greek discussion, and suggested by the experience, already considerable, of the Greeks in the results of discussion. The age of debate is beginning, and even Herodotus, the least of a wrangler of any man, and the most of a sweet and simple narrator, felt the effect. When we come to Thucydides, the results of discussion are as full as they have ever been; his light is pure, "dry light," free from the "humors" of habit, and purged from consecrated usage. As Grote's history often reads like a report to Parliament, so half Thucydides reads like a speech, or materials for a speech, in the Athenian Assembly. Of later times it is unnecessary to speak. Every page of Aristotle and Plato bears ample and indelible trace of the age of discussion in which they lived; and thought cannot possibly be freer. The deliverance of the speculative intellect from traditional and customary authority was altogether complete.

No doubt the "detachment" from prejudice, and the subjection to reason, which I ascribe to ancient Athens, only went down a very little way among the population of it. Two great classes of the people, the slaves and women, were almost excluded from such qualities; even the freer population doubtless contained a far greater proportion of very ignorant and very superstitious persons than we are in the habit of imagining. We fix our attention on the best specimens of Athenian culture—on the books which have descended to us—and we forget that the corporate action of the Athenian people at various critical junctures exhibited the most gross superstition. Still, as far as the intellectual and cultivated part of society is concerned, the triumph of reason was complete; the minds of the highest philosophers were then as ready to obey evidence and reason as they have ever been since; probably they were more ready. The rule of custom over them at least had been wholly broken, and the primary conditions of intellectual progress were in that respect satisfied. . . .

It is true that the influence of discussion is not the only force which has produced this vast effect. Both in ancient and in modern times other forces co-operated with it. Trade, for example, is obviously a force which has done much to bring men of different customs and different beliefs into close contiguity, and has thus aided to change the customs and the beliefs of them all. Colonization is another such influence: it settles men among aborigines of alien race and usages; and it commonly compels the colonists not to be over-strict in the choice of their own elements. They are obliged to coalesce with and "adopt" useful bands and useful men, though their ancestral customs may not be identical—nay, though they may be, in fact, opposite to their own. In modern Europe, the existence of a cosmopolite Church, claiming to be above nations and really extending through nations, and the scattered remains of Roman law and Roman civilization co-operated with the liberating influence of political discussion. And so did other causes also. But perhaps in no case have these subsidiary causes alone been able to generate intellectual freedom; certainly in all the most remarkable cases the influence of discussion has presided at the creation of that freedom, and has been active and dominant in it. . . .

In this manner politics or discussion broke up the old bonds of custom which were now strangling mankind, though they had once aided and helped it. But this is only one of the many gifts which those polities have conferred, are conferring, and will confer on mankind. I am not going to write a eulogium on liberty, but I wish to set down three points which have not been sufficiently noticed.

Civilized ages inherit the human nature which was victorious in barbarous ages, and that nature is, in many respects, not at all suited to civilized circumstances. A main and principal excellence in the early times of the human race is the impulse to action. The problems before men are then plain and simple. The man who works hardest, the man who kills the most deer, the man who catches the most fish—even later on, the man who tends the largest herds, or the man who tills the largest field—is the man who succeeds; the nation which is quickest to kill its enemies, or which kills most of its enemies, is the nation which succeeds. All the inducements of early society tend to foster immediate action; all its penalties fall on the man who pauses; the traditional wisdom of those times was never weary of inculcating that "delays are dangerous," and that the sluggish man—the man "who roasteth not that which he took in hunting"—will not prosper on the earth, and indeed will very soon perish out of it. And in consequence an inability to stay quiet, an irritable desire to act directly, is one of the most conspicuous failings of mankind.

Pascal said that most of the evils of life arose from "man's being unable to sit still in a room"; and, though I do not go that length, it is certain that we should have been a far wiser race than we are if we had been readier to sit quiet—we should have known much better the way in which it was best to act when we came to act. The rise of physical science, the first great body of practical truth probable to all men, exemplifies this in the plainest way. If it had not been for quiet people, who sat still and studied the sections of the cone; if other quiet people had not sat still and studied the theory of infinitesimals, or other quiet people had not sat still and worked out the doctrine of chances, the most "dreamy moonshine," as the purely practical mind would consider, of all human pursuits; if "idle stargazers" had not watched long and carefully the motions of the heavenly bodies—then our modern astronomy would have been impossible, and without our astronomy "our ships, our colonies, our seamen," all which makes modern life modern life, could not have existed. Ages of sedentary, quiet, thinking people were re-quired before that noisy existence began, and without those pale preliminary students it never could have been brought into being. And nine-tenths of modern science is in this respect the same: it is the produce of men whom their contemporaries thought dreamers; who were laughed at for caring for what did not concern them; who, as the proverb went, "walked into a well from looking at the stars"; who were believed to be useless, if anyone could be such. And the conclusion is plain that if there had been more such people, if the world had not laughed at those there were, if rather it had encouraged them—then there would have been a great accumula-tion of proved science ages before there was. It was the irritable activity, the "wish to be doing something," that prevented it. Most men inherited a nature too eager and too restless to be quiet and find out things; and, even worse, with their idle clamor they "dis-turbed the brooding hen"; they would not let those be quiet who wished to be so, and out of whose calm thought much good might have come forth.

If we consider how much science has done and how much it is doing for mankind, and if the over-activity of men is proved to be the cause why science came so late into the world, and is so small and scanty still, that will convince most people that our over-activity is a very great evil. But this is only part, and perhaps not the greatest part, of the harm that over-activity does. As I have said, it is inherited from times when life was simple, objects were plain, and quick action generally led to desirable ends. If A kills B before B kills A, then A survives, and the human race is a race of A's. But the issues of life are plain no longer. To act rightly in modern society requires a great deal of previous study, a great deal of assimilated information, a great deal of sharpened imagination; and these prerequisites of sound action require much time, and, I was going to say, much "lying in the sun," a long period of "mere passiveness." Even the art of killing one another, which at first particularly trained men to be quick, now requires them to be slow. A hasty general is the worst of generals nowadays; the best is a sort of Von Moltke,[13] who is passive if any man ever was passive, who is "silent in seven languages," who possesses more and better accumulated information as to the best way of killing people than anyone who ever lived. This man plays a restrained and considerate game of chess with his enemy. I wish the art of benefiting men had kept pace with the art of destroying them; for, though war has become slow, philanthropy has remained hasty. The most melancholy of human reflections perhaps is that, on the whole, it is a question whether the benevolence of mankind does most good or harm. Great good, no doubt, philanthropy does, but then it also does great evil. It augments so much vice, it multiplies so much suffering, it brings to life such great populations to suffer and to be vicious, that it is open to argument whether it be or be not an evil to the world, and this is entirely because excellent people fancy that they can do much by rapid action—that they will most benefit the world when they most relieve their own feelings; that as soon as an evil is seen "something" ought to be done to stay and prevent it. One may incline to hope that the balance of good over evil is in favor of benevolence; one can hardly bear to think that it is not so; but anyhow it is certain that there is a most heavy debit of evil, and that this burden might almost all have been spared us if philanthropists as well as others had not inherited from their barbarous forefathers a wild passion for instant action.

Even in commerce, which is now the main occupation of mankind,

[13] Helmuth von Moltke (1800–1891), chief of Prussian general staff (1858–1888)

and one in which there is a ready test of success and failure wanting in many higher pursuits, the same disposition to excessive action is very apparent to careful observers. Part of every mania is caused by the impossibility to get people to confine themselves to the amount of business for which their capital is sufficient, and in which they can engage safely. In some degree, of course, this is caused by the wish to get rich; but in a considerable degree, too, by the mere love of activity. There is a greater propensity to action in such men than they have the means of gratifying. Operations with their own capital will only occupy four hours of the day, and they wish to be active and to be industrious for eight hours, and so they are ruined. If they could only have sat idle the other four hours, they would have been rich men. The amusements of mankind, at least of the English part of mankind, teach the same lesson. Our shooting, our hunting, our traveling, our climbing have become laborious pursuits. It is a common saying abroad that "an Englishman's notion of a holiday is a fatiguing journey"; and this is only another way of saying that the immense energy and activity which have given us our place in the world have in many cases descended to those who do not find in modern life any mode of using that activity, and of venting that energy. . . .

But it will be said: What has government by discussion to do with these things? Will it prevent them, or even mitigate them? It can and does do both in the very plainest way. If you want to stop instant and immediate action, always make it a condition that the action shall not begin till a considerable number of persons have talked over it, and have agreed on it. If those persons be people of different temperaments, different ideas, and different educations, you have an almost infallible security that nothing, or almost nothing, will be done with excessive rapidity. Each kind of persons will have their spokesman; each spokesman will have his characteristic objection, and each his characteristic counter-proposition, and so in the end nothing will probably be done, or at least only the minimum which is plainly urgent. In many cases this delay may be dangerous; in many cases quick action will be preferable. A campaign, as Macaulay well says, cannot be directed by a "debating society"; and many other kinds of action also require a single and absolute general. But for the purpose now in hand—that of preventing hasty action, and ensuring elaborate consideration—there is no device like a polity of discussion.

The enemies of this object—the people who want to act quickly —see this very distinctly. They are forever explaining that the present is "an age of committees," that the committees do nothing, that all evaporates in talk. Their great enemy is parliamentary government; they call it, after Mr. Carlyle, the "national palaver"; they add up the hours that are consumed in it, and the speeches which are made in it, and they sigh for a time when England might again be ruled, as it once was, by a Cromwell—that is, when an eager, absolute man might do exactly what other eager men wished, and do it immediately. All these invectives are perpetual and many-sided; they come from philosophers, each of whom wants some new scheme tried; from philanthropists, who want some evil abated; from revolutionists, who want some old institution destroyed; from "new eraists," who want their new era started forthwith. And they all are distinct admissions that a polity of discussion is the greatest hindrance to the inherited mistake of human nature—to the desire to act promptly, which in a simple age is so excellent, but which in a later and complex time leads to so much evil.

The same accusation against our age sometimes takes a more general form. It is alleged that our energies are diminishing; that ordinary and average men have not the quick determination nowadays which they used to have when the world was younger; not only that committees and parliaments do not act with rapid decisiveness, but that no one now so acts. And I hope that in fact this is true, for, according to me, it proves that the hereditary barbaric impulse is decaying and dying out. So far from thinking the quality attributed to us a defect, I wish that those who complain of it were far more right than I much fear they are. Still, certainly, eager and violent action *is* somewhat diminished, though only by a small fraction of what it ought to be. And I believe that this trend is in great part due, in England at least, to our government by discussion, which has fostered a general intellectual tone, a diffused disposition to weigh evidence, a conviction that much may be said on every side of everything which the elder and more fanatic ages of the world lacked. This is the real reason why our energies seem so much less than those of our fathers. When we have a definite end in view, which we know we want, and which we think we know how to obtain, we can act well enough. The campaigns of our soldiers are as energetic as any campaigns ever were; the speculations of our merchants have greater promptitude, greater audacity, greater vigor than any such speculations ever had before. In old times a few ideas got possession of men and communities, but this is happily now possible no longer. We see how incomplete these old ideas were; how almost by chance one seized on one nation, and another on another; how often one set of men have persecuted another set for opinions on subjects of which neither, we now perceive, knew anything. It might be well if a greater number of effectual demonstrations existed among mankind; but while no such demonstrations exist, and while the evidence which completely convinces one man seems to another trifling and insufficient, let us recognize the plain position of inevitable doubt. Let us not be bigots with a doubt, and persecutors without a creed. We are beginning to see this, and we are railed at for so beginning. But it is a great benefit, and it is to the incessant prevalence of detective discussion that our doubts are due; and much of that discussion is due to the long existence of a government requiring constant debates, written and oral. . . .

Lastly, a polity of discussion not only tends to diminish our inherited defects, but also, in one case at least, to augment a heritable excellence. It tends to strengthen and increase a subtle quality or combination of qualities singularly useful in practical life—a quality which it is not easy to describe exactly, and the issues of which it would require not a remnant of an essay, but a whole essay to elucidate completely. This quality I call "animated moderation."

If anyone were asked to describe what it is which distinguishes the writings of a man of genius who is also a great man of the world from all other writings, I think he would use these same words, "animated moderation." He would say that such writings are never slow, are never excessive, are never exaggerated; that they are always instinct with judgment, and yet that the judgment is never a dull judgment; that they have as much spirit in them as would go to make a wild writer, and yet that every line of them is the product of a sane and sound writer. . . .

In action it is equally this quality in which the English—at least so I claim it for them—excel all other nations. There is an infinite deal to be laid against us; and as we are unpopular with most others, and as we are always grumbling at ourselves, there is no want of people to say it. But, after all, in a certain sense, England is a success in the world; her career has had many faults, but still it has been a fine and winning career upon the whole. And this on account of the exact possession of this particular quality. What is the making of a successful merchant? That he has plenty of energy, and yet that he does not go too far. And if you ask for a description of a great practical Englishman, you will be sure to have this, or something like it: "Oh, he has plenty of go in him; but he knows when to pull up." He may have all other defects in him; he may be coarse, he may be illiterate, he may be stupid to talk to; still this great union of spur and bridle, of energy and moderation, will remain to him. Probably he will hardly be able to explain why he stops when he does stop, or why he continued to move as long as he, in fact, moved; but still, as by a rough instinct, he pulls up pretty much where he should, though he was going at such a pace before. . . .

It is plain that this is a quality which as much as, if not more than, any other multiplies good results in practical life. It enables men to see what is good; it gives them intellect enough for sufficient perception; but it does not make men all intellect; it does not "sickly them o'er with the pale cast of thought"; it enables them to do the good things they see to be good, as well as to see that they are good. And it is plain that a government by popular discussion tends to produce this quality. A strongly idiosyncratic mind, violently disposed to extremes of opinion, is soon weeded out of political life, and a bodiless thinker, an ineffectual scholar, cannot even live there for a day. A vigorous moderateness in mind and body is the rule of a polity which works by discussion; and, upon the whole, it is the kind of temper most suited to the active life of such a being as man in such a world as the present one.

These three great benefits of free government, though great, are entirely secondary to its continued usefulness in the mode in which it originally was useful. The first great benefit was the deliverance of mankind from the superannuated yoke of customary law, by the gradual development of an inquisitive originality. And it continues to produce that effect upon persons apparently far remote from its influence, and on subjects with which it has nothing to do. Thus Mr. Mundella, a most experienced and capable judge, tells us that the English artisan, though so much less sober, less instructed, and less refined than the artisans of some other countries, is yet more inventive than any other artisan. The master will get more good suggestions from him than from any other.

Again, upon plausible grounds—looking, for example, to the position of Locke and Newton in the science of the last century, and to that of Darwin in our own—it may be argued that there is some quality in English thought which makes them strike out as many, if not more, first-rate and original suggestions than nations of greater scientific culture and more diffused scientific interest. In both cases I believe the reason of the English originality to be that government by discussion quickens and enlivens thought all through society; that it makes people think no harm may come of thinking; that in England this force has long been operating, and so it has developed more of all kinds of people ready to use their mental energy in their own way, and not ready to use it in any other way, than a despotic government. And so rare is great originality among mankind, and so great are its fruits, that this one benefit of free government probably outweighs what are in many cases its accessory evils. Of itself it justifies, or goes far to justify, our saying with Montesquieu: "Whatever be the cost of this glorious liberty, we must be content to pay it to heaven."

8. LUDWIG FEUERBACH:
THE ESSENCE OF CHRISTIANITY

Ludwig Feuerbach (1804–1872), a German philosopher, was the son of one of the most famous jurists and reformers of criminal law of his time, Anselm von Feuerbach (1775–1833). Influenced as a young man by Hegel, he soon turned from metaphysics to the study of human nature. "Theology I can study no more," he wrote to a friend of his. "I long to take nature to my heart, that nature before whose depth the faint-hearted theologian shrinks back; and with nature man, man in his entire quality." His book, *The Essence of Christianity*, published in 1841 and translated into English in 1853 by George Eliot (Mary Ann Evans, 1819–1880), the English novelist, is the fundamental statement in the growing humanist and secularist trend, which held that Christianity is no longer the decisive force in modern civilization.

In this book Feuerbach developed an "anthropological" interpretation of religion, viewed as man's consciousness of the infinite, which is part of human nature itself. He said that God is no essence separate from and over man, but the outward projection of man's inward nature. In 1848 Feuerbach delivered a number of lectures in Heidelberg, in which he declared as his principal aim, "to change the friends of God into friends of man, believers into thinkers, worshippers into workers, candidates for the other world into students of this world, Christians who see themselves as half-animal and half-angel into men—whole men." Men had been servants of a celestial and terrestrial monarchy; they were henceforth to become free, self-reliant citizens of the earth. In that sense Feuerbach represented the spirit of 1848 and of the nineteenth century.

Feuerbach had a great influence on the young Marx; many see in him the link between Hegel and Marx. Feuerbach's "humanization" of religion formed, together with Darwinism, one of the essential roots of the growing secularization of moral and intellectual life in the second part of the nineteenth century. The conflict between the new rational and humanist ethics and traditional religious morality was presented in many "nonconformist" novels and plays of the period—those of George Eliot as well as Henrik Ibsen's (1828–1906) *Rosmers-*

holm. Through all of them runs the undercurrent of a "profound belief in man's responsibility to a moral law higher" than any taught by dogmatic religion.

Feuerbach's book consists of twenty-seven chapters. The following excerpts are from the last chapter, called "Concluding Applications."[14]

In the contradiction between Faith and Love which has just been exhibited, we see the practical, palpable ground of necessity that we should raise ourselves above Christianity, above the peculiar stand-point of all religion. We have shown that the substance and object of religion is altogether human; we have shown that divine wisdom is human wisdom; that the secret of theology is anthropology; that the absolute mind is the so-called finite subjective mind. But religion is not conscious that its elements are human; on the contrary, it places itself in opposition to the human, or at least it does not admit that its elements are human. The necessary turning-point of history is therefore the open confession that the consciousness of God is nothing else than the consciousness of the species; that man can and should raise himself only above the limits of his individuality, and not above the laws, the positive essential conditions of his species; that there is no other essence which man can think, dream of, imagine, feel, believe in, wish for, love and adore as the absolute, than the essence of human nature itself.

Our relation to religion is therefore not a merely negative, but a critical one; we only separate the true from the false;—though we grant that the truth thus separated from falsehood is a new truth, essentially different from the old. Religion is the first form of self-consciousness. Religions are sacred because they are the traditions of the primitive self-consciousness. But that which in religion holds the first place—namely, God—is, as we have shown, in itself and according to truth, the second, for it is only the nature of man regarded objectively; and that which to religion is the second—namely, a man—must therefore be constituted and declared the first. Love to man must be no derivative love; it must be original. If human nature is the highest nature to man, then practically also the highest and first law must be the love of man to man. *Homo homini Deus est:*—this is the great practical principle:—this is the axis on which revolved the history of the world. The relations of child and parent, of husband and wife, of brother and friend—in general, of man to man—in short, all the moral relations are *per se*

[14] Ludwig Feuerbach, *The Essence of Christianity,* Translation by George Eliot (New York: Harper Torchbooks, 1957), pp. 270–280

religious. Life as a whole is, in its essential, substantial relations, throughout of a divine nature. Its religious consecration is not first conferred by the blessing of the priest. But the pretension of religion is that it can hallow an object by its essentially external co-operation; it thereby assumes to be itself the only holy power; besides itself it knows only earthly, ungodly relations; hence it comes forward in order to consecrate them and make them holy.

But marriage—we mean, of course, marriage as the free bond of love—is sacred in itself, by the very nature of the union which is therein effected. That alone is a religious marriage, which is a true marriage, which corresponds to the essence of marriage—of love. And so it is with all moral relations. Then only are they moral,— then only are they enjoyed in a moral spirit, when they are regarded as sacred in themselves. True friendship exists only when the boundaries of friendship are preserved with religious conscientiousness, with the same conscientiousness with which the believer watches over the dignity of his God. Let friendship be sacred to thee, property sacred, marriage sacred,—sacred the well-being of every man; but let them be sacred in and by themselves.

In Christianity the moral laws are regarded as the commandments of God; morality is even made the criterion of piety; but ethics have nevertheless a subordinate rank, they have not in themselves a religious significance. This belongs only to faith. Above morality hovers God, as a being distinct from man, a being to whom the best is due, while the remnants only fall to the share of man. All those dispositions which ought to be devoted to life, to man—all the best powers of humanity, are lavished on the being who wants nothing. The real cause is converted into an impersonal means; a merely conceptional, imaginary cause usurps the place of the true one. Man thanks God for those benefits which have been rendered to him even at the cost of sacrifice by his fellow-man. The gratitude which he expresses to his benefactor is only ostensible; it is paid, not to him, but to God. He is thankful, grateful to God, but unthankful to man. Thus is the moral sentiment subverted into religion! Thus does man sacrifice man to God! The bloody human sacrifice is in fact only a rude, material expression of the inmost secret of religion. Where bloody human sacrifices are offered to God, such sacrifices are regarded as the highest thing, physical existence as the chief good. For this reason life is sacrificed to God, and it is so on extraordinary occasions; the supposition being that this is the way to show him the greatest honour. If Christianity no longer, at least in our day, offers bloody sacrifices to its God, this arises, to say nothing of other reasons, from the fact that physical existence is no longer regarded as the highest good. Hence the soul, the emotions are now offered to God, because these are held to be something higher. But the common case is, that in religion man sacrifices some duty towards man—such as that of respecting the life of his fellow, of being grateful to him—to a religious obligation,—sacrifices his relation to man to his relation to God. The Christians, by the idea that God is without wants, and that he is only an object of pure adoration, have certainly done away with many pernicious conceptions. But this freedom from wants is only a metaphysical idea, which is by no means part of the peculiar nature of religion. When the need for worship is supposed to exist only on one side, the subjective side, this has the invariable effect of one-sidedness, and leaves the religious emotions cold; hence, if not in express words, yet in fact, there must be attributed to God a condition corresponding to the subjective need, the need of the worshipper, in order to establish reciprocity. All the positive definitions of religion are based on reciprocity. The religious man thinks of God because God thinks of him; he loves God because God has first loved him. God is jealous of man; religion is jealous of morality; it sucks away the best forces of morality; it renders to man only the things that are man's, but to God the things that are God's; and to him is rendered true, living emotion,—the heart.

When in times in which peculiar sanctity was attached to religion, we find marriage, property, and civil law respected, this has not its foundation in religion, but in the original, natural sense of morality and right, to which the true social relations are sacred as such. He to whom the Right is not holy for its own sake will never be made to feel it sacred by religion. Property did not become sacred because it was regarded as a divine institution, but it was regarded as a divine institution because it was felt to be in itself sacred. Love is not holy because it is a predicate of God, but it is a predicate of God because it is in itself divine. The heathens do not worship the light or the fountain because it is a gift of God, but because it has of itself a beneficial influence on man, because it refreshes the sufferer; on account of this excellent quality they pay it divine honours.

Wherever morality is based on theology, wherever the right is made dependent on divine authority, the most immoral, unjust, infamous things can be justified and established. I can found morality on theology only when I myself have already defined the Divine Being by means of morality. In the contrary case, I have no criterion of the moral and immoral, but merely an unmoral, arbitrary basis, from which I may deduce anything I please. Thus, if I would found morality on God, I must first of all place it in God: for Morality, Right, in short, all substantial relations, have their only basis in themselves, can only have a real foundation—such as truth demands—when they are thus based. To place anything in God, or to derive anything from God, is nothing more than to withdraw it from the test of reason, to institute it as indubitable, unassailable, sacred, without rendering an account why. Hence self-delusion, if not wicked, insidious design, is at the root of all efforts to establish morality, right, on theology. Where we are in earnest about the right, we need no incitement or support from above. We need no Christian rule of political right: we need only one which is rational, just, human. The right, the true, the good, has always its ground of sacredness in itself, in its quality. Where man is in earnest about ethics, they have in themselves the validity of a divine power. If morality has no foundation in itself, there is no inherent necessity for morality; morality is then surrendered to the groundless arbitrariness of religion.

9. ERNEST RENAN: *THE LIFE OF JESUS*

Ernest Renan (1823–1890), Orientalist, philosopher, and historian, was the most influential French thinker in the third quarter of the nineteenth century. Originally trained for the Catholic priesthood, he turned later to an agnostic attitude and was a man of great moral influence. He was deprived of his chair at the Collège de France in 1864 for calling Jesus "an incomparable man." His profound familiarity with the Bible and with theology, as well as with the Biblical and Eastern Mediterranean lands and languages, made it possible for him to write the seven volumes of his *History of the Origin of Christianity,* the first of which, *The Life of Jesus,* appeared in 1863 and sold within the first four months 60,000 copies.

The brilliance of his style and his poetical and respectful appreciation of religious figures and landscapes marked the book in its own time a classic even though it was violently attacked by fundamentalist circles. In the year of its appearance (1863) it was translated into English by C. E. Wilbour and published the following year. This translation is being used here. The book is divided into twenty-eight chapters; the following excerpts are taken from Chapter 1, "Place of

Jesus in the History of the World," and Chapter 28, "Essential Character of the Work of Jesus."[15]

To write the history of a religion, it is necessary, firstly, to have believed it (otherwise we should not be able to understand how it has charmed and satisfied the human conscience): in the second place, to believe it no longer in an absolute manner, for absolute faith is incompatible with sincere history. But love is possible without faith. To abstain from attaching one's self to any of the forms which captivate the adoration of men, is not to deprive ourselves of the enjoyment of that which is good and beautiful in them. No transitory appearance exhausts the Divinity; God was revealed before Jesus—God will reveal Himself after him. Profoundly unequal, and so much the more Divine, as they are grander and more spontaneous, the manifestations of God hidden in the depths of the human conscience are all of the same order. Jesus cannot belong solely to those who call themselves his disciples. . . .

. . . A superior personage, who, by his bold originality, and by the love which he was able to inspire, became the object and fixed the starting-point of the future faith of humanity. . . .

Up to the time of the Maccabees, Judaism, in spite of its persistence in announcing that it would one day be the religion of the human race, had had the characteristic of all the other worships of antiquity; it was a worship of the family and the tribe. The Israelite thought, indeed, that his worship was the best, and spoke with contempt of strange gods; but he believed also that the religion of the true God was made for himself alone. Only when a man entered into the Jewish family did he embrace the worship of Jehovah. No Israelite cared to convert the stranger to a worship which was the patrimony of the sons of Abraham. The development of the pietistic spirit, after Ezra and Nehemiah, led to a much firmer and more logical conception. Judaism became the true religion in a more absolute manner; to all who wished, the right of entering it was given; soon it became a work of piety to bring into it the greatest number possible. Doubtless the refined sentiment which elevated John the Baptist, Jesus, and St. Paul above the petty ideas of race, did not yet exist, for, by a strange contradiction, these converts were little respected and were treated with disdain. But the idea of a sovereign religion, the idea that there was something in the world superior to country, to blood, to laws—the idea which makes apostles and martyrs—was founded. Profound pity for the pagans,

[15] Ernest Renan, *The Life of Jesus* (Garden City, N.Y.: Dolphin Books, n.d.), pp. 43–53, 307–317

however brilliant might be their worldly fortune, was henceforth the feeling of every Jew. By a cycle of legends destined to furnish models of immovable firmness, such as the histories of Daniel and his companions, the mother of the Maccabees and her seven sons, the romance of the race-course of Alexandria—the guides of the people sought above all to inculcate the idea that virtue consists in a fanatical attachment to fixed religious institutions. . . .

The reigns of the last Asmoneans, and that of Herod, saw the excitement grow still stronger. They were filled by an uninterrupted series of religious movements. In the degree that power became secularized, and passed into the hands of unbelievers, the Jewish people lived less and less for the earth, and became more and more absorbed by the strange fermentation which was operating in their midst. The world, distracted by other spectacles, had little knowledge of that which passed in this forgotten corner of the East. . . . The quite recent formation of the empire exalted the imagination; the great era of peace on which it entered and that impression of melancholy sensibility which the mind experiences after long periods of revolution, gave birth on all sides to unlimited hopes.

In Judea expectation was at its height. Holy persons—among whom may be named the aged Simeon, who, legend tells us, held Jesus in his arms; Anna, daughter of Phanuel, regarded as a prophetess—passed their life about the temple, fasting, and praying, that it might please God not to take them from the world without having seen the fulfillment of the hopes of Israel. They felt a powerful presentiment; they were sensible of the approach of something unknown.

This confused mixture of clear views and dreams, this alteration of deceptions and hopes, these ceaseless aspirations, driven back by an odious reality, found at last their interpretation in the incomparable man, to whom the universal conscience has decreed the title of Son of God, and that with justice, since he has advanced religion as no other has done, or probably ever will be able to do. . . .

Jesus, it will be seen, limited his action entirely to the Jews. Although his sympathy for those despised by orthodoxy led him to admit pagans into the kingdom of God—although he had resided more than once in a pagan country, and once or twice we surprise him in kindly relations with unbelievers—it may be said that his life was passed entirely in the very restricted world in which he was born. . . . The essential work of Jesus was to create around him a circle of disciples, whom he inspired with boundless affection, and amongst whom he deposited the germ of his doctrine. To have made himself beloved, "to the degree that after his death they ceased not to love him," was the great work of Jesus, and that which most struck his contemporaries. His doctrine was so little dogmatic, that he never thought of writing it or of causing it to be written. Men did not become his disciples by believing this thing or that thing, but in being attached to his person and in loving him. A few sentences collected from memory, and especially the type of character he set forth, and the impression it had left, were what remained of him. Jesus was not a founder of dogmas, or a maker of creeds; he infused into the world a new spirit. The least Christian men were, on the one hand, the doctors of the Greek Church, who, beginning from the fourth century, entangled Christianity in a path of puerile metaphysical discussions, and, on the other, the scholastics of the Latin Middle Ages, who wished to draw from the Gospel the thousands of articles of a colossal system. To follow Jesus in expectation of the kingdom of God, was all that at first was implied by being Christian. . . .

The Church has had its epochs and its phases; it has shut itself up in creeds which are, or will be, but temporary: but Jesus has founded the absolute religion, excluding nothing, and determining nothing unless it be the spirit. His creeds are not fixed dogmas, but images susceptible of indefinite interpretations. We should seek in vain for a theological proposition in the Gospel. All confessions of faith are travesties of the idea of Jesus, just as the scholasticism of the Middle Ages, in proclaiming Aristotle the sole master of a completed science, perverted the thought of Aristotle. . . . In this sense we are Christians, even when we separate ourselves on almost all points from the Christian tradition which has preceded us. . . .

The faith, the enthusiasm, the constancy of the first Christian generation is not explicable, except by supposing at the origin of the whole movement, a man of surpassing greatness. . . .

I know that our modern ideas have been offended more than once in this legend, conceived by another race, under another sky, and in the midst of other social wants. There are virtues which, in some respects, are more conformable to our taste. The virtuous and gentle Marcus Aurelius, the humble and gentle Spinoza, not having believed in miracles, have been free from some errors that Jesus shared. Spinoza, in his profound obscurity, had an advantage which Jesus did not seek. By our extreme delicacy in the use of means of conviction, by our absolute sincerity and our disinterested love of the pure idea, we have founded—all we who have devoted our lives to science—a new ideal of morality. But the judgment of general history ought not to be restricted to considerations of personal merit. Marcus Aurelius and his noble teachers have had no permanent influence on the world. Marcus Aurelius left behind him delightful books, an execrable son, and a decaying nation. Jesus remains an inexhaustible principle of moral regeneration for humanity. . . .

The terms healthy and diseased are entirely relative. Who would not prefer to be diseased like Pascal, rather than healthy like the common herd? The narrow ideas which are spread in our times respecting madness, mislead our historical judgments in the most serious manner, in questions of this kind. A state in which a man says things of which he is not conscious, in which thought is produced without the summons and control of the will, exposes him to being confined as a lunatic. Formerly this was called prophecy and inspiration. The most beautiful things in the world are done in a state of fever; every great creation involves a breach of equilibrium, a violent state of the being which draws it forth. . . .

To show that the religion founded by Jesus was the natural consequence of that which had gone before, does not diminish its excellence; but only proves that it had a reason for its existence, that it was legitimate, that is to say, conformable to the instinct and wants of the heart in a given age. . . .

Doubtless, circumstances much aided the success of this marvellous revolution; but circumstances only second that which is just and true. Each branch of the development of humanity has its privileged epoch, in which it attains perfection by a sort of spontaneous instinct, and without effort. No labor of reflection would succeed in producing afterward the masterpieces which Nature creates at those moments by inspired geniuses. That which the golden age of Greece was for arts and literature, the age of Jesus was for religion. Jewish society exhibited the most extraordinary moral and intellectual state which the human species has ever passed through. It was truly one of those divine hours in which the sublime is produced by combinations of a thousand hidden forces, in which great souls find a flood of admiration and sympathy to sustain them. The world, delivered from the very narrow tyranny of small municipal republics, enjoyed great liberty. Roman despotism did not make itself felt in a disastrous manner until much later, and it was, moreover, always less oppressive in those distant provinces than in the centre of the empire. Our petty preventive interferences (far more destructive than death to things of the spirit) did not exist. Jesus, during three years, could lead a life which, in our societies, would have brought him twenty times before the magistrates. . . .

This sublime person, who each day still presides over the destiny of the world, we may call divine, not in the sense that Jesus has absorbed all the divine, or has been adequate to it (to employ an expression of the schoolmen), but in the sense that Jesus is the one who has caused his fellowmen to make the greatest step toward the divine. Mankind in its totality offers an assemblage of low beings, selfish, and superior to the animal only in that its selfishness is more reflective. From the midst of this uniform mediocrity, there are pillars that rise toward the sky, and bear witness to a nobler destiny. Jesus is the highest of these pillars which show to man whence he comes, and whither he ought to tend. In him was condensed all that is good and elevated in our nature. He was not sinless; he has conquered the same passions that we combat; no angel of God comforted him, except his good conscience; no Satan tempted him, except that which each one bears in his heart. In the same way that many of his great qualities are lost to us, through the fault of his disciples, it is also probable that many of his faults have been concealed. But never has any one so much as he made the interests of humanity predominate in his life over the littleness of self-love. Unreservedly devoted to his mission, he subordinated everything to it to such a degree that, toward the end of his life, the universe no longer existed for him. It was by this access of heroic will that he conquered heaven. There never was a man, Çakya-Mouni[16] perhaps excepted, who has to this degree trampled under foot, family, the joys of this world, and all temporal care. Jesus only lived for his Father and the divine mission which he believed himself destined to fulfill.

10. LOUIS VEUILLOT:

REAFFIRMATION OF ORTHODOXY

Against the liberal spirit in religion, represented by Ludwig Feuerbach, George Eliot, and Ernest Renan, powerful voices were raised in favor of dogmatic orthodoxy. The struggle between the two currents of thought was especially significant among French Catholics. Liberal Catholics led by Jean Baptiste Henri Lacordaire (1802–1861) and Count Charles de Montalembert (1810–1870) sought a reconciliation of Catholic piety with the modern world which had emerged in 1789. They favored "a free Church in a free state." Any compro-

---

[16] Çakya-Mouni, in English generally Sakya-muni, a name of Gautama Buddha, 563–483 B.C. Sakya-muni (correctly Shakya-muni) means the Shakya sage, Buddha being of the Shakya clan.

mise with modern society and with liberalism was rejected by
Louis Veuillot (1818–1883), the editor of the Catholic paper
L'Univers.

A disciple of Joseph Comte de Maistre (1753–1821),
Veuillot rejected the entire liberal tradition. "The Church,"
he wrote in 1855, "gives you all the freedom that decent people
want and which is essential to human dignity." In 1866 he
published a pamphlet against "the liberal illusion," from which
the following excerpts are taken.[17]

The children of the Christ, the children of the King, are kings.
They form an absolutely superior society, whose duty it is to take
possession of the earth and reign over it for the purpose of baptizing
all men and of raising them to that selfsame glory for which Christ
has destined them. They ought to strive for that goal, because the
only way of realizing the ideal of universal liberty, universal equality, universal fraternity is to establish the universal reign of Christ.
For the liberty that is man's due is liberty to attain his supernatural
end, which is union with Christ; and the only society ever known
to recognize all men as equals and as brothers is the society of the
disciples of Christ.

In the normal order, Christian society is maintained and extended by means of two powers that ought to be distinct—not
separated, united—not confused, one above the other—not equal.
The one is the head, the other the arm; the one is the supreme and
sovereign word of the Pontiff, the other the social power. . . .

The Christians despoiled pagan society of its weapons and its
temples to transform them, not to destroy them. From the temple,
they expelled the idol; upon might they imposed right. The foolish
idea of abolishing force never even came to them. Force allowed
itself to be transposed, allowed itself to be disciplined; allowed
itself to be sanctified. Who is so rash as to think he can abolish
might? and why, after all, should anyone wish to abolish it at all?
Might is a very good thing; it is a gift of God, nay, a very attribute
of God, "I am the most mighty God of thy father."

As right is of itself a force, so force can be of itself a right. Mankind and the Church recognize a right of war. From the iron of
which it despoils barbarous force, Christianity made coats of mail
for the weak and noble swords with which it armed the right.
Force in the hands of the Church is the force of right, and we have

[17] Louis Veuillot, *The Liberal Illusion*, translated by George Barry O'Toole,
Washington, 1939, pp. 37–39, 47–48, 62–64, 76–77

no desire that right should remain without force. Force in its proper place and doing its duty, that is the orderly way. . . .

Force ought to protect, to affirm, to vindicate the grandest, the noblest, the most necessary right of man, which is to acknowledge and to serve God; it should enable the Church to extend to every man on earth the benefit of this right. Let us never relinquish this right which liberal Catholicism surrenders, so that it can drift down the current, along with the crowd. . . .

The revolutionary sphinx, under the name of the modern mind, propounds a series of riddles with which the liberal Catholics occupy themselves a great deal more than befits the dignity of children of Christ. Not one of them, however, answers the riddle in a way calculated to satisfy either the sphinx, or themselves, or anybody else, and it is a matter of record, that the monster devours soonest just those who flatter themselves on having guessed its meaning best.

Scant is the self-respect and scant the faith that remains in these last! They come, not without arrogance, to ask, in the name of the sphinx and in their own name, how "intolerant" Catholics can get around the "conquests" of the dissenting mind with its rights of man, its liberty of religions, its constitutions grounded on these principles, etc. etc. Nothing could be easier to answer.

To begin with, the dissenting mind invariably starts off with an unwarranted assumption of its own superiority, which we flatly refuse to recognize. Error is never the equal, much less the superior of truth, neither can it hope to overawe truth, or ever to prevail legitimately against it, and, by consequence, the disciples of error, infidels, unbelievers, atheists, renegades and the like, are never the superiors nor even the legitmate equals of the disciples of Jesus Christ, the one true God. From the standpoint of unalterable right, the perfect society that constitutes the Church of Christ is by no means on a level with the gang that collects around error. We know right well to whom it has been said: Going therefforth, teach— a word, we may remark in passing, like the great Increase and multiply, which was spoken at the beginning of things; and these two words are living words despite the ruses and triumphs of death— error has nothing to teach by divine right, neither has it the divine right to increase and multiply. Truth is at liberty to tolerate error, but error is obliged to grant to truth the right of liberty. . . .

In a word, Catholic society will be Catholic, and the dissenters whom it will tolerate will know its charity, but they will not be allowed to disrupt its unity. . . .

It behooves us to lock arms around the Sovereign Pontiff, to follow unswervingly his inspired directions, to affirm with him the truths that alone can save our souls and the world. It behooves us to abstain from any attempt to twist his words to our own sense: "When the Sovereign Pontiff has proclaimed a pastoral decision, no one has the right to add or to suppress the smallest vowel, no *addere*, no *minuere*. Whatever he affirms, that is true forever." Any other course can but result in dividing us further and in fatally disrupting our unity. That is the misfortune of misfortunes. The doctrines known as liberal have riven us apart. Before their inroad, favored only too much, alas! by a spell of political bad humor, few as we were, we amounted, nevertheless, to something: we formed an unbroken phalanx. We rallied in such a phalanx whenever we chose to do so; it was no more than a pebble if you will: that pebble had at least its compactness and its weight. Liberalism has shattered it and reduced it to so much dust. I doubt if it still holds its place: dispersal is not expansion. At all events, a hundred thousand pecks of dust would not furnish ammunition for a single sling. Let us aim now at but one goal, let us work with but one mind to attain it: let us throw ourselves wholeheartedly into obedience, it will give us the cohesion of rock, and upon this rock, *hanc petram*, Truth shall plant her victorious foot.

11. *THE PONTIFICATE OF PIUS IX*

After 1848 the dominant wing of the Catholic Church, represented by men like Veuillot, looked to papal authority in the then still independent papal states "beyond the mountains"; hence the name "ultramontane party." Veuillot was powerfully supported from Rome, where, during a pontificate of unusual duration, Pius IX (Giovanni Maria Mastai-Ferretti, 1792–1878) restored the influence of the Catholic Church and the papacy, which had been shaken by the skepticism of the eighteenth century and by the revolutions of 1789 and 1848.

The reign of Pius IX began at a critical time—in 1846—when, under the pressure of the general climate of the period and in order to counter the general dissatisfaction of the people with the regime, the Pope introduced some cautious liberal reforms in the administration of the papal states. But the revolution, which turned Rome temporarily into a republic under Mazzini's leadership, made the Pope the foremost leader in the fight against the spirit of modern times.

This victory of the ultramontanist party found its expression in three documents of great historical importance which strengthened the central authority and the dogmatic inflexibility of the Church. The Bull *Ineffabilis Deus* (1854) declared it as a divinely revealed truth that the Virgin Mary was conceived without any stain of hereditary sin. Ten years later the *Syllabus of the Principal Errors of Our Age* (A), published together with the encyclical *Quanta cura,* proclaimed the impossibility of reconciling the papacy with progress, liberalism, and modern civilization. It rejected freedom of conscience and the idea of tolerance and claimed for the Church the control of all cultural, scientific, and educational activities.

Finally in 1869 the Pope called the Twentieth Ecumenical Council of the Roman Church, the first since the one which met at Trent from 1545 to 1563. The council, which assembled at the Vatican, proclaimed on July 18, 1870, the dogma of papal infallibility (B). Two months later the papal states ceased to exist, and Rome was incorporated into the Italian nation-state created by the Sardinian monarchy, a state which introduced the separation of Church and state.[18]

A. Syllabus of Errors

. . . That the Church ought to tolerate the error of philosophy; leaving to philosophy the care of their correction. That the decree of the Apostolic See and of the Roman Congregations fetter the free progress of science. That the method and principles, by which the old scholastic Doctors cultivated Theology, are no longer suitable to the demands of the age. . . .

That every man is free to embrace and profess the religion he shall believe true, guided by the light of reason. . . . That the eternal salvation may (at least) be hoped for, of all those who are not at all in the true Church of Christ. That Protestantism is nothing more than another form of the same true Christian religion in which it is possible to please God equally as in the Catholic Church.

That the Roman Pontiffs and Oecumenical Councils have exceeded the limits of their power, have usurped the rights of princes, and have even committed errors in defining matters of faith and morals. That the Church has not the power of availing herself of force, or of any direct or indirect temporal power. . . . The ecclesiastical jurisdiction for the temporal causes—whether civil or crim-

[18] *Documents of the Christian Church* (including A & B), selected and edited by Henry Bettenson (London: The World's Classics, 1943), pp. 379–382

inal—of the clergy, ought by all means to be abolished. . . . That National Churches can be established, after being withdrawn and separated from the authority of the holy Pontiff. That many Pontiffs have, by their arbitrary conduct, contributed to the division of the Church into Eastern and Western.

. . . That the civil government—even when exercised by an infidel sovereign—possesses an indirect and negative power over religious affairs; and possesses, not only the right called that of *exequatur*, but also that of the (so called) *appellatio ab abusu*. . . . That the best theory of civil society requires that popular schools, open to the children of all classes, should be freed from all ecclesiastical authority. . . . That the Church ought to be separated from the State, and the State from the Church.

. . . That it is allowable to refuse obedience to legitimate princes; nay more, to rise in insurrection against them. . . .

. . . That the abrogation of the temporal power of which the Apostolic See is possessed, would be the greatest contribution to the liberty and prosperity of the Church. . . .

That in the present day, it is no longer necessary that the Catholic religion be held as the only religion of the State, to the exclusion of all other modes of worship: whence it has been wisely provided by the law, in some countries nominally Catholic, that persons coming to reside therein shall enjoy the free exercise of their own worship. . . . That the Roman Pontiff can, and ought to, reconcile himself to, and agree with, progress, liberalism, and modern civilization.

B. Papal Infallibility

That which the Prince of Shepherds and great Shepherd of the sheep, Jesus Christ our Lord, established in the person of the Blessed Apostle Peter, to secure the perpetual welfare and lasting good of the Church, must, by the same institution, necessarily remain unceasingly in the Church; which, being founded upon the Rock, will stand firm to the end of the world. For none can doubt, and it is known to all ages, that the holy and Blessed Peter, the Prince and Chief of the Apostles, the pillar of the Catholic Church, received the keys of the kingdom from our Lord Jesus Christ, the Saviour and Redeemer of mankind, and lives, presides, and judges, to this day and always, in his successors the Bishops of the Holy See of Rome, which was founded by him, and consecrated by his blood. Whence, whosoever succeeds to Peter in this See does by the institution of Christ Himself obtain the Primacy of Peter over the whole Church. The disposition made by Incarnate Truth therefore remains, and Blessed Peter, abiding in the rock strength which he received, has not abandoned the direction of the Church. Wherefore it has at all times been necessary that every particular Church—that is to say, the faithful throughout the world—should come to the Church of Rome, on account of the greater princedom it has received; so that in this See, whence the rights of venerable communion spread to all, they might, as members joined together in their head, grow closely into one body.

If, then, any shall say that it is not by the institution of Christ the Lord, or by divine right, that Blessed Peter has a perpetual line of successors in the Primacy over the universal Church; or that the Roman Pontiff is not the successor of Blessed Peter in this primacy; let him be anathema.

. . . Faithfully adhering to the tradition received from the beginning of the Christian faith, for the glory of God our Saviour, the exaltation of the Catholic Religion, and the salvation of Christian people, with the approval of the Sacred Council. We teach and define that it is a dogma divinely revealed: That the Roman Pontiff, when he speaks *ex cathedra*, that is, when in discharge of the office of Pastor and Teacher of all Christians, by virtue of this supreme Apostolic authority, he defines a doctrine regarding faith or morals to be held by the universal Church, is, by the divine assistance promised to him in Blessed Peter, possessed of that infallibility with which the divine Redeemer willed that His Church should be endowed in defining doctrine regarding faith or morals; and that therefore such definitions of the Roman Pontiff are of themselves, and not from the consent of the Church, irreformable.

12. AUGUSTE COMTE: *POSITIVIST RELIGION*

Auguste Comte (1798–1857) was in his younger years a secretary to the early French socialist Claude Henri de Rouvroy Comte de Saint-Simon (1769–1825). Like his teacher, he was conscious of the profound spiritual and social crisis which the French Revolution and the Industrial Revolution had produced. Comte, who became the father of modern sociology, wished to solve the problems of the age through the methods of science. He expected his philosophy of positive science to end the political and intellectual anarchy of the transitional revolutionary age and thus to re-establish, on a higher level, the harmony of society and thought which had existed in the medieval Catholic Church. Through his new religion Comte wished to fuse order and progress. The new religion, while retaining the hierarchy and the dogmatism of the Church, wished to replace the idea of God with the idea of mankind, and the priests with positivist scientists.

In 1852 Comte published his *Catechism of Positive Religion: Summary and Exposition of the Universal Religion,* which appeared in 1858 in an English translation by Richard Congreve. Comte saw in history a continuous process in which three states, or attitudes, succeeded each other: the religious one, the metaphysical one, and the scientific positivist one. In this last stage, which mankind was now entering, "the servants of Humanity" —both the scientists and the practical men—had to assume the direction of mankind's progress to social regeneration.[19]

We come forward to deliver the Western world from an anarchical democracy and from a retrograde aristocracy. We come forward to constitute, as far as practicable, a real sociocracy; one which will be able to combine wisely, in furtherance of the common regeneration, all the powers of man, each of course brought to bear according to its own nature. In fact, we Sociocrats are as little democratical as we are aristocratical. In our eyes these two opposite parties—that is, their respectable portions—represent, though not in theory, on the one hand Solidarity, on the other, Continuity. These two ideas have hitherto been unfortunately antagonistic. Positivism removes this antagonism and replaces it with a subordination of the one to the other, by showing Solidarity to be subordinate to Continuity. So we adopt both these tendencies, in themselves and singly incomplete and incoherent; and we rise above them both equally. Yet at the present time we will by no means equally condemn the two parties which represent them. During the whole of my philosophical and social career, a period of thirty years, I have ever felt a profound contempt for that which, under our different governments, bore the name of the Opposition; I have felt a secret affinity for all constructive statesmen of whatever order. Even those who would build with evidently worn-out materials, I have never hesitated to prefer to the pure destructives in a century in which a general reconstruction is everywhere the chief want. Our official conservatives are behindhand, it is true.

[19] Auguste Comte, *Catechism of Positive Religion: Summary and Exposition of the Universal Religion,* translated by Richard Congreve (London: John Chapman, 1858), pp. 1–5, 11–14, 28–36, 407–28

And yet, the mere revolutionist seems to me still more alien to the true spirit of the time; for in the middle of the nineteenth century, he blindly continues the negative line of action which could only suit the eighteenth. And he does not redeem the stagnation caused by his error, by the generous aspirations for a universal renovation, which were characteristic of his predecessors. . . .

Be this as it may, the retrograde nature of the wornout ideas which our conservatives provisionally employ absolutely disqualifies them for directing political action in the midst of the present anarchy. For that anarchy has its origin in the irremediable weakness of the old beliefs. Western Europe no longer submits its reason to the guidance of opinions which evidently admit of no demonstrations, nay, which are radically illusory. For such is the character of all opinions of theological origin whatever the theology, be it even the purest Deism. All now recognize the fact that the practical activity of man must no longer waste itself on mutual hostilities, but must set itself peaceably to the resources of the earth—man's residence. Still less can we persist in the state of intellectual and moral childhood in which for the conduct of our life we look to motives which are absurd and degrading. The nineteenth century must never repeat the eighteenth, but neither must it break from it and reject it. It must continue the work of the eighteenth and realize at length the noble object of its wishes, a religion resting on demonstration, which directs the pacific activity of man. . . .

Positive religion gives full satisfaction to the intelligence of man and to his activity. Impelled onwards by the character of reality which distinguishes it, it has embraced the region of sentiment. We see no reason to fear that any thinkers worthy of the name, whether theoretical or practical, can commit the mistake made in the early period of Catholicism, and fail to see the superiority of a faith which is real and complete, which is social not by any accident, but by its own inherent nature. For the rest, it is for the nascent priesthood of Positivism and for all its true disciples, to secure, by their conduct as men and citizens, a due appreciation of its excellence. Even those who cannot be expected to form a judgment on its principles may be led by experience to a favorable conclusion. A doctrine which shall be seen to develop all human virtue—personal, domestic and civic—will soon gain the respect of all honest opponents, however strong may be their preference for an absolutist and egoistic rather than a relative and altruistic synthesis. . . .

My present work claims to furnish a systematic basis for the active propagation of Positivism. By so doing it necessarily forwards my principal construction, for it brings the new religion to bear on the classes which constitute its true social audience. The intellectual discipline instituted by Positive Philosophy rests on logical and scientific foundations of the utmost solidity; but no solidity can secure its prevalence, so antipathetic is its severe regime to minds trained as at present, unless it can gain the support of women and the proletarian class. That support should lend it irresistible strength. . . . The deep-seated intellectual anarchy of our time is another reason why Positive religion should appeal more particularly to the female sex. For that anarchy renders more necessary than ever the predominance of feeling, as it is feeling alone which preserves Western society from a complete and irreparable dissolution. Since the close of the Middle Ages, the influence of woman has been the sole though unacknowledged check on the moral evils naturally resulting from a state of mental alienation, the state which the West has been approximating more and more—and in the West, especially its centre—France. This chronic state of unreason is now at its height, and since no maxim of social experience can resist the corrosive effects of discussion as actually conducted, it is feeling alone that maintains order in the West. And even feeling is already seriously impaired. . . .

Four great classes constitute modern society. The four were destined to experience in succession the shock which the final regeneration of society rendered inevitable. The convulsion began in the last century with the intellectual element. The class which represented it rose in insurrection against the entire existing system based on the ideas of theology and war. The political explosion which was the natural result soon followed. It began with the middle classes who had long been eager to take the place of the nobility. Throughout Europe the nobility resisted and its resistance could only be overcome by calling on the French proletariat to support their new political chiefs. Thus induced to mix in the great political struggle, the proletariat of Western Europe put forward its claim—a claim which there was no resisting because of its justice—to be incorporated into the system of modern society. It was advanced as soon as peace allowed the proletariat to make its wishes sufficiently clear. Still the revolutionary chain is incomplete, for it does not embrace the most fundamental element of the system of human order rightly viewed. The revolution, in regard to women, must be the complement of the revolution which enveloped the proletariat, just as this last, consolidating the revolution of the middle classes, sprung in its turn originally from the philosophical revolution. . . .

Woman's object is the same everywhere: to secure the due supremacy of moral force. She is led, therefore, to regard with especial reprobation all collective violence. She is still less ready to accept the yoke of numbers than that of wealth. Her influence will facilitate the industrial patriciate's advent to political power and that of the Positive priesthood; it will do this by leading both to unentangle themselves once and for all from the heterogeneous and ephemeral classes who headed the transition when it was in its negative phase. So completed, so purified, the revolution of Western Europe will proceed in a free and systematic course towards its peaceful termination, under the general direction of the true servants of Humanity. Their guidance will have an organic and progressive character which will completely reject all retrograde and anarchical parties. They will look upon anyone who persists in the theological or metaphysical state as disqualified by weakness of the brain for government. . . .

At the opening of the fourteenth century, then, begins the vast revolution in Western Europe, whose cessation is the mission of Positivism. The whole medieval regime was thoroughly broken up by conflicts between its component parts, while its doctrinal system remained intact. The chief struggle naturally was between the temporal and spiritual powers. This decisive revolution was completed in the fifteenth century when in every case, the national clergy became subordinate to the temporal authority. The Pope became a mere illusion as a spiritual centre; he sunk into the role of an Italian prince. With its independence, the priesthood lost its morality; first public, then private. To ensure its material existence, it placed its teaching at the service of the stronger authority. . . .

At the very commencement of the second phase of modern history, the negative doctrine directly broaches its anarchical principle, by its assertion of absolute individualism. This follows from its permit that anyone, with no conditions of competence exacted, may decide every question. Once this is allowed, all spiritual authority is at an end. The living rise in open insurrection against the dead, as is evidenced by the blind reprobation for the whole medieval system, for which the irrational admiration of antiquity was but a poor compensation. Protestantism lent its influence to widen the fatal breach in the continuity of the race which Catholicism had first opened. . . .

The anarchical character of its principles did not prevent Protestantism from aiding, at its commencement, the progress of science and the development of industry; for it gave a stimulus to individual effort, and it set aside oppressive rules. We owe two revolutions to it—that of Holland against the tyranny of Spain, and that of England to secure internal reform. The second was premature, and therefore ultimately failed. But it did not fail till it had given indications, under the admirable dictatorship of Cromwell, of the inevitable tendency of the European movement.

From this time forward the requirements of order and of progress, both equally imperative, became absolutely irreconcilable. The nations of Western Europe ranged themselves on one side or the other, according as they felt more strongly the need of order or of progress. . . .

It is easy then to understand the stormy character of the crisis, of the vast revolution which was the final issue of the whole five centuries which lie between us and the Middle Ages. That stormy character was the necessary result of the fatal inequality in the progression of the positive and negative movements. The two together make up the whole movement of Western Europe. The negative movement had been very rapid, and the positive had not been able to supply its demand for organization. The leadership in the work of modern regeneration, at the time of its greatest difficulty, had developed on the class least qualified for the post, the class of mere writers. The sole object of their aspirations was the pedantocracy dreamed of by their Greek masters. They would concentrate all power in their own persons. . . .

After a few years of hesitation under the Constituent Assembly, a decisive shock overthrew forever the retrograde institution of monarchy, last vestige of the caste system. The theocratic consecration given it by the servile clergy of modern times points to it as such. The glorious Convention, the only assembly that enjoys a real popularity in France, when it overthrew the monarchy as a preliminary step to social regeneration, had no power to supply any deficiencies in the intellectual movement of Western Europe. It lacked the requisites for a real organic policy. It was competent to direct in a heroic manner the defence of the French Republic, but it could not do more than express in vague form the program of social wants; and even this was obscured by a metaphysical philosophy which has always been incapable of any constructiveness whatever.

The political triumph of the negative doctrine brought its thoroughly subversive tendencies to light. This soon led to a retrograde reaction. The reaction began under the ephemeral ascendancy of a bloodthirsty Deism in the person of Robespierre. The reaction grew in the official restoration of Catholicism under the military tyranny of Buonaparte. But the primary tendencies of modern civilization reject alike theology and war. Though every egoistic instinct was stimulated at that time to an unparalleled extent, the military spirit was yet obliged in its last orgies, to rest on a system of compulsory recruitment. The universal adoption of conscription is a sign that the abolition of standing armies is approaching. Their substitute will be a police force. The expedients to which a retrograde policy has since been driven to avert such a result have all failed; it has been found as impossible to revive a warlike spirit as a theological

one. The expedition to Algiers was the most immoral of these expedients; and I venture in this place, in the name of true Positivists,
solemnly to proclaim my wish that the Arabs may forcibly expel
the French, unless the French consent to an act of noble restitution.

The retrograde movement under the first Napoleon drew its
apparent strength solely from war. The extent of its failure was
evident on the final restoration of peace. In the absence, however,
of all organic views, the spiritual anarchy reached its height. All
the previous convictions of men, whether of the revolutionary or
retrograde school, lost their hold. If discipline is partial it cannot
be real and lasting. If it is to be universal, it must rest on one
principle—the constant supremacy of the heart over the intellect.
But the principle had been losing ground ever since the close of
the Middle Ages. It had the support of women, but this holy support was powerless; for Western Europe, in its madness, paid less
and less respect to women. The result was that even in the scientific
sphere, the provisional order which Bacon and Descartes had tried
to institute, was set aside; and free course was given on empirical
grounds to the unconnected study of special sciences. All philosophical control was scorned by those who engaged in such pursuits.
Every effort was made to give each science an indefinite extension
by isolating it from the whole. At each step in this process the
whole was lost sight of more completely. The movement became
retrograde as well as anarchical, for it threatened to destroy even
the great results of former labors while it gave increased power to
academic mediocrity. In the domain of art we find anarchy and
retrogression still more rampant. Art is by its nature eminently
synthetic; it rejects analytic empiricism more absolutely than science
does. Yet even in poetry the degradation was so great that the
learned could appreciate nothing but style. This was carried to such
an extent that they often placed real masterpieces below compo-
sitions which were both poor and immoral. . . .

. . . The result of the whole positive movement was to facilitate
the advent of sociology—a birth which had been heralded by
Condorcet in his attempt to bring the future into systematic subordination to the past. His attempt failed, but it is nonetheless
immortal. It was made at a time when men's minds were in a state
most entirely averse to all sound historical conceptions.

By the universal adoption of an exclusively human point of view,
it was possible for a subjective synthesis to construct a philosophy
which should be proof against all objections. The next step after the
synthesis was to found the final religion. To this I was led as soon
as the renovation of the intellect had been followed by a regeneration of the moral nature. . . .

All noble hearts and all great intellects may converge for the future. They accept this termination of the long and difficult initiation through which Humanity has had to pass, under the sway of powers which have been constantly on the decline—theology and war. . . . The relative finally takes the place of the absolute; altruism tends to control egoism; systematic progress is substituted for spontaneous growth. In a word, Humanity definitely occupies the place of God, but she does not forget the services which the idea of God provisionally rendered. . . .

13. RUSSIAN SERFDOM AND EMANCIPATION

Though Russia had entered, during the Napoleonic wars, into full diplomatic partnership with the rest of Europe, the vast empire remained, until the last decades of the nineteenth century, a socially and politically underdeveloped country sharply set apart from the rest of Europe—with the possible exceptions of the Balkan and, to a lesser degree, the Iberian peninsulas. Characteristic of this underdeveloped condition and the social and political backwardness of Russia was the continuation of serfdom, which was not abolished until March, 1861.

Few foreigners traveled in Russia before the end of the nineteenth century; consequently, few became well acquainted with the existing conditions. But among those who did was Sir Donald Mackenzie Wallace (1841–1919), a British journalist and linguist of distinction whose volume, *Russia* (1877), dealt comprehensively with the country and has been recognized as a classic. Wallace "was impressed by the profound difference between the historically rooted institutions of Russia and those which he knew in the West, and his ability to convey an understanding of this difference was one of the principal qualities of his work" (Cyril E. Black). Though he came to Russia only after the emancipation, he made very detailed studies of the documents concerning the conditions of the Russian peasants under serfdom and immediately after emancipation. The following excerpts survey the reasons for the relative failure of the emancipation.[20]

[20] D. M. Wallace, *Russia* (New York: Holt & Co., 1877), pp. 478 ff., 500 ff.

As to the means which the proprietors possessed of oppressing their peasants, we must distinguish between the legal and the actual. The legal were almost as complete as anyone could desire. "The proprietor," it is said in the Laws (Vol. IZ., 1045, ed.an. 1857), "may impose on the serfs every kind of labor, may take from them money dues (obrok) and demand from them personal service, with this one restriction, that they should not be thereby ruined, and that the number of days fixed by law should be left to them for their own work." Besides this, he had the right to transform peasants into domestic servants, and might, instead of employing them in his own service, hire them out to others who had the rights and privileges of noblesse (1047–48). For all offenses committed against himself or against any one under his jurisdiction, he could subject the guilty ones to corporal punishment not exceeding forty lashes with the birch or fifteen blows with the stick (1052); and if he considered any of his serfs as incorrigible he could present them to the authorities to be drafted into the army or transported to Siberia as he might desire (1053–55). In cases of insubordination, where the ordinary domestic means of discipline did not suffice, he could call in the police and the military to support his authority.

Such were the legal means by which the proprietor might oppress his peasants, and it will be readily understood that they were very considerable and very elastic. By law he had the power to impose any dues in labor or money which he might think fit, and in all cases the serfs were ordered to be docile and obedient (1027). Corporal punishment, though restricted by law, he could in reality apply to any extent. Certainly none of the serfs, and very few of the proprietors, were aware that the law placed any restriction on this right. All the proprietors were in the habit of using corporal punishment as they thought proper, and unless a proprietor became notorious for inhuman cruelty, the authorities never thought of interfering. But in the eyes of the peasants corporal punishment was not the worst. What they feared infinitely more than the birch or the stick was the proprietor's power of giving them or their sons as recruits. The law assumed that this extreme means would be employed only against those serfs who showed themselves incorrigibly vicious or insubordinate; but the authorities accepted those presented without making any investigations, and consequently the proprietor might use his power as an effective means of extortion. . . .

We might naturally suppose that an unscrupulous proprietor, armed with the enormous legal and actual power which I have just described, could easily extort from his peasants anything he desired. In reality, however, the process of extortion, when it exceeded a certain measure, was a very difficult operation. The

Russian peasant has a capacity of patient endurance that would do honor to a martyr, and a power of continued, dogged, passive resistance such as is possesssed, I believe, by no other class of men in Europe; and these qualities formed a very powerful barrier against the rapacity of unconscientious proprietors. . . .

It might be reasonably supposed that the serfs received with boundless gratitude and delight the Manifesto proclaiming these principles. Here at last was the realization of their long cherished hopes. Liberty was accorded to them, and not only liberty, but a goodly portion of the soil—more than a half of all the arable land possessed by the proprietors.

In reality the Manifesto created among the peasantry a feeling of disappointment rather than delight. To understand this strange fact we must endeavor to place ourselves at the peasant's point of view.

In the first place, it must be remarked, that all vague, rhetorical phrases about free labor, human dignity, national progress, and the like, which may readily produce among educated men a certain amount of temporary enthusiasm, fall on the ears of the Russian peasant like drops of rain on a granite rock. If, therefore, the Government would make a law by which his share of the Communal land would be increased, or his share of the Communal burdens diminished, he would in return willingly consent to be therein designated by the most ugly name that learned ingenuity can devise.

In their minds the proprietors were merely temporary occupants, who were allowed by the Tsar to exact labor and dues from the serfs. What then was Emancipation? Certainly the abolition of all obligatory labor and money dues, and perhaps the complete ejectment of the proprietors. On this latter point there was a difference of opinion. All assumed, as a matter of course, that the Communal land would remain the property of the Commune, but it was not so clear what would be done with the rest of the estate. Some thought that it would be retained by the proprietor, but very many believed that the nobles would receive salaries from the Tsar, and that all the land would be given to the Communes. In this way the Emancipation would be in accordance with historical right and with the material advantage of the peasantry, for whose exclusive benefit, it was assumed, the reform had been undertaken.

Instead of this the peasants found that they were still to pay dues, even for the Communal land which they regarded as unquestionably their own! So at least said the expounders of the law. But the thing was incredible. Either the proprietors must be concealing or misinterpreting the law, or this was merely a preparatory measure, which would be followed by the real Emancipation. Thus were awakened among the peasantry a spirit of mistrust and suspicion and a widespread belief that there would be a second Emancipation, by which all the land would be divided and all the dues abolished. . . .

The peasants naturally imagined that, as soon as the Tsar said they were free, they were no longer obliged to work for their old masters—that all obligatory labor ceased as soon as the Manifesto was read. In vain the proprietors endeavored to convince them that, in regard to labor, the old relations must continue, as the law enjoined, until a new arrangement had been made. To all explanations and exhortations the peasants turned a deaf ear, and to the efforts of the rural police they too often opposed a dogged, passive resistance. In many cases the simple appearance of the authorities sufficed to restore order, for the presence of one of the Tsar's servants convinced many that the order to work for the present as formerly was not a mere invention of the proprietors. But not unfrequently the birch had to be applied. Indeed, I am inclined to believe, from the numerous descriptions of this time which I have received from eye-witnesses, that rarely, if ever, had the serfs seen and experienced so much flogging as during these first three months, after their liberations. . . .

14. HERZEN: *LIBERTY IN RUSSIA*

After 1848 the movement of protest against the lack of freedom and the backwardness of the social conditions in Russia grew stronger. It was voiced by relatively small circles of intellectuals, of whom many in the beginning came from the landowning aristocracy. The leading liberal spokesman of this group in the 1850's was Alexander Herzen (1812–1870). In 1847 he left Russia for Europe, but was deeply disappointed by the defeat of the European revolutions of 1848 and the triumph of absolutism and reaction at that time. This feeling of disappointment explains the beginning of the following excerpt from his book, *The Development of Revolutionary Ideas in Russia* (written in French).

Herzen did not return to Russia from his exile. He clearly saw in the Russia of St. Petersburg under Nicolai I the un-European backwardness which had characterized the Russia of Moscow under Ivan III and Ivan IV. When Alexander II followed Nicolai in 1855 and raised the hope of reform (the emancipation of the serfs in March, 1861, was followed by many administrative reforms), Herzen founded in 1857 the first free Russian newspaper, *The Bell*, in London, where, like his contemporaries Marx and Mazzini, he found a refuge. In spite of some confusion in his thought, Herzen upheld the tradition of Western liberty as a model for Russia. "Only the mighty thought of the West," he wrote in his autobiography, "to which all its long history has led is able to fertilize the seeds slumbering in the patriarchal mode of life" of the Russians.[21]

It is horrible to live in Russia, it is as horrible to live in Europe. Why did I leave Russia? To answer this question I shall quote some words of the farewell letter to my [Russian] friends: "Don't be mistaken! I have found here neither joy nor rest. I can't even imagine anybody finding rest or joy in Europe today. Sadness breathes in every word of my letters. Life here is very painful. I believe in nothing but the movement. I regret nothing but the victims; I love only the persecuted. I esteem only the tortured, and yet I stay. I stay to suffer twice: our own pain and that which I find here, perhaps to sink in the general dissolution. But I stay because here the struggle is wide open, because here it has a voice. Woe to the defeated here! But here he does not succumb without making his voice heard and without having tried his strength in the struggle. For the sake of this voice, for the sake of this open struggle, for the sake of this publicity, I stay!" This I wrote on March 1, 1849. . . . But if in Europe also they succeed in gagging us and if oppression no longer permits us to curse our oppressors openly, then we shall leave for America, sacrificing everything to the dignity of man and to the freedom of expression. . . .

One thought only united the Petersburg period of Russian history with that of Moscow, the thought of the aggrandizement of the state. Everything was sacrificed to it, the dignity of the rulers, the blood of the subjects, justice towards one's neighbors, and the welfare of the whole country. . . .

This discontent of which we speak cannot be easily seen. Russia always seems so tranquil that one has difficulty in believing that something is happening there. Few people know what happens beneath the shroud with which the government covers the corpses,

[21] Hans Kohn, ed., *The Mind of Modern Russia* (New Brunswick, N.J.: Rutgers University Press, 1955), pp. 159 f., 163

the stains of blood, the military executions, while maintaining hypocritically and arrogantly that there is neither blood nor corpse beneath the shroud. . . .

Can one really believe that servitude, passive obedience and a despotic government can develop the abilities of the Russian people? A long servitude cannot be an accident, it must correspond to some national trait. This trait can be absorbed and overcome by other traits, but it can also remain victorious; if Russia accommodates herself to the existing order, she will not have the future which we wish for her. If she continues the period of St. Petersburg, or if she returns to the period of Moscow, she will have no future but to throw herself upon Europe, like a semibarbarian and semicorrupted horde devastating the civilized countries and perishing in the midst of general destruction. Was it not necessary therefore to call upon the Russian people to recognize its tragic conditions? . . . Instead, the Slavophiles preached submission. . . . They preached the contempt of the West, and yet the West alone could enlighten the dark gulf of Russian life; they glorified the past, instead of emphasizing the need of liberation from this past in favor of a future common to Russia and the West. . . .

One has remarked that an opposition which leads a frontal attack upon a government always has itself, in an inverted sense, something of the character of the government attacked. I believe that there is some justification for the fear of communism which the Russian government begins to feel: Communism is the Russian autocracy turned upside down. . . .

II
1871–1914

THE four decades between the triumph of Bismarck (1871) and the outbreak of the great European war (1914), in which the Bismarckian Reich collapsed, were for Europe outwardly a time of peace and growing self-confidence. Yet under the surface the armament race brought about huge standing armies on the European continent and technological inventions which threatened to increase both the destructiveness of war and the financial burden imposed upon the population. Though an organized peace movement in the various countries reached a wider audience and favored, for the first time, the creation of machinery for the reform and administration of international law, the aggressive trends of nationalism and imperialism proved stronger. In the 1880's Africa was "opened up" and divided among the European powers, and the weakness shown by the Chinese Empire in the 1890's seemed to indicate its approaching partitioning. However, it was the competition for the inheritance of another ramshackle empire, that of the Ottoman sultans, in the welter of conflicting nationalisms and imperialisms, that was the immediate cause of the war of 1914—the war which put an end to the outwardly "idyllic" period of the nineteenth-century European order and the era of European predominance in the world.

With the growth of industrialism, stimulated by armaments, imperialism, and scientific progress, the socialist movement gained in breadth and depth. In the 1880's socialist societies were formed in Britain, and unskilled labor undertook its first mass strike. On the European continent, especially in Germany, Marxism became an established doctrine. In 1889, six years after Marx's death, at the centennial celebration of the French Revolution the Second Workers' International was organized. Socialist parties became well represented in Germany and other countries, where, in spite of the survival of pre-modern social structures and value-systems, parliamentary forms copied from the West gained acceptance. At the beginning of the twentieth century the first steps toward a modern constitutionalism were taken even in the most backward parts of Europe, in Russia (1905) and in Turkey (1908). This development seemed to bear out the prevailing feeling of security and continuous progress.

Though this feeling of progress toward a better mankind was shared by the majority of Europeans, in no way did it remain unopposed. Under two prominent popes, Pius IX and Leo XIII, who wore the papal tiara for an unusually long time, the Catholic Church as the defender of traditional verities gained a greater influence than it had enjoyed for centuries. On the other hand, intellectual movements spearheaded by Friedrich Nietzsche rejected the past and the present in their willful and hopeful quest for new values. The works of the great Russian novelists, Fyodor Dostoevsky and Leo Tolstoy, became known outside Russia, and their doubt and criticism of the values of modern Western civilization spread in the West.

At the end of the nineteenth century the quest for new values and forms became productive in European arts and letters. Henrik Ibsen may be regarded as the father of the modern theatre; a new poetry became characteristic of "modern" sensibility and diction in practically all European literatures from Russia to Britain; in the field of music Gustav Mahler and Arnold Schönberg found new ways of expression; in the visual arts Paul Cézanne and Vincent Van Gogh formed the bridge from impressionism to contemporary art. In the year of Cézanne's death (1906) Pablo Picasso painted "Les Demoiselles d'Avignon," inaugurating cubist painting. Movies brought a new art form. The fermentation of intellectual and cultural life was increased by the new psychology of Sigmund Freud (1900) and the new physics of Max Planck (1900) and Albert Einstein (1905). But all these movements reached a wider influence only after the First World War, which more and more appears to be the great divide in contemporary political and intellectual history.

15. WILLIAM E. GLADSTONE:
EUROPEAN PEACE AND LIBERTY

William Ewart Gladstone (1809–1898) was Britain's greatest Liberal statesman of the nineteenth century. From 1832 to 1895, with only one break of a year and a half, he was a member of the House of Commons. He entered the cabinet for the first time in 1843 and later was four times prime minister. During his first tenure of office as prime minister (1868–1874) the Franco-Prussian War of 1870–1871 broke out.

In an unsigned article published in the *Edinburgh Review* for October, 1870, Gladstone foresaw as a consequence of the war the development of a warlike spirit, which dominated the era of 1871–1914 and finally led to the First World War. Gladstone strongly opposed the piling up of huge armaments and huge budgets, a trend of the age.[1]

Is there then no charge, which lies against the [French] Empire as especially its own? Unhappily there is. They were warlike and not peaceful memories which, clustering round the name of the First Napoleon, made that name a passport to public favour in the person of his nephew; and, founded in its origin on a combination of force and fraud, the Empire perforce became thereby, in no small measure, an example of that degrading form of human things, in which right is based only upon power. The Emperor promised, and possibly at times desired, to give to France freer institutions. But it was only after he had held supreme power for seventeen years, that he dared to set about what was too soon shown to be after all only a nominal fulfillment of the promise. Unhappily, he then, by the reservation of the right of appeal to the people over the heads of their representatives, deprived the new-born system of all that vitality which belongs to genuine freedom. So that through the whole reign the French nation was really under despotic rule. A people so intellectual, and so advanced, could not thus forego its liberty without profound injury to its national life. . . .

While all was thus unsound beneath, on the surface all was gorgeous; and the glare of Parisian gaiety and splendour more than ever imposed upon the eye, and tainted the conscience, of the world. It was a close and foul atmosphere, of which the evil odour was only kept down by clouds of incense and floods of perfume. Admitting freely that there were good deeds, and great deeds, which leave trails of light upon the course of the Second Empire, we feel that for France it was a snare, a calamity, a hopeless impediment to solid well-being. Strange indeed that, being such, it should have received thrice over the solemn sanction of an overwhelming popular suffrage; and happy the release from the illusion, even though it will be achieved in the midst not only of disaster but of agony. Nothing can compensate a people for the loss of what we may term civic individuality. Without it, the European type becomes politically debased to the Mahometan and Oriental model. For many

[1] The following excerpts are from the article in the *Edinburgh Review*, as reprinted in Gladstone's *Gleanings of Past Years* (London: John Murray, 1879), vol. IV, pp. 233–57

generations it has been waning away in France. The great Revolution did not restore the institutions necessary to rear it. Napoleon I. ruthlessly destroyed, in the municipality and the commune, the remaining depositaries of public spirit, responsibility, and manhood. The system of Napoleon III., which worked despotic power under the mask of universal suffrage, aggravated the evil by concealing it. . . .

Unhappily, however, M. Jules Favre[2] reports that in the conference of September 20, Count Bismarck used the following extraordinary language, in speaking of the inhabitants of Alsace and a portion of Lorraine, which he had announced his intention to appropriate: "Je sais fort bien qu'ils ne veulent pas de nous. Ils nous imposeront une rude corvée; mais nous ne pouvons pas ne pas les prendre."[3] This, if it were really made, is a harsh, almost a brutal announcement. Of the whole sum of human life, no small part is that which consists of a man's relations to his country, and his feelings concerning it. To wrench a million and a quarter of a people from the country to which they have belonged for some two centuries, and carry them over to another country of which they have been the almost hereditary enemies, is a proceeding not to be justified in the eyes of the world and of posterity by any mere assertion of power, without even the attempt to show that security cannot be had by any other process.

We hear much of the civilisation of the Germans. Let them remember, that Italy has been built up, at least from 1860 onwards, upon the groundwork of the expressed desires of the people of its several portions; that England surrendered the possession of the Ionian Islands in deference to the popular desire, expressed through the representative Chamber, to be united to Greece; that even the Emperor Napoleon took Savoy and Nice under cover of a vote, as to which no one can say that it clearly belied the real public sentiment. This is surely a great advance on the old and cruel practice of treating the population of a civilised European country as mere chattels. Are we to revert to that old practice? Will its revival be in harmony with the feeling, the best feeling, of Europe? Will it conduce to future peace? Can Germany afford, and does she mean, to set herself up above European opinion? We can hardly hope that M. Favre has misrepresented Count Bismarck, since the commentary of the Chancellor on Mr. Favre's report takes no exception to this

[2] Jules Favre (1809–1890), leader of the opposition to the Second Empire, negotiated with Bismarck as minister of foreign affairs in the government of National Defense, 1870–71.

[3] "I know well that they do not wish to have anything in common with us. They will impose upon us an irksome task; but we cannot do otherwise than to take them."

part of it; but we still trust that Count Bismarck has misrepresented his country. But if neither is the case, then we must take leave to say that Germany will yet have to prove her civilisation by some other means than by boasting that six, or that six hundred, letters have been written in good Sanscrit by the soldiers of her army to their friends at home. . . .

Amidst the many additions which this age has contributed to the comfort and happiness of man, it has made some also to his miseries. And among these last is the deplorable discovery of methods by which we can environ peace with many of the worst attributes of war; as, for instance, with its hostility to the regular development of freedom, through the influence of great standing armies, and the prevalence of military ideas; with its hostility to sound and stable government, through crushing taxation, financial embarrassment, and that constant growth of public debt which now, with somewhat rare exceptions, marks the policy of the States of Europe; with the jealous and angry temper, which it kindles between nations; and lastly, with the almost certainty of war itself, as the issue of that state of highly armed preparation, which, we are affectedly told, is the true security for the avoidance of quarrels among men. . . .

We have not yet spoken of England; but of her we confidently hope that, . . . her hand will be not unready to be lifted up, on every fit and hopeful occasion, in sustaining the general sense of Europe against a disturber of the public peace.

In truth the nations of Europe are a family. Some one of them is likely, if not certain, from time to time to be the strongest, either by inherent power or by favouring opportunity. To this strength great influence will attach; and great power over the lot of others. Such influence and power may be abused. In one important respect, Germany may be peculiarly open to temptation to abuse the power which she has undoubtedly acquired. She alone among modern nations has discovered a secret, which releases her from one of the main checks on a disposition to go to war. She has learned to make it pay; to exact from the enemy the cost of her operations in the shape of pecuniary indemnity. . . .

One accomplishment yet remains needful to enable us to hold without envy our free and eminent position. It is that we should do as we would be done by; that we should seek to found a moral empire upon the confidence of the several peoples, not upon their fears, their passions, or their antipathies. Certain it is that a new law of nations is gradually taking hold of the mind, and coming to sway the practice, of the world; a law which recognises independence, which frowns upon aggression, which favours the pacific, not the bloody settlement of disputes, which aims at permanent and not temporary adjustments; above all, which recognises, as a tribunal of paramount authority, the general judgment of civilised mankind. It has censured the aggression of France; it will censure, if need arise, the greed of Germany. "Securus judicat orbis terrarum." It is hard for all nations to go astray. Their ecumenical council sits above the partial passions of those who are misled by interest and disturbed by quarrel. The greatest triumph of our time, a triumph in a region loftier than that of electricity and steam, will be the enthronement of this idea of Public Right, as the governing idea of European policy; as the common and precious inheritance of all lands, but superior to the passing opinion of any. The foremost among the nations will be that one, which by its conduct shall gradually engender in the mind of the others a fixed belief that it is just. In the competition for this prize, the bounty of Providence has given us a place of vantage; and nothing save our own fault or folly can wrest it from our grasp.

16. ERNEST RENAN: *EUROPEAN PEACE*

At the beginning of the Franco-Prussian war in the summer of 1870, Renan wrote an article, "The War Between France and Germany," which appeared in the *Revue des Deux Mondes* on September 15, 1870. In this article he foresaw some of the worst consequences for Europe and Russia, consequences which have since come true. The future course of the German Reich created in the war and proclaimed by the German princes at the gates of Paris, in the Hall of Mirrors of the French Royal Palace at Versailles; the possibility of a conflict between the Slavs and the Germans; the need for a European federation to preserve the peace of Europe—all these show how correct Renan was in his predictions.

One year later, in a letter dated September 15, 1871, to the German scholar David Friedrich Strauss (1808–1874), Renan warned once more that "by abandoning herself to the statesmen and warriors of Prussia, Germany has mounted a frisky horse which will lead her where she does not wish to go. . . . Germany risks, with her military splendor, to lose her true vocation. Let all of us together take up the great and true problems, the social problems, . . . to find a rational organisation of mankind which would be as just as is humanly possible."[4]

I always regarded the war between France and Germany as the greatest misfortune which could happen to the cause of civilization. . . . In fact, if we leave aside the United States of America, whose undoubtedly brilliant future is still obscure and which in any case occupies a secondary rank in the original labor of the human mind, the intellectual and moral greatness of Europe rests on the Triple Alliance of France, Germany and England. Its rupture would be deeply grievous for progress. United, these three great forces would lead the world and lead it well. They would necessarily lead the other elements, each of considerable importance, which compose Europe. They would, above all, imperiously trace a road for another force which one should neither exaggerate nor depreciate— Russia. Russia is a danger only if the rest of Europe abandons her to the false idea of an originality which she perhaps does not possess, and allows her to unite the barbaric peoples of central Asia. These peoples are entirely powerless by themselves, but they are capable of discipline and unity around a Muscovite Genghis Khan if heed is not taken. The United States can become a danger only if a divided Europe allows it to abandon itself to the lures of a presumptuous youth and to hold resentments against the motherland. . . . That was only a dream. One day was sufficient to overthrow the edifice which housed our hopes and to open the world to all kinds of dangers, creeds, and brutalities. . . .

And now who will conclude the peace? . . . The worst consequence of war is to render powerless those who did not desire the war. . . . It opens a fatal circle where common sense is called cowardice and sometimes even treason. Let us speak frankly. One force alone in the world will be able to repair the evil which feudal pride, exaggerated patriotism, the excess of personal power and the low state of parliamentary government on the continent, has cost to civilization. This force is Europe. Europe has a major interest that neither of the two nations should be too victorious or too vanquished. The disappearance of France from among the great powers would mean the end of the European balance. I dare say that Britain especially would feel the conditions of her existence completely changed when such an event should happen. France is one of the conditions of Britain's prosperity. The alliance of France and Britain is well-established for centuries to come. Let

[4] Ernest Renan, *La Réforme Intellectuelle et Morale* (Cambridge University Press, 1950), pp. 79–104

Britain think of the United States, of Constantinople, of India; she will always find that she needs France and a strong France. . . .

How could such a horrifying event occur which will leave a memory of terror connected with the year 1870? Because the various European nations are too independent from each other and have no authority above them. There exists neither a congress nor a parliament which would be superior to national sovereignties. Though especially since 1814, Europe has acted frankly as a collective force, the central power has not been strong enough to prevent terrible wars. It must become so strong. That dream of pacifist utopians, a code of justice without an army to uphold its decisions, is a chimera. Nobody will obey it. On the other hand, the opinion that peace can be assured when one nation would have an uncontested superiority over the others is the opposite of the truth; each nation which exercises hegemony prepares its own ruin by this fact alone, because it brings about a coalition of all the other countries against itself. Peace cannot be established and maintained except by the common interest of Europe, or, if one prefers it, by a league of neutral powers ready to enforce peace. Justice has no chance to triumph between two contending parties, but between ten contending parties, justice wins out; for she alone offers a common basis of agreement. The only force capable of upholding a decision for the welfare of the European family against its most powerful member state lies in the power of the various states to unite, to intervene and to mediate. Let us hope that this force will assume ever more concrete and regular forms and will lead in the future to a real congress, meeting periodically if not permanently. It will become the heart of the United States of Europe, bound by a federal pact. . . .

I know there exist in the world foci of fanaticism which are still entirely dominated by temperament. In certain countries a military nobility exists which is fundamentally hostile to reasonableness and which dreams of exterminating whatever does not resemble it. The feudal elements in Prussia and Russia are still at an age in which one possesses the acridity of barbarian blood, an age in which one forbears to look back lest he should fall into disillusionment. . . . For these enthusiasts the idea of the German Reich is not that of a limited nationality, free at home, which does not occupy itself with the rest of the world. What they desire is a universal action of the German race, an action which would renew and dominate Europe.

Their frenzy is chimeric; for let us assume, to please these chagrined minds, that France were destroyed, Belgium, Holland and Switzerland wiped out, and Britain passive and silent: what should we say then of the great ghost which haunts the German future, namely, the Slav race, which would aspire more strongly to separate itself from Germany the more the latter individualized herself? Slav consciousness grows in proportion to the growth of German consciousness. They oppose each other and create each other. The German has the right to a fatherland like everyone else; but he has no more the right to dominate than anyone else. . . .

The greatest mistake which liberals could make in the midst of the horrors which surround us would be to despair. The future belongs to liberalism. This war, the object of future maledictions, has come because the principles of liberalism have been abandoned, principles which at the same time concern peace and the union of nations. The baneful desire for revenge—a desire which would indefinitely prolong the extermination—will be averted by a wise development of liberal policy. . . .

The federal principle, the guardian of justice, is the foundation of humanity. It is the guarantee of the rights of all of us. There is no European people which must not bow before such a tribunal. The great German race, greater in reality than its bungling apologists wish to make it appear, will certainly have another high claim for consideration in the future, if one will be able to say that its powerful action has definitely introduced so essential a principle into European law. All the great military hegemonies, that of Spain in the sixteenth century and those of France under Louis XIV and Napoleon, have ended in quick exhaustion. Let Prussia take heed. Her radical policy can engage her in a series of complications from which it will not be easy to disentangle herself. A penetrating eye could perhaps now perceive the formation of future coalitions. The wise friends of Prussia will tell her, not as a threat but as a warning: *vae victoribus*, woe to the victors.

17. BISMARCK:

GERMANY'S SYSTEM OF ALLIANCES

Otto von Bismarck (1815–1898), a member of the Prussian rural nobility, has been regarded by many as the greatest German statesman of the nineteenth century. Prussian prime minister since 1862 and chancellor of the German Reich, which he created, from 1871 to 1890, he was for many years the decisive force in German and European history. Through his brief and successful wars against Denmark, against the German Confederation, and against France he created the German Reich, which was an extension and expression of Prussian power. A grateful monarch raised him first to the dignity of a count, later to that of a prince.

After his victory over France, Bismarck's domestic policy combatted the liberal and democratic forces in Germany and the rise there of a parliamentary system of government. In his foreign policy he initiated that system of alliances which continued until, and partly caused, the war of 1914. His system of alliances had not only the task of protecting Germany and her leading European position, but also of safeguarding the conservative Central and Eastern European military monarchies against liberal influences coming from the West. In Chapter XXIX of his famous *Reflections and Reminiscences* Bismarck explained, in his masterly style, not only his system of alliances but also the principles of his *Realpolitik,* so different from those of Gladstone or Renan.[5]

The triple alliance [of the three Eastern Emperors] which I originally sought to conclude after the peace of Frankfort [1871] and about which I had already sounded Vienna and St. Petersburg in September 1870, was an alliance of the three Emperors with the further idea of bringing into it monarchical Italy. It was designed for the struggle which, as I feared, was before us; between the two European tendencies which Napoleon I called Republican and Cossack, and which I, according to our present ideas, should designate on the one side as the system of order on a monarchical basis, and on the other as the social republic to the level of which the anti-monarchical development is wont to sink, either slowly or by leaps and bounds, until the conditions thus created become intolerable, and the disappointed populace are ready for a violent return to monarchical institutions in a Cæsarean form. I consider that the task of escaping from this vicious circle, or, if possible, of sparing the present generation and their children an entrance into it, ought to be more closely incumbent on the strong existing monarchies, those monarchies which still have a vigorous life, than any rivalry over the fragments of nations which people the Balkan peninsula. If the monarchical governments have no understanding of the necessity for holding together in the interests of political and social order, but make themselves subservient to the chauvinistic impulses

[5] Otto von Bismarck, *Gedanken und Erinnerungen* in *Gesammelte Werke,* vol. XV (Berlin, 1932), English translation Leipzig, Bernhard Tauchnitz, n.d.

of their subjects, I fear that the international revolutionary and social struggles which will have to be fought out will be all the more dangerous, and take such a form that the victory on the part of monarchical order will be more difficult. Since 1871 I have sought for the most certain assurance against those struggles in the alliance of the three Emperors, and also in the effort to impart to the monarchical principle in Italy a firm support in that alliance. I was not without hope of a lasting success when the meeting of the three Emperors took place at Berlin in September 1872, and this was followed by the visits of my Emperor [William I] to St. Petersburg in May, of the King of Italy to Berlin in September, and of the German Emperor to Vienna in the October of the next year. . . .

Count Shuvalov[6] was perfectly right when he said that the idea of [anti-German] coalitions gave me nightmares. We had waged victorious wars against two of the European Great Powers; everything depended on inducing at least one of the two mighty foes whom we had beaten in the field to renounce the anticipated design of uniting with the other in a war of revenge. To all who knew history and the character of the Gallic race, it was obvious that the Power could not be France, and if a secret treaty of Reichstadt was possible without our consent, without our knowledge, so also was a renewal of the old coalition of France, Austria, and Russia, whenever the elements which it represented, and which beneath the surface were still present in Austria, should gain the ascendancy there. They might find points of connexion which might serve to infuse new life into the ancient rivalry, the ancient struggle for the hegemony of Germany, making it once more a factor in Austrian policy, whether by an alliance with France, or by a closer accord with Russia, the existence of which was attested by the secret convention of Reichstadt. The question of what support Germany had in such a case to expect from England I will not answer without more in the way of historical retrospect of the Seven Years' war and the congress of Vienna. I merely take note of the probability that, but for the victories of Frederick the Great, the cause of the King of Prussia would have been abandoned by England even earlier than it actually was.

This situation demanded an effort to limit the range of the possible anti-German coalition by means of treaty arrangements placing our relations with at least one of the Great Powers upon a firm footing. The choice could only lie between Austria and Russia, for the English constitution does not admit of alliances of assured permanence, and a union with Italy alone did not promise an ade-

[6] Count Paul Shuvalov (1830–1908), Russian general and diplomat, was his country's ambassador in Germany, 1885–1894

quate counterpoise to a coalition of the other three Great Powers, even supposing her future attitude and formation to be considered independently not only of French but also of Austrian influence. The area available for the formation of the coalition would therefore be narrowed till only the alternative remained which I have indicated.

In point of material force I held a union with Russia to have the advantage. I had also been used to regard it as safer, because I placed more reliance on traditional dynastic friendship, on community of conservative monarchical instincts, on the absence of indigenous political divisions, than on the fits and starts of public opinion among the Hungarian, Slav, and Catholic populations of the monarchy of the Habsburgs. Complete reliance could be placed upon the durability of neither union, whether one estimated the strength of the dynastic bond with Russia, or of the German sympathies of the Hungarian populace. If the balance of opinion in Hungary were always determined by sober political calculation, this brave and independent people, isolated in the broad ocean of Slav populations, and comparatively insignificant in numbers, would remain constant to the conviction that its position can only be secured by the support of the German element in Austria and Germany. But the Kossuth episode, and the suppression in Hungary itself of the German elements that remained loyal to the Empire, with other symptoms showed that among Hungarian hussars and lawyers self-confidence is apt in critical moments to get the better of political calculation and self-control. Even in quiet times many a Magyar will get the gypsies to play to him the song, *"Der Deutsche ist ein Hundsfott"* ("The German is a blackguard").

In the forecast of the future relations of Austria and Germany an essential element was the imperfect appreciation of political possibilities displayed by the German element in Austria, which has caused it to lose touch with the dynasty and forfeit the guidance which it had inherited from its historical development. Misgivings as to the future of an Austro-German confederation were also suggested by the religious question, by the remembered influence of the father confessors of the imperial family, by the anticipated possibility of renewed relations with France, on the basis of a *rapprochement* by that country to the Catholic Church, whenever such a change should have taken place in the character and principles of French statesmanship. How remote or how near such a change may be in France is quite beyond the scope of calculation. . . .

While occupied with the consideration of these questions I was compelled by the threatening letter of Czar Alexander II (1879) to take decisive measures for the defence and preservation of our independence of Russia. An alliance with Russia was popular with nearly all parties, with the Conservatives from an historical tradition, the entire consonance of which with the point of a modern Conservative group, is perhaps doubtful. The fact, however, is that the majority of Prussian Conservatives regard alliance with Austria as congruous with their tendencies, and did so none the less when there existed a sort of temporary rivalry in Liberalism between the two governments. The Conservative halo of the Austrian name outweighed with most of the members of this group the advances, partly out of date, partly recent, made in the region of Liberalism, and the occasional leaning to *rapprochements* with the Western Powers, and especially with France. The considerations of expediency which commended to Catholics an alliance with the preponderant Catholic Great Power came nearer home. In a league, having the form and force of a treaty, between the new German Empire and Austria the National-Liberal party discerned a way of approximating to the quadrature of the political circle of 1848, by evading the difficulties which stood in the way of the complete unification, not only of Austria and Prussia-Germany, but also of the several constituents of the Austro-Hungarian Empire. Thus, outside of the Social Democratic party, whose approval was not to be had for any policy whatever which the government might adopt, there was in parliamentary quarters no opposition to the alliance with Austria, and much partiality for it.

Moreover, the traditions of international law from the time of the Holy Roman Empire, German by nation, and of the German Confederation tended to the theory that between Germany as a whole and the Habsburg monarchy there existed a legal tie binding these central European territories together for purposes of mutual support. Practical effect had indeed rarely been given to this *consortium* in former ages; but it was possible to vindicate in Europe, and especially in Russia, the position that a permanent confederation of Austria and the modern German Empire was, from the point of view of international law, no new thing. These questions, whether the alliance would be popular in Germany, how far it could be justified by international law, were to me matters of subordinate importance, merely subsidiary to its eventual completion. In the foreground stood the question whether the execution of the design should be begun at once or deferred for a time, and with what degree of decision it would be advisable to combat the opposition which might be anticipated on the part of Emperor William I—an opposition sure to be determined rather by his idiosyncrasy than by policy. So cogent seemed to me the considerations which in the political situation pointed us to an alliance with Austria that I would have striven to conclude one even in the face of a hostile public opinion.

When Emperor William I went to Alexandrovo in Sept. 1879, I had already made arrangements at Gastein for a meeting with Count Andrassy,[7] which took place on August 27–28. When I had explained the situation to him he drew therefrom the following conclusion: To a Russo-French alliance the natural counterpoise is an Austro-German alliance. I answered that he had formulated the question to discuss which I had suggested at our meeting, and we came readily to a preliminary understanding for a merely defensive alliance against a Russian attack on one of the two sides; but my proposition to extend the alliance to other than Russian attacks found no favour with the Count.

Before my departure from Gastein I addressed (Sept. 10) the following letter to the King of Bavaria:

"Your majesty was so gracious on a former occasion as to express your most exalted satisfaction with the efforts which I directed to the object of securing for the German Empire peace and friendship with both her great neighbours, Austria and Russia alike. In the course of the last three years this problem has increased in difficulty, as Russian policy has come to be entirely dominated by the partly warlike revolutionary tendencies of Panslavism. . . . The leading minister, in so far as such a minister there is at present in Russia, is the War Minister, Milutin.[8] At his demand the peace, in which Russia is threatened by no one, has yet been followed by the might preparations which have raised the footing of the army of the West, which is kept ready for active service, by about 400,000 men. These preparations can only be intended as a menace to Austria or Germany, and the military establishments in the [Russian] kingdom of Poland correspond to such a design. The War Minister has also unreservedly declared that Russia must prepare for a war 'with Europe.'

"If it is indubitable that Czar Alexander (II), without desiring the war with Turkey, nevertheless waged it under stress of Panslavist influence, and if, meanwhile, the same party has gained in influence in consequence of the greater and more dangerous impression which the agitation at the back of it now makes on the mind of the Czar, we may readily apprehend that it may also succeed in obtaining Czar Alexander's sanction for further warlike enterprises on the western frontier. . . .

"Austria regards the restless Russian policy with as much dis-

[7] Count Julius Andrassy (1823–1890), Hungarian statesman and foreign minister of Austria-Hungary, 1871–1879
[8] General Dmitri Milutin (1816–1912), Russian minister of war, 1862–1881

quietude as we, and seems to be inclined for an understanding with us for common defence against a possible Russian attack on either of the two Powers.

"If the German Empire were to come to such an understanding with Austria, an understanding which should have in view the cultivation of peace with Russia as sedulously as before, but should also provide for joint defence in the event of an attack by her upon either of the allied powers, I should see in it an essential security for the peace of Europe. Thus mutually assured, both empires might continue their efforts for the further consolidation of the Three Emperors' Alliance. The German Empire in alliance with Austria would not lack the support of England, and the peace of Europe, the common interest of both empires, would be guaranteed by 2,000,000 fighting men. In this alliance, purely defensive as it would be, there would be nothing to excite jealousy in any quarter: for in the German Confederation the same mutual guarantee subsisted with the sanction of international law for fifty years after 1815. If no such understanding is come to, Austria will not be to blame if, under the influence of Russian threats, and uncertain of the attitude of Germany, she finally seeks an *entente cordiale* with either France or Russia. In the latter case, Germany, by reason of her relation to France, would be in danger of entire isolation on the Continent. Supposing, however, that Austria were to effect an *entente cordiale* with France and England, as in 1854, Germany, unless prepared for isolation, would be forced to unite with Russia alone, and, as I fear, to follow in the mistaken and perilous course of Russian domestic and foreign policy.

"If Russia compels us to choose between her and Austria, I believe that the disposition which Austria would display towards us would be conservative and peaceable, while that of Russia would be uncertain." . . .

The Emperor's [William I] chivalrous temper demanded that the Czar of Russia should be confidentially informed that in the event of his attacking either of the two neighbour-powers he would find himself opposed by both, in order that Czar Alexander might not make the mistake of supposing that he could attack Austria alone. I deemed this solicitude groundless inasmuch as the cabinet of St. Petersburg must by our answer to the questions sent us from Livadia have already learned that we were not going to let Austria fall, and so our treaty with Austria had not created a new situation, but only legalised that which existed.

A renewal of Kaunitz's[9] coalition might be confronted without

[9] Count Wenzel Anton von Kaunitz (1711–1794), Austrian statesman, effected an Austro-French alliance against Prussia.

despair by a United Germany which conducted her campaigns with skill; nevertheless it would be a very serious combination, the formation of which it must be the aim of our foreign policy, if possible, to prevent. If the united Austro-German power had by the closeness of its cohesion and the unity of its counsels as assured a position as either the Russian or the French power regarded *per se,* I should not consider a simultaneous attack by our two great neighbour-empires, even though Italy were not the third in the alliance, as a matter of life and death. But if in Austria anti-German proclivities, whether national or religious, were to gain strength; if Russian tentatives and overtures in the sphere of eastern policy, such as were made in the days of Catherine and Joseph II, were to be thrown into the scale, if Italian ambitions were to threaten Austria's possession on the Adriatic sea, and require the exertion of her strength—then the struggle, the possibility of which I anticipate, would be unequal. And if we suppose the French monarchy restored, and France and Austria in league with the Roman Curia and our enemies for the purpose of making a clean sweep of the results of 1866, no words are needed to show how greatly aggravated would then be the peril of Germany. This idea, pessimistic, but by no means chimerical, nor without justification in the past, induced me to raise the question whether it might not be advisable to establish between the German Empire and Austria-Hungary an organic connexion which should not be published like ordinary treaties, but should be incorporated in the legislation of both Empires, and require for its dissolution a new legislative Act on the part of one of them.

Such a guarantee has a tranquillising effect on the mind; but whether it would stand the actual strain of events may reasonably be doubted, when it is remembered that the constitution of the Holy Roman Empire, which in theory had much more effective sanctions, yet failed to assure the cohesion of the German nation, and that we should never be able to embody our relation with Austria in any more binding treaty form than the earlier confederation treaties, which in theory excluded the possibility of the battle of Königgrätz.[10] All contracts between great states cease to be unconditionally binding as soon as they are tested by "the struggle for existence." No great nation will ever be induced to sacrifice its existence on the altar of fidelity to contract when it is compelled to choose between the two. The maxim *"ultra posse nemo obligatur"* holds good in spite of all treaty formulas whatsoever, nor can any treaty guarantee the degree of zeal and the amount of force that will be devoted to the

[10] Decisive Prussian victory over Austria and the German Confederation in July, 1866

discharge of obligations when the private interest of those who lie under them no longer reinforces the text and its earlier interpretation. If, then, changes were to occur in the political situation of Europe of such a kind as to make an anti-German policy appear *salus publica* for Austria-Hungary, public faith could no more be expected to induce her to make an act of self-sacrifice than we saw gratitude do during the Crimean war, though the obligation was perhaps stronger than any that can be established by the wax and parchment of a treaty.

An alliance under legislative sanction would have realised the constitutional project which hovered before the minds of the most moderate members of the assembly of the Paulskirche, both those who stood for the narrower Imperial-German and those who represented the wider Austro-German confederation; but the very reduction of such a scheme to contractual form would militate against the durability of its mutual obligations. The example of Austria between 1850 and 1866 was a warning to me that the political changes which such arrangements essay to control outrun the credits which independent states can assure to one another in the course of their political transactions. I think, therefore, that to ensure the durability of a written treaty it is indispensable that the variable element of political interest, and the perils involved therein, should not be left out of account. The German alliance is the best calculated to secure for Austria a peaceful and conservative policy.

The dangers to which our union with Austria are exposed by tentatives towards a Russo-Austrian understanding, such as was made in the days of Joseph II, and Catherine, may, so far as possible, be minimised by keeping the strictest possible faith with Austria, and at the same time taking care that the road from Berlin to St. Petersburg is not closed. Our principal concern is to keep the peace between our two imperial neighbours. We shall be able to assure the future of the fourth great dynasty in Italy in proportion as we succeed in maintaining the unity of the three empire states, and in either bridling the ambition of our neighbours on the east or satisfying it by an *entente cordiale* with both. Both are for us indispensable elements in the European political equilibrium; the lack of either would be our peril—but the maintenance of monarchical government in Vienna and St. Petersburg, and in Rome as dependent upon Vienna and St. Petersburg, is for us in Germany a problem which coincides with the maintenance of our own [imperial-conservative] state *régime*. . . .

Peace between Germany and Russia may be imperilled by the systematic fomentation of ill-feeling, or by the ambition of Russian or German military men who desire war before they grow too old to distinguish themselves, but is hardly to be imperilled in any other way. The Russian press must needs be characterised by stupidity and disingenuousness in an unusual degree for it to believe and affirm that German policy was determined by aggressive tendencies in concluding the Austrian, and thereafter the Italian, defensive alliance. The disingenuousness was less of Russian than of Polish-French, the stupidity less of Polish-French than of Russian origin. In the field of Russian credulity and ignorance Polish-French finesse won a victory over that want of finesse in which, according to circumstances, consists now the strength, now the weakness of German policy. In most cases an open and honourable policy succeeds better than the subtlety of earlier ages, but it postulates, if it is to succeed, a degree of personal confidence which can more readily be lost than gained. The future of Austria, regarded in herself, cannot be reckoned upon with that certainty which is demanded when the conclusion of durable and, so to speak, organic treaties is contemplated. The factors which must be taken into account in this shaping are as manifold as is the mixture of her populations, and to their corrosive and occasionally disruptive force must be added the incalculable influence that the religious element may from time to time, as the power of Rome waxes or wanes, exert upon the directing personalities. Not only Panslavism and the Bulgarian or Bosnian, but also the Serbian, the Roumanian, the Polish, the Czech questions, nay even today the Italian question in the district of Trent, in Trieste, and on the Dalmatian coast, may serve as points of crysallisation not merely for Austrian, but for European crises, by which German interests will be directly affected only in so far as the German Empire enters into a relation of close solidarity with Austria. In Bohemia the antagonism between Germans and Czechs has in some places penetrated so deeply into the army that the officers of the two nationalities in certain regiments hold aloof from one another even to the degree that they will not meet at mess. There is more immediate danger for Germany of becoming involved in grievous and dangerous struggles on her western frontier, by reason of the aggressive, plundering instincts of the French people, which have been greatly developed by her monarchs since the time of Emperor Charles V., in their lust of power at home as well as abroad. . . .

We must and can honourably maintain the alliance with the Austro-Hungarian monarchy; it corresponds to our interests, to the historical traditions of Germany, to the public opinion of our people. The influences and forces under and amid which the future policy of Vienna must be shaped are, however, more complex than with us, by reason of the manifold diversity of the nationalities, the divergence of their aspirations and activities, the influence of the clergy, and the temptations to which the Danubian countries are exposed in the Balkan and Black Sea latitudes.

We cannot abandon Austria, but neither can we lose sight of the possibility that the policy of Vienna may willy-nilly abandon us. The possibilities which in such a case remain open to us must be clearly realised and steadily borne in mind by German statesmen before the critical moment arrives, nor must their action be determined by prejudice or misunderstanding, but by an entirely dispassionate weighing of the national interests. . . .

International policy is a fluid element which under certain conditions will solidify, but on a change of atmosphere reverts to its original diffuse condition. The clause *rebus sic stantibus* is tacitly understood in all treaties that involve performance. The Triple Alliance is a strategic position, which in the face of the perils that were imminent at the time when it was concluded was politic, and, under the prevailing conditions, feasible. It has been from time to time prolonged, and may be yet further prolonged, but eternal duration is assured to no treaty between Great Powers; and it would be unwise to regard it as affording a permanently stable guarantee against all the possible contingencies which in the future may modify the political, material, and moral conditions under which it was brought into being. It has the significance of a strategic position adopted after strict scrutiny of the political situation of Europe at the time when it was concluded, but it no more constitutes a foundation capable of offering perennial resistance to time and change than did many another alliance (triple or quadruple) of recent centuries, and in particular the Holy Alliance and the German Confederation. It does not dispense us from the attitude of *toujours en vedette*.

18. TREITSCHKE:

THE NATURE OF THE STATE AND POLITICS

The attitude of the Bismarckian age with regard to the nature of the state and of politics was best expressed by the German historian and political writer Heinrich von Treitschke (1834–1896). From 1874 on, he held the chair for modern history at the University of Berlin. A brilliant and prolific writer and an enthusiastic teacher, he helped to imbue generations of German teachers and intellectuals with the Bismarckian ideal of power and heroism and with the then widespread confidence in the superiority of German arms and culture and a belief in Germany's right to lead and rule.

Among his lecture courses none was as popular as his course on politics. It was the favored course of Treitschke himself, as well as of his students. None of his courses he gave as often as this one. From 1874 on, he repeated it every year. Only after his death in 1897 were the lectures published, in two volumes, mostly from the stenographic notes of some of his students. They appeared in an English translation in 1916 with an introduction by the English statesman Arthur James Balfour, in which the latter wrote that Treitschke's "utopia appears to be a world in which all small States had been destroyed, and in which the large States are all either fighting, or preparing for battle."[11]

The State is not an Academy of Arts. If it neglects its strength in order to promote the idealistic aspirations of man, it repudiates its own nature and perishes. This is in truth for the State equivalent to the sin against the Holy Ghost, for it is indeed a mortal error in the State to subordinate itself for sentimental reasons to a foreign Power, as we Germans have often done to England. . . .

We have described the State as an independent force. This pregnant theory of independence implies firstly so absolute a moral supremacy that the State cannot legitimately tolerate any power above its own, and secondly a temporal freedom entailing a variety of material resources adequate to its protection against hostile influences. Legal sovereignty, the State's complete independence of any other earthly power, is so rooted in its nature that it may be said to be its very standard and criterion. . . .

It is clear that the international agreements which limit the power of a State are not absolute, but voluntary self-restrictions. Hence, it follows that the establishment of a permanent international Arbitration Court is incompatible with the nature of the State, which could at all events only accept the decision of such a tribunal in cases of second- or third-rate importance. When a nation's existence is at stake there is no outside Power whose impartiality can be trusted. Were we to commit the folly of treating the Alsace-Lorraine problem as an open question, by submitting it to arbitration, who would seriously believe that the award could be impartial? It is, moreover,

[11] Heinrich von Treitschke, *Politics,* English translation by Mrs. Blanche Dugdale (London: Constable, 1916)

a point of honour for a State to solve such difficulties for itself. International treaties may indeed become more frequent, but a finally decisive tribunal of the nations is an impossibility. The appeal to arms will be valid until the end of history, and therein lies the sacredness of war. . . .

The entire development of European polity tends unmistakably to drive the second-rate Powers into the background, and this raises issues of immeasurable gravity for the German nation, in the world outside Europe. Up to the present Germany has always had too small a share of the spoils in the partition of non-European territories among the Powers of Europe, and yet our existence as a State of the first rank is vitally affected by the question whether we can become a power beyond the seas. If not, there remains the appalling prospect of England and Russia dividing the world between them, and in such a case it is hard to say whether the Russian knout or the English money bags would be the worst alternative. . . .

When we examine more closely the whole fabric of these conditions of mutual interdependence which we call society we find that under all its forms it tends naturally towards aristocracy. The Social Democrats imply in their very title the absurdity of their aspirations. Just as the State presupposes an irremovable distinction between those in whom authority is vested and those who must submit to it, so also does the nature of society imply differences of social standing and economic condition amongst its members. In short, all social life is built upon class organization. Wise legislation may prevent it from being oppressive and make the transition from class to class as easy as possible, but no power on earth will ever be able to substitute a new and artificial organization of society for the distinctions between its groups which have arisen naturally and automatically.

It is a fundamental rule of human nature that the largest portion of the energy of the human race must be consumed in supplying the primary necessities of existence. The chief aim of a savage's life is to make that life secure, and mankind is by nature so frail and needy that the immense majority of men, even on the higher levels of culture must always and everywhere devote themselves to bread-winning and the material cares of life. To put it simply: the masses must for ever remain the masses. There would be no culture without kitchen-maids.

Obviously education could never thrive if there was nobody to do the rough work. Millions must plough and forge and dig in order that a few thousands may write and paint and study.

It sounds harsh, but it is true for all time, and whining and complaining can never alter it. Moreover the outcry against it does not spring from love of humanity but from the materialism and modern conceit of education. It is profoundly untrue to regard education as the essential factor in history, or as the rock on which human happiness is founded. . . .

It is precisely in the differentiation of classes that the moral wealth of mankind is exhibited. The virtues of wealth stand side by side with those of poverty, with which we neither could nor should dispense, and which by their vigour and sincerity put to shame the jaded victim of over-culture. There is a hearty joy in living which can only flourish under simple conditions of life. Herein we find a remarkable equalization of the apparently cruel classifications of society. Want is a relative conception. It is the task of government to reduce and mitigate distress, but its abolition is neither possible nor desirable. The economy of Nature has here set definite limits upon human endeavour, and on the other hand man's pleasure in life is so overwhelming that a healthy race will increase and spread wherever there is space for them.

We are told indeed that the innumerable inventions of a highly developed commercial community will make the supply of the primary necessities of life increasingly easier, but this is a delusion, for needs and desires lie so near the root of human nature that every material want which is satisfied generates another in endless succession. When the first railway was built it was generally assumed that a great number of horses would in future be superfluous, since the mail-coaches would cease to run upon the highroads. Exactly the contrary has happened, because more horses are now used on the byeroads which lead to the railways than were formerly required in the whole of Germany.

So it will remain true that the great mass of humanity is always labouring for the elementary requirements of the race. Nor can any one seriously wish that everybody should receive a highly intellectual education. We have already overstepped the limits of prudence in this direction and it would be a disaster if still more Germans wished to matriculate. The modern Greeks have squandered away their future by developing two characteristics with an appalling one-sidedness: firstly by cultivating an appetite for information which has raised the number of students in Athens to more than 3000, whose highest ideal is that of the schoolmaster, and secondly by neglecting their army. They cannot strike, and therefore it has become doubtful whether they will ever possess Constantinople, however much it is to be desired that they should. There are then nations who, to their great detriment, are over-cultured, and there is still truth in the old saying about the hallowed soil of manual work.

Let us hear no clap-trap about the disinherited. No doubt there have been times when those in possession have grossly abused their power, but as a rule the social balance is kept. . . .

The next essential function of the State is the conduct of war. The long oblivion into which this principle had fallen is a proof of how effeminate the science of government had become in civilian hands. In our century this sentimentality was dissipated by Clausewitz,[12] but a one-sided materialism arose in its place, after the fashion of the Manchester school, seeing in man a biped creature, whose destiny lies in buying cheap and selling dear. It is obvious that this idea is not compatible with war, and it is only since the last war [1870–71] that a sounder theory arose of the State and its military power.

Without war no State could be. All those we know of arose through war, and the protection of their members by armed force remains their primary and essential task. War, therefore, will endure to the end of history, as long as there is multiplicity of States. The laws of human thought and of human nature forbid any alternative, neither is one to be wished for. The blind worshipper of an eternal peace falls into the error of isolating the State, or dreams of one which is universal, which we have already seen to be at variance with reason.

Even as it is impossible to conceive of a tribunal above the State, which we have recognized as sovereign in its very essence, so it is likewise impossible to banish the idea of war from the world. It is a favourite fashion of our time to instance England as particularly ready for peace. But England is perpetually at war; there is hardly an instant in her recent history in which she has not been obliged to be fighting somewhere. The great strides which civilization makes against barbarism and unreason are only made actual by the sword. Between civilized nations also war is the form of litigation by which States make their claims valid. The argument brought forward in these terrible law suits of the nations compel as no argument in civil suits can ever do. Often as we have tried by theory to convince the small States that Prussia alone can be the leader in Germany, we had to produce the final proof upon the battlefields of Bohemia and the [river] Main [in 1866].

Moreover war is a uniting as well as a dividing element among nations; it does not draw them together in enmity only, for through its means they learn to know and to respect each other's peculiar qualities.

It is important not to look upon war always as a judgment from

[12] Karl von Clausewitz (1780–1831), Prussian general, author of "On War" (three volumes, 1833)

God. Its consequences are evanescent; but the life of a nation is reckoned by centuries, and the final verdict can only be pronounced after the survey of whole epochs.

Such a State as Prussia might indeed be brought near to destruction by a passing phase of degeneracy; but being by the character of its people more reasonable and more free than the French, it retained the power to call up the moral force within itself, and so to regain its ascendancy. Most undoubtedly war is the one remedy for an ailing nation. Social selfishness and party hatreds must be dumb before the call of the State when its existence is at stake. Forgetting himself, the individual must only remember that he is a part of the whole, and realize the unimportance of his own life compared with the common weal.

The grandeur of war lies in the utter annihilation of puny man in the great conception of the State, and it brings out the full magnificence of the sacrifice of fellow-countrymen for one another. In war the chaff is winnowed from the wheat. Those who have lived through 1870 cannot fail to understand Niebuhr's[13] description of his feelings in 1813, when he speaks of how no one who has entered into the joy of being bound by a common tie to all his compatriots, gentle and simple alike, can ever forget how he was uplifted by the love, the friendliness, and the strength of that mutual sentiment.

It is war which fosters the political idealism which the materialist rejects. What a disaster for civilization it would be if mankind blotted its heroes from memory. The heroes of a nation are the figures which rejoice and inspire the spirit of its youth, and the writers whose words ring like trumpet blasts become the idols of our boyhood and our early manhood. He who feels no answering thrill is unworthy to bear arms for his country. To appeal from this judgment to Christianity would be sheer perversity, for does not the Bible distinctly say that the ruler shall rule by the sword, and again that greater love hath no man than to lay down his life for his friend? To Aryan races, who are before all things courageous, the foolish preaching of everlasting peace has always been vain. They have always been men enough to maintain with the sword what they have attained through the spirit. . . .

Such matters must not be examined only by the light of the student's lamp. The historian who moves in the world of the real Will sees at once that the demand for eternal peace is purely reactionary. He sees that all movement and all growth would disappear with war, and that only the exhausted, spiritless, degenerate periods of history have toyed with the idea. . . .

[13] Barthold Georg Niebuhr (1776–1831), historian and Prussian ambassador

But it is not worth while to speak further of these matters, for the God above us will see to it that war shall return again, a terrible medicine for mankind diseased.

Despite all this it is not denied that the progress of culture must make wars both shorter and rarer, . . .

. . . Therefore wars must become rarer and shorter, owing to man's natural horror of bloodshed as well as to the size and quality of modern armies, for it is impossible to see how the burdens of a great war could long be borne under the present conditions. But it would be false to conclude that wars can ever cease. They neither can nor should, so long as the State is sovereign and stands among its peers. . . .

The individual should feel himself a member of his State, and as such have courage to take its errors upon him. There must be no question of subjects having the right to oppose a sovereignty which in their opinion is not moral. Cases may arise when the State's action touches the foundation of the moral life, namely, religious feeling. When the Huguenots in France had their religion proscribed and were commanded to worship their God under forms which their deepest conviction held to be unchristian, conscience drove them out from their fatherland, but we must not praise the fine temper of these martyrs for religion from the standpoint of the theologian without recognizing the degree of tragic guilt which is always blended with such moral compulsion. The Huguenots who left their homes were gallant men, no doubt, but each of them had a bitter conflict to fight out within himself before he placed his love for the Heidelberg Catechism above his hereditary love for his country and his king. In modern times there have been Radical parties who have in their vanity imagined themselves faced with a similar struggle, which had in fact only a subjective existence in their own exalted imagination. This was the reason why a number of the German-Americans [after 1848] forsook their fatherland. It is foolish to admire them for this. We must always maintain the principle that the State is in itself an ethical force and a high moral good. . . .

All great nations in the fulness of their strength have desired to set their mark upon barbarian lands. All over the globe today we see the peoples of Europe creating a mighty aristocracy of the white races. Those who take no share in this great rivalry will play a pitiable part in time to come. The colonizing impulse has become a vital question for a great nation. . . .

Thus every colonizing effort which retains its single nationality has become a factor of immense importance for the future of the world. Upon it depends the share which each people will take in

the domination of the earth by the white races. It is quite conceivable that a country without colonies may cease to rank as a great
European Power, however strong it may be. Therefore we must
never become rigid, as a purely Continental policy must make us,
but see to it that the outcome of our next successful war must be
the acquisition of colonies by any possible means. . . .

The normal condition naturally is that the political victor should
be in a position to impose his culture and manners upon the people
he has subjugated. This the Germans did, as we have seen, in the
territories belonging to the Teutonic Order, but farther east, in
Esthonia and Kurland, we were not strong enough to effect this
complete colonization. The German invasion rolled its full tide over
Prussia, but the Hanseatic Fleet conveyed only a few shiploads of
settlers to Livonia and Esthonia, these principally from Westphalia.
In these two countries the Teutonic immigrants only formed as it
were a thin crust over the mass of the population, who remained un-
Germanized. The nobility and the upper classes were German, and
assumed dominion over a people who were not. But since every
nation is rejuvenated from below, it is the peasant population which
decides nationality. We may depend upon the re-Germanizing of
Alsace, but not of Livonia and Kurland. There no other course is
open to us but to keep the subject race in as uncivilized a condition
as possible, and thus prevent them from becoming a danger to the
handful of their conquerors.

19. RICHARD WAGNER:

CHRISTIANITY, GERMANISM AND RACIALISM

The famous composer of great operas, Richard Wagner
(1813–1883), wrote also profusely on fundamental problems
of civilization and politics. Like Marx, he participated actively
in the German revolution of 1848–49, and then had to flee into
exile. But whereas Marx died in exile and poverty, Wagner
returned in 1864 to Germany as an artist-prince who regarded
it his task to renew civilization not only through his art but
also through his leadership on national and religious issues.

In 1876, at the height of his fame and influence, he opened
a festival house in Bayreuth in northern Bavaria, which was
exclusively dedicated to performances of his own works. The
opening production was his monumental *The Ring of the*

Nibelung, which revived in Germany a fascination for the ancient mythology of Germanic gods and demons.

In Bayreuth he became the head and center of a circle of followers who accepted his sharply pronounced, extremist ideas of racialism, Germanism, and anti-Judaism with great fervor and dedication. This circle created its own organ, *Bayreuther Blätter,* in which Wagner published in 1878 his article "Public and Popularity" and in 1881 two articles, one called "Know Thyself, a Continuation of Religion and Art" and "Herodom and Christendom." The following excerpts are taken from these three articles.[14]

Christianity still endures; its oldest churchly institutions stand even with a firmness that makes desperate cowards of many toilers for State-culture. That a heartfelt, truly blest relation to Christ's precepts exists among the generality of present Christians, is certainly not so easy to aver. The educated doubts, the common man despairs. Science makes God the Creator more impossible each day; but from the beginning of the Church the God revealed to us by Jesus has been converted by the Theologians from a most sublime reality into an ever less intelligible problem. That the God of our Saviour should have been identified with the tribal god of Israel, is one of the most terrible confusions in all world-history; it has avenged itself in every age, and avenges itself today by the more and more outspoken atheism of the coarsest, as the finest minds. We have lived to see the Christian God condemned to empty churches, while ever more imposing temples are reared among us to Jehova. And it almost seems right that Jehova at last should quite suppress the God so monstrously mistakenly derived from him. If Jesus is proclaimed Jehova's son, then every Jewish rabbi can triumphantly confute all Christian theology, as has happened indeed in every age. What a melancholy, what a discreditable plight, is that of our whole Theology, maintained to give our doctors of the church and popular preachers little else than the guidance to an insincere interpretation of the truths contained in our priceless Gospels! To what is the preacher bound fast in the pulpit, but to compromises between the utmost contradictions, whose subtleties must necessarily confound our very faith itself and make us ask: Who now knows Jesus?— Historical criticism, perchance? It casts in its lot with Judaism, and, just like every Jew, it wonders that the bells on Sunday morn should

[14] Richard Wagner's *Prose Works,* translated by William Ashton Ellis, vol. VI (London, 1897)

still be ringing for a Jew once crucified two thousand years ago. How often and minutely have the Gospels been critically searched, their origin and compilation exposed beyond a doubt; so that one might have thought the very evidence of the spuriousness and irrelevance of their contradictory matter would at last have opened the eyes of Criticism to the lofty figure of the Redeemer and his work. But the God whom Jesus revealed to us; the God no god, no sage or hero of the world, had known before; the God who, amid Pharisees, Scribes and sacrificial Priests, made himself known to poor Galilean shepherds and fishermen with such soulcompelling power and simplicity that whoso once had recognized him, beheld the world and all its good as null; this God who never more can be revealed, since this first time was He revealed to us for ever:—this God the critic always views with fresh distrust, because he feels obliged to take Him for the maker of the Jewish world, Jehova! . . .

Is it so utterly impossible to Theology, to take the great step that would grant to Science its irrefutable truths through surrender of Jehova, and to the Christian world its pure God revealed in Jesus the only?

A hard question, and undoubtedly a still harder demand. Yet both might take a more menancing form if the problems still soluble upon the basis of a noble Science should one day be propounded by the Folk itself, and solved in its wonted fashion. As I already have hinted, the doubting and the despairing sections of mankind may finally combine in the so trivial confession of Atheism. We are already witnessing it. Nothing else seems expressed in this confession, as yet, than great dissatisfaction. Whither that may lead, however, is food for reflection. The politician handles a capital in which a large part of the nation has no share. Never, since the abolition of slavery, has the world been more conspicuously divided into those who own and those who do not. Perhaps it was imprudent to admit the unpropertied to a voice in legislation intended solely for possessors. The consequent entanglements have not been slow to arise; to face them, it might reward wise statesmen to give the non-possessors at least an interest in the maintenance of Property. Much shows that such an act of wisdom is improbable, whereas repression is deemed easier and more swiftly efficacious. Indisputably the instinct of preservation is stronger than one commonly supposes: the Roman Empire maintained itself in a state of dissolution for half a thousand years. The period of two thousand years, which great historic civilizations have hitherto covered in their evolution from barbarism back to barbarism, would carry ourselves to somewhere about the middle of the next millennium. Can one imagine the state of barbarism at which we shall have arrived, if our social system continues for another six hundred years or so in the footsteps of the declining Roman world-dominion? I believe that the Saviour's second advent, expected by the earliest Christians in their lifetime, and later cherished as a mystic dogma, might have a meaning for that future date, and perchance amid occurrences not totally unlike those sketched in the Apocalypse. For, in the conceivable event of a relapse of our whole Culture into barbarism, we may take one thing for granted: namely, that our Historical science, our criticism and chemistry of knowledge would also have come to end; whilst it may be hoped, on the contrary, that Theology would by then have come to a final agreement with the Gospels, and the free understanding of Revelation be opened to us without Jehovaistic subtleties —for which event the Saviour promised us his coming back. . . .

What has given the Jews their now so dreaded power among and over us, not one man seems to stop and ponder; or if he goes into the question, he seeks no farther than the facts and phases of the last ten years, or at most a few years earlier; nowhere can we trace as yet an inclination to a deeper search into ourselves, in this case to a thorough criticism of the will and spirit of all that conglomerate of nature and civilization which we, for instance, call the "German."

Yet the movement here alluded to perhaps is more adapted than any other to set us marvelling at ourselves: in it we seem to see the late reawakening of an instinct that appeared extinct. A man [Wagner himself] who some thirty years ago drew notice to the Jews' inaptitude for taking a productive share in our Art, and felt impelled to renew that attempt just eighteen years thereafter, was met by the utmost indignation of Jews alike and Germans; it became quite dangerous to breathe the word "Jew" with a doubtful accent. But what once roused the bitterest ill-will when spoken on the field of ethical aesthetics, we suddenly hear cried in vulgar brutal tones upon the field of civic intercourse and party politics. The fact that lies between these two expressions is the bestowal [in 1871] of full rights upon the Jews to regard themselves in all respects as Germans —much as a blanket authorised the blacks in Mexico to hold themselves for whites. Whoever weighs this matter well, even if its real absurdity escapes him, must at least be highly astonished at the levity—nay, the frivolity of our State authorities, who could decree so vast, so incomputable a transformation of our national system without the smallest sense of what they were doing. . . .

How was it possible for there to be Germans, at any time, who could conceive of all that keeps the Jewish race so wide apart from us under the idea of a religious "confession," seeing it was first and solely in German history that divisions arose in the *Christian*

Church which led to the State-acknowledgment of various confessions? However, if only we will turn that "Know thyself" with ruthless energy upon ourselves, this curiously perverted formula may afford us one of the principal clues to explanation of the seemingly inexplicable. The first thing then to strike us, will be the recent experience that our clerics feel lamed at once in their agitation against the Jews when Judaism itself is seized by the root, and the patriarchs for instance, great Abraham in particular, are submitted to a criticism involving the actual text of the Mosaic books. At once the groundwork of the Christian Church, its "positive" religion, seems to reel beneath their feet; a "Mosaic confession" is recognised; and its adherents are accorded the right to take their place beside us, to examine the credentials of a second revelation through Jesus Christ—whom even in the opinion of the late English Prime Minister[15] they regard as one of their countless minor prophets, of whom we have made by far too much ado. To tell the truth, it will fall hard to prove by the aspect of the Christian world, and the character of the culture shed upon it by a Church so soon decayed, the superiority of the revelation through Jesus Christ to that through Abraham and Moses: in spite of its dispersion, the Jewish stock has remained one whole with the Mosaic laws to this very day, whereas our culture and civilisation stand in the most crying contradiction to Christ's teaching.

However, an inner motive plainly lies at bottom of the present movement, little as it may be evinced by the behaviour of its leaders so far. We expressed our belief, above, that this motive was the re-awakening of an instinct lost to the German nation. People speak of an antagonism of *races*. In this sense we should have fresh cause for self-inspection, as it would necessitate our defining the relation of certain given breeds of man to one another. Here it would probably have to be recognised at the outset that, in talking of a German "race," it would be very difficult, nay, wellnigh impossible to compare it with a race so strongly pronounced, and still unaltered, as the Jewish. When learned men debate the relative value of mixed or pure-bred races, for the evolution of mankind, the decision must surely hinge on what we mean by man's developmental progress. The so-called Romanic nations, and the English too, are praised as hybrid stocks that obviously surpass in cultural progress the peoples of a haply pure Germanic breed. On the other hand, if one declines to be blinded by the glamour of this culture and civilisation, and seeks the welfare of mankind in its bringing-to-birth of great characters, one finds that these far rather come to light—nay, almost

[15] Benjamin Disraeli, Earl of Beaconsfield

solely—in pure-bred races; where it seems that the still unbroken nature-force of Race at first makes up for every higher human virtue yet unformed, and only to be won through life's sore trials, by that of *pride*. . . .

Our nation, one may say, has not the natural instinct for that which suits it, for what becomes it, helps and furthers it; estranged from itself, it dabbles in foreign manners. On none other have great and original spirits been bestowed, as on it, without its having known in time to treasure them: yet if the silliest news-writer or political cheap-jack but brazens out his lying phrases, it chooses him to represent its weightiest interests; whilst if the Jew comes tinkling with his bell of paper, it throws its savings at his feet, and makes him in one night a millionaire.

The Jew, on the contrary, is the most astounding instance of racial congruence ever offered by world-history. Without a fatherland, a mother-tongue, midst every people's land and tongue he finds himself again, in virtue of the unfailing instinct of his absolute and in-delible idiosyncrasy: even commixture of blood does not hurt him; let Jew or Jewess intermarry with the most distinct of races, a Jew will always come to birth. Not into the remotest contact is he brought with the religion of any of the civilised nations; for in truth he has no religion at all—merely the belief in certain promises of his god which in nowise extend to a life beyond this temporal life of his, as in every true religion, but simply to this present life on earth, whereon his race is certainly ensured dominion over all that lives and lives not. Thus the Jew has need to neither think nor chatter, not even to calculate, for the hardest calculation lies all cut and dried for him in an instinct shut against all ideality. A wonderful, unparalleled phenomenon: the plastic dæmon of man's downfall in triumphant surety; and German citizen of State, to boot, with a Mosaic confession; the darling of Liberal princes, and warrant of our national unity!

Despite the enormous disadvantage at which the German race (if so we still may call it) appears to stand against the Jewish, we yet have ventured to suggest the re-awakening of a German instinct as one factor in the present agitation. As, however, we have been obliged to discard all idea of its being a purely racial instinct, we perhaps might search for something higher: a bent that, merely vaguely (*wahnvoll*) felt by the Folk of today, would at first appear indeed as instinct, though really of far nobler origin and loftier aim, and which might haply be defined as the spirit of the purely human.

From the cosmopolitan proper, if such a man exists in fact, we probably should have little to expect for the solution of our problem. It is no small thing, to run through the history of the world and yet preserve love for the human species. Here nothing but a rooted feeling of kinship with the immediate nation whence we sprang, can serve to re-knit the strand dissevered by a survey of the whole: here operates the thing we feel ourselves to be; we pity, and strive our best to hope, as for the future of our nearer family. Fatherland, mother-tongue: woe to the man bereft of these! But what un-measured happiness, to recognise in one's mother-tongue the speech of one's ancestors! Through such a tongue our feelings and beholdings stretch right back to early Man himself; no fence and pale there hedge our nobles in, and far beyond the fatherland at last assigned us, beyond the landmarks of historic knowledge and all our outer trappings thence derived, we feel ourselves one kin with pristine Man's creative beauty. Such is our German language, the only heritage retained intact from our forefathers. Do we feel our breath fast quitting us, beneath the pressure of an alien civilization; do we fall into uncertainty about ourselves: we have only to dig to the roots in the true father-soil of our language, to reap at once a reassuring answer on ourselves, nay, on the truly human. And this possibility, of always drawing from the pristine fount of our own nature, that makes us feel ourselves no more a race, no mere variety of man, but one of mankind's primal branches,—it is this that ever has bestowed on us great men and spiritual heroes, as to whom we have no need to trouble whether fashioners of foreign fatherless civilisations are able to understand and prize them; whilst we again, inspired by the deeds and gifts of our forefathers, and gazing with unclouded eye, are able to rightly estimate those foreigners, and value them according to the spirit of pure humanity indwelling in their work. For the sterling German instinct asks and seeks for nothing but this purely-human, and through that search alone can it be helpful—not merely to itself, but to all that shews the pure and genuine under never so great disguise.

We cannot withhold our acknowledgment that the human family consists of irremediably disparate races, whereof the noblest well might rule the more ignoble, yet never raise them to their level by commixture, but simply sink to theirs.

The first point will be, to examine the special attributes of those noblest races, through whose enfeeblement they lost themselves among ignoble races. The more definitely has recent science inclined us to accept the natural descent of man's lower races from the ani-mal species most resembling them, the harder is it to assent to a derivation of the so-called white race from those black and yellow: as to the explanation of the white tint itself our physiologists are still at variance. Whilst yellow races have viewed themselves as sprung from monkeys, the white traced back their origin to gods, and deemed themselves marked out for rulership. It has been made quite clear that we should have no History of Man at all, had there been no movements, creations and achievements of the white men; and we may fitly take world-history as the consequence of these white men mixing with the black and yellow, and bringing them in so far into history as that mixture altered them and made them less unlike the white. Incomparably fewer in individual numbers than the lower races, the ruin of the white races may be referred to their having been obliged to mix with them; whereby, as remarked already, they suffered more from the loss of their purity than the others could gain by the ennobling of their blood.

The plainest type of heroism is that evolved by the Hellenic sagas in their *Herakles*. Labours put upon him to destroy him, he executes in proud obedience, and frees the world thereby from direct plagues. Seldom, in fact scarcely ever, do we find the hero otherwise than in a state of suffering prepared for him by fate: Herakles is persecuted by Hera out of jealousy of his divine begetter, and kept in menial subjection. In this main trait we surely should not do wrong to recognise an allusion to that school of arduous labours in which the noblest Aryan races throve to grandeur of demigods: the by no means mildest climates whence they enter history at last, as men matured, supply us with a clue to the fortunes of their ancestry. Here we find the fruit of suffering and deprivations vanquished by heroic toil, that proud selfconsciousness whereby these stocks are once for all distinguished from the others throughout our whole world-history. Like Herakles and Siegfried, they were conscious of divine descent: a lie to them was inconceivable, and a free man meant a truthful man. Nowhere in history do these root-qualities of the Aryan race show forth more plainly than in the contact of the last pure-bred Germanic branches with the failing Roman world. The accident of their becoming masters of the great Latino-Semite realm was fatal to them. Pride is a delicate virtue and brooks no compromise, such as crossing of breed: but the Germanic race without this virtue has nothing to tell us. For this Pride is the soul of the truthful, of the free though serving. He knows no fear (*Furcht*), but respect (*Ehrfurcht*)—a virtue whose very name, in its proper sense, is known to none save those oldest Aryan peoples; whilst honour (*Ehre*) itself is the sum of all personal worth, and therefore can neither be given nor received, as is our practice today, but, a witness of divine descent, it keeps the hero unashamed even in his most shameful of sufferings. From Pride and Honour sprang the rule that, not property ennobles man, but man this property;

which, again, was expressed in the custom that excessive possessions were speedily shared out, for very shame, by him to whom they haply fell.

Upon looking back to these characteristics and the inviolably noble code that flowed therefrom we certainly are justified in seeking the cause of their loss and its decay in a depravation of those races' blood, since we see the fall undoubtedly accompany their hybridising. This fact has been so completely established by the talented and energetic author[16] named above, that we need only refer our friends to his work on the Disparity of the Races of Man, to rest assured that what we now propose to link thereto will not be viewed as superficial guess-work. For we now must seek the Hero where he turns against the ruin of his race, the downfall of its code of honour, and girds his erring will to horror: the hero wondrously become divine—the *Saint*.

20. GRIFFITH: *ECONOMIC NATIONALISM*

Besides the pseudoreligious and biological nationalism as represented by Richard Wagner, there was a growing insistence, hardly known before 1848, on economic power and self-sufficiency as a necessary foundation of national strength, an expansion of the nationalist power struggle into the field of economics.

This trend was well expressed by Arthur Griffith (1872–1922), an Irish nationalist leader, who helped to found the Sinn Fein (Ourselves) movement. In 1899 he started to edit the paper *The United Irishman,* the name of which he changed in 1906 to *Sinn Fein* and in 1917 to *Nationality.*

At the first annual convention of the National Council of Sinn Fein on November 28, 1905, Griffith delivered a speech in which he demanded the production and use of home manufactures and the boycott of foreign (English) goods. He asked the Irish to be willing to pay, if necessary, higher prices for Irish goods and appealed for the help of Irish American capital.[17]

[16] Count Arthur Gobineau (1816–1882) author of *Essay on the Inequality of the Human Races,* four volumes, 1853–1855
[17] The following characteristic passages are from the speech as printed in Griffith's paper *The United Irishman* of December, 1905.

I am in economics largely a follower of the man who thwarted England's dream of the commercial conquest of the world, and who made the mighty confederation before which England has fallen commercially and is falling politically—Germany. His name is a famous one in the outside world, his works are the text books of economic science in other countries—in Ireland his name is unknown and his works unheard of—I refer to Frederick List,[18] the real founder of the German Zollverein— . . .

Brushing aside the fallacies of Adam Smith and his tribe, List points out that between the individual and humanity stands, and must continue to stand, a great fact—the nation. The nation, with its special language and literature, with its peculiar origin and history, with its special manners and customs, laws and institutions, with the claims of all these for existence, independence, perfection, and continuance for the future, with its separate territory, a society which, united by a thousand ties of minds and interests, combines itself into one independent whole, which recognizes the law of right for and within itself, and in its united character is still opposed to other societies of a similar kind in their national liberty, and consequently can, under the existing conditions of the world, maintain self-existence and independence only by its own power and resources. As the individual chiefly obtains by means of the nation and in the nation, mental culture, power and production, security and prosperity, so is the civilization of the human race only conceivable and possible by means of the civilization and development of individual nations. . . .

21. JAMES BRYCE: *IRISH HOME RULE*

In the second half of the nineteenth century Irish nationalists began to claim home rule for Ireland. Under Gladstone's leadership English liberals accepted the demand, but the Conservatives resisted it, fearing that home rule for Ireland would be—as it turned out to be—the first step on the road to the liquidation of the British Empire. The struggle for Irish home rule in England led also to a broader democratization of British life and institutions, a democratization which started under the Liberal administration of the 1880's and was continued

[18] Friedrich List (1789–1846), economist, born in Germany, naturalized in the United States, foremost advocate of a nationalist protective-tariff policy in Germany

under the Liberal administration in the last decade before the outbreak of the war of 1914.

During his second ministry (1880–1885) Gladstone had a new Irish Land Act passed which fundamentally improved the economic and legal position of the Irish tenant peasant. In 1886 he introduced his first Home Rule Bill, which split the Liberal Party and was defeated. But the liberal agitation for home rule for Ireland did not cease.

One of the prominent academic Liberals of the day was James Bryce (1838–1922), author of *The American Commonwealth* (1888), in which he discussed, in a most appreciative spirit, the United States institutions from the point of view of a constitutional lawyer. In 1907 Bryce became British ambassador to the United States and on his retirement (1913) was created a viscount.

After the defeat of the first Home Rule Bill, Bryce, then a member of parliament, edited a *Handbook of Home Rule, Being Articles on the Irish Question* (2nd printing, London, 1887), to which he himself contributed an article describing the reasons why many Liberals followed Gladstone in favoring home rule for Ireland.[19]

Very few words are needed to summarize the outline which, omitting many details which would have illustrated and confirmed its truth, I have attempted to present of the progress of opinion among Liberal members of the Parliament of 1880.

1. Our experience of the Coercion Bills of 1881 and 1882 disclosed the enormous mischief which such measures do in alienating the minds of Irishmen, and the difficulty of enlisting Irish sentiment on behalf of the law. The results of the Act of 1881 taught us that the repression of open agitation means the growth of far more dangerous conspiracy; those of the Act of 1882 proved that even under an administration like Lord Spencer's repression works no change for the better in the habits and ideas of the people.

2. The conduct of the House of Lords in 1880 and 1881, and the malign influence which its existence exerted whenever remedial legislation for Ireland came in question, convinced us that full and complete justice will never be done to Ireland by the British

---

[19] James Bryce, ed., *Handbook of Home Rule, Being Articles on the Irish Question* (second printing, London, 1887)

Parliament while the Upper House (as at present constituted) remains a part of that Parliament.

3. The break-down of the procedure of the House of Commons, and the failure of the efforts to amend it, proved that Parliament cannot work so long as a considerable section of its members seek to impede its working. To enable it to do its duty by England and Scotland, it was evidently necessary, either to make the Irish members as loyal to Parliament as English and Scotch members usually are, or else to exclude them.

4. The discussions of Irish Bills in the House of Commons made us realize how little English members knew about Ireland; how utterly different were their competence for, and their attitude towards, Irish questions and English questions. We perceived that we were legislating in the dark for a country whose economic and social condition we did not understand—a country to which we could not apply our English ideas of policy; a country whose very temper and feeling were strange to us. We were really fitter to pass laws for Canada or Australia than for this isle within sight of our shores.

5. I have said that we were legislating in the dark. But there were two quarters from which light was proferred, the Irish members and the Irish Executive. We rejected the first, and could hardly help doing so, for to accept it would have been to displace our own leaders. We followed the light which the Executive gave. But in some cases (as notably in the case of the Coercion Bill of 1881) it proved to be a "wandering fire," leading us into dangerous morasses. And we perceived that at all times legislation at the bidding of the Executive, against the wishes of Irish members, was not self-government or free government. It was despotism. The rule of Ireland by the British Parliament was really "the rule of a dependency through an official, responsible no doubt, but responsible not to the ruled, but to an assembly of which they form less than a sixth part." As this assembly closed its ears to the one-sixth, and gave effect to the will of the official, this was essentially arbitrary government, and wanted those elements of success which free government contains.

This experience had, by 1884, convinced us that the present relations of the British Parliament to Ireland were bad, and could not last; that the discontent of Ireland was justified; that the existing system, in alienating the mind of Ireland, tended, not merely to Repeal, but to Separation; that the simplest, and probably the only effective, remedy for the increasing dangers was the grant of an Irish Legislature. Two events clinched these conclusions. One was the Tory surrender of June, 1885. Self-government, we had come to

see, was the only alternative to Coercion, and now Coercion was
gone. The other was the General Election of December, 1885, when
newly-enfranchised Ireland, through five-sixths of her representatives, demanded a Parliament of her own.

These were not, as is sometimes alleged, conclusions of despair.
We were mostly persons of a cautious and conservative turn of
mind, as men imbued with the spirit of the British Constitution
ought to be. The first thing was to convince us that the existing relations of the islands were faulty, and could not be maintained. This
was a negative result, and while we remained in that stage we were
despondent. Many Liberal members will remember the gloom
that fell on us in 1882 and 1883 whenever we thought or spoke of
Ireland. But presently the clouds lifted. We still felt the old objections to any Home Rule scheme, though we now saw that they were
less formidable than the evils of the present system. But we came
to feel that the grant of self-government was a right thing in itself.
It was not merely a means of ridding ourselves of our difficulties,
not merely a boon yielded because long demanded. It was a return
to broad and deep principles, a conformity to those natural laws
which govern human society as well as the inanimate world—an
effort to enlist the better and higher feelings of mankind in the
creation of a truer union between the two nations than had ever
yet existed. When we perceived this, hope returned. It is strong
with us now, for, though we see troubles, perhaps even dangers, in
the immediate future, we are confident that the principles on which
Liberal policy towards Ireland is based will in the long run work
out a happy issue for her, as they have in and for every other
country that has trusted to them.

One last word as to Consistency. We learned in the Parliament of
1880 many facts about Ireland we had not known before; we felt
the force and bearing of other facts previously accepted on hearsay,
but not realized. We saw the Irish problem change from what it
had been in 1880 into the new phase which stood apparent at the
end of 1885, Coercion abandoned by its former advocates, Self-
government demanded by the nation. Were we to disregard all
these new facts, ignore all these new conditions, and cling to old
ideas, some of which we perceived to be mistaken, while others,
still true in themselves, were outweighed by arguments of far wider
import? We did not so estimate our duty. We foresaw the taunts
of foes and the reproaches of friends. But we resolved to give effect
to the opinions we slowly, painfully, even reluctantly formed,
opinions all the stronger because not suddenly adopted, and
founded upon evidence whose strength no one can appreciate till

he has studied the causes of Irish discontent in Irish history, and been forced (as we were) to face in Parliament the practical difficulties of the government of Ireland by the British House of Commons.

22. RUDYARD KIPLING:
THE GLORY AND BURDEN OF EMPIRE

Home rule for Ireland was the first step in the decolonization started by the British at the beginning of the twentieth century and followed in its middle years by all modern Western nations. The decades around the turn of the century witnessed in all these nations, including the United States, an upsurge of imperialism, compounded of social Darwinism, of alleged economic needs, of nationalist pride, and of the belief in the manifest destiny of the advanced nations to spread their progressive civilization.

The glory and burden of this imperialism was expressed in the poems and writings of Rudyard Kipling (1865–1936). Born in British India and working there in his early years as writer and journalist, he later lived several years in the United States, marrying an American in 1895. He was awarded the Nobel Prize for literature in 1907.

Following the victory of the United States in its war with Spain (1898), Kipling published the poem "The White Man's Burden" (A), which summed up the then popular arguments for the civilizing mission of imperialism and for its invigorating effect on the imperial nations. In the 1890's Kipling, then regarded as the "Prophet of Empire," saw, as did Cecil Rhodes (1853–1902) and Theodore Roosevelt (1858–1919), in the English speaking peoples the main instruments of civilization then active in the world. His poem, "Recessional" (B), which he published in London at the time of the jubilant celebration (1897) of Queen Victoria's sixty years of a reign of solid magnificence and growing prosperity, proved that Kipling, in his heart-searching, was aware of the darker and more ominous colors in the then radiant panoply of modern imperialism.[20]

[20] From *Rudyard Kipling's Verse Inclusive Edition.* Reprinted by permission of Mrs. George Bambridge and Doubleday & Company, Inc.

A. White Man's Burden

Take up the White Man's burden—
Send forth the best ye breed—
Go bind your sons to exile
To serve your captives' need;
To wait in heavy harness,
On fluttered folk and wild—
Your new caught, sullen peoples,
Half-devil and half-child.

Take up the White Man's burden—
In patience to abide,
To veil the threat of terror
And check the show of pride;
By open speech and simple,
An hundred times made plain
To seek another's profit,
And work another's gain.

Take up the White Man's burden—
The savage wars and peace—
Fill full the mouth of Famine
And bid the sickness cease;
And when your goal is nearest
The end for others sought,
Watch sloth and heathen Folly
Bring all your hopes to nought.

Take up the White Man's burden—
No tawdry rule of kings,
But toil of serf and sweeper—
The tale of common things.
The ports ye shall not enter,
The roads ye shall not tread,
Go make them with your living,
And mark them with your dead.

Take up the White Man's burden—
And reap his old reward:
The blame of those ye better,
The hate of those ye guard—
The cry of hosts ye humour

(Ah, slowly!) toward the light:—
"Why brought he us from bondage,
Our loved Egyptian night?"

Take up the White Man's burden—
Ye dare not stoop to less—
Nor call too loud on Freedom
To cloke your weariness;
By all ye cry or whisper,
By all ye leave or do,
The silent, sullen peoples
Shall weigh your Gods and you.

Take up the White Man's burden—
Have done with childish days—
The lightly proffered laurel,
The easy, ungrudged praise.
Comes now, to search your manhood
Through all the thankless years,
Cold, edged with dear-bought wisdom,
The judgment of your peers!

B. Recessional

God of our fathers, known of old,
  Lord of our far-flung battle-line,
Beneath whose awful hand we hold
  Dominion over palm and pine—
Lord God of Hosts, be with us yet,
Lest we forget—lest we forget!

The tumult and the shouting dies;
  The captains and the kings depart:
Still stands Thine ancient sacrifice,
  An humble and a contrite heart.
Lord God of Hosts, be with us yet,
Lest we forget—lest we forget!

Far-called, our navies melt away;
  On dune and headland sinks the fire:
Lo, all our pomp of yesterday
  Is one with Nineveh and Tyre!
Judge of the Nations, spare us yet,
Lest we forget—lest we forget!

If, drunk with sight of power, we loose
    Wild tongues that have not Thee in awe,
Such boastings as the Gentiles use,
    Or lesser breeds without the Law—
Lord God of Hosts, be with us yet,
Lest we forget—lest we forget!

For heathen heart that puts her trust
    In recking tube and iron shard,
All valiant dust that build on dust,
    And, guarding, calls not Thee to guard,
For frantic boast and foolish word—
Thy Mercy on Thy People, Lord!

23. WILLIAM MORRIS: *A SOCIALIST SONG*

The impact of socialism was, in the last decades of the nineteenth century, less powerful than the impact of nationalism
and imperialism. Only after the First World War did socialism
grow in influence and effectiveness in Europe and in the world,
and frequently its appeal fused with that of nationalism. Nevertheless, the two last decades of the nineteenth century laid the
foundations for the future growth of socialism.

When Karl Marx died in England in 1883, hardly any notice
was taken of the event. Only six years later the Second International was founded in Paris. The German Social Democratic Party was then the strongest and best organized, whereas
in France the movement was split into various factions which
Jean Jaurès (1859–1914) consolidated into one party in 1905.
Even slower was the development in Britain. In 1900, for the
first time, two members entered the House of Commons as
official representatives of labor. This was due to the initiative
of Keir Hardie (1856–1915), who in 1893 founded the Independent Labor Party, independent of the two historical parties.
In the elections of 1906 the number of Labor M.P.'s increased
to thirty.

The Labor Party originated in a committee set up by the
Trade Union Congress in cooperation with small socialist
groups, mostly consisting of intellectuals, the formation of
which went back to the 1880's. Among these groups was the

Fabian Society in which George Bernard Shaw (1856–1944) and Sidney (1859–1947) and Beatrice Webb (1858–1943) took a leading part, and the small Marxist Social Democratic Federation, organized by Henry M. Hyndman (1842–1921).

Among the members of the latter group was the English poet and artist William Morris (1834–1896). He seceded and, in 1884, founded the Socialist League and edited its organ *The Commonweal*. There he published *News From Nowhere*, which appeared in book form in 1891 and in which he described an England in which the principles of socialism had been realized. Besides literature and art, Morris was also interested and creative in arts and crafts; his protest against commercialism and cheapness of manufacture was part of his socialism. In 1885 he published his *Chants for Socialism*, in which the following song was printed.[21]

The Day is Coming

Come hither lads, and hearken, for a tale there is to tell,
Of the wonderful days a'coming when all shall be better than well.

And the tale shall be told of a country, a land in the midst of the sea,
And folk shall call it England in the days that are going to be.

There more than one in a thousand in the days that are yet to come,
Shall have some hope of the morrow, some joy of the ancient home.

For then—laugh not, but listen, to this strange tale of mine—
All folk that are in England shall be better lodged than swine.

Then a man shall work and bethink him, and rejoice in the deeds of
    his hand,
Nor yet come home in the even too faint and weary to stand.

Men in that time a'coming shall work and have no fear
For to-morrow's lack of earning and the hunger-wolf anear.

I tell you this for a wonder, that no man then shall be glad
Of his fellow's fall and mishap to snatch at the work he had.

For that which the worker winneth shall then be his indeed,
Nor shall half be reaped for nothing by him that sowed no seed.

[21] William Morris, *Chants for Socialism* (London, 1885)

O strange new wonderful justice! But for whom shall we gather the
    gain?
For ourselves and for each of our fellows, and no hand shall labour
    in vain.

Then all *mine* and all *thine* shall be ours, and no more shall any
    man crave
For riches that serve for nothing but to fetter a friend for a slave.

And what wealth then shall be left us when none shall gather gold
To buy his friend in the market, and pinch and pine the sold?

Nay, what save the lovely city, and the little house on the hill,
And the wastes and the woodland beauty, and the happy fields we
    till.

And the homes of ancient stories, the tombs of the mighty dead;
And the wise men seeking out marvels, and the poet's teeming head;

And the painter's hand of wonder; and the marvellous fiddle-bow,
And the banded choirs of music:—all those that do and know.

For all these shall be ours and all men's, nor shall any lack a share
Of the toil and the gain of living in the days when the world grows
    fair.

Ah! such are the days that shall be! But what are the deeds of today
In the days of the years we dwell in, that wear our lives away?

Why, then, and for what are we waiting? There are three words to
    speak
WE WILL IT, and what is the foeman but the dreamstrong wakened
    and weak?

Oh why and for what are we waiting? while our brothers droop
    and die,
And on every wind of the heavens a wasted life goes by.

How long shall they reproach us where crowd on crowd they dwell,
Poor ghosts of the wicked city, the gold-crushed hungry hell?

Through squalid life they laboured, in sordid grief they died,
Those sons of a mighty mother, those props of England's pride.

They are gone; there is none can undo it, nor save our souls from
    the curse;
But many a million cometh, and shall they be better or worse?

It is we must answer and hasten, and open wide the door
For the rich man's hurrying terror, and the slow-foot hope of the
    poor.

Yea, the voiceless wrath of the wretched, and their unlearned
    discontent,
We must give it voice and wisdom till the waiting-tide be spent.

Come, then, since all things call us, the living and the dead,
And o'er the weltering tangle a glimmering light is shed.

Come, then, let us cast off fooling, and put by ease and rest,
For the CAUSE alone is worthy till the good days bring the best.

Come, join in the only battle wherein no man can fail,
Where whoso fadeth and dieth, yet his deed shall still prevail.

Ah! come, cast off all fooling, for this, at least, we know:
That the Dawn and the Day is coming, and forth the Banners go.

24. DOSTOEVSKY: *THE POSSESSED*

In the nineteenth century nationalism and socialism penetrated the boundaries of the secluded Russian empire, which,
beginning with the reforms of Alexander II (1855–1881), entered into closer contact with the West. Under the entirely
different social conditions and intellectual traditions of Russia,
the European movements, detached from their environmental
roots, assumed radical and extreme forms. The continuing
autocratic regime allowed no political activity or freedom of
expression until 1906. Russia, conscious of her potential
strength and suffering from a cultural inferiority, endlessly discussed during the nineteenth century her relationship with
Europe and the future role which a Christian or a socialist
Russia would play in the world.

Fyodor Dostoevsky (1821–1881) was not only a great Russian novelist but also a political journalist who actively participated in the debate on the meaning of Russia's history and mission. In his writings he upheld the claim of the Russian people to a unique leading role in the service of civilization, peace, and social justice. He regarded the Russian people, if they remained true to their own tradition, as the bearers of salvation for Europe. He was one of the leading spokesmen of the Slavophils, who identified the Russians with the Slavs—a group of peoples speaking related languages, among whom the Russians were the most numerous and powerful—and who believed in the superiority of the Russian way of life and traditions over those of Europe. The Slavophils were opposed to the Westernizers in Russia, who wished to reform Russian life and government according to Western models and in cooperation with Western Europe.

One of the four famous great novels by Dostoevsky is *The Possessed,* which he published in 1871–72. It is a bitter attack upon, and partly a caricature of, the radical revolutionary movement among a large section of the Russian intelligentsia of the day. In the novel, Shatov, a former serf—and therefore close to the "real" Russian people—has after a short time as a revolutionary found his way to Slavophilism and thus expresses its views in a famous discussion of Russia's national and ideological mission with the enigmatic Nicolai Stavrogin.[22]

"Do you know," he began with flashing eyes, almost menacingly, bending right forward in his chair, raising the forefinger of his right hand above him (obviously unaware that he was doing so), "do you know who are the only 'God-bearing' people on earth, destined to regenerate and save the world in the name of a new God, and to whom are given the keys of life and of the new world. . . . Do you know which is that people and what is its name?"

"From your manner I am forced to conclude, and I think I may as well do so at once, that it is the Russian people."

"And you can laugh, oh, what a race!" Shatov burst out.

"Calm yourself, I beg of you; on the contrary, I was expecting something of the sort from you." . . .

[22] Fyodor Mikhailovich Dostoevsky, *The Possessed,* part II, chapter 1, translated by Constance Garnett (New York: The Macmillan Company). Reprinted by permission. First published in 1914 by Heinemann, London.

Shatov interrupted, waving his hand.

"Do you remember your expression that 'an atheist can't be a Russian,' that 'an atheist at once ceases to be a Russian'? "Do you remember saying that?"

"Did I?" Nikolai Vsyevolodovitch questioned him back.

"You ask? You've forgotten? And yet that was one of the truest statements of the leading peculiarity of the Russian soul, which you divined. You can't have forgotten it! I will remind you of something else: you said then that 'a man who was not orthodox could not be Russian.' "

"I imagine that's a Slavophile idea."

"The Slavophiles of today disown it. Nowadays, people have grown cleverer. But you went further: you believed that Roman Catholicism was not Christianity; you asserted that Rome proclaimed Christ subject to the third temptation of the devil. Announcing to all the world that Christ without an earthly kingdom cannot hold his ground upon earth. Catholicism by so doing proclaimed Antichrist and ruined the whole Western world. You pointed out that if France is in agonies now it's simply the fault of Catholicism, for she has rejected the iniquitous God of Rome and has not found a new one. That's what you could say then! I remember our conversation." . . .

Shatov bent forward in his chair again and again held up his finger for a moment.

"Not a single nation," he went on, as though reading it line by line, still gazing menacingly at Stavrogin, "not a single nation has ever been founded on principles of science or reason. There has never been an example of it, except for a brief moment, through folly. Socialism is from its very nature bound to be atheism, seeing that it has from the very first proclaimed that it is an atheistic organization of society, and that it intends to establish itself exclusively on the elements of science and reason. Science and reason have, from the beginning of time, played a secondary and subordinate part in the life of nations; so it will be till the end of time. Nations are built up and moved by another force which sways and dominates them, the origin of which is unknown and inexplicable: that force is the force of an insatiable desire to go on to the end, though at the same time it denies that end. It is the force of the persistent assertion of one's own existence, and a denial of death. It's the spirit of life, as the Scriptures call it, 'the river of living water,' the drying up of which is threatened in the Apocalypse. It's the aesthetic principle, as the philosophers call it, the ethical principle with which they identify it, 'the seeking for God,' as I call it more simply. The object of every national movement, in every people and at every period of its existence is only the seeking for its god, who must be its own god, and the faith in him as the only true one. God is the synthetic personality of the whole people, taken from its beginning to its end. It has never happened that all, or even many, peoples have had one common god, but each has always had its own. It's a sign of the decay of nations when they begin to have gods in common. When gods begin to be common to several nations the gods are dying and the faith in them, together with the nations themselves. The stronger a people the more individual their god. There never has been a nation without a religion, that is, without an idea of good and evil. Every people has its own conception of good and evil, and its own good and evil. When the same conceptions of good and evil become prevalent in several nations, then these nations are dying, and then the very distinction between good and evil is begining to disappear. Reason has never had the power to define good and evil, or even to distinguish between good and evil, even approximately; on the contrary, it has always mixed them up in a disgraceful and pitiful way; science has even given the solution by the fist. This is particularly characteristic of the half-truths of science, the most terrible scourge of humanity, unknown till this century, and worse than plague, famine, or war. A half-truth is a despot such as has never been in the world before. A despot that has its priests and its slaves, a despot to whom all do homage with love and superstition hitherto inconceivable, before which science itself trembles and cringes in a shameful way. These are your own words, Stavrogin, all except that about the half-truth; that's my own because I am myself a case of half-knowledge, and that's why I hate it particularly. I haven't altered anything of your ideas or even of your words, not a syllable."

"I don't agree that you've not altered anything," Stavrogin observed cautiously. "You accepted them with ardour, and in your ardour have transformed them unconsciously. The very fact that you reduce God to a simple attribute of nationality. . . ."

He suddenly began watching Shatov with intense and peculiar attention, not so much his words as himself.

"I reduce God to the attribute of nationality?" cried Shatov. "On the contrary, I raise the people to God. And has it ever been otherwise? The people is the body of God. Every people is only a people so long as it has its own god and excludes all other gods on earth irreconcilably; so long as it believes that by its god it will conquer and drive out of the world all other gods. Such, from the beginning of time, has been the belief of all great nations, all, anyway, who have been specially remarkable, all who have been leaders of humanity. There is no going against facts. The Jews

lived only to await the coming of the true God and left the world
the true God. The Greeks deified nature and bequeathed the world
their religion, that is, philosophy and art. Rome deified the people
in the State, and bequeathed the idea of the State to the nations.
France throughout her long history was only the incarnation and
development of the Roman god, and if they have at last flung
their Roman god into the abyss and plunged into atheism, which,
for the time being, they call socialism, it is solely because socialism
is, anyway, healthier than Roman Catholicism. If a great people
does not believe that the truth is only to be found in itself alone
(in itself alone and in it exclusively); if it does not believe that it
alone is fit and destined to raise up and save all the rest by its
truth, it would at once sink into being ethnographical material, and
not a great people. A really great people can never accept a secondary part in the history of Humanity, nor even one of the first,
but will have the first part. A nation which loses this belief ceases
to be a nation. But there is only one truth, and therefore only a
single one out of the nations can have the true God, even though
other nations may have great gods of their own. Only one nation
is 'god-bearing,' that's the Russian people, and . . . and . . ."

"Certainly I'll ask differently." Nikolai Vsyevolodovitch looked
coldly at him. "I only wanted to know, do you believe in God,
yourself?"

"I believe in Russia. . . . I believe in her orthodoxy. . . . I believe
in the body of Christ. . . . I believe that the new advent will take
place in Russia. . . . I believe. . . ." Shatov muttered frantically.

"And in God? In God?"

"I . . . I will believe in God. . . ."

"I'm sorry I can't feel affection for you, Shatov," Stavrogin re-
plied coldly.

"I know you can't, and I know you are not lying. Listen. I can
set it all right, I can 'catch your hare' for you."

Stavrogin did not speak.

"You're an atheist because you're a snob, a snob of the snobs.
You've lost touch with your own people. A new generation is
coming, straight from the heart of the people, and you will know
nothing of it, neither you nor the Verhovenskys, father or son; nor
I, for I'm a snob too—I, the son of your serf and lackey, Pashka. . . .
Listen. Attain to God by work; it all lies in that; or disappear like
rotten mildew. Attain to Him by work."

"God by work? What sort of work?"

"Peasants' work. Go, give up all your wealth. . . . Ah! you laugh,
you're afraid of some trick?"

But Stavrogin was not laughing.

"You suppose that one may attain to God by work, and by peasants' work," he repeated, reflecting as though he had really come across something new and serious which was worth considering.

25. POBYEDONOSTSEV:
AGAINST WESTERN DEMOCRACY

Dostoevsky had sharply criticized modern Western civilization and its institutions as a creative and imaginative writer. A similar criticism, from the point of view of a leading jurist and statesman, was voiced by Constantine Pobyedonostsev (1827–1907), a friend of Dostoesvky and a former professor of Russian law at the University of Moscow. He became the tutor and then the chief advisor of Alexander III (1881–1894) and of his son Nicolai II (1894–1917). From 1880 to 1905 Pobyedonostsev was the chief procurator or chairman of the Holy Synod, the supreme ecclesiastical authority of the Russian Orthodox Church. Under his influence the weak reformist trends of the reign of Alexander II were reversed.

Pobyedonostsev was a firm believer in the virtues of autocracy and of Orthodoxy as the unshakable bulwarks of Russian power. He had no doubt about the moral and practical evil of modern Western democratic institutions and their inapplicability to Russia. He rejected parliamentary representation and freedom of opinion of the press and claimed that he was doing it as a champion of the common people. In the Western capitalist democracies, according to him, the real rulers were the dexterous manipulators of votes, so that the so-called free elections in no way expressed the true will of the people. According to him the masses in the Western countries groaned under the despotism of parliamentarism and recognized its faults.

Pobyedonostsev's conviction that parliamentary democracy necessarily led to the corruption of the people and that freedom of speech and press meant the right to lie and to pervert the people's mind was expressed by him in his *Moskovsky Sbornik* ("Moscow Collection of Essays," 1896). The book was translated into English two years later under the title *Reflections of a Russian Statesman*, with a preface by Olga Novikoff, who regarded the views of the Russian statesman as expressing "true" people's democracy.[23]

In a Democracy, the real rulers are the dexterous manipulators of votes, with their placemen, the mechanics who so skillfully operate the hidden strings which move the puppets in the arena of democratic elections. Men of this kind are ever ready with loud speeches lauding equality; in reality, they rule the people as any despot or military dictator might rule it. The extension of the right to participate in elections is regarded as progress and as the conquest of freedom by democratic theorists, who hold that the more numerous the participants in political rights, the greater is the probability that all will employ this right in the interests of the public welfare, and for the increase of the freedom of the people. Experience proves a very different thing. The history of mankind bears witness that the most necessary and fruitful reforms—the most durable measures—emanated from the supreme will of statesmen, or from a minority enlightened by lofty ideas and deep knowledge, and that, on the contrary, the extension of the representative principle is accompanied by an abasement of political ideas and the vulgarisation of opinions in the mass of the electors. It shows also that this extension—in great States—was inspired by secret aims to the centralization of power, or led directly to dictatorship. In France, universal suffrage was suppressed with the end of the Terror, and was re-established twice merely to affirm the autocracy of the two Napoleons. In Germany, the establishment of universal suffrage served merely to strengthen the high authority of a famous statesman who had acquired popularity by the success of his policy. What its ultimate consequences will be, Heaven only knows! . . .

In what does the theory of Parliamentarism consist? It is supposed that the people in its assemblies makes its own laws, and elects responsible officers to execute its will. Such is the ideal conception. Its immediate realisation is impossible. The historical development of society necessitates that local communities increase in numbers and complexity; that separate races be assimilated, or, retaining their polities and languages, unite under a single flag, that territory extend indefinitely: under such conditions direct government by the people is impracticable. The people must, therefore, delegate its right of power to its representatives, and invest them with administrative autonomy. These representatives in turn cannot govern

[23] K. P. Pobyedonostsev, *Reflections of a Russian Statesman*, translated by R. C. Long (London: Grant Richards, 1898).

immediately, but are compelled to elect a still smaller number of trustworthy persons—ministers—to whom they entrust the preparation and execution of the laws, the apportionment and collection of taxes, the appointment of subordinate officials, and the disposition of the militant forces.

In the abstract this mechanism is quite symmetrical: for its proper operation many conditions are essential. . . . Given such conditions the machine would work exactly, and would accomplish its purpose. The law would actually embody the will of the people: administrative measures would actually emanate from Parliament; the pillars of the State would rest actually on the elective assemblies, and each citizen would directly and conscientiously participate in the management of public affairs.

Such is the theory. Let us look at the practice. Even in the classic countries of Parliamentarism it would satisfy not one of the conditions enumerated. The elections in no way express the will of the electors. The popular representatives are in no way restricted by the opinions of their constituents, but are guided by their own views and considerations, modified by the tactics of their opponents. In reality, ministers are autocratic, and they rule, rather than are ruled by, Parliament. They attain power, and lose power, not by virtue of the will of the people, but through immense personal influence, or the influence of a strong party which places them in power, or drives them from it. They dispose of the force and resources of the nation at will, they grant immunities, and favours, they maintain a multitude of idlers at the expense of the people, and they fear no censure while they enjoy the support in Parliament of a majority which they maintain by the distribution of bounties from the rich tables which the State has put at their disposal. In reality, the ministers are as irresponsible as the representatives of the people. Mistakes, abuse of power, and arbitrary acts, are of daily occurrence, yet how often do we hear of the grave responsibility of a minister? It may be once in fifty years a minister is tried for his crimes, with a result contemptible when compared with the celebrity gained by the solemn procedure. . . .

Thus the representative principle works in practice. The ambitious man comes before his fellow-citizens, and strives by every means to convince them that he more than any other is worthy of their confidence. What motives impel him to this quest? It is hard to believe that he is impelled by disinterested zeal for the public good. . . .

On the day of polling few give their votes intelligently; these are the individuals, influential electors whom it has been worth while to convince in private. The mass of electors, after the practice of the herd, votes for one of the candidates nominated by the committees. Not one exactly knows the man, or considers his character, his capacity, his convictions; all vote merely because they have heard his name so often. It would be vain to struggle against this herd. If a level-headed elector wished to act intelligently in such a grave affair, and not to give way to the violence of the committee, he would have to abstain altogether, or to give his vote for his candidate according to his conviction. However he might act, he could not prevent the election of the candidate favoured by the mass of frivolous, indifferent, and prejudiced electors.

In theory, the elected candidate must be the favourite of the majority; in fact, he is the favourite of a minority, sometimes very small, but representing an organized force, while the majority, like sand, has no coherence, and is therefore incapable of resisting the clique and the faction. In theory, the election favours the intelligent and capable; in reality, it favours the pushing and impudent. It might be thought that education, experience, conscientiousness in work, and wisdom in affairs, would be essential requirements in the candidate; in reality, whether these qualities exist or not, they are in no way needed in the struggle of the election, where the essential qualities are audacity, a combination of impudence and oratory, and even some vulgarity, which invariably acts on the masses; modesty, in union with delicacy of feeling and thought, is worth nothing. . . .

. . . What is a Parliamentary party? In theory, it is an alliance of men with common convictions, joining forces for the realisation of their views in legislation and administration. But this description applies only to small parties; the large party, which alone is an effective force in Parliament, is formed under the influence only of personal ambition, and centres itself around one commanding personality. By nature, men are divided into two classes—those who tolerate no power above them, and therefore of necessity strive to rule others; and those who by their nature dread the responsibility inseparable from independent action, and who shrink from any resolute exercise of will. These were born for submission, and together constitute a herd, which follows the men of will and resolution, who form a minority. Thus the most talented persons submit willingly, and gladly entrust to stronger hands the control of affairs and the moral responsibility for their direction. Instinctively they seek a leader, and become his obedient instruments, inspired by the conviction that he will lead them to victory—and, often, to spoil. Thus all the important actions of Parliament are controlled by the leaders of the party, who inspire all decision, who lead in combat, and profit by victory. The public sessions are no more than a spectacle for the mass. Speeches are delivered to sustain the fiction of Parliamentarism, but seldom a speech by itself affects the decision of Parliament in a grave affair. Speechmaking serves for the glory of orators, for the increase of their popularity, and the making of their careers; only on rare occasions does it affect the distribution of votes. Majorities and minorities are usually decided before the session begins. Such is the complicated mechanism of the Parliamentary farce; such is the great political lie which dominates our age. . . .

Such is the Parliamentary institution, exalted as the summit and crown of the edifice of State. It is sad to think that even in Russia there are men who aspire to the establishment of this falsehood among us; that our professors glorify to their young pupils representative government as the ideal of political science; that our newspapers pursue it in their articles and feuilletons, under the name of justice and order, without troubling to examine without prejudice the working of the parliamentary machine. Yet even where centuries have sanctified its existence, faith already decays; the Liberal intelligence exalts it, but the people groans under its despotism, and recognizes its falsehood. We may not see, but our children and grandchildren assuredly will see, the overthrow of this idol, which contemporary thought in its vanity continues still to worship. . . .

26. SOLOVEV: *AGAINST THE SLAVOPHILES*

Vladimir Solovev (1853–1900), the son of the famous Russian historian Sergei Solovev (1820–1879), was in his youth a Slavophile and an ardent admirer of Dostoevsky. Later he became an advocate of close Russian relations with the West. Unlike other Westernizers, Solovev remained a faithful Orthodox Christian, but his faith was important to him not because it was the religion of the Russian masses—as it was for Dostoevsky—but because it was part of the universal Church, for the reunion of which he prayed and strove.

Besides his work as philosopher and religious thinker, Solovev was "the best poet of his generation," and the brilliant array of Russian poets in the first two decades of the twentieth century owed a great deal to him. His greatest concern was personal freedom. He rejected all kinds of subjugation, in politics as well as in religion.

The chief work of Pan-Slavism and Slavophilism, called *Russia and Europe, An Inquiry into the Cultural and Political Relations of the Slav World and of the German-Latin World,* was published in 1869 by Nikolai Danilevsky (1822–1885) and ardently admired by Dostoevsky. Danilevsky tried to prove in his book that Russia represented a distinctive and specific civilization of its own, to which the future belonged, while Western civilization was in a state of decline. In 1888 Solovev published a criticism of it, from which the following excerpt is taken.[24]

Although Russian science and scholarship, whose serious beginnings we can date from Lomonosov,[25] had less time for its development than Western European science, it had on the other hand the great advantage that the Russian scholars found a soil well prepared for them by their European colleagues and could thus build on secure foundations. The Russians have certainly proved their qualifications for every scholarly or scientific activity. These qualifications together with the excellent training which the Russian scholars received, aroused the hope among the Slavophiles that the Russian nation would accomplish real miracles in the scientific field, in view of the extraordinarily fast intellectual development of our time. Reality has not fulfilled these hopes. Born under unusually favorable circumstances, Russian scholarship has not been able to make any startlingly new contributions. In mathematics, chemistry and biology we can, it is true, find some Russian scholars who occupy a considerable and honorable position in the European world of scholarship. Yet their work bears no stamp of a specifically Russian science. It has no sharply defined national character. Moreover, the scientific works of our greatest scholars, in spite of their excellent qualities, are not so profoundly significant as to influence definitively the general course of scientific development. None is of epoch-making importance in the history of even one of the various fields of scientific endeavor. . . .

German idealistic philosophy in its final Hegelian form has nowhere in Europe aroused as much interest and understanding as it has awakened in our educated circles in the thirties and forties. Yet in spite of the enthusiasm that it aroused among so many excellent minds, this philosophic movement bore no fruit. A promi-

---

[24] Reprinted by permission from Hans Kohn, ed., *The Mind of Modern Russia: Historical and Political Thought of Russia's Great Age* (New Brunswick, N.J.: Rutgers University Press, 1955), pp. 215–20

[25] Mikhail Lomonosov (1711–1765), the first Russian scientist

nent thinker, Ivan Kireyevsky,[26] came to the conclusion that true wisdom and real science could be found only in the ascetic writers of the Orthodox East. His friends hoped that he would draw from this deep well the living waters of a new Eastern philosophy; and that he would oppose it triumphantly to the desiccated intellectual life of the rotting West. But Kireyevsky failed to produce anything beyond a few general remarks. The entire Russian philosophical movement of that period left nothing but a few essays, which were partly inspired by the outlook of Western philosophers and partly directed against that outlook. These essays, however, contained no positive foundations of an independent and original philosophical system. . . .

Russian intellectual life oscillates between two points of view, an extreme scepticism and an extreme mysticism. It is evident that both points of view preclude a real philosophy. It is true that every profound philosophical system contains a sceptical and a mystical element. Philosophical scepticism is directed against all arbitrary authority and against all apparent reality. Philosophical mysticism is the consciousness of the inner and indestructible connection of the thinking mind with the absolute. But the attitude which underlies Russian thought has no relation to this kind of scepticism or mysticism. Russian scepticism has little in common with the legitimate doubts of Descartes or Kant who wished to find the limits of cognition. Russian scepticism wishes to destroy the idea of truth itself and to undermine the interest in cognition. In a similar way our national mysticism leads to the subordination of our spiritual individuality to an absolute object recognized as something superior. This irretrievable loss of self in a higher entity expresses itself sometimes in an unshakable indifference and passivity and sometimes in a suicidal fanaticism. Under these conditions there can be no foundation for a great and independent Russian future in the field of thought and knowledge.

Without doubt the best examples of Russian creative writing have a specific character and intrinsic value. However, this is also true of German, Spanish, and English literature; and yet these qualities do not imply a special cultural-historical type of these nations. Why should it do so for Russia? Nobody contests the existence of a Russian national character which manifests itself, among other things, in literature. The Russian and the English novel certainly differ, but not more than the English and the Spanish. The Russian novel represents one type among the many types of Euro-

---

[26] Ivan Kireyevsky (1806–1856), one of the early Slavophile thinkers

pean novels. And as Russian literature can be regarded only as a form of European literature, so Russia, in spite of her distinctive character, is only a Euopean state among the other European states. Danilevsky's contrary position cannot adduce a single proof for its point of view.

In periods of national egoism and isolation from the rest of the Christian world, Russia has not been able to produce anything great or significant. Only through the closest internal and external ties with Europe can Russia become great. . . .

Danilevsky opens his book "Russia and Europe" with the question, "Why doesn't Europe love Russia?" His answer is well known. Europe, he thinks, fears us as a new and higher cultural-historical type which is destined to replace the obsolescent Roman-Germanic civilization. However, the contents of his book and his own confessions suggest another answer. Europe views Russia with hostility and anxiety, for she recognizes the dark and enigmatic elemental forces alive in the Russian people, and, together with Russia's spiritual and cultural poverty, that country's vast and well defined ambition. Europe fears above all the voice of our "nationalism," a nationalism which desires to destroy Turkey and Austria, to divide Germany, to annex Constantinople, and, should an opportunity arise, even India. If, however, we are asked what we have to offer mankind as compensation for what we take and destroy, what spiritual and cultural principles we have contributed to world history, then we must either be silent or indulge in meaningless phrases.

If Danilevsky's bitter confession that Russia is a "sick and enfeebled colossus,"[27] is true, then the question "Why doesn't Europe love us?" must be replaced by a more obvious and important one, namely, "What is the nature and cause of our malady?" Physically Russia is strong enough, as the last Russian war in the East[28] has demonstrated. Our illness must therefore be of a moral nature. We carry the burden, as an old writer says, of our people's sins, which we do not wish to acknowledge. That is a fact which must be foremost in our minds. As long as we remain morally crippled, our elemental energies can only harm us. Therefore the most important, nay, the only important question for a true, clear-sighted Russian patriot, is not the question of our power or of our mission, but the question of "Russia's sin." . . .

[27] Danilevsky explained Russia's "sickness" by the "subservience" of her intelligentsia to Western influences.
[28] Russia's war against Turkey (1877–1878), in which Russia gained victories in the Balkan Peninsula and in eastern Anatolia.

27. LEO TOLSTOY: *THE CHRISTIAN DOCTRINE OF NON-RESISTANCE*

Count Leo Tolstoy (1828–1910), a wealthy Russian aristocrat and landowner and one of the century's greatest novelists (*War and Peace,* 1866, and *Anna Karenina,* 1875–77), was torn between his love of life, which as an artist he depicted with a rare freshness and gusto, and his quest for meaning in life, which taught him as a moralist to reject conventional society and self-indulging art. His "conversion," described in his *Confession* (Geneva, 1882), led him to a Rousseauist belief in the goodness of free and natural man, a condemnation of the "superstition of progress," and a faith in the "true" teaching of Christ's gospel—the brotherhood of man, humility, and the duty of returning good for evil. He found the essence of Christ's teachings in the Sermon on the Mount: "I say unto you, That you resist not evil" (Matt. V, 39).

Like some writers of the 1960's (e.g. Samuel Beckett), Tolstoy rejected the "illusions" about society, state, and politics, and worked to educate his readers to a realization of the emptiness of their lives. But to him, as to Rousseau, life was not fundamentally absurd and meaningless. On the contrary, he believed in its divine and rational substance. He was convinced that the growing contradiction between the conventional life of organized society, based upon force and threatening the extermination of man by war, and individual conscience, through which the insight in divine truth speaks in the heart of man, will bring men and peoples to renounce violence and war and to lead a truly civilized life in harmony with the divine order and the intentions of the gospel.

Tolstoy's pacifist and cosmopolitan doctrine runs counter to the growing nationalism which ultimately caused the outbreak of the great wars of the twentieth century. But Tolstoy's thought was not without some influence before and after the First World War. Oppressed sects and individuals in Russia looked for support to Yasnaya Polyana, Tolstoy's country estate, but the power of his personality radiated far beyond Russia. The life and teaching of the Indian leader Mohandas Karamchand Gandhi (1869–1948) bore witness to Tolstoy's influence, as did the introduction to *Vie de Tolstoi* (1911) by the French writer Romain Rolland (1866–1944) and the attitude of many conscientious objectors in the First World War.[29]

The Christian religion is not a legal system which, being imposed by violence, may transform men's lives. Christianity is a new and higher conception of life. A new conception of life cannot be imposed on men; it can only be freely assimilated. And it can only be freely assimilated in two ways: one spiritual and internal, the other experimental and external.

Some people—a minority—by a kind of prophetic instinct divine the truth of the doctrine, surrender themselves to it and adopt it. Others—the majority—only through a long course of mistakes, experiments, and suffering are brought to recognize the truth of the doctrine and the necessity of adopting it.

And by this experimental external method the majority of Christian men have now been brought to this necessity of assimilating the doctrine. One sometimes wonders what necessitated the corruption of Christianity which is now the greatest obstacle to its acceptance in its true significance.

If Christianity had been presented to men in its true, uncorrupted form, it would not have been accepted by the majority, who would have been as untouched by it as the nations of Asia are now. The peoples who accepted it in its corrupt form were subjected to its slow but certain influence, and by a long course of errors and experiments, and their resultant sufferings, have now been brought to the necessity of assimilating it in its true significance. . . .

Christianity is at once a doctrine of truth and a prophecy. Eighteen centuries ago Christianity revealed to men the truth in which they ought to live, and at the same time foretold what human life would become if men would not live by it but continued to live by their previous principles, and what it would become if they accepted the Christian doctrine and carried it out in their lives.

Laying down in the Sermon on the Mount the principles by which to guide men's lives, Christ said: "Whosoever heareth these sayings of mine, and doeth them, I will liken him unto a wise man who built his house upon a rock; and the rain descended, and the floods came, and the winds blew and beat upon that house; and it fell not, for it was founded on a rock. And everyone that heareth these sayings and doeth not them shall be likened unto a foolish man who built

[29] The following excerpts are taken from chapter VIII of Tolstoy's *The Kingdom of God is Within You*, written in 1892–3 and published in an English translation by Heinemann (London, 1894).

his house upon the sand; and the rain descended, and the floods came, and the winds blew and beat upon that house; and it fell: and great was the fall of it" (Matt. vii. 24–27).

And now after eighteen centuries the prophecy is being fulfilled. Not having followed Christ's teaching generally and its application to social life in non-resistance to evil, men have been brought in spite of themselves to the inevitable destruction foretold by Christ for those who do not fulfil his teaching. . . .

The question of resistance or non-resistance to evil arose when the first conflict between men took place, since every conflict is nothing else than resistance by force to what each of the combatants regards as evil. But before Christ, men did not see that resistance by force to what each regards as evil, simply because one thinks evil what the other thinks good, is only one of the methods of settling the dispute, and that there is another method—that of not resisting evil by force at all. . . .

But men were not ready to accept the solution given by Christ, and the old definitions of evil, which ought to be resisted, continued to be laid down by means of making laws binding on all and enforced by forcible means. The authority that decided what ought to be regarded as evil and resisted by force was at one time the pope, at another an emperor or king, an elective assembly or a whole nation. . . .

Things went on like this for eighteen centuries and at last reached the present position in which it is absolutely obvious that there is, and can be, no external definition of evil binding upon all. . . .

. . . If fifty years ago the idle rich man and the illiterate labourer were both alike convinced that their state of everlasting holiday for one and everlasting toil for the other was ordained by God himself, we know very well that nowadays, thanks to the growth of population and the diffusion of books and education, it would be hard to find in Europe, or even in Russia, either among rich or poor, a man to whom in one shape or another a doubt as to the justice of this state of things had never presented itself. The rich know that they are guilty in the very fact of being rich, and try to expiate their guilt by sacrifices to art and science, as of old they expiated their sins by sacrifices to the Church. And even the larger half of the working people openly declare that the existing order is iniquitous and bound to be destroyed or reformed. . . . The governments of our day—all of them, the most despotic and the liberal alike—have become what Herzen so well called "Ghengis Khan with the telegraph": that is to say, organisations of violence based on no principle but the grossest tyranny, and at the same time taking advantage of all the means invented by science for the peaceful collective social activity of free and equal men, used by them to enslave and oppress their fellows. . . .

While socialists and communists regard the individualistic, capitalistic organisation of society as an evil, and the anarchists regard as an evil all government whatever, there are royalists, conservatives, and capitalists who consider any socialistic or communistic organisation or anarchy as an evil, and all these parties have no means other than violence to bring men to agreement. Whichever of these parties were successful in bringing their schemes to pass, must resort to support its authority to all the existing methods of violence and even invent new ones.

The oppressed would be another set of people, and coercion would take some new form; but the violence and oppression would be unchanged or even more cruel, since hatred would be intensified by the struggle, and new forms of oppression would have been devised. So it has always been after all revolutions and all attempts at revolution, all conspiracies, and all violent changes of government. Every conflict only strengthens the means of oppression in the hands of those who happen at a given moment to be in power. . . .

The position of our Christian humanity, if you look at it from the outside, with all its cruelty and degradation of men, is terrible indeed. But if one looks at it within, in its inner consciousness, the spectacle it presents is absolutely different.

All the evil of our life seems to exist only because it has been so for so long; those who do the evil have not had time yet to learn how to act otherwise, though they do not want to act as they do. . . .

I think it is Max Müller[30] who describes the amazement of an Indian convert to Christianity who, after absorbing the essence of the Christian doctrine, came to Europe and saw the actual life of Christians. He could not recover from his astonishment at the complete contrast between the reality and what he had expected to find among Christian nations. If we feel no astonishment at the contrast between our convictions and our conduct, that is because the influences, tending to obscure the contrast, produce an effect upon us too. We need only look at our life from the point of view of that Indian, who understood Christianity in its true significance, without any compromises or concessions, we need but look at the savage brutalities of which our life is full, to be appalled at the contradictions in the midst of which we live often without observing them.

We need only recall the preparations for war, the mitrailleuses, the silver-gilt bullets, the torpedoes and—the Red Cross; the solitary prison-cells, the experiments of execution by electricity—and

[30] Max Müller (1823–1900), Orientalist and comparative philologist at Oxford

the care of the hygienic welfare of prisoners; the philanthropy of the rich, and—their life, which produces the poor they are benefiting.

And these inconsistencies are not, as it might seem, because men pretend to be Christians while they are really pagans, but because of something lacking in men, or some kind of force hindering them from being what they already feel themselves to be in their consciousness, and what they genuinely wish to be. Men of the present day do not merely pretend to hate oppression, inequality, class distinction, and every kind of cruelty to animals as well as human beings. They genuinely detest all this, but they do not know how to put a stop to it, or perhaps cannot decide to give up what preserves it all, and seems to them necessary.

Indeed, ask every man separately whether he thinks it laudable and worthy of a man of this age to hold a position from which he receives a salary disproportionate to his work; to take from the people—often in poverty—taxes to be spent on constructing cannon, torpedoes, and other instruments of butchery, so as to make war on people with whom we wish to be at peace, and who feel the same wish in regard to us; or to receive a salary for devoting one's whole life to constructing these instruments of butchery, or to preparing oneself and others for the work of murder. And ask him whether it is laudable and worthy of a man, and suitable for a Christian, to employ himself, for a salary, in seizing wretched, misguided, often illiterate and drunken, creatures because they appropriate the property of others—on a much smaller scale than we do—or because they kill men in a different fashion from that in which we undertake to do it —and shutting them in prison for it, ill-treating them, and killing them? And whether it is laudable and worthy of a man and a Christian to preach for a salary to the people, not Christianity, but superstitions which one knows to be stupid and pernicious. And whether it is laudable and worthy of a man to rob his neighbour for his gratification, of what he wants to satisfy his simplest needs, as the great landowners do? Or to force him to exhausting labour beyond his strength, to augment one's wealth, as do factory owners and manufacturers? Or to profit by the poverty of men to increase one's gains, as merchants do? And every one taken separately, especially if one's remarks are directed at some one else, not himself, will answer "No!" And yet the very man who sees all the baseness of those actions, of his own free will, uncoerced by any one, often even for no pecuniary profit, but only from childish vanity, for a china cross, a scrap of ribbon, a bit of fringe he is allowed to wear, will enter military service, become a magistrate or justice of the peace, commissioner, archbishop or beadle, though in fulfilling these offices he must commit acts the baseness and shamefulness of which he cannot fail to recognise.

I know that many of these men will confidently try to prove that they have reasons for regarding their position as legitimate and quite indispensable. They will say in their defence that authority is given by God, that the functions of the state are indispensable for the welfare of humanity, that property is not opposed to Christianity; that the rich young man was only commanded to sell all he had and give to the poor if he wished to be perfect; that the existing distribution of property and our commercial system must always remain as they are, and are to the advantage of all, and so on. But, however much they try to deceive themselves and others, they all know that what they are doing is opposed to all the beliefs which they profess, and in the depths of their souls, when they are left alone with their conscience, they are ashamed and miserable at the recollection of it, especially if the baseness of their action has been pointed out to them. A man of the present day, whether he believes in the divinity of Christ or not, cannot fail to see that to assist in the capacity of Tsar, minister, governor, or commissioner, in taking from a poor family its last cow for taxes to be spent on cannons, or on the pay and pensions of idle officials, who live in luxury and are worse than useless; or in putting into prison some man we have ourselves corrupted, and throwing his family on the streets; or in plundering and butchering in war; or in inculcating savage and idolatrous superstitions in the place of the law of Christ; or in impounding the cow found on one's land though it belongs to a man who has no land; or to cheat the workman in a factory by imposing fines for accidentally spoiled articles; or making a poor man pay double the value for anything simply because he is in the direst poverty;—not a man of the present day can fail to know that all these actions are base and disgraceful, and that they need not do them. They all know it. They know that what they are doing is wrong, and would not do it for anything in the world if they had the power of resisting the forces which shut their eyes to the criminality of their actions and impel them to commit them.

In nothing is the pitch of inconsistency modern life has attained to so evident as in universal conscription, which is the last resource and the final expression of violence.

Indeed, it is only because this state of universal armament has been brought about gradually and imperceptibly, and because governments have exerted, in maintaining it, every resource of intimidation, corruption, brutalisation and violence, that we do not see its flagrant inconsistency with the Christian ideas and sentiments by which the modern world is permeated. . . .

And even that is not all. In 1892 the Emperor of Germany William, the *enfant terrible* of state authority who says plainly what other people only think, in addressing some soldiers gave public utterance to the following speech, which was reported next day in thousands of newspapers:—"Conscripts!" he said, "you have sworn fidelity to *me* before the altar and the minister of God! You are still too young to understand all the importance of what has been said here; let your care before all things be to obey the orders and instructions given you. You have sworn fidelity *to me*, lads of my guard; *that means that you are now my soldiers*, that *you have given yourselves to me body and soul*. For you there is now but one enemy, *my* enemy. *In these days of Socialistic sedition it may come to pass that I command you to fire on your own kindred, your brothers, even your own fathers and mothers—which God forbid!* even then you are bound to obey my orders without hesitation."

This man expresses what all sensible rulers think, but studiously conceal. He says openly that the soldiers are in *his* service, at *his* disposal, and must be ready for *his* advantage to murder even their brothers and fathers. . . .

The last, the most extreme test is put before men in its coarsest form. And they do not seem even to notice that it is a test, that there is any choice about it. They seem to think there is no course open but slavish submission. One would have thought these insane words, which outrage everything a man of the present day holds sacred, must rouse indignation. But there has been nothing of the kind. . . .

Every savage has something he holds sacred, something for which he is ready to suffer, something he will not consent to do. But what is it that is sacred to the civilised man of today? They say to him: "You must become my slave, and this slavery may force you to kill even your own father;" and he, often very well educated, trained in all the sciences at the university, quietly puts his head under the yoke. They dress him up in a clown's costume, and order him to cut capers, turn and twist and bow, and kill—he does it all submissively. And when they let him go, he seems to shake himself and go back to his former life, and he continues to discourse upon the dignity of man, liberty, equality and fraternity as before.

"Yes, but what is one to do?" people often ask in genuine perplexity; "if every one would stand out it would be something, but by myself I shall only suffer without doing any good to any one."

And that is true. A man with the social conception of life cannot resist. The aim of his life is his personal welfare. It is better for his personal welfare for him to submit and he submits. . . .

. . . It is often said that the invention of terrible weapons of destruction will put an end to war. That is an error. As the means of extermination are improved, the means of reducing men who hold the state conception of life to submission can be improved to correspond. They may slaughter them by thousands, by millions, they may tear them to pieces, still they will march to war like senseless cattle. . . .

And of this mass of men so brutalised as to be ready to promise to kill their own parents, the social reformers—conservatives, liberals, socialists, and anarchists—propose to form a rational and moral society. What sort of moral and rational society can be formed out of such elements? With warped and rotten planks you cannot build a house, however you put them together. And to form a rational moral society of such men is just as impossible a task. They can be formed into nothing but a herd of cattle, driven by the shouts and whips of the herdsmen. As indeed they are. . . .

The contradiction between life and conscience and the misery resulting from it have reached the extreme limit and can go no further. The state organisation of life based on violence, the aim of which was the security of personal, family and social welfare, has come to the point of renouncing the very objects for which it was founded —it has reduced men to absolute renunciation and loss of the welfare it was to secure.

28. *THE PONTIFICATE OF LEO XIII*

Leo XIII (Gioacchimo Pecci, 1810–1903) followed Pope Pius IX in February, 1878, as Supreme Pontiff. He was an eminent scholar and statesman. He was concerned with the stricter training of the Catholic clergy in the philosophy of Thomas Aquinas (1225–1274), an Italian scholastic philosopher who entered the Dominican order and taught mainly at the University of Paris. Canonized by Pope John XXII in 1323, Thomas was declared in 1880 the patron of all Catholic schools and learning.

Like Pius IX, Leo XIII was convinced that the Church should superintend and direct civil life, but he showed a greater adaptability to modern society and civilization. Thus he promulgated in 1885 the encyclical *Immortale Dei* (A), which allowed the French Catholics to cooperate with the liberal regime of the Third French Republic. In 1891 the Pope, in the encyclical *Rerum novarum* (B), dealt with the situation of the working class in the capitalist society of the nineteenth century. Leo XIII did much to raise the prestige of the papacy, especially among European governments.[31]

A. Church and State

Sad it is to call to mind how the harmful and lamentable rage for innovation which rose to a climax in the sixteenth century threw first of all into confusion the Christian religion, and next, by natural sequence, invaded the precincts of philosophy, whence it spread amongst all classes of society. From this source, as from a fountain-head, burst forth all those later tenets of unbridled license which, in the midst of the terrible upheavals of the last century, were wildly conceived and boldly proclaimed as the principles and foundation of that new jurisprudence which was not merely previously unknown, but was at variance on many points with not only the Christian, but even the natural law.

Amongst these principles the main one lays down that as all men are alike by race and nature, so in like manner all are equal in the control of their life; that each one is so far his own master as to be in no sense under the rule of any other individual; that each is free to think on every subject just as he may choose, and to do whatever he may like to do; that no man has any right to rule over other men. In a society grounded upon such maxims all government is nothing more nor less than the will of the people, and the people, being under the power of itself alone, is alone its own ruler. It does choose nevertheless, some to whose charge it may commit itself, but in such wise that it makes over to them not the right so much as the business of governing, to be exercised, however, in its name. . . .

And it is part of this theory that all questions than concern religion are to be referred to private judgment; that every one is to be free to follow whatever religion he prefers, or none at all if he disapproves of all. From this the following consequences logically flow: that the judgment of each one's conscience is independent of all law; that the most unrestrained opinions may be openly expressed as to the practice or omissions of divine worship; and that everyone has unbounded license to think whatever he chooses and to publish abroad whatever he thinks. . . .

From these pronouncements of the Popes it is evident that the origin of public power is to be sought for in God Himself, and not in the multitude and that it is repugnant to reason to allow free scope for sedition. Again, that it is not lawful for the State, any

---

[31] Published in English (including A & B) and distributed by Catholic Truth Society, London.

more than for the individual, either to disregard all religious duties or to hold in equal favor different kinds of religion; that the unrestrained freedom of thinking and of openly making known one's thoughts is not inherent in the rights of citizens, and is by no means to be reckoned worthy of favor and support. In like manner it is to be understood that the Church no less than the State itself is a society perfect in its own nature and its own right, and that those who exercise sovereignty ought not so to act as to compel the Church to become subservient or subject to them, or to hamper her liberty in the management of her own affairs, or to despoil her in any way of the other privileges conferred upon her by Jesus Christ. In matters, however, of mixed jurisdiction, it is in the highest degree consonant to nature, as also to the design of God, that so far from one of the powers separating itself from the other, or still less coming into conflict with it, complete harmony, such as is suited to the end for which each power exists, should be preserved between them.

This, then, is the teaching of the Catholic Church concerning the constitution and government of the State. By the words and decrees just cited, if judged dispassionately, no one of the several forms of government is in itself condemned, inasmuch as none of them contains anything contrary to Catholic doctrine, and all of them are capable, if wisely and justly managed, to insure the welfare of the State. Neither is it blameworthy in itself, in any manner, for the people to have a share greater or less, in the government: for at certain times, and under certain laws, such participation may not only be of benefit to the citizens, but may even be of obligation. Nor is there any reason why any one should accuse the Church of being wanting in gentleness of action or largeness of view, or of being opposed to real and lawful liberty. The Church, indeed, deems it unlawful to place the various forms of divine worship on the same footing as the true religion, but does not, on that account, condemn those rulers who, for the sake of securing some great good or of hindering some great evil, allow patiently custom or usage to be a kind of sanction for each kind of religion having its place in the State. And, in fact, the Church is wont to take earnest heed that no one shall be forced to embrace the Catholic faith against his will, for, as St. Augustine wisely reminds us, "Man cannot believe otherwise than of his own will." . . .

B. The Working Class

The foremost duty, therefore, of the rulers of the State should be to make sure that the laws and institutions, the general character and administration of the commonwealth, shall be such as of themselves to realize public well-being and private prosperity. This is the proper scope of wise statesmanship and the work of the heads of the State. Now a State chiefly prospers and thrives through moral rule, well regulated family life, respect for religion and justice, the moderation and fair imposing of public taxes, the progress of the arts and of trade, the abundant yield of the land—through everything, in fact, which makes the citizen better and happier. Hereby, then, it lies in the power of a ruler to benefit every class in the State, and amongst the rest to promote to the utmost the interests of the poor; and this in virtue of his office, and without being open to suspicion of undue interference—since it is the province of the State to consult the common good. And the more that is done for the benefit of the working classes by the general laws of the country, the less need will there be for special means to relieve them. . . .

Rights must be religiously respected wherever they exist; and it is the duty of the public authority to prevent and to punish injury, and to protect every one in the possession of his own. Still, when there is question of defending the rights of individuals, the poor and badly-off have a claim to especial consideration. The richer class have many ways of shielding themselves, and stand less in need of help from the State; whereas the mass of the poor have no resources of their own to fall back upon, and must chiefly depend upon the assistance of the State. And it is for this reason that wage-earners, since they mostly belong to that class, should be specially cared for and protected by the Government.

Here, however it is expedient to bring under special notice certain matters of moment. The chief thing is the duty of safeguarding private property by legal enactment and protection. Most of all it is essential, where the passion of greed is so strong, to keep the people within the line of duty; for if all may justly strive to better their condition, neither justice nor the common good allows any individual to seize upon that which belongs to another, or, under the futile and shallow pretext of equality, to lay violent hands on other people's possessions. Most true it is that by far the larger part of the workers prefer to better themselves by honest labor rather than by doing any wrong to others. But there are not a few who are imbued with evil principles and eager for revolutionary change, whose main purpose is to stir up disorder and incite their fellows to acts of violence. The authority of the State should intervene to put restraint upon such firebrands, to save the working classes from being led astray by their manoeuvres, and to protect lawful owners from spoliation.

When work-people have recourse to a strike, it is frequently because the hours of labor are too long, or the work too hard, or because they consider their wages insufficient. The grave inconvenience of this not uncommon occurrence should be obviated by public remedial measures; for such paralyzing of labor not only affects the masters and their work-people alike, but is extremely injurious to trade and to the general interests of the public; moreover, on such occasions, violence and disorder are generally not far distant, and thus it frequently happens that the public peace is imperilled. The laws should forestall and prevent such troubles from arising; they should lend their influence and authority to the removal in good time of the causes which lead to conflicts between employers and employed. . . .

Let the working man and the employer make free agreements, and in particular let them agree freely as to wages; nevertheless there underlies a dictate of natural justice more imperious and ancient than any bargain between man and man, namely that wages ought not to be insufficient to support a frugal and well behaved wage-earner. If through necessity or fear of a worse evil the workman accepts harder conditions because an employer or contractor will afford him no better, he is made the victim of force and injustice. In these and similar questions however,—such as, for example, the hours of labor in different trades, the sanitary precautions to be observed in factories and workshops, etc.—in order to supersede undue interference on the part of the State, especially as circumstances, times and localities differ so widely, it is advisable that recourse be had to Societies or Boards such as we shall mention presently, or to some other mode of safeguarding the interests of the wage-earners; the State being appealed to, should circumstances require, for its sanction and protection. . . .

Many excellent results will follow from this; and first of all, property will certainly become more equitably divided. For the result of civil change and revolution has been to divide society into two widely differing castes. On the one side there is the party which holds power because it holds wealth; which has in its grasp the whole of labor and trade; which manipulates for its own benefit and its own purposes all the sources of supply, and which is even represented in the councils of the State itself. On the other side there is the needy and powerless multitude, sick and sore in spirit and ever ready for disturbance. If working people can be encouraged to look forward to obtaining a share in the land, the consequence will be that the gulf between vast wealth and sheer poverty will be bridged over, and the respective classes will be brought nearer to one another. A further consequence will result in the greater abundance of the fruits of the earth. Men always work harder and more readily when they work on that which belongs to them; nay, they learn to love the very soil that yields in response to the labor of their hands, not only food to eat, but an abundance of good things for themselves and those dear to them. That such a spirit of willing labor would add to the produce of the earth and to the wealth of the community is self-evident. And a third advantage would spring from this: men would cling to the country in which they were born; for no one would exchange his country for a foreign land if his own afforded him the means of living a decent and happy life. These three important benefits, however, can be reckoned on only provided that a man's means be not drained and exhausted by excessive taxation. The right to possess private property is derived from nature, not from man; and the State has the right to control its use in the interest of the public good alone, but by no means to absorb it altogether. The State would therefore be unjust and cruel if under the name of taxation it were to deprive the private owner of more than is fair. . . .

The most important of all organizations are Working-men's Unions; for these virtually include all the rest. History attests what excellent results were brought about by the Artificers's Guilds of olden times. They were the means of affording not only many advantages to the workmen, but in no small degree of promoting the advancement of art, as numerous monuments remain to bear witness. Such Unions should be suited to the requirements of this our age— an age of wider education, of different habits, and of far more numerous requirements in daily life. It is gratifying to know that there are actually in existence not a few associations of this nature, consisting either of workmen alone, or of workmen and employers together; but it were greatly to be desired that they should become more numerous and more efficient. . . .

29. FRIEDRICH NIETZSCHE:
THE WILL TO POWER

Friedrich Nietzsche (1844–1900), the son of a Lutheran minister, was trained as a classical philologist. At the age of twenty-four he became professor of Greek at the University of Basel and came under the powerful influence of Arthur Schopenhauer and Richard Wagner. He emancipated himself from these influences and freed himself from the professorship during the following ten years. The next decade he lived in independence, poverty, and loneliness and wrote his main works, which after his death exercized a far-reaching impact not on the philosophy but on the general thought of Europe in the first part of the twentieth century. At the beginning of 1889 he became insane.

Nietzsche's first book was *The Birth of Tragedy Out of the*

Spirit of Music, later carrying the subtitle *The Greek Spirit and Pessimism.* His chief later works bore the significant titles which have now become famous: *Untimely Meditations, Human, All-Too-Human, The Gay Science* (B), *Beyond Good and Evil, Toward a Genealogy of Morals.* These works consisted largely of essays and aphorisms. More rhapsodic was the style of the book he regarded as his chief work, a kind of bible which he called *Thus Spake Zarathustra* (C) and which he wrote in four parts between 1883 and 1885. The last year of his creative life was especially fruitful. He wrote *The Twilight of the Idols,* the remarkable autobiography *Ecce Homo* (A), and *The Anti-Christ.* This last he regarded as a part of his ultimate work, which he intended first to call *The Will to Power* and later on *The Re-Valuation* (or *Trans-Valuation*) *of All Values.*

Nietzsche's outlook on life and history may be defined as a tragic optimism, an affirmation of existence in spite of all its frightfulness, an appeal to individual strength and fearlessness. In the midst of the apparently secure Victorian or Bismarckian age he sensed the approaching nihilism of values and the approaching crises of history. An "immoralist," as he called himself, he rejected all conformism and self-deception; also a psychologist, he "unmasked" the hidden escapist motives of men. As a lonely individual, free of all social responsibility, and as a playful master of the word, he tends to extreme and irresponsible formulations. He was no systematic thinker, nor did he write for professional scholars. He rejected followers and disciples and wished each one to be himself. He did not try to remake society but to re-form man.[32]

A. Ecce Homo (*1888*)

THE CONCEPT OF THE DIONYSIAN IN "THE BIRTH OF TRAGEDY" (1872)

The two decisive innovations in the book are, first, the comprehension of the Dionysian phenomenon among the Greeks[33]—it provides the first psychological analysis of this phenomenon, and sees in

---

[32] The following excerpts are taken partly from *Ecce Homo,* in the translation by Anthony M. Ludovici, *The Complete Works of Friedrich Nietzsche,* edited by Oscar Levy, vol. XVII (London, 1911), and partly from *The Gay Science* and *Thus Spake Zarathustra,* translated from the German original, Friedrich Nietzsche, *Werke* (Munich: Carl Hanser Verlag, n.d.), vol. II.

[33] In his first book Nietzsche opposed Apollo, the Olympian god of harmony and radiant light, to Dionysus, a god of exuberance, intoxication, and the more chaotic sides of nature and life, at the same time patron of the drama.

it the single root of all Greek art; and, secondly, the comprehension of Socraticism—Socrates being presented for the first time as a typical decadent: Reason against Instinct, Reason at any cost, as a dangerous, life-undermining force. The whole book is profoundly and politely silent concerning Christianity, which is neither Apollonian nor Dionysian; it denies all esthetic values, which are the only values that "The Birth of Tragedy" recognizes. Christianity is most profoundly nihilistic, whereas the Dionysian symbol expresses the most extreme limits of a yes-saying attitude to life. . . .

I was the first to see the actual contrast: the degenerate instinct which turns upon life with a subterranean lust of vengeance (Christianity, Schopenhauer's philosophy, and in some respects even Plato's philosophy—in short, the whole of idealism in its typical forms), as opposed to a formula of the highest yes-saying to life, born of an abundance and a super-abundance of life—a yes-saying free from all reserves, applying even to suffering and guilt and all that is questionable and strange in existence. . . . Nothing that exists must be suppressed, nothing can be dispensed with. . . . . In order to understand this, a certain courage is necessary, and, as a prerequisite of this, a certain superfluity of strength: for a man can approach only as near to truth as he has the courage to advance. . . . Knowledge, and the affirmation of reality, are just as necessary to the strong man as cowardice, the flight from reality—in fact, the "ideal"—are necessary to the weak. . . . Decadents stand in need of lies, it is one of their self-preservative measures.

DIONYSUS AND ZARATHUSTRA

One day Zarathustra[34] severely determined his life task—and it is also mine. Let no one misunderstand its meaning. It is a yes-saying to the point of justifying, to the point of redeeming even all that is past.

"I walk among men as among fragments of the future: of that future which I see. And all my creativeness and effort is but this, that I may be able to think and recast all these fragments and riddles and dismal accidents into one piece. And how could I bear to be a man, if man were not also a poet, a riddle reader, and a redeemer of chance!" . . .

In another passage Zarathustra defines what to him "man" can be,—not a subject for love nor yet for pity—Zarathustra became master even of his loathing of man: man is to him a thing unshaped, raw material, an ugly stone that needs the sculptor's chisel:

---

[34] Nietzsche's spokesman in *Thus Spake Zarathustra*, not the historic Zarathustra, or Zoroaster, the founder of the religion of the ancient Persians who lived in the sixth century B.C.

"No longer to will, no longer to value, no longer to create! Oh, that this great weariness may never be mine! Even in the lust of knowledge, I feel only the joy of my will to create and to grow; . . . Away from God and gods did this will lure me: what would there be to create if there were gods? But to man does it ever drive me anew, my burning creative will. Thus drives it the hammer to the stone. Within the stone there sleeps an image for me, the image of all my dreams! Alas, that it should have to sleep in the hardest and ugliest stone! Now my hammer ruthlessly rages against its prison. From the stone the fragments fly: what is that to me? . . . The beauty of the superman came to me like a shadow. What are the—gods to me now?"

A Dionysian life-task needs the hardness of the hammer, and one of its first essentials is without doubt the joy even of destruction. The command "Harden yourselves!" and the deep conviction that all creators are hard, is the really distinctive sign of a Dionysian nature.

NIETZSCHE, WAGNER, AND GERMANY

I must express a word or two of gratitude for that which has given me the most hearty and profound comfort. This, without the slightest doubt, was my intimate relationship with Richard Wagner. All my other relationships with men I treat quite lightly; but I would not have the days I spent at Tribschen[35]—those days of confidence, of cheerfulness, of sublime flashes, and of profound moments—blotted from my life at any price. I do not know what Wagner may have been to others; but no cloud ever darkened *our* sky. . . .

With a nature like mine, which is so alien to everything German, that even the presence of a German disturbs my digestion, my first meeting with Wagner was the first moment in my life in which I breathed freely. I felt him and honored him as the opposite and the incarnate contradiction of all "German virtues." . . . As an artist, a man has no home in Europe save in Paris; that subtlety of all the five senses which Wagner's art presupposes, those fingers that can detect slight gradations, psychological morbidity—all these things can be found only in Paris. . . . In Germany no one has an idea of the tremendous ambition that fills the heart of a Parisian artist. The German is a good fellow. Wagner was by no means a good fellow. . . . He is one of the late French romanticists, like Delacroix and Berlioz, . . . Who was the first intelligent fol-

[35] Tribschen, near Lucerne, where Nietzsche frequently visited Wagner between 1868 and 1872

lower of Wagner? Charles Baudelaire, that typical decadent in whom a whole generation of artists recognized themselves.[36] . . . What is it that I have never forgiven Wagner? The fact that he condescended to the Germans, that he became a German imperialist. Wherever Germany spreads, she ruins culture.

Taking everything into consideration, I could never have survived my youth without Wagnerian music. For I was condemned to the society of Germans. If a man wishes to get rid of a feeling of insufferable oppression, he has to take to hashish. Well, I had to take to Wagner. Wagner is the counter-poison to everything essentially German—the fact that he is a poison too, I do not deny.

I suppose I know better than anyone the prodigious feats of which Wagner was capable, the fifty worlds of strange ecstasies to which no one else had wings to soar; and as I am alive today and strong enough to turn even the most suspicious and most dangerous things to my own advantage, and thus to grow stronger, I declare Wagner to have been the greatest benefactor of my life. . . . Just as Wagner is merely a misunderstanding among Germans, so, in truth, am I, and ever will be. You lack two centuries of psychological and artistic discipline, my dear countrymen! . . . But you can never recover the time lost.

This book [*Human, All-Too Human*, 1878] was begun during the first musical festival at Bayreuth [1876]; . . . Where on earth was I? I recognized nothing that I saw; I scarcely recognized Wagner. It was in vain that I called up reminiscences. Tribschen— remote island of bliss: not the shadow of a resemblance! What has happened? Wagner had been translated into German! The Wagnerite had become master of Wagner. . . . We who know only too well the kind of refined artists and cosmopolitanism in taste, to which alone Wagner's art can appeal, were beside ourselves at the sight of Wagner bedecked with German virtues.

B. The Gay Science

FROM BOOK FIVE, "WE FEARLESS ONES"— "THE GREAT HEALTH"

We who are new and nameless and difficult to understand, we prematurely born creatures of a future still unproved—we require new means for a new end, that means, a new health, a health stronger, keener, tougher, bolder and more joyful than any that

---

[36] Charles Baudelaire (1821–1867), the poet; Louis Hector Berlioz (1803–1869), the composer; Ferdinand Victor Eugène Delacroix (1799–1863), the painter, were leaders of romanticism in France, though this is true of Baudelaire, the "decadent," only with reservations. Baudelaire was an early enthusiastic admirer of Wagner's music.

has existed so far. He whose soul longs to experience the whole range of values and aims that have existed so far . . . ; who from the adventures of his own inmost experience wishes to know how it feels to be a conqueror and a discoverer of the ideal or an artist, a saint, a legislator, a sage, a scholar, a pious man, a prophet or a divine hermit in the manner of old times; such a man requires above all great health, such health as he not only possesses but also constantly acquires, because he continually abandons it again and must abandon it.

Now, after thus having been long on the road, we Argonauts of the ideal, who are perhaps more courageous than is prudent and who are often shipwrecked and damaged, but as I have said, healthier than people would like to allow us, dangerously healthy —and for ever regaining our health—it seems as if we had ahead of us, as a reward for all this, a country still undiscovered, the frontiers of which no one has yet seen, a country beyond every existing country and every existing refuge of the ideal that man has ever known, a world so overflowing with beauty, strangeness, doubt, terror and divinity, that our curiosity and our lust of possession cannot be satisfied by anything else. Now faced by such prospects and with such burning desire in our conscience and consciousness, could we still remain satisfied with present-day man? . . .

Another ideal now leads us on, a wonderful seductive ideal, full of danger, which we would not urge upon anyone, because we do not wish so easily to acknowledge any one's right to it: the ideal of a mind who plays naively, that means involuntarily and out of overflowing richness and power, with everything that has so far been called sacred, good, untouchable, and divine; a mind to whom even the loftiest thing that the people have rightly made their measure of value would mean a danger, decay and abasement, or at least a relaxation, a blindness and temporary self-forgetfulness: the ideal of a humanly superhuman well-being and good will, which often enough may seem inhuman—e.g., when it stands beside all past earnestness on earth, all past solemnities in gesture, word, tone, look, morality, and task, like their most lifelike and involuntary parody—but with which true great earnestness perhaps begins for the first time, with which the first true sign of interrogation is set, the fate of the soul arrives at a turning point, the hour hand moves, and tragedy begins.

FROM BOOK THREE, "THE MAD MAN"

Have you not heard of that mad man who on a bright morning lit a lantern, ran to the market place, and shouted incessantly,

"I seek God! I seek God!" Among the many of those who do not believe in God and who were standing around there, he provoked much laughter. Why, did God get lost? asked one. Did he lose his way like a child? asked another. Or is he hiding? Is he afraid of us? Has he left on a boat? Has he emigrated? Thus they shouted and laughed. The man jumped into their midst and pierced them with his glances.

"Whither is God?" he shouted. "I shall tell you. We have killed him—you and I. We all are his murderers. But how have we done it? How were we able to drink up the ocean? Who gave us the sponge to wipe out the whole horizon? What did we do when we unchained this earth from its sun? Whither is it moving now? Whither are we moving? Away from all suns? Are we not falling continually? Falling backward, sideward, forward, in all directions? Is there any up or down left? Are we not straying as through infinite nothingness? Do we not feel the breath of empty space? Has it not become colder? Is not night and more night coming on all the time? Must not lanterns be lit in the morning? Do we not yet hear the noise of the gravediggers who are burying God? Do we not begin to smell God's putrefaction? Gods, too, putrefy. God is dead. God will remain dead. And we have killed him. How shall we, the murderers of all murderers comfort ourselves? The holiest and mightiest of all that the world has ever owned has bled to death under our knives: who will wipe this blood off us? With what water can we clean ourselves? . . . Is not the greatness of this deed too great for us? Must not we ourselves become gods in order to seem worthy of it? There has never been a greater deed: whoever will be born after us, will be on account of this deed part of a higher history than all prior history."

Here the mad man became silent and glanced at his listeners; they too had become silent and stared at him with a strange feeling. Finally, he threw his lantern on the ground so that it broke into pieces and was extinguished. Then he said: "I have come too soon, my time has not come yet. This tremendous event is still on its way, it has not yet reached the ears of man. Lightning and thunder require time, the light of the stars requires time, deeds require time even after they are done, to be seen and heard. This deed is still more distant from them than the most distant stars—and yet they themselves have done it."

On the same day, we are told, the mad man entered a number of churches and there sang his *requiem aeternam deo*. Led out and questioned, he, according to the report, gave always the same reply, "What are these churches now if they are not the tombs and sepulchers of God?"

"GUILT"

Though the most discerning judges in the witch trials and even the witches themselves were convinced of the reality of the crime of witchcraft, nevertheless the crime of which they were guilty, did not exist. Thus it is with all guilt.

FROM BOOK FOUR, "SANCTUS JANUARIUS" (ON NEW YEAR'S DAY, 1882)

I am still alive, I am still thinking: I must continue to live, for I must continue to think. *Sum, ergo cogito: cogito, ergo sum.* Today everyone allows himself to express his wish and most beloved thought: thus, I too wish to say what I am wishing today for myself as a gift from myself, and which thought first occurred to my heart this year, a thought which shall become the foundation, the security and sweetness of all my future life! I wish to learn evermore, to regard as beautiful whatever is necessary in the things: thus I shall become one of those who make the things beautiful. *Amor fati:* this be from now on my love! I do not wish to wage war against the ugly. I do not wish to accuse, I do not wish to accuse even the accusers. To look away shall be my only negation. And, all in all, I wish one day to be one who only says yes!

"TO BE ABLE TO CONTRADICT"

Everyone knows by now that the ability to accept contradiction is a high sign of culture. Some even know that the higher type of man desires and provokes contradiction, to become better aware of his own injustice which has so far remained unknown to him. But more than these two is the ability to contradict, the good conscience which one has acquired in one's hostility to the accustomed, the traditional, the sanctified. This is the truly great, new and astonishing element in our culture, the decisive step forward of the liberated mind: who knows this?

"IN MEDIA VITA!"

No! Life has not disappointed me! On the contrary, I find it every year richer, more desirable and mysterious. This started on that day when the great liberating thought overcame me, that life may be an experiment in the pursuit of knowledge, and not a duty, a fatality to be accepted, or a fraud.—The pursuit of knowledge may be for others something else, perhaps a place for rest or relaxation, conversation or idleness, for me it is a world of dangers and victories, in which heroism, too, finds its dancing ground and arena. If one regards life as pursuit of knowledge, then one cannot only live courageously but even joyfully and laugh joyfully. And who could understand to laugh and live well, if he would not understand to war and win well?

"PREPARATORY MEN"

I welcome all signs that a more manly, a warlike age is now starting, an age which above all will honor valor again. For this age shall prepare the way for one yet higher and it shall gain the strength which one day this higher age will need, this age which is to carry heroism into the pursuit of knowledge and to wage wars for the sake of thoughts and their consequences. For that many preparatory courageous men are now needed. Yet they cannot leap into being out of nothing—anymore than out of the sand and slime of today's civilization and metropolitan culture: men who understand how to be silent, solitary, determined, constant and satisfied with inconspicuous activity; who in everything seek for that which must be overcome; men characterized by cheerfulness, patience, simplicity and contempt for all great vanities, as well as by magnanimity in victory and forbearance regarding the small vanities of all vanquished; men judging sharply and freely all victors and the share of chance in every victory and every fame; . . . men who live in greater danger, more fruitful and happier. For, believe me, the secret which enables us to harvest in life the greatest fruitfulness and the greatest enjoyment is: to live danger-ously! Build your cities under Vesuvius! Send your ships into un-charted seas! Live at war with your peers and yourselves! . . . At long last the pursuit of knowledge will reach out for its due: it will wish to rule and own, and you with it.

C. "Thus Spake Zarathustra"

"ON OLD AND NEW TABLETS"

I

Here I sit waiting, broken old tablets around me and new tablets half covered with writing. When will my hour come? The hour of my descent among men, to whom I must go once more. But first the signs must come to me that it is *my* hour. . . . Meanwhile I talk to myself having much time. Nobody tells me anything new, so I myself tell it to myself.

II

When I arrived among men I found that they were clinging to an old illusion: all of them imagined that they have long known what is good and evil for man. All talk of virtue seemed an old and weary matter to them, and whoever wanted to sleep well, talked of good and evil before going to sleep.

I disturbed this sleepiness when I taught: no one knows yet what is good and evil, unless it be the creative man, the man who sets man's goal and gives the earth its meaning and its future. He is the one who makes that anything at all is good and evil.

I ordered them to overthrow the old academic chairs and wherever that old illusion had been sitting; I ordered them to laugh at their great teachers of virtue, saints, poets and world redeemers. I ordered them to laugh at their gloomy sages and at those who ever sat on the tree of life warning them like a black scarecrow. I sat down by their great tomb-road among corpses and vultures, and I laughed at all their past and its brittle decaying glory. . . .

VIII

When there are planks across the water and bridges and railings cover the river, then no one believes the man who says "Everything is in flux." Even the stupid people speak out against him. "How now?" they say. "Everything should be in flux? After all, planks and railings are over the river. Thus over the river everything is firm, all the values of things, the bridges, the concepts, all 'good' and 'evil'—all that is firm."

And when the hard winter comes, the tamer of the river-animal, then . . . not only the stupid people say, "Does not everything stand still?"

"At bottom everything stands still"—that is truly a winter doctrine, a good thing for sterile times, a good comfort for those who hibernate or sit behind the warm stove.

But the thaw-wind preaches against "At bottom everything stands still." The thaw-wind, . . . a raging bull, a destroyer who breaks the ice with wrathful horns. Ice breaks bridges!

Is not everything in flux now, my brothers? Have not all railings and bridges fallen into the water? Who can continue to cling to "good" and "evil?"

XII

O my brothers, I dedicate and direct you to a new nobility. You shall procreate and cultivate . . . , not a nobility that you could buy like shopkeepers and with shopkeepers' gold: for whatever has its price is of little value.

Not whence you come shall from now on be your pride and honor but whither you are going. Your will and your foot which wishes to go beyond yourselves—they should create your new honor. . . . Your nobility should not look backward but forward! You shall be exiled from all fatherlands and all ancestral lands! You shall love your children's land: this love shall be your new nobility—the undiscovered land in the most distant sea. For that I order your sails search and search.

XX

Am I really cruel? But I say that man should push what is falling. Who would try to hold today all that falls and decays? But I—I wish to push it.

Do you know the voluptuous delight which rolls stones into steep depths? Look at these man of today, how they roll into my depth.

I am a prelude of better players, o my brothers, I am a precedent. Follow my precedent! And those whom you cannot teach to fly, teach to fall faster!

XXVI

O my brothers, where do you find the greatest danger for man's future: is it not with the good and the just? With those who say and feel in their heart, "We already know what is good and just, and we have it too; woe unto those who still seek here!" Whatever harm the evil may do, the harm done by the good is the most harmful harm. . . .

"Whom do they hate most?" They hate most the creative mind who breaks tablets and old values. They call him a law breaker. For the good cannot create; they are always the beginning of the end: they crucify him who writes new values on new tablets; they sacrifice the future to themselves—they crucify all man's future.

XXIX

The kitchen-coal once asked the diamond: "Why so hard? Are we not close kin?"

But I ask you, my brothers, why so soft? Are you not my brothers? If your hardness will not flash and sever and cut to pieces, how can you one day create with me? For creators are hard. To impress your hand on millennia as on wax, must appear to you as bliss.

I place over you, o my brothers, this new tablet: become hard!

"ON THE GIFT-BESTOWING VIRTUE"

I

When Zarathustra had taken leave of the town, he was followed and escorted by many who called themselves his disciples. When they came to a crossroads, Zarathustra told them that he wanted to go on alone, for he liked to walk alone. Then his disciples gave him as a farewell present a staff with a golden handle on which a serpent coiled around the sun. Zarathustra, delighted with the staff, leaned on it and then spoke to his disciples:

Tell me, how did it come about that gold became the highest value? Because it is uncommon and useless and radiant and gentle in its splendor; it always gives itself. . . . I understand you well, my disciples: like myself, you strive for the gift-bestowing virtue. . . . You thirst to become yourselves sacrifices and gifts, and therefore you thirst to pile up all the riches in your soul. Insatiably your soul strives for treasures and gems, because your virtue is insatiable in its wish to bestow. . . .

Tell me my brothers, what do we regard as bad and worst? Is it not decadence? Wherever the gift-bestowing soul is lacking, there we suspect decadence. . . . We shudder at the decadent sense which says, "Everything for me." Upward flies our sense: thus it is a parable of our body, a parable of elevation. . . .

When you despise the agreeable and the soft bed and cannot bed yourselves far enough from the soft: there is the origin of your virtue. . . . This new virtue is power, a dominant thought with a wise soul around: a golden sun, and around it the serpent of knowledge.

11

Here Zarathustra fell silent for a while and looked lovingly at his disciples. Then he continued to speak with a changed voice:

With the power of your virtue, my brothers, remain faithful to the earth. May your gift-bestowing love and your knowledge serve the meaning of the earth. Do not let them fly away from earthly things and beat with their wings against eternal walls. Alas, there has always been so much virtue that has flown away. Follow me in leading back to the earth the virtue that has flown away, yes, back to body and life, so that this virtue may give the earth its meaning, a human meaning. . . .

There are a thousand paths that have never yet been trodden— a thousand healths and hidden islands of life. Man and man's earth are still unexhausted and undiscovered.

Wake and listen, you lonely men. Out of the future come winds with secret wing-beats, and good tidings are proclaimed to delicate ears. You lonely men of today, who live as outsiders, you shall one day be a people: out of you, who have chosen yourselves, there shall grow a chosen people—and out of it, the superman. Truly, the earth shall become a site of recovery. Even now a new fragrance surrounds it, a fragrance which promises salvation and a new hope.

III

After having said this, Zarathustra became silent in the manner of those who had not yet said their last word. For a long time he doubtfully weighed the staff in his hand. At last he spoke, and his voice had changed:

Now I go alone, my disciples. You too go now and go alone. Thus I wish it. I advise you: leave me and defend yourselves against Zarathustra! Even better: be ashamed of him! Perhaps he deceived you. . . .

One repays a teacher badly if one remains nothing but a pupil. Why do you not wish to pluck at my wreath?

You say you believe in Zarathustra. But what matters Zarathustra? You are my believers. But what matter all believers? . . . Now I order you to lose me and to find yourselves; and only when you all have denied me, I will return to you . . . to celebrate the great noon with you.

That is the great noon when man stands in the middle of his road between animal and superman and celebrates his way toward evening as his highest hope: for it is the way to a new morning. . . . "Dead are all gods: now we want the superman to live"—this be, on that great noon, our last will.

30. FREUD: *ON THE ORIGIN OF PSYCHOANALYSIS*

Around 1900 the physical and biological sciences entered into a new phase of their development which deepened and changed our understanding of the universe, of the physical world, and of the physiology and psychology of men. One of the pioneers of the new science was Sigmund Freud (1856–1939), an Austrian physician who accounted for many of the irrational factors in man's behaviour in his theory of the hold of the subconscious on the human mind. His influence went far beyond the limits of science, and was soon to be felt in almost every field of intellectual activity, above all in literature and in the arts.

In 1932, in his last lecture in *New Introductory Lectures on Psychoanalysis,* Freud defined the relation of psychoanalysis, or of science in general, to the question of a world outlook or *Weltanschauung.* In his truly scientific modesty, he warned against all exaggerated claims on behalf of science:

Psychoanalysis is not, in my opinion, in a position to create a *Weltanschauung* of its own. It has no need to do so, for it is a branch of science, and can subscribe to the scientific world outlook. The latter, however, hardly merits such a high-sounding name, for it does not take everything into its scope, it is incomplete, and it makes no claim to being comprehensive or to constituting a system. Scientific thought is still in its infancy; there are very many of the great problems with which it has as yet been unable to cope. A *Weltanschauung* based upon science has, apart from its emphasis upon the real world, essentially negative characteristics, such as that it limits itself to truth and rejects illusions. Those of our fellow-men who are dissatisfied with this state of things and who desire something more for their momentary peace of mind may look for it where they can find it. We shall not blame them for doing so; but we cannot help them and cannot change our own way of thinking on their account.

In September, 1909, Freud was invited to deliver five lectures on the Origin and Development of Psychoanalysis, at the celebration of the twentieth anniversary of Clark University in Worcester, Massachusetts. The following excerpts are taken from those lectures which were published in the *American Journal of Psychology* in 1910.[37]

I was a student, busy with the passing of my last examinations, when another physician of Vienna, Dr. Joseph Breuer [was experimenting with methods of treating hysterical patients (1880–2)]. . . .

When, a number of years later, I began to use Breuer's researches and treatment on my own patients, my experiences completely coincided with his. . . . If you will permit me to generalize, as is indispensable in so brief a presentation, we may express our results up to this point in the formula: *Our hysterical patients suffer from reminiscences.* Their symptoms are the remnants and the memory symbols of certain (traumatic) experiences . . . they cannot escape from the past and neglect present reality in its favor. This fixation of the mental life on the pathogenic traumata is an essential, and practically a most significant characteristic of the neurosis. . . .

We have so far only explained the relation of the hysterical symptoms to the life history of the patient; now by considering two further factors which Breuer observed, we may get a hint as to the processes of the beginning of the illness and those of the cure. With regard to the first, it is especially to be noted that Breuer's patient in almost all pathogenic situations had to sup-

[37] Reprinted by permission from *A General Selection from the Works of Sigmund Freud,* edited by John Rickman (London: The Hogarth Press, 1937), by permission of Liveright Publishers, New York.

press a strong excitement, instead of giving vent to it by appropriate words and deeds. . . .

. . . Through the study of hypnotic phenomena, the conception, strange though it was at first, has become familiar, that in one and the same individual several mental groupings are possible, which may remain relatively independent of each other, "know nothing" of each other, and which may cause a splitting of consciousness along lines which they lay down. . . .

When I undertook to continue on my own account the investigations begun by Breuer I soon came to another view of the origin of hysterical dissociation (or splitting of consciousness). . . . The cathartic treatment, as Breuer had made use of it, presupposed that the patient should be put in deep hypnosis, for only in hypnosis was available the knowledge of his pathogenic associations, which were unknown to him in his normal state. Now hypnosis, as a fanciful, and so to speak, mystical, aid, I soon came to dislike; and when I discovered that, in spite of all my efforts, I could not hypnotize by any means all of my patients, I resolved to give up hypnotism and to make the cathartic method independent of it.

Since I could not alter the psychic state of most of my patients at my wish, I directed my efforts to working with them in their normal state. This seems at first sight to be a particularly senseless and aimless undertaking. The problem was this: to find out something from the patient that the doctor did not know and the patient himself did not know. How could one hope to make such a method succeed? The memory of a very noteworthy and instructive proceeding came to my aid, which I had seen in Bernheim's clinic at Nancy. Bernheim showed us that persons put in a condition of hypnotic somnambulism, and subjected to all sorts of experiences, had only apparently lost the memory of those somnambulic experiences, and that their memory of them could be awakened even in the normal state. If he asked them about their experiences during somnambulism, they said at first that they did not remember, but if he persisted, urged, assured them that they did know, then every time the forgotten memory came back.

Accordingly I did this with my patients. When I had reached in my procedure with them a point at which they declared that they knew nothing more, I would assure them that they did know, that they must just tell it out, and I would venture the assertion that the memory which would emerge at the moment that I laid my hand on the patient's forehead would be the right one. In this way I proceeded, without hypnosis, in learning from the patient all that was necessary for a construction of the connection between the forgotten pathogenic scenes and the symptoms which they had left behind. This was a troublesome and in its length an exhausting proceeding, and did not lend itself to a finished technique. But I did not give it up without drawing definite conclusions from the data which I had gained. I had substantiated the fact that the forgotten memories were not lost. They were in the possession of the patient, ready to emerge and form associations with his other mental content, but hindered from becoming conscious, and forced to remain in the unconscious by some sort of a force. The existence of this force could be assumed with certainty, for in attempting to drag up the unconscious memories into the consciousness of the patient, in opposition to this force, one got the sensation of his own personal effort striving to overcome it. One could get an idea of this force, which maintained the pathological situation, from the resistance of the patient.

It is on this idea of *resistance* that I based my theory of the psychic processes of hystericals. It had been found that in order to cure the patient it was necessary that this force should be overcome. Now with the mechanism of the cure as a starting point, quite a definite theory could be constructed. These same forces, which in the present situation as resistances opposed the emergence of the forgotten ideas into consciousness, must themselves have caused the forgetting, and repressed from consciousness the pathogenic experiences. I called this hypothetical process "repression," and considered that it was proved by the undeniable existence of resistance.

But now the question arose: What were those forces and what were the conditions of this repression, in which we were now able to recognize the pathogenic mechanism of hysteria? A comparative study of the pathogenic situations, which the cathartic treatment has made possible, allows us to answer this question. In all those experiences, it had happened that a wish had been aroused, which was in sharp opposition to the other desires of the individual, and was not capable of being reconciled with the ethical, aesthetic and personal pretensions of the patient's personality. There had been a short conflict, and the end of this inner struggle was the repression of the idea which presented itself to consciousness as the bearer of this irreconcilable wish. This was, then, repressed from consciousness and forgotten. The incompatibility of the idea in question with the "ego" of the patient was the motive of the repression, the ethical and other pretensions of the individual were the repressing forces. The presence of the incompatible wish, or the duration of the conflict, had given rise to a high degree of mental pain; this pain was avoided by the repression. This latter process is evidently in such a case a device for the protection of the personality. . . .

The difference between our theory and that of Janet [is that we] do not derive the psychic fission from a congenital lack of capacity on the part of the mental apparatus to synthesize its experiences, but we explain it dynamically by the conflict of opposing mental forces, we recognize in it the result of an active striving of each mental complex against the other.

New questions at once arise in great number from our theory. The situation of psychic conflict is a very frequent one; an attempt of the ego to defend itself from painful memories can be observed everywhere, and yet the result is not a mental fission. We cannot avoid the assumption that still other conditions are necessary, if the conflict is to result in dissociation. I willingly concede that with the assumption of "repression" we stand, not at the end, but at the very beginning of a psychological theory. But we can advance only one step at a time, and the completion of our knowledge must await further and more thorough work. . . .

We come to the conclusion, from working with hysterical patients and other neurotics, that they have not fully succeeded in repressing the idea to which the incompatible wish is attached. They have, indeed, driven it out of consciousness and out of memory, and apparently saved themselves a great amount of psychic pain, *but in the unconscious the suppressed wish still exists,* only waiting for its chance to become active, and finally succeeds in sending into consciousness, instead of the repressed idea, a disguised and unrecognizable surrogate-creation, to which the same painful sensations associate themselves that the patient thought he was rid of through his repression. This surrogate of the suppressed idea—the symptom—is secure against further attacks from the defenses of the ego, and instead of a short conflict there originates now a permanent suffering. We can observe in the symptom, besides the tokens of its disguise, a remnant of traceable similarity with the originally repressed idea; the way in which the surrogate is built up can be discovered during the psychoanalytic treatment of the patient, and for his cure the symptom must be traced back over the same route to the repressed idea. If this repressed material is once more made part of the conscious mental functions—a process which supposes the overcoming of considerable resistance—the psychic conflict which then arises, the same which the patient wished to avoid, is made capable of a happier termination, under the guidance of the physician, than is offered by repression. . . .

It is very useful to designate a group of ideas which belong together and have a common emotive tone, . . . as a "complex." So we can say that if we set out from the last memories of the patient to look for a repressed complex, that we have every prospect of discovering it, if only the patient will communicate to us a sufficient number of the ideas which come into his head. . . .

This method of work with whatever comes into the patient's head when he submits to psychoanalytic treatment, is not the only technical means at our disposal for the widening of consciousness. Two other methods of procedure serve the same purpose, the interpretation of his dreams and the evaluation of acts which he bungles or does without intending to. . . .

The manifest dream-content is the disguised surrogate for the unconscious dream thoughts, and this disguising is the work of the defensive forces of the ego, of the resistances. These prevent the repressed wishes from entering consciousness during the waking life, and even in the relaxation of sleep they are still strong enough to force them to hide themselves by a sort of masquerading. . . .

I may now pass to that group of everyday mental phenomena whose study has become a technical help for psychoanalysis. These are the bungling of acts [parapraxes] among normal men as well as among neurotics, to which no significance is ordinarily attached; the forgetting of things which one is supposed to know and at other times really does know (for example the temporary forgetting of proper names); mistakes in speaking, which occur so frequently; analogous mistakes in writing and in reading; the automatic execution of purposive acts in wrong situations and the loss or breaking of objects, etc. These are trifles for which no one has ever sought a psychological determination, which have passed unchallenged as chance experiences, as consequences of absent-mindedness, inattention, and similar conditions. Here, too, are included the acts and gestures executed without being noticed by the subject, to say nothing of the fact that he attaches no psychic importance to them; as playing and trifling with objects, humming melodies, handling one's person and clothing and the like. . . .

It follows that they deserve the rank of symptoms, and their observation, like that of dreams, can lead to the discovery of the hidden complexes of the psychic life. With their help one will usually betray the most intimate of his secrets. If these occur so easily and commonly among people in health, with whom repression has on the whole succeeded fairly well, this is due to their insignificance and their inconspicuous nature. But they can lay claim to high theoretic value, for they prove the existence of repression and surrogate creations even under the conditions of health. You have already noticed that the psychoanalyst is distinguished by an especially strong belief in the determination of the psychic life. For him there is in the expressions of the psyche nothing trifling, nothing arbitrary and lawless. . . .

Psychoanalytic investigations trace back the symptoms of disease with really surprising regularity to impressions from the sexual life, show us that the pathogenic wishes are of the nature of erotic impulse-components, and necessitate the assumption that to disturbances of the erotic sphere must be ascribed the greatest significance among the etiological factors of the disease. This holds true of both sexes. I know that this assertion will not willingly be credited. Even those investigators who gladly follow my psychological labors, are inclined to think that I overestimate the etiological share of the sexual factors. They ask me why other mental excitations should not lead to the phenomena of repression and surrogate-creation which I have described. I can give them this answer; that I do not know why they should not do this, I have no objection to their doing it, but experience shows that they do not possess such a significance, and that they merely support the effect of the sexual factors, without being able to support them. . . .

Is there an infantile sexuality? you will ask. Is childhood not rather that period of life which is distinguished by the lack of the sexual impulse? No . . . it is not at all true that the sexual impulse enters into the child at puberty, as the devils in the gospel entered into the swine. The child has his sexual impulses and activities from the beginning, he brings them with him into the world, and from these the so-called normal sexuality of adults emerges by a significant development through manifold stages. It is not very difficult to observe the expressions of this childish sexual activity; it needs rather a certain art to overlook them or to fail to interpret them. . . .

You will now perhaps make the objection: "But all that is not sexuality," I have used the word in a very much wider sense than you are accustomed to understand it. This I willingly concede. But it is a question whether you do not rather use the word in much too narrow a sense when you restrict it to the realm of procreation. You sacrifice by that the understanding of perversions; of the connection between perversion, neurosis, and normal sexual life; and have no means of recognizing, in its true significance, the easily observable beginning of the somatic and mental sexual life of the child. But however you decide about the use of the word, remember that the psychoanalyst understands sexuality in that full sense to which he is led by the evaluation of infantile sexuality. . . .

. . . The relation of the child to his parents is, as both direct observation of the child and later analytic investigation of adults agree, not at all free from elements of sexual accessory-excitation. The child takes both parents, and especially one, as an object of his erotic wishes. Usually he follows in this the stimulus given by his parents, whose tenderness has very clearly the character of a sex manifestation, though inhibited as far as its goal is concerned. As a rule, the father prefers the daughter, the mother the son;

the child reacts to this situation, since, as son, he wishes himself in the place of his father; as daughter, in the place of the mother. The feelings awakened in these relations between parents and children, and, as a resultant of them, those among the children in relation to each other, are not only positively of a tender, but negatively of an inimical sort. The complex built up in this way is destined to quick repression, but it still exerts a great and lasting effect from the unconscious. We must express the opinion that this with its ramifications presents the *nuclear complex* of every neurosis, and so we are prepared to meet with it in a not less effectual way in the other fields of mental life. The myth of King Oedipus, who kills his father and wins his mother as a wife, is only the slightly altered presentation of the infantile wish, rejected later by the opposing barriers of incest. Shakespeare's tale of Hamlet rests on the same basis of an incest complex, though better concealed. . . .

I am of the opinion that there are, on the intellectual side, two hindrances to acknowledging the value of the psychoanalytic viewpoint: first, the fact that we are not accustomed to reckon with a strict determination of mental life, which holds without exception, and second, the lack of knowledge of the peculiarities through which unconscious mental processes differ from those conscious ones with which we are familiar. One of the most widespread resistances against the work of psychoanalysis with patients as with persons in health reduces to the latter of the two factors. One is afraid of doing harm by psychoanalysis, one is anxious about calling up into consciousness the repressed sexual impulses of the patient, as though there were danger that they could overpower the higher ethical strivings and rob him of his cultural acquisitions. . . .

. . . In relation to this anxiety we must consider what our experiences have taught us with certainty, that the somatic and mental power of a wish, if once its repression has not succeeded, is incomparably stronger when it is unconscious than when it is conscious, so that by being made conscious it can only be weakened. The unconscious wish cannot be influenced, is free from all strivings in the contrary direction, while the conscious is inhibited by those wishes which are also conscious and which strive against it. The work of psychoanalysis accordingly presents a better substitute, in the service of the highest and most valuable cultural strivings, for the repression which has failed.

Now what is the fate of the wishes which have become free by psychoanalysis, by what means shall they be made harmless for the life of the individual? There are several ways. The general consequence is that the wish is consumed during the work by the correct mental activity of those better tendencies which are opposed to it. The repression is supplanted by a condemnation carried through with the best means at one's disposal. This is possible, since for the most part we have to abolish only the effects of earlier developmental stages of the ego. The individual for his part only repressed the useless impulse, because at that time he was himself still incompletely organized and weak; in his present maturity and strength he can, perhaps, conquer without injury to himself that which is inimical to him. A second issue of the work of psychoanalysis may be that the revealed unconscious impulses can now arrive at those useful applications which, in the case of undisturbed development, they would have found earlier. The extirpation of the infantile wishes is not at all the ideal aim of development. The neurotic has lost, by his repressions, many sources of mental energy whose contributions would have been very valuable for his character building and his life activities. We know a far more purposive process of development, the so-called *sublimation,* by which the energy of infantile wish-excitations is not secluded, but remains capable of application, while for the particular excitations, instead of becoming useless, a higher, eventually no longer sexual, goal is set up. The components of the sexual instinct are especially distinguished by such a capacity for the sublimation and exchange of their sexual goal for one more remote and socially more valuable. We probably owe the highest achievements of our culture to energy which has been liberated in this way. A repression taking place at an early period precludes the sublimation of the repressed impulse; after the removal of the repression the way to sublimation is again free.

We must not neglect, also, to glance at the third of the possible issues. A certain part of the suppressed libidinous excitation has a right to direct satisfaction and ought to find it in life. The claims of our civilization make life too hard for the greater part of humanity, and so further the aversion to reality and the origin of neuroses, without producing an excess of cultural gain by this excess of sexual repression. We ought not to go so far as fully neglect the original animal part of our nature, we ought not to forget that the happiness of individuals cannot be dispensed with as one of the aims of our culture. The plasticity of the sexual-components, manifest in their capacity for sublimation, may induce the temptation to accomplish ever greater achievements of culture by a more and more far-reaching sublimation. But just as with our machines we expect to change only a certain fraction of the applied heat into useful mechanical work, so we ought not to try to separate the sexual impulse in its whole extent of energy from its peculiar goal. It cannot be done, and if the narrowing of sexuality is pushed too far it will have all the evil effects of a robbery.

III
1914–1960

THE war of 1914 started as a European war, but the entrance of the United States as a decisive factor in the struggle (April, 1917) and Lenin's seizure of power in Russia (November, 1917) transformed the war into the First World War, which opened a new era of global history. This was not clearly seen in the 1920's. The prevailing opinion in Europe and the United States was in favor of the continuation of the nineteenth century, with its faith in liberalism and progress, its preponderance of European power on a world-wide scale, plus an intensification of the national and imperial ambitions which had characterized the Bismarckian and post-Bismarckian age. Only the Second World War, which was the result of these intensified power conflicts, made manifest what had happened a quarter of a century before.

In the interim period, the great economic depression which set in at the end of the 1920's, the staying power of communism (which had been regarded by many as a transitory phenomenon), and the triumphant rise of fascism in European countries in the early 1930's undermined the confident nineteenth-century faith in progress, in the appeal of liberty, even in the survival of modern Western civilization. Already in World War I Oswald Spengler predicted the approaching doom of the Occident, and the Leninists were convinced of the inevitable collapse of "capitalist" and free society. The cynicism about the values of liberal democracy made deep inroads even into Western intellectual circles and in its turn, enhanced the self-confidence of the totalitarian movements. The overvaluation of totalitarianism was one of the factors that brought about the Second World War, which started with the united front of all totalitarian movements against Western democracy.

Immediately after the First World War the French poet and critic Paul Valéry (1871–1945) expressed the new feeling that modern European civilization was fragile and mortal like the others had been:

The storm has died away, still we are restless, uneasy, as if the storm were about to break. Almost all the affairs of men remain in a terrible uncertainty. . . . We confess that the charm of life is behind us, abundance is behind us, but doubt and disorder are in us and with us. There is no thinking man who can hope to dominate this anxiety, to measure the probable duration of this period when the vital relations of humanity are disturbed profoundly. One can say that all the fundamentals of our world have been affected by the war, or more exactly, by the circumstances of the war; something deeper has been worn away than the renewable parts of the machine. . . . Among all the injured things is the Mind. The Mind has indeed been cruelly wounded; its complaint is heard in the hearts of intellectual men; it passes a mournful judgment on itself. It doubts itself profoundly.

This age of anxiety created a revival of Catholic and Protestant orthodoxy. But unorthodox were the arts. The experimental novels of Marcel Proust and James Joyce, abstract painting and sculpture, surrealism with its contempt for all traditional esthetic and moral values and its emphasis on the subconscious, the theater of the grotesque and absurd, "ultramodern" music—all these movements inaugurated a new era of sensitivity around and after the First World War. In all these movements a sense of bewilderment, of anguish at rising dark forces, and a revolt against the traditional order seemed mingled in varying degrees.

The outcome of the Second World War has again shifted the emphasis. A new age of radio and television, of electronics and computers, of supersonic airplanes and space flights made the world of 1960 infinitely more "new" to a man of 1860 than the world of 1860 would have appeared to a man of 1760. New was also the unprecedented rapidity and ubiquity of these developments. Their universality corresponded to another new phenomenon of the 1960's: the emergence of the "underdeveloped" countries, of Asia and Africa, into active partnership in world history. The Europe-centered view which had predominated until the end of World War II gave way to new global concepts. Thus, with the 1960's, a new period in the political and intellectual history of mankind may be forming.

31. LENIN: *ON REVOLUTIONARY THEORY AND PRACTICE*

The First World War resulted in a wasteland of cynical disillusionment and utopian expectations. The faith in the recuperative powers of orderly progress through democratic forms of political and social life was dangerously undermined

in countries where Western democracy was not firmly rooted—
such as Russia, Italy, and Germany. As a result, the Russian
Revolution of March, 1917, which had to proceed in the midst
of chaos created by war and defeat, provided the opportunity
for a closely knit group of revolutionary Marxists under the
leadership of Vladimir Ilyich Ulyanov (1870–1924), who became famous under the name of Lenin, to seize power in
November, 1917. At that time the party which Lenin led called
itself Bolshevik; in 1918 it changed its name to Communist; the
government which Lenin established was simultaneously the
first communist and the first totalitarian government in history.

Decades of industrial underdevelopment in Russia caused the
Marxist party, the Russian Social Democratic Party, to be
founded there only in 1898. At its second Congress, held in the
summer of 1903 in Brussels and London, it split into a majority
group of Bolsheviks under Lenin's leadership, and a minority
group (Mensheviks) who followed a more evolutionary socialist line akin to that of the Western social democratic parties.

In 1899 Lenin wrote an article, "Our Program" (A), an early
anticipation of the theories which he then applied as the leader
of the Bolshevik Party. During World War I he lived in Switzerland, where he propagated the turning of the war among the
European nations into an international class war in which the
proletariat would overthrow its "own" national governments
and establish throughout Europe an international proletarian
dictatorship.

The revolution of March, 1917, allowed Lenin to return to
Russia. In April he arrived in Petrograd, now Leningrad, and
from that moment on ceaselessly strove for the overthrow of
the democratic revolutionary regime in Russia. Applying his
theory of revolution, he preached that "armed uprising is inevitable and the situation has fully matured." At the end of
September he wrote his article "Marxism and Uprising" (B)
in order to overcome the hesitation the members of the Central
Committee of his own party had against the immediate seizure
of power. On the eve of the sixth of November he wrote the
"Call to Action" (C), to the members of the central committee
of the party.[1]

---

[1] *A Handbook of Marxism* (including A, B, & C.) (New York: International
Publishers, 1935), pp. 570 ff., 799 ff.

A. *"Our Program"*

International social democracy is at present going through a period of theoretical vacillations. Up to the present the doctrines of Marx and Engels were regarded as a firm foundation of revolutionary theory—nowadays voices are raised everywhere declaring these doctrines to be inadequate and antiquated. Anyone calling himself a social-democrat and having the intention to publish a social-democratic organ, must take up a definite attitude as regards this question, which by no means concerns German social-democrats alone.

We base our faith entirely on Marx's theory; it was the first to transform socialism from a Utopia into a science, to give this science a firm foundation and to indicate the path which must be trodden in order further to develop this science and to elaborate it in all its details. It discovered the nature of present-day capitalist economy and explained the way in which the employment of workers—the purchase of labour power—the enslavement of millions of those possessing no property by a handful of capitalists, by the owners of the land, the factories, the mines, etc., is concealed. It has shown how the whole development of modern capitalism is advancing towards the large producer ousting the small one, and is creating the prerequisites which make a socialist order of society possible and necessary. It has taught us to see, under the disguise of ossified habits, political intrigues, intricate laws, cunning theories, the class struggle, the struggle between, on the one hand, the various species of the possessing classes, and, on the other hand, the mass possessing no property, the proletariat, which leads all those who possess nothing. It has made clear what is the real task of a revolutionary socialist party—not to set up projects for the transformation of society, not to preach sermons to the capitalists and their admirers about improving the position of the workers, not the instigation of conspiracies, but the organization of the class struggle of the proletariat and the carrying on of this struggle, the final aim of which is the seizure of political power by the proletariat and the organization of a socialist society.

We now ask: What new elements have the touting "renovators" introduced into this theory, they who have attracted so much notice in our day and have grouped themselves round the German socialist Bernstein? Nothing, nothing at all; they have not advanced by a single step the science which Marx and Engels adjured us to develop; they have not taught the proletariat any new methods of fighting; they are only marching backwards in that they adopt the fragments of antiquated theories and are preaching to the proletariat not the theory of struggle but the theory of submissiveness—submissiveness to the bitterest enemies of the proletariat, to the governments and bourgeois parties who never tire of finding new methods of persecuting socialists. . . .

We know that on account of these words we shall be drenched with a flood of accusations; they will cry out that we want to turn the Socialist Party into a holy order of the "orthodox," who persecute the "heretics" for their aberrations from the "true dogma," for any independent opinion, etc. We know all these nonsensical phrases which have become the fashion nowadays. Yet there is no shadow of truth in them, no iota of sense. There can be no strong socialist party without a revolutionary theory which unites all socialists, from which the socialists draw their whole conviction, which they apply in their methods of fighting and working. To defend a theory of this kind, of the truth of which one is completely convinced, against unfounded attacks and against attempts to debase it, does not mean being an enemy of criticism in general. We by no means regard the theory of Marx as perfect and inviolable; on the contrary, we are convinced that this theory has only laid the foundation stones of that science on which the socialists must continue to build in every direction, unless they wish to be left behind by life. We believe that it is particularly necessary for Russian socialists to work out the Marxist theory independently, for this theory only gives general precepts, the details of which must be applied in England otherwise than in France, in France otherwise than in Germany, and in Germany otherwise than in Russia. For this reason we will willingly devote space in our paper to articles about theoretical questions, and we call upon all comrades openly to discuss the matters in dispute.

What are the main questions which arise in applying the common programme of all social-democrats to Russia?

We have already said that the essence of this programme consists in the organization of the class struggle of the proletariat and in carrying on this struggle, the final aim of which is the seizure of political power by the proletariat and the construction of a socialist society. The class struggle of the proletariat is divided into: The economic fight (the fight against individual capitalists, or against the individual groups of capitalists by the improvement of the position of the workers) and the political fight (the fight against the Government for the extension of the rights of the people, i.e., for democracy, and for the expansion of the political power of the proletariat). Some Russian social-democrats (among them apparently those who conduct the paper *Rabochaia Mysl*[2]) regard the economic fight as incomparably more important and almost go

[2] A Menshewik publication. The title means "Workers' Opinion."

as far as to postpone the political fight to a more or less distant future. This standpoint is quite wrong. All social-democrats are unanimous in believing that it is necessary to carry on an agitation among the workers on this basis, i.e., to help the workers in their daily fight against the employers, to direct their attention to all kinds and all cases of chicanery, and in this way to make clear to them the necessity of unity. To forget the political for the economic fight would, however, mean a digression from the most important principle of international social-democracy; it would mean forgetting what the whole history of the Labour movement has taught us. Fanatical adherents of the bourgeoisie and of the Government which serves it, have indeed repeatedly tried to organise purely economic unions of workers and thus to deflect them from the "politics" of socialism. It is quite possible that the Russian Government will also be clever enough to do something of the kind, as it has always endeavoured to throw some largesse or other sham presents to the people in order to prevent them becoming conscious that they are oppressed and are without rights.

No economic fight can give the workers a permanent improvement of their situation, it cannot, indeed, be carried on on a large scale unless the workers have the free right to call meetings, to join in unions, to have their own newspapers and to send their representatives to the National Assembly as do the workers in Germany and all European countries (with the exception of Turkey and Russia). In order, however, to obtain these rights, a political fight must be carried on. In Russia, not only the workers but all the citizens are deprived of political rights. Russia is an absolute monarchy. The Tsar alone promulgates laws, nominates officials and controls them. For this reason it seems as though in Russia the Tsar and the Tsarist Government were dependent on no class and cared for all equally. In reality, however, all the officials are chosen exclusively from the possessing class, and all are subject to the influence of the large capitalists who obtain whatever they want—the Ministers dance to the tune the large capitalists play. The Russian worker is bowed under a double yoke; he is robbed and plundered by the capitalists and the landowners, and, lest he should fight against them, he is bound hand and foot by the police, his mouth is gagged and any attempt to defend the rights of the people is followed by persecution. Any strike against a capitalist results in the military and police being let loose on the workers. Every economic fight of necessity turns into a political fight, and social-democracy must indissolubly combine the economic with the political fight into a united class struggle of the proletariat.

The first and chief aim of such a fight must be the conquest of political rights, the conquest of political freedom. Since the workers of St. Petersburg alone have succeeded, in spite of the inadequate support given them by the socialists in obtaining concessions from the Government within a short time—the passing of a law for shortening the hours of work—the whole working class, led by a united "Russian Social-Democratic Labour Party," will be able, through obstinate fighting, to obtain incomparably more important concessions.

The Russian working class will see its way to carrying on an economic and political fight alone, even if no other class comes to its help. The workers are not alone, however, in the political fight. The fact that the people is absolutely without rights and the unbridled arbitrary rule of the officials rouses the indignation of all who have any pretensions to honesty and education, who cannot reconcile themselves with the persecution of all free speech and all free thought; it rouses the indignation of the persecuted Poles, Finns, Jews, Russian sects, it rouses the indignation of small traders, of the industrialists, the peasants, of all who can nowhere find protection against the chicanery of the officials and the police. All these groups of the population are incapable of carrying on an obstinate political fight alone; if, however, the working class raises the banner of a fight of this kind it will be supported on all sides. Russian social-democracy will place itself at the head of all fights for the rights of the people, of all fights for democracy, and then it will be invincible.

B. Marxism and Uprising

Among the most vicious and perhaps most widespread distortions of Marxism practised by the prevailing "Socialist" parties, is to be found the opportunist lie which says that preparations for an uprising, and generally the treatment of an uprising as an art, is "Blanquism."[3]

Bernstein,[4] the leader of opportunism, long since gained sad notoriety by accusing Marxism of Blanquism; and our present opportunists, by shouting about Blanquism, in reality do not in any way improve or "enrich" the meagre "ideas" of Bernstein.

To accuse Marxists of Blanquism for treating uprising as an art! Can there be a more flagrant distortion of the truth, when there is not a single Marxist who denies that it was Marx who expressed

[3] Louis Auguste Blanqui (1805–1881), an extreme French socialist, stressed action and conspiracy. He spent thirty-four years in jail and ten in exile.

[4] Eduard Bernstein (1850–1932), German moderate socialist, was a proponent (1889) of revisionism stressing evolution, not revolution.

himself in the most definite, precise and categorical manner on this score; that it was Marx who called uprising nothing but an *art*, who said that uprising must be treated as an art, that one must *gain* the first success and then proceed from success to success without stopping the *offensive* against the enemy and making use of his confusion, etc., etc.

To be successful, the uprising must be based not on a conspiracy, not on a party, but on the advanced class. This is the first point. The uprising must be based on the revolutionary upsurge of the people. This is the second point. The uprising must be based on the *crucial point* in the history of the maturing revolution, when the activity of the vanguard of the people is at its height, when the *vacillations* in the ranks of the enemies, and *in the ranks of the weak, half-hearted, undecided friends of the revolution are at their highest point.* This is the third point. It is in pointing out these three conditions as the way of approaching the question of an uprising, that Marxism differs from Blanquism.

But once these conditions exist, then to refuse to treat the uprising *as an art* means to betray Marxism and the revolution. . . .

We have before us all the objective prerequisites for a successful uprising. We have the advantages of a situation where *only* our victory in an uprising will put an end to the most painful thing on earth, the vacillations that have sickened the people; a situation where *only our* victory in an uprising will *put an end* to the game of a separate peace against the revolution by openly offering a more complete, more just, more immediate peace *in favor of* the revolution.

Only our party, having won a victory in an uprising, *can* save Petrograd, for if our offer of peace is rejected, and we obtain not even a truce, then *we* shall become "defensists," then we shall place ourselves *at the head of the war parties,* we shall be the most "warring" party, and we shall carry on a war in a truly revolutionary manner. We shall take away from the capitalists all the bread and all the shoes. We shall leave them crumbs. We shall dress them in bast shoes. We shall send all the bread and all the shoes to the front.

And then we shall save Petrograd.

The resources, both material and spiritual, of a truly revolutionary war are still immense in Russia; there are ninety-nine chances in a hundred that the Germans will at least grant us a truce. And to secure a truce at present means to conquer the *whole world*.

Having recognized the absolute necessity of an uprising of the workers of Petrograd and Moscow for the sake of saving the revolution and of saving Russia from being "separately" divided among the imperialists of both coalitions, we must first adapt our political tactics at the conference to the conditions of the maturing uprising; secondly, we must prove that we accept, and not only in words, the idea of Marx about the necessity of treating uprising as an art.

At the conference, we must immediately consolidate the Bolshevik fraction without worrying about numbers, without being afraid of leaving the vacillators in the camp of the vacillating: they are more useful *there* to the cause of revolution than in the camp of the resolute and courageous fighters.

We must compose a brief declaration in the name of the Bolsheviks in which we sharply emphasise the irrelevance of long speeches, the irrelevance of "speeches" generally, the necessity of quick action to save the revolution, the absolute necessity of breaking completely with the bourgeoisie, of completely ousting the whole present government, of completely severing relations with the Anglo-French imperialists who are preparing a "separate" partition of Russia, the necessity of all power immediately passing into the hands of *revolutionary democracy headed by the revolutionary proletariat.*

Our declaration must be the briefest and sharpest formulation of this conclusion; it must connect up with the points in the programme of peace to the people, land to the peasants, confiscation of scandalous profits, and a halt to the scandalous damage to production done by the capitalist. . . .

The other point. In offering an immediate peace without annexations, in breaking at once with the Allied imperialists and with all imperialists, we obtain either an immediate truce or a going over of the entire revolutionary proletariat to the side of defence, and a truly just, truly revolutionary war will then be waged by revolutionary democracy under the leadership of the proletariat.

Having made this declaration, having appealed for *decisions* and not talk; for *actions,* not writing resolutions, we must *push* our whole fraction *into the factories and barracks:* its place is there; the pulse of life is there; the source of saving the revolution is there; the moving force of the Democratic Conference is there.

In heated, impassioned speeches we must make our programme clear and we must put the question this way: either the conference accepts it *fully,* or an uprising follows. There is no middle course. Delay is impossible. The revolution is perishing.

Having put the question this way, having concentrated our entire fraction in the factories and barracks, *we shall correctly estimate the best moment to begin the uprising.*

And in order to treat uprising in a Marxist way, i.e., as an art, we must at the same time, without losing a single moment, organise the staff of the insurrectionary detachments; designate the forces; move the loyal regiments to the most important points; surround the Alexander theatre; occupy the Peter and Paul Fortress; arrest the general staff and the government; move against the military cadets, the Wild Division, etc., such detachments as will die rather than allow the enemy to move to the centre of the city; we must mobilise the armed workers, call them to a last desperate battle, occupy at once the telegraph and telephone stations, place *our* staff of the uprising at the central telephone station, connect it by wire with all the factories, the regiments, the points of armed fighting, etc.

Of course, this is all by way of an example, to *illustrate* the idea that at the present moment it is impossible to remain loyal to the revolution *without treating uprising as an art.*

C. *"Call to Action"*

Comrades!

I am writing these lines on the evening of the 6th. The situation is extremely critical. It is as clear as can be that delaying the uprising now really means death.

With all my power I wish to persuade the comrades that now everything hangs on a hair, that on the order of the day are questions that are not solved by conferences, by congresses (even by Congresses of Soviets), but only by the people, by the masses, by the struggle of armed masses. . . .

Who should seize power?

At present this is not important. Let the Military Revolutionary Committee seize it, or "some other institution" which declares that it will relinquish the power only to the real representatives of the interests of the people, the interests of the Army (immediate offer of peace), the interests of the peasants (take the land immediately, abolish private property), the interests of the hungry.

It is necessary that all the boroughs, all regiments, all forces should be mobilised and should immediately send delegations to the Military Revolutionary Committee, to the Central Committee of the Bolsheviks, insistently demanding that under no circumstances is power to be left in the hands of Kerensky[5] and Co. until the 7th, by no means!—that the matter must absolutely be decided this evening or tonight.

History will not forgive delay by revolutionists who could be

[5] Alexander Kerensky (1881——), moderate Socialist, member of Provisional Russian Government after the February revolution and prime minister, from July to November, 1917

victorious today (and will surely be victorious today), while they risk losing much tomorrow, they risk losing all.

If we seize power today, we seize it not against the Soviets but for them.

Seizure of power is the point of the uprising; its political task will be clarified after the seizure.

It would be a disaster or formalism to wait for the uncertain voting of November 7. The people have a right and a duty to decide such questions not by voting but by force; the people have a right and duty in critical moments of a revolution to give directions to their representatives, even their best representatives, and not to wait for them.

This has been proven by the history of all revolutions, and the crime of revolutionists would be limitless if they let go the proper moment, knowing that upon them depends the *saving of the revolution*, the offer of peace, the saving of Petrograd, the saving from starvation, the transfer of the land to the peasants.

The government is tottering. We must *deal it the death blow* at any cost.

To delay action is the same as death.

Written November 6, 1917.

32. SPENGLER: *THE DECLINE OF THE WEST*

The contempt for Western democracy, the feeling that a great historical turning point had been reached which meant the end of the predominance of Western liberalism, and the impatience for fast and decisive action were not confined to Russian extremists. Similar sentiments prevailed in Germany and Italy. They were all signs of a deep crisis of the European mind. The West and Western civilization, as it had taken shape in the eighteenth and nineteenth centuries, seemed in decline, a mood which disappeared in the West only after the Second World War.

The conviction that Western liberalism was doomed was expressed by the German scholar Oswald Spengler (1880–1936), who wrote, during the First World War, at a time when the German armies still were victorious, the first volume of his *Der Untergang des Abendlandes* ("The Decline of the West"), which appeared in 1918. A second volume appeared in 1922.

Both went through many printings, in the German original as well as in the English translation. The title of the book became a term of general usage. One fundamental difference between Lenin and Spengler should be noted here: the former's theory was fundamentally equalitarian, the latter's aristocratic. Thus, they appeared more hostile than they actually were. As a follower of Marx, Lenin stressed the rationality of history; Spengler stressed its irrationality. Spengler regarded himself as a disciple of Nietzsche, though only with very partial justification. In his turn he influenced the thought of fascism.[6]

A. Philosophy of Politics

Here the attempt will be made to give, instead of an ideological system, a PHYSIOGNOMY of politics as it has actually been practised. The problem was, and is, to penetrate to the final meaning of great events, to "see" them, to feel and to transcribe the symbolically important in them. The projects of world-improvers and the actuality of History have nothing to do with one another.

The being-streams of humanity are called History when we regard them as movement, and family, estate, people, nation, when we regard them as the object moved. Politics is the way in which this fluent Being maintains itself, GROWS, triumphs over other life-streams. ALL LIVING IS POLITICS, in every trait of instinct, in the inmost marrow. That which we nowadays like to call life-energy (vitality), the "it" in us, at all costs strives forward and upward, the blind cosmic drive to validity and power that at the same time remains plantwise and racewise, bound up with the earth, the "home"-land; the directedness, the need to actualize— it is this that appears in every higher mankind, as its political life, seeking naturally and inevitably the great decisions that determine whether it shall be, or shall suffer, a Destiny. For it grows or IT DIES OUT; there is no third possibility. . . .

It is only in and between these being-streams that fill the field of the high Culture that high policy exists. They are only possible, therefore, in the plural. A people IS, really, only in relation to peoples. But the natural relation between them is for that very reason a relation of war—this is a fact that no truths avail to alter.

[6] The following excerpts are reprinted from chapters XII and XIV (the final chapter) of vol. II of *The Decline of the West* (A) and from *The Hour of Decision* (B) which appeared in German in 1933. Both works were translated by Charles Francis Atkinson, and the excerpts are reprinted here with the permission of the publisher Alfred A. Knopf (New York) and George Allen & Unwin (London). Copyright 1928, 1932, and 1934 by Alfred A. Knopf, Inc.

War is the primary politics of EVERYTHING that lives, and so much so that in the deeps battle and life are one, and being and will-to-battle expire together. Old Germanic words for this, like "ORRUSTA" and "ORLOG," mean seriousness and destiny in contrast to jest and play—and the contrast is one of intensity, not of qualitative difference. And even though all high politics tries to be a substitution of more intellectual weapons for the sword and though it is the ambition of the statesman at the culminations of all the Cultures to feel able to dispense with war, yet the primary relationship between diplomacy and the art of war endures. The character of battle is common to both and the tactics and stratagems, and the necessity of material forces in the background to give weight to the operations. The aim, too, remains the same— namely, the growth of one's life-unit (class or nation) at the cost of the others. . . .

To be the centre of action and effective focus of a multitude, to make the inward form of one's own personality into that of whole peoples and periods, to be history's commanding officer, with the aim of bringing one's own people or family or purposes to the top of events—that is the scarce-conscious but irresistible impulse in every individual being that has a historical vocation in it. There is only PERSONAL history and consequently only PERSONAL politics. The struggle of, not principles but men, not ideals but vital qualities, for executive power is the alpha and omega. Even revolutions are no exception, for the "sovereignty of the people" only expresses the fact that the ruling power has assumed the title of people's leader instead of that of king. The method of governing is scarcely altered thereby, and the position of the governed not at all. And even world-peace, in every case where it has existed, has been nothing but the slavery of an entire humanity under the rule imposed by a few strong natures determined to rule.

The essential, therefore, is to understand the time FOR which one is born. He who does not sense and understand its most secret forces, who does not feel in himself something cognate that drives him forward on a path neither hedged nor defined by concepts, who believes in the surface, public opinion, large phrases and ideals of the day—he is not of the stature for its events. He is in their power, not they in his. Look not back to the past for measuring-rods! Still less sideways for some system or other! There are times, like our own present and the Gracchan age, in which there are two most deadly kinds of idealism, the reactionary and the democratic. The one believes in the reversibility of history, the other in a teleology of history. But it makes no difference to the inevitable failure with which both burden a nation over whose destiny they have power, whether it is to a memory or to a concept that they sacrifice it. The genuine statesman is incarnate history, its directedness expressed as individual will and its organic logic as character. . . .

Politics is the form in which is accomplished the history of a nation within a plurality of nations. The great art is to maintain one's own nation inwardly "in form" for events outside; this is the natural relation of home and foreign politics, holding not only for Peoples and States and Estates, but for living units of every kind, down to the simplest animal swarms and down into the individual bodies. And, as between the two, THE FIRST EXISTS EXCLUSIVELY FOR THE SECOND AND NOT VICE VERSA. The true democrat is accustomed to treat home politics as an end in itself; the rank and file of diplomats think solely of foreign affairs; but just because of this the individual successes of either "cut no ice." No doubt, the political master exhibits his powers most obviously in the tactics of home reform; in his economic and social activities; in his cleverness in maintaining the public form of the whole, the "rights and liberties," both in tune with the tastes of the period and AT THE SAME TIME effective; and in the education of the feelings without which it is impossible for a people to be "in condition"—namely, trust, respect for the leaders, consciousness of power, contentment, and (when necessary) enthusiasm. But the value of all this depends upon its relation to this basic fact of higher history—that a people is not alone in the world, and that its future will be decided by its force-relationships towards other peoples and powers and not by its mere internal ordering. And, since the ordinary man is not so far-sighted, it is the ruling minority that must possess this quality on behalf of the rest, and not unless there is such a minority does the statesman find the instrument wherewith he can carry his purposes into effect.

The coming of Cæsarism breaks the dictorship of money and its political weapon, democracy. After a long triumph of urban economy and its interests over political creative force, the political side of life manifests itself after all as the stronger of the two. The sword is victorious over the money, the master-will subdues again the plunder-will. If we call these money-powers "Capitalism," then we may designate as Socialism the will to call into life a mighty politico-economic order that transcends all class interests, a system of LOFTY thoughtfulness and duty-sense that keeps the whole in fine condition for the decisive battle of its history, and this battle is also the battle of money and law. The PRIVATE powers of the economy want for their acquisition of great resources. No legislation must stand in their way. They want to make the laws themselves, in their interests, and to that end they make use of the tool they have made for themselves, democracy, the subsidized party. Law needs, in order to resist this onslaught, a high tradition and an ambition of strong families that finds its satisfaction not in the heaping-up of riches, but in the tasks of true rulership, above and beyond all money-advantage. A POWER CAN BE OVER-THROWN ONLY BY ANOTHER POWER, not by a principle, and no power that can confront money is left but this one. Money is overthrown and abolished only by vitality and breeding. LIFE is alpha and omega, the cosmic onflow in microcosmic form. It is THE fact of facts within the world-as-history. Before the irresistible rhythm of the generation-sequence, everything built up by the conscious mind in its vitality, the triumph of the will-to-power—and not the victory of truths, discoveries, or money that is significant. WORLD-HISTORY IS THE WORLD COURT, and it has ever decided in favour of the stronger, fuller, and more self-assured life—decreed to it, namely, the right to exist, regardless of whether its right would hold before a tribunal of the rational mind. Always it has sacrificed truth and justice to might and vitality, and passed doom of death upon men and peoples to whom truth was more than deeds, and justice more than power. And so the drama of a high Culture—that wondrous world of deities, arts, thoughts, battles, cities—closes with the return of the pristine facts of the blood eternal that is one and the same as the ever-circling cosmic flow. . . .

For us, however, whom a Destiny has placed in this Culture and at this moment of its development—the moment when money is celebrating its last victories, and the Cæsarism that is to succeed approaches with quiet, firm step—our direction, willed and obligatory at once, is set for us within narrow limits, and on any other terms life is not worth the living. We have not the freedom to reach to this or to that, but the freedom to do the necessary or to do nothing. And a task that historic necessity has set WILL be accomplished with the individual or against him.

Faced as we are with this destiny, there is only one world-outlook that is worthy of us, that which has already been mentioned as the Choice of Achilles—better a short life, full of deeds and glory, than a long life without content. Already the danger is so great, for every individual, every class, every people, that to cherish any illusion whatever is deplorable. Time does not suffer itself to be halted; there is no question of prudent retreat or wise renunciation. Only dreamers believe that there is a way out. Optimism is COWARDICE.

We are born into this time and must bravely follow the path to the destined end. There is no other way. Our duty is to hold on to the lost position, without hope, without rescue, like that Roman soldier whose bones were found in front of a door in Pompeii, who, during the eruption of Vesuvius, died at his post because they forgot to relieve him. That is greatness. That is what it means to be a thoroughbred. The honourable end is the one thing that can NOT be taken from a man.

B. World Politics

The great game of world politics is not over. Only now are the highest stakes being played for. Every living nation must rise to greatness or go under. But the events of this year allow us to hope that the decision in our case has not yet been made—that we, as in Bismarck's day, shall sooner or later again be subjects and not mere objects of history. The decades in which we live are stupendous—and accordingly terrifying and void of happiness. Greatness and happiness are incompatible and we are given no choice. No one living in any part of the world of today will be happy, but many will be able to control by the exercise of their own will the greatness or insignificance of their life-course. As for those who seek comfort merely, they do not deserve to exist. . . .

It is the great task of the historical EXPERT (in the true sense) to understand the facts of his time and through them to envisage, interpret, and delineate the future—which will come whether we will or no. An epoch so conscious of itself as the present is impossible of comprehension without creative, anticipating, warning, LEADING criticism. . . .

If few can stand a long war without deterioration of soul, none can stand a long peace. This peace period from 1870 to 1914, and the memory of it, rendered all White men self-satisfied, covetous, void of understanding, and incapable of bearing misfortune. We see the result in the Utopian conceptions and challenges which today form part of every demagogue's program; challenges to the age, to the State, to parties, and in fact to "everyone else," in complete disregard of the limits of possibility or of duty, doing, and forgoing. . . .

And thus we deceive ourselves, blind to the fact that we have here one of those incalculable great catastrophes that are the NORMAL form in which history takes its major turns.

For we live in a mighty age. . . . The First World War was but the first flash and crash from the fateful thundercloud which is passing over this century. . . . But who understands this? Who is facing it? Does one of us consider himself lucky to be there to see it? The age is mighty, but all the more diminutive are the people in it. They can no longer bear tragedy, either on the stage or in real life. They crave happy endings of insipid novels, so miserable and weary are they. But the destiny which pitched them into these decades now takes them by the collar and does with them what has to be done, whether they will or no. The coward's security of 1900 is at an end. Life in danger, the real life of history, comes once more into its own. Everything has begun to slide, and now only that man counts who can take risks, who has the courage to see and accept things as they are. The age is approaching—nay, is already here—which has no more room for soft hearts and weakly ideals. The primeval barbarism which has lain hidden and bound for centuries under the form-rigour of a ripe Culture, is awake again now that the Culture is finished and the Civilization has set in: that warlike, healthy joy in one's own strength which scorns the literature-ridden age of Rationalist thought, that unbroken vital-instinct, which desires a different life from one spent under the weight of books and bookish ideals. . . .

The man who is incapable of experiencing or enduring tragedy can never be a figure of world significance. He cannot MAKE history unless he experiences it as it really is—tragic, permeated by destiny, and in consequence meaningless, aimless, and unmoral in the eyes of the worshippers of utility. It marks the parting of the ways between the superior and the subordinate ethos of human existence. The individual's life is of importance to none besides himself: the point is whether he wishes to escape from history or give his life for it. History recks nothing of human logic. Thunderstorms, earthquakes, lava-streams: these are near relatives of the purposeless, elemental events of world history. Nations may go under, ancient cities of ageing Cultures burn or sink in ruins, but the earth will continue to revolve calmly round the sun, and the stars to run their courses.

Man is a beast of prey. I shall say it again and again. All the would-be moralists and social-ethics people who claim or hope to be "beyond all that" are only beasts of prey with their teeth broken, who hate others on account of the attacks which they themselves are wise enough to avoid. Only look at them. They are too weak to read a book on war, but they herd together in the street to see an accident, letting the blood and the screams play on their nerves. And if even that is too much for them, they enjoy it on film and in the illustrated papers. If I call man a beast of prey, which do I insult: man or beast? For remember, the larger beasts of prey are NOBLE creatures, perfect of their kind, and without the hypocrisy of human moral due to weakness.

They shout: "No more war" — but they desire class war. They are indignant when a murder is executed for a crime of passion, but they feel a secret pleasure in hearing of the murder of a political opponent. What objection have they raised to the Bolshevist slaughters? There is no getting away from it: Conflict is the original fact of life, is life itself, and not the most pitiful pacifist is able entirely to uproot the pleasure it gives his inmost soul. Theoretically, at least, he would like to fight and destroy all opponents of pacifism.

Human history in the period of the high cultures is the history of political forces. The form of this history is war. But peace is also part of it, for it is the continuation of war with different means. A State represents the "being in condition" of a national unit trained and set up by it for real and potential wars. When the "form" is very high, it has in itself the value of a victorious war, which is won without weapons and solely by the weight of the force ready to come into play. If form is poor, it approximates to continuous defeat in the State's relation to other powers. States are PURELY POLITICAL units, units of radiated power. They are NOT units bound up with race, language, or religion, but stand ABOVE these. Whenever they coincide or mingle with such elements, their strength usually declines and never increases, in consequence of the inward contradiction. Internal politics exist only to secure the strength and unity of external politics, and when they pursue different aims of their own, decay sets in and the State gets "out of form."

For a power to be "in form," as a State among states, it must have strength and unity in its leadership, its government, and its authority, without which the State has no real existence.

Is the United States a power with a future? Before 1914 superficial observers talked of unlimited possibilities after they had looked about them for a week or two, and post-war "society" from Western Europe, compounded of snobs and mobs, was full of enthusiasm for "husky" young America as being far superior to ourselves—nay, positively a model for us to follow. But for purposes of durable form, records and dollars must not be taken to represent the spiritual strength of the people to whom they belong; neither must sport be confused with race-soundness nor business intelligence with spirit and mind. What IS "hundred per cent Americanism"? A mass existence standardized to a low average level, a primitive pose, or a promise for the future?

All we know is that so far there is neither a real nation nor a real State. Can both of these develop out of the knocks of fate, or is this possibility excluded by the very fact of the Colonial type, whose spiritual past belongs elsewhere and is now dead? The American does not talk of State or Mother Country like the Englishman, but of "THIS country." Actually what it amounts to is a boundless field and a population of trappers, drifting from town to town in the dollar-hunt, unscrupulous and dissolute; for the law is only for those who are not cunning or powerful enough to ignore it.

The resemblance to Bolshevik Russia is far greater than one imagines. . . . There is the same dictatorship there as in Russia (it does not matter that it is imposed by society instead of a party), affecting everything—flirtation and church-going, shoes and lipstick, dances and novels A LA MODE, thought, food, and recreation—that in the Western world is left to the option of individuals. There is one standardized type of American, and above all, American woman, in body, clothes, and mind; any departure from or open criticism of the type arouses public condemnation in New York as in Moscow. Finally, there is an almost Russian form of State socialism or State capitalism, represented by the mass of trusts, which, like the Russian economic administrations, systematically standardize and control every detail of production and marketing. These are the real lords of the land in both cases. It is the Faustian will-to-power, but translated from organic growth to soulless mechanization.

Not many years since, anyone using the word "revolution" in connexion with this country would have been called an idiot. Today such ideas are quite in order. What will the masses of the unemployed do—I repeat, the majority are NOT "hundred per cent Americans"—when their sources of relief are exhausted and there is no State support because there is no organized State with exact and honest statistics and control of those in want? Will they fall back on their fists and their common economic interest with the underworld? And will the intellectually primitive upper class, obsessed as it is by the thought of money, reveal all at once, in face of this danger, dormant moral forces that will lead to the real construction of a State and to spiritual preparedness to sacrifice possessions and blood to it, instead of regarding war as a means of gaining wealth as hitherto? Or will the special economic interests of individual areas still pull the most weight and, as once before in 1861, lead to the disintegration of the country into separate states such as, say, the industrial North-East, the farming region of the Middle West, the Negro states of the South, and the area beyond the Rockies?

Leaving out Japan, which only desires to carry out undisturbed her imperialistic plans in eastern Asia and Australia, there is but one power which would do anything and make any sacrifice to bring about this distintegration: England.

And how if Russia and America came to an agreement as a result of England's tradition-ridden pride? That is NOT beyond the bounds of possibility.

I have now reached the point when the definitive word must be said about "Prussianism" and "Socialism." In 1919 I compared the two, the one a living IDEA and the other the catchword of a whole century, and was—not understood. People no longer know how to read—this great art, still known in the age of Goethe, has died out. They skim printed pages "mass-wise," and, as a rule, the reader demoralizes the book. I showed that in the German working class, as Bebel[7] welded it into a powerful army, in its discipline and loyal subordination, its good comradeship, its readiness for the ultimate sacrifice, there still lived that Old-Prussian "style" which first proved itself in the battles of the Seven Years' War. What mattered then was the INDIVIDUAL Socialist as a character, his "moral imperative," not the Socialism hammered into his head, which was a wholly un-Prussian mixture of foolish ideology and vulgar greed. I pointed out also that this type of BEING "IN FORM" FOR A TASK was a tradition going back to the Teutonic Order, by which in the Gothic centuries—as again today—the frontier guard of the Faustian Culture was kept up against Asia. This ethical attitude, unconscious as is every genuine life-style, and therefore to be awakened and trained only by living example and not by talk and writing, stood forth in its splendour in August 1914—the army had trained Germany—and was betrayed by the parties in 1918 when the STATE went under. Since then this disciplined will has again raised its head in the Nationalist movement; not in its programs and parties, but in the ethical attitude of an élite, as individuals; and it is possible that, starting from this foundation, the German people may by perseverance be slowly trained for its difficult future. This is essential if we are not to succumb in the battles that lie ahead.

Germany is the KEY country of the world, not only on account of her geographical situation on the borders of Asia (which is today the most important continent in world policy), but also because Germans are still young enough to experience world-historical problems, to form them and solve them, INWARDLY, while other nations have become too old and rigid to do more than raise defences. But in tackling great PROBLEMS, as in other matters, it is the attack that holds the greater promise of victory.

[7] August Bebel (1840–1913), German Social-Democratic leader

33. MUSSOLINI: *THE DOCTRINE OF FASCISM*

Fascism, the other great authoritarian mass movement of the twentieth century which, though of European origin, opposed modern Western civilization, represented an inflammation of nationalism brought about partly by the First World War. It no longer believed, as Mazzini did, in the harmony of the national interests of free nations. It dedicated itself to the preparation for the "inevitable" struggle that forms the life of nations. Fascism absolutized nationalism. The nation became the supreme arbiter, its service the one supreme duty. The absolute devotion to the nation guides all fascist education, which, like communist education, wishes to determine every thought and every sentiment.

Fascism came first to power in Italy with the March on Rome in October, 1922, under the leadership of Benito Mussolini (1883–1945), who until 1914 was an extremist socialist and editor of the representative socialist paper in Italy. In the 1930's fascist principles were accepted, to a varying degree, in most countries in central, eastern, and southern Europe, and they penetrated into Latin America and Japan. On October 25, 1932, Mussolini assured his jubilant audience at Milan of the coming world leadership of fascist Italy. "Today with a fully tranquil conscience, I say to you, that the twentieth century will be the century of fascism, the century of Italian power, the century during which Italy will become for the first time the leader of mankind."

Mussolini himself expressed the political doctrine of fascism in an article in the official *Enciclopedia Italiana* in 1932. It was republished in an official translation in a somewhat changed form in Benito Mussolini, *The Doctrine of Fascism.*[8]

Thus many of the practical expressions of Fascism, such as party organization, educational systems, discipline, can only be understood when considered in relation to its general attitude towards life. Fascism does not see in the world only those superficial, material aspects in which man appears as a self-centered individual, standing alone, subject to natural laws and instincts which urge

[8] Translated by E. Cope, 3rd ed. (Florence, 1938). The following excerpts are from pp. 10–25, 30–40, 49.

him towards a life of selfish momentary pleasure; it does not only see the individual, but also the nation and the country; individuals and generations bound together by a moral law, moral traditions and a mission which, repressing the instinct for life enclosed in a brief circle of pleasure, builds up a higher life founded on duty, a life free from the limitations of time and space, in which the individual may achieve that purely spiritual existence in which his worth as a man consists, by self-sacrifice, in the renunciation of self-interest, by death itself. . . .

Fascism wants men to be active and to engage in activity with all their energy; it requires that they should be manfully aware of the difficulties besetting them and ready to face them. Life is conceived as a struggle in which a man is bound to win for himself a really worthy place, first of all by fitting himself physically, morally and intellectually, and to have the necessary qualities for winning it. As it is for the individual, so is it for the nation, and for all mankind. Hence the high value of culture in all its forms, religious, scientific and artistic, and the outstanding importance of education. Hence also the essential value of work, by which man subdues nature and creates the human world in its economic, political, ethical and intellectual aspects.

This positive conception of life is obviously an ethical one. It covers the entire field of reality as well as the human activities which master it. No action is exempt from moral judgment: no activity can be deprived of the value which a moral purpose confers on all things. Therefore life, as conceived by the Fascist, is serious, austere, religious; all its manifestations take place in a world sustained by moral forces and subject to spiritual responsibilities. The Fascist disdains an easygoing life.

The Fascist conception of life is a religious one in which man is viewed in his permanent relation to a higher law, endowed with an objective will transcending the individual and raising him to conscious membership of a spiritual society. Those who perceive nothing beyond opportunist considerations in the religious policy of the Fascist Regime, fail to realize that Fascism is not only a system of government, but also and chiefly a system of thought. . . .

Being anti-individualistic, the Fascist system of life stresses the importance of the State and recognizes the individual only in so far as his interests coincide with those of the State, which stands for the consciousness and the universality of man as an historic entity. It is opposed to classic Liberalism which arose as a reaction to absolutism and exhausted its historical function when the State became the expression of the consciousness and the will of the people. Liberalism denied the State in the name of the individual;

Fascism reasserts the rights of the State as expressing the real essence of the individual. And if liberty is to be the attribute of living men and not that of abstract dummies invented by individualistic Liberalism, then Fascism stands for liberty and for the only liberty worth having, the liberty of the State and of the individual within the State. The Fascist conception of the State is all-embracing; outside of it no human or spiritual values may exist, much less have any value. Thus understood, Fascism is totalitarian and the Fascist State, as a synthesis and a unit which includes all values, interprets, develops and lends additional power to the whole life of people.

A nation, as expressed in the State, is a living, ethical entity only in so far as it is progressive. Inactivity means death. Therefore the State does not only stand for Authority which governs and confers legal form and spiritual value on individual wills, but it is also Power which makes its will felt and respected beyond its own boundaries, thus affording practical evidence of the universal character of the decisions necessary to ensure its development. This implies organization and expansion, potential if not actual. . . .

Fascism, in short, is not only a lawgiver and a founder of institutions, but an educator and a promoter of spiritual life. It does not merely aim at remoulding the forms of life, but also their content, man, his character and his faith. To achieve this purpose it enforces discipline and makes use of authority, entering into the mind and ruling with undisputed sway. Therefore it has chosen as its emblem the Lictor's rods, the symbol of unity, strength and justice. . . .

Yet if anybody cares to read over again the faded minutes of the meetings at which the Italian Fasci di Combattimento were founded, he will not find a doctrine, but a series of hints, pointers, forecasts which, after being freed from unavoidable contemporary confusion, were to develop in a few years' time into a series of theoretical positions entitling Fascism to rank as a political doctrine differing from all others, past or present.

"If the bourgeoisie"—I stated at that time—"believe that they have found in us their lightning conductors, they are mistaken. We must go towards the people. . . . We wish the working classes to accustom themselves to the responsibilities of management, so that they may realize that it is no easy matter to run a business. . . .

. . . Now that the succession of the Regime is open we must not be faint-hearted. We must rush forward; when the present Regime is superseded we must take its place. The right to the succession is ours, for we urged the country to enter the war and we led it to victory. . . . The existing forms of political representation cannot satisfy us; we want direct representation of all separate interests. . . .

It may be objected that this programme implies a return to the guilds. No matter! . . . I therefore hope this assembly will accept the economic claims advanced by National Syndicalism. . . ."

Fascism is definitely and absolutely opposed to the doctrines of Liberalism, both in the political and in the economic sphere. The importance of Liberalism in the XIX century must not be exaggerated for present-day controversial purposes, nor should we make of one of the many theories which flourished in that century, a religion for mankind for the present and for all time to come. It is symptomatic that throughout the nineteenth century the religion of Liberalism was totally unknown to so highly civilized a people as the Germans, except for a single case, which has been described as the "ridiculous Parliament of Frankfurt" which lasted just one season. Germany attained her national unity outside Liberalism and in opposition to Liberalism, a doctrine which seems to be foreign to the German temperament, an essentially Monarchist one, whereas Liberalism is the historic and logical prelude to anarchy. The three stages of the achievement of German unity were the three wars of 1864, 1866 and 1870, directed by such "Liberals" as Moltke and Bismarck. And Liberalism played a very minor part in building up Italian unity, if we compare it to the contribution made by Mazzini and Garibaldi who were not Liberals. But for the intervention of the illiberal Napoleon III we would not have had Lombardy, and without that of the illiberal Bismarck at Sadowa and Sedan very probably we would not have had Venetia in 1866, nor would we have entered Rome in 1870. . . .

The Fascist negation of Socialism, Democracy, Liberalism should not, however, be interpreted as implying a desire to drive the world backwards to positions occupied prior to 1789. Monarchist absolutism is of the past, and so is Church rule. Dead and done for are feudal privileges and the division of society into closed, secluded castes. Neither has the Fascist conception of authority anything in common with that of the police-ridden State.

The State educates its members to citizenship, makes them aware of their mission, urges them to unity; its justice harmonizes their divergent interests; it hands down to future generations the conquests of the mind in the fields of science, art, law, human solidarity; it leads them up from primitive tribal life to imperial rule, the highest expression of human power. The State hands down to future generations the memory of those who laid down their lives to ensure its safety or to obey its laws; it sets up as examples and records for future ages the names of captains who enlarged its territory and of the men of genius who have made it famous. Whenever respect for the State declines and the disintegrating and centrifugal tendencies of individuals and groups prevail, nations are heading for decay. . . ."

If Liberalism spells individualism, Fascism spells collectivism. The Fascist State, however, is an unique and original creation. It is not reactionary but revolutionary, for it anticipates the solution of certain universal problems which have been raised elsewhere in the political field by the disintegration of parties, the usurpation of powers by parliaments, the irresponsibility of assemblies; in the economic field by the increasingly numerous and important functions discharged by trade unions and trade associations with their disputes and agreements, affecting both capital and labour; in the ethical field by the need felt for order, discipline, obedience to the moral principles of patriotism.

Fascism desires the State to be strong and organic, based on solid foundations of popular support. The Fascist State lays claim to rule in the economic field no less than in others; it makes its action felt throughout the length and breadth of the country by means of its corporate, social and educational institutions, and all the political, economic and spiritual forces of the nation, organized in their respective associations, spread all over the State. . . .

Today I hold that Fascism as an idea, a doctrine, a realization, is universal; it is Italian in its particular institutions, but it is universal by reason of its nature. Therefore anyone may foresee a Fascist Europe drawing inspiration for her institutions from the doctrine and practice of Fascism; Europe, in other words, giving a Fascist turn to the solution of problems which beset the modern State, the Twentieth Century State which is very different from the States existing before 1789, and the States formed immediately after. Today Fascism answers to universal requirements.

34. ADOLF HITLER: *MEIN KAMPF*

National Socialism was the German form of fascism. It stressed even more than Italian fascism the antibourgeois, anti-capitalist, mass aspect of the movement. Its official name was the German National Socialist Workers' Party; its official flag was basically red, with a small white circle around a black swastika in the center, thus recalling, at the same time, the colors of the imperial flag of the Bismarckian Reich—black-white-red. Above all, it was the insistence on race, racial purity, and ruthless race war as the "iron law of nature" and history which distinguished German from Italian fascism.

The belief in race—the Germans as the noblest and most creative race, and the Jews as the very opposite—was accepted among some German intellectuals in the nineteenth century when they rejected the Western Enlightenment and its trends to emancipation, equality, and democracy. With Adolf Hitler (1889–1945) the racial interpretation of history and the faith in the Germans as its chosen people became an obsessive passion. This passion explains the great attraction of his oratory for so many Germans. It is expressed also in his book *Mein Kampf*. He wrote its first volume during a brief term of a very mild imprisonment to which he was sentenced after his unsuccessful uprising of November 9, 1923, and the second volume in the fall of 1926. He dedicated it to the memory of the sixteen Nazis killed in the uprising. The book partly described in a somehow legendary fashion Hitler's youth and early activities, and partly displayed the "theories" of his racial and pan-German movement.

Hitler was born in the German-speaking part of the multi-ethnic Austrian monarchy, which he hated. He started his book by proclaiming that people of common descent belong in a common state. At the outbreak of the war of 1914 Hitler, then living in Munich, joined the German army, in which he served throughout the war. It is interesting that Hitler stressed the German people's eagerness to go to war in 1914. The war of 1914, he wrote, probably this time correctly, "was not forced upon the [German] masses, Good God! but desired by the entire people itself. . . . To me personally those hours [of August, 1914] appeared like the redemption from the annoying moods of my youth. Therefore . . . overwhelmed by impassionate enthusiasm, I fell on my knees and thanked Heaven out of my overflowing heart that it had granted me the good fortune of being allowed to live in these times." The greater was Hitler's and Germany's disappointment when the welcome war and the far-reaching dreams of dominion connected with victory were lost.

Hitler explained in *Mein Kampf* that the war was lost by German weakness at home and by poor leadership. He promised the Germans that by racialism at home and under his leadership Germany would become invincible and the master of the world. But Hitler's war ended in greater disaster for

Germany than the war of 1914. Racialism proved a poor guide for the understanding of historical forces.[9]

A. *Nation and Race*

Just as little as Nature desires a mating between weaker individuals and stronger ones, far less she desires the mixing of a higher race with a lower one, as in this case her entire work of higher breeding, which has perhaps taken hundreds of thousands of years, would tumble at one blow.

Historical experience offers countless proofs of this. It shows with terrible clarity that with any mixing of the blood of the Aryan with lower races the result was the end of the culture-bearer. North America, the population of which consists for the greatest part of Germanic elements—which mix only very little with the lower, colored races—displays a humanity and a culture different from those of Central and South America, where chiefly the Romanic immigrants have sometimes mixed with the aborigines on a large scale. By this example alone one may clearly and distinctly recognize the influence of the race mixture. The Germanic of the North American continent, who has remained pure and less intermixed, has become the master of that continent; he will remain so until he, too, falls victim to the shame of blood-mixing.

The result of any crossing, in brief, is always the following:

(a) Lowering of the standard of the higher race,

(b) Physical and mental regression, and, with it, the beginning of a slowly but steadily progressive lingering illness.

To bring about such a development means nothing less than sinning against the will of the Eternal Creator.

This action, then, is also rewarded as a sin.

Man, by trying to resist this iron logic of Nature, becomes entangled in a fight against the principles to which alone he, too, owes his existence as a human being. Thus his attack is bound to lead to his own doom.

Of course, now comes the typically Jewish, impudent, but just as stupid, objection by the modern pacifist: "Man conquers Nature!" . . .

Everything that today we admire on this earth—science and

[9] The following excerpts are from chapter XI ("Nation and Race") of vol. I (A) and from chapters XIII ("German Policy of Alliance after the War"), XIV ("Eastern Orientation or Eastern Policy"), and XV ("Emergency Defense as a Right") of vol. II (B). They are reprinted by permission from the complete and unabridged translation of *Mein Kampf* published by Reynal and Hitchcock (New York, 1940), copyright 1939, Houghton Mifflin Company.

art, technique and inventions—is only the creative product of a few peoples and perhaps originally of *one* race. On them now depends also the existence of this entire culture. If they perish, then the beauty of this earth sinks into the grave with them. . . .

If one were to divide mankind into three groups: culture-founders, culture-bearers, and culture-destroyers, then, as representative of the first kind, only the Aryan would come in question. . . .

Therefore, it is no accident that the first cultures originated in those places where the Aryan, by meeting lower peoples, subdued them and made them subject to his will. They, then, were the first technical instrument in the service of a growing culture.

With this the way that the Aryan had to go was clearly lined out. As a conqueror he subjected the lower peoples and then he regulated their practical ability according to his command and his will and for his aims. But while he thus led them towards a useful, though hard activity, he not only spared the lives of the subjected, but perhaps he even gave them a fate which was better than that of their former so-called "freedom." As long as he kept up ruthlessly the master's standpoint, he not only really remained "master" but also the preserver and propagator of the culture. For the latter was based exclusively on his abilities, and, with it, on his preservation in purity. But as soon as the subjected peoples themselves began to rise (probably) and approached the conqueror linguistically, the sharp separating wall between master and slave fell. The Aryan gave up the purity of his blood and therefore he also lost his place in the Paradise which he had created for himself. . . .

The blood-mixing, with the lowering of the racial level caused by it, is the sole cause of the dying-off of old cultures; for the people do not perish by lost wars, but by the loss of that force of resistance which is contained only in the pure blood.

All that is not race in this world is trash. . . .

The Jew forms the strongest contrast to the Aryan. Hardly in any people of the world is the instinct of self-preservation more strongly developed than in the so-called "chosen-people." The fact of the existence of this race alone may be looked upon as the best proof of this. Where is the people that in the past two thousand years has been exposed to so small changes of the inner disposition, of character, etc., as the Jewish people? Which people finally has experienced greater changes than this one—and yet has always come forth the same from the most colossal catastrophes of mankind? What an infinitely persistent will for life, for preserving the race do these facts disclose! . . .

The Jews were always a people with definite racial qualities and never a religion, only their progress made them probably look very early for a means which could divert disagreeable attention from their person. . . .

Upon this first and greatest lie, that the Jew is not a race but simply a religion, further lies are then built up in necessary consequence. To them, also belongs the language spoken at the time by the Jew. For him it is never a means of expressing his thoughts, but for hiding them. When he speaks French, he thinks Jewish, and when he turns out German poetry, he only gives an outlet to the nature of his people. . . .

. . . Thus, despite all disgraceful actions of the Courts, the people instinctively sees in the Jew the alien elements in its own body and it takes a corresponding attitude towards him.

This was to become different now. In the course of a thousand years he has learned to master the language of his host people to such an extent as to believe that he can in the future risk to accent his Judaism a little less and to put his "Germanity" more into the foreground; for no matter how ridiculous, nay, absurd, it may seem at first, yet he permits himself the impudence of changing himself into a "Germanic"; in this case therefore a "German." Thereby begins one of the most infamous lies conceivable. Since of Germanity he possesses really nothing but the ability to speak its language badly in the most terrible manner, since for the rest, however, he never blended with it, therefore his whole Germanity rests only on the language. The race, however, is not based upon the language, but upon the blood exclusively, something that nobody knows better than the Jew, who puts only very little value upon the preservation of his language, but everything on the preservation of the purity of his blood. One can change the language of a man without ado, that means he can use another language; but then he will express his old thoughts in his new language, his inner nature will not be changed. This is shown best of all by the Jew who is able to speak in a thousand languages and yet remain always the one Jew. . . .

. . . Thus he applies all knowledge which he takes in in the schools of the others, only to the service of his race.

This nationality, however, he guards as never before. While he seems to overflow with "enlightenment," "progress," "freedom," "humanity," etc., he exercises the strictest seclusion of his race. Although he sometimes hangs his women onto the coattails of influential Christians, yet he always keeps his male line pure in principle. He poisons the blood of the others, but he guards his own. The Jew does not marry a Christian woman, but always the Christian a Jewess. Yet the bastards take to the Jewish side. Especially a part of the higher nobility degrades itself completely.

He knows this only too well, and for this reason he systematically carries out this kind of "disarmament" of the spiritually leading class of his racial adversaries. Yet, in order to disguise his activity and to put his victims to sleep, he speaks now more and more of the equality of all men, without consideration of race and of color. And those who are stupid begin to believe him. . . .

If we let all the causes of the German collapse pass before our eyes, there remains as the ultimate and decisive cause the non-recognition of the race problem and especially of the Jewish danger.

The defeats in the battlefield of August, 1918, would have been easily bearable. They were out of proportion to the victories of our people. Not the defeats have overthrown us, but we were overthrown by that power which prepared these defeats by robbing our people systematically, for many decades, of its political and moral instincts and forces which alone enable and entitle peoples to exist in this world.

All really important symptoms of decay of the pre-War time ultimately go back to racial causes. . . .

Therefore, in August, 1914, it was not a people, determined to attack, which rushed to the battlefield, but what took place was only the last flaring-up of the national instinct of self-preservation in face of the progressing pacifist Marxist paralyzation of our national body. As even in those fateful days one did not recognize the internal enemy, all outward resistance was in vain, and Providence gave the reward, not to the victorious sword, but it followed the law of eternal revenge.

Out of this inner realization there were to be formed for us the leading principles, as well as the tendency of the new movement which alone, in our conviction, was enabled to bring the decline of the German people not only to a standstill, but also to create the granite foundation upon which one day there can exist a State which represents not a mechanism of economic considerations and interests, alien to the people, but a folkish organism: *A Germanic State of the German Nation.*

B. Foreign Policies

The most essential maxim and guiding principle which must always shine before us in estimating this matter is that foreign policy, too, is only a means to an end, but the end must be exclusively the advancement of our own nationality. No consideration of foreign policy can be guided by any point of view but this: *Does it benefit our nation now or in the future, or will it be harmful to it?*

This is the sole preconceived opinion permitted in dealing with this question. Partisan, religious, humanitarian, and all other points of view in general are completely beside the point.

If, before the War, the task of German foreign policy was to guarantee the sustenance of our nation and its children on this globe through the preparation of ways which could lead to this goal, as well as the winning of the auxiliary forces necessary thereto in the form of suitable allies, then today it is the same, with only one difference: *Before the War it was necessary to serve the preservation of the German nationality, having in mind a certain available force of the independent free power State; today it is imperative first to restore to the people, in the form of the free power State, that strength which is the presumption for the later carrying-out of a practical foreign policy signifying the maintenance, promotion, and sustenance of our people for the future.*

In other words: *The goal of a German foreign policy of today must be the preparation of the reconquest of freedom for tomorrow.*

Moreover, one thing above all must be kept in mind as a directive: *A nation's chance of reconquering its independence is not absolutely bound up with the integrity of a State territory, but rather with the existence of a never so small remnant of this nation and State which, having the necessary freedom, has it in its power to be not only the bearer of the spiritual communion of the entire nationality, but also the preparer of the military struggle for freedom.*

If a people of one hundred million men, to protect the State's integrity, jointly tolerates the yoke of slavery, then that is worse than if such a State and such a people had been demolished and only a part of it could remain in possession of full freedom, of course on condition that this last remnant were filled with the sacred mission not only constantly to proclaim spiritual and cultural inseparability, but also to achieve the armed preparation for final liberation and the reuniting of the unhappy oppressed portions with the motherland.

It should further be noted that the question of the regaining of lost portions of territory of a people and State is always in the first instance the question of regaining the political power and independence of the motherland; that consequently in such a case the interests of the lost regions as compared with the sole interest of the regaining of the freedom of the main territory must be unhesitatingly set aside. For the liberation of oppressed, since separated splinters of a nationality or province of a realm takes place, not on the basis of a desire of the oppressed or a protest of those remaining behind, but through the instruments of power of those remnants of the former common fatherland which have remained more or less sovereign.

Consequently, the premise for the winning of lost territories is the intensive advancement and strengthening of the remaining remnant State as well as the unshakable decision, slumbering in the heart, to consecrate at the given moment to the service of the liberation and unification of the whole nation that new force, forming itself through this process: that is, *setting aside* the interests of the separated regions as opposed to the sole interest of winning for the remaining remnant that measure of political power and strength which is the premise for a rectification of the will of a hostile victor. *For oppressed countries will not be brought back into the bosom of a common Reich by means of fiery protests, but by a mighty sword.*

To forge this sword is the task of the domestic political leadership of a people; to guard the work of forging and to seek comrades in arms is the task of the foreign-policy leadership.

Whoever undertakes, from the above viewpoint, an estimate of the present *possibilities of an alliance* for Germany must reach the conviction that the last practicable tie remaining is only *English* support. However horrible the results of English war policy were and are for Germany, one must not ignore the view that there is *today* no longer a necessary English interest in *crushing* Germany, but that, on the contrary, England's desire must from year to year be increasingly for a limitation of the unbounded French drive for hegemony. . . .

Practical application for today can, consequently, mean only: *which States at the moment have no vital interest in French economic and military power achieving an absolute ruling position of hegemony by means of the total elimination of a German Middle Europe, yes, which States, owing to their instinct of self-preservation and their previous traditional political rule, would see in such a development a threat to their own future.*

Because we must at last become entirely clear about this: the German people's irreconcilable mortal enemy is and remains France. It does not matter who ruled or who will rule in France, whether Bourbons or Jacobins, Bonapartists or *bourgeois* democrats, clerical republicans or red Bolsheviks, the final goal of her foreign-policy activity would always be an effort to hold the Rhine frontier and to guarantee this stream by means of a disintegrated and dismembered Germany.

England desires no German world power, but France desires no power at all called Germany: a really quite essential difference.

Today, however, we are not fighting for position as a world power, but we must struggle for the existence of our fatherland, our national unity, and for daily bread for our children. If, with this viewpoint, we want to keep our eyes open for European allies, then there remain practically two States: *England and Italy.*

England does not want a France whose military might, unchecked by the rest of Europe, can undertake to push a policy which, one way or another, must some day cross English interests. England can never desire a France which, by possessing the enormous western European iron and coal deposits, has the premises of a threatening world economic status. And England, further, can never desire a France whose continental political status, thanks to the smashing of the rest of Europe, seems so secure that the resumption of a broader line of French world policy is not only made possible but actually forced. The Zeppelin bombs of another day could multiply a thousandfold any night: the military predominance of France weighs heavy on the heart of the British Empire.

But Italy, too, can and would not desire further reinforcement of French superiority in Europe. Italy's future must always lie in a development territorially centered in the Mediterranean Basin. What Italy pursued in the War was not really a desire to see France made greater, but rather the object of giving a deathblow to her hated rivals in the Adriatic. Every added continental reinforcement of France means, nevertheless, a future restriction on Italy, and thereupon let nobody deceive himself—kinship relations among nations cannot at all eliminate rivalries. . . .

There are two reasons which induce me to subject the relations of Germany to Russia to a special examination:

(1) In this case we are concerned with perhaps the most decisive matter of German foreign affairs as a whole; and

(2) this question is also the touchstone of the political capacity of the young National Socialist movement to think clearly and to act correctly. . . .

The foreign policy of a folkish State is charged with guaranteeing the existence on this planet of the race embraced by the State, by establishing between the number and growth of the population, on the one hand, and the size and value of the soil and territory, on the other hand, a viable, natural relationship.

Only a sufficiently extensive area on this globe guarantees a nation freedom of existence. . . .

Hence the German people can defend its future only as a world power. For almost two thousand years the defense of our nation's interests, as we shall term our more or less happy foreign policy, was *world history.* We ourselves witnessed this, because the great struggle of the nations in the years 1914–18 was only the German people's struggle for its existence on this planet, although we describe the type of event itself as *World War.* . . .

Looked at purely territorially, the area of the German Reich compared with that of the so-called world powers altogether vanishes. One can really not take England as a standard of comparison, because the English mother country is really only the great capital of the British world empire which calls its own almost a fourth of the entire earth's surface. We must also consider as giant States first of all the American Union, then Russia and China. All magnitudes of greater area, some of them ten times greater than the present-day German Reich. And even France must be counted among these States. Not only because the colored human stock of its enormous empire supplements its army to an ever greater extent, she is racially making such progress in negrofying herself that one can really speak of the establishment of an African State on European soil. The colonial policy of present-day France cannot be compared with that of Germany in the past. Let the development of France continue three centuries more in the present manner, and the last remnants of Frankish blood will have succumbed in the developing European-African mulatto State. A mighty self-contained area of settlement from the Rhine to the Congo filled with an inferior race developing out of continual hybridization. . . .

If the National Socialist movement really desires to be consecrated by history to a great mission for our people, it must, penetrated by knowledge of, and filled with suffering for, her real situation on this earth, valiantly and conscious of its goal, take up the fight against the aimlessness and incompetence which have heretofore guided the German people on the course of foreign affairs. It must, then, without regard to "traditions" and prejudices, find the courage to assemble our people and their might for a march forward on that road which leads out of the present constriction of the domain of life, and hence also permanently liberates from the danger of vanishing off this earth or having to enter the service of others as a slave nation.

The National Socialist Movement must endeavor to eliminate the discrepancy between our population and our area—the latter viewed not only as a source of nourishment, but also as a point of support for power politics—between our historical past and the hopelessness of our impotence today. It must, moreover, remain conscious that we are also obligated to a high duty as the guardians of the highest human race on this earth, and it will be all the more able to fulfill this duty, the more it contrives that the German people recovers its racial sense and, in addition to breeding dogs, horses, and cats, takes mercy on its *own* blood. . . .

Much as we all today recognize the necessity for a reckoning with France, it will remain largely ineffective if our foreign-policy aim is restricted thereto. It has and will retain significance if it provides the rear cover for an enlargement of our national domain of life in Europe. For we will find this question's solution not in colonial acquisitions, but exclusively in the winning of land for settlement which increases the area of the motherland itself, and thereby not only keeps the new settlers in the most intimate community with the land of origin, but insures to the total area those advantages deriving from its united magnitude. . . .

We National Socialists, however, must go further: *the right to soil and territory can become a duty if decline seems to be in store for a great nation unless it extends its territory.* Even more especially if what is involved is not some little Negro people or other, but the German mother of all life, which has given its cultural picture to the contemporary world. *Germany will be either a world power or will not be at all.* To be a world power, however, it requires that size which nowadays gives its necessary importance to such a power, and which gives life to its citizens.

But if we talk about new soil and territory in Europe today, we can think primarily only of *Russia* and its vassal border states.

Fate itself seems to seek to give us a tip at this point. In the surrender of Russia to bolshevism, the Russian people was robbed of that intelligentsia which theretofore produced and guaranteed its State stability. For the organization of a Russian State structure was not the result of Russian Slavdom's State-political capacity, but rather a wonderful example of the State-building activity of the German element in an inferior race. Thus have innumerable mighty empires of the earth been created. Inferior nations with German organizers and lords as leaders have more than once expanded into powerful State structures, and endured as long as the racial nucleus of the constructive State-race maintained itself. For centuries Russia drew nourishment from this Germanic nucleus of its superior strata of leaders. Today it is uprooted and obliterated almost without a trace. The Jew has replaced it. Impossible as it is for the Russians alone to shake off the yoke of the Jews through their own strength, it is equally impossible in the long run for the Jews to maintain the mighty empire. Jewry itself is not an organizing element, but a ferment of decomposition. The Persian Empire, once so powerful, is now ripe for collapse; and the end of Jewish dominion in Russia will also be the end of the Russian State itself. We have been chosen by Fate to be the witnesses of a catastrophe which will be the most powerful substantiation of the correctness of the folkish theory of race. . . .

I still recall the equally childish and incomprehensible hopes that England was facing a collapse in India which suddenly arose in folkish circles in the years 1920–21. Some Asiatic fakir or other, perhaps, for all I care, some real Indian "fighters for freedom", who were then running around Europe, contrived to stuff even otherwise quite intelligent people with the fixed idea that the British Empire, whose keystone is in India, was on the verge of collapse right there. Naturally, it did not occur to them that in this case, too, the father of all thoughts was only their own wish. Equally little the para-doxicality of their own hopes. For, in so far as they expected the end of the British Empire and English power to result from a col-lapse of English rule in India, they admitted themselves that pre-cisely India was of the most paramount importance to England.

This question of the greatest life import, however, would prob-ably be known not only to a German folkish prophet as a most profound secret, but presumably also even to the guides of English destiny themselves. It is really rather childish to assume that in England they do not know how properly to estimate the importance of the Indian Empire for the British world union. And if anybody flatters himself that England will let India go without risking her last drop of blood, that is simply a bad sign of the absolute failure to learn from the World War and the complete misunderstanding and ignorance of Anglo-Saxon determination. It is, furthermore, a proof of the German's total lack of any notion of the whole method of British penetration and administration of this empire. *England will lose India only if it either falls victim to racial degeneration within its own administrative machinery* (something which, at the moment, is entirely excluded in India), *or if it is compelled to by the sword of a powerful enemy.* Indian rebels will, however, never achieve this. We Germans have learned well enough how hard it is to force England. Entirely aside from the fact that, as a German, I would, despite everything, still far rather see India under Eng-lish than under some other rule.

Hopes in the legendary uprising in Egypt are exactly as wretched. The *"Holy War"* can produce in our German muttonheads the pleasant thrill that now others are ready to shed their blood for us—because this cowardly speculation has, to speak bluntly, been the silent father of all such hopes—but in reality it will meet a ghastly end under the fire of English machine-gun companies and the hail of explosive bombs.

It is simply an impossibility for a coalition of cripples to storm a powerful State determined, if need be, to risk the last drop of blood for its existence. As a folkish man, who estimates the value of humanity on racial bases, I may not, simply because of my knowledge of their racial inferiority, link my own nation's fate with that of these so-called "oppressed nations."

But today we must adopt exactly the same attitude with respect to Russia. The former Russia, divested of its German upper stratum, is, entirely aside from its new rulers' private plans, no ally for a struggle of the German nation for freedom. . . .

The danger which once overwhelmed Russia always faces Germany. Only a *bourgeois* simpleton can flatter himself that bolshevism is banished. In this superficial thinking, he has no notion that this is a question of an instinctive matter—*i.e.,* the drive of the Jewish nation to world rule—a matter just as natural as the impulse of the Anglo-Saxons on their side to secure dominion over this earth for themselves. And, just as the Anglo-Saxon pursues this course in his way and fights his struggle with his weapons, so also does the Jew. He pursues his course, the course of sneaking in among the nations and of gouging them internally, and he fights with his weapons, with lies and slanders, poison and destruction, intensifying the struggle to the point of bloodily exterminating his hated opponents. *In Russian bolshevism we must see Jewry's twentieth-century effort to take the world dominion unto itself,* just as it sought to strive towards the same goal in other periods by other, if inwardly related, doings. Its effort is most profoundly based on the nature of its essence. As little as any other nation renounces of its own volition to yield to its impulse towards expanding its nature and power, but must be forced to do so by external relations or falls into senile impotence, so little also will the Jew abandon his course towards world dictatorship by voluntary self-denial or by suppressing his eternal drive. He, too, must be thrown back in his course either by forces lying outside himself or all his impulse towards world rule must be finished by dying of itself. The impotence of nations, their own death of old age, however, comes from the abandonment of their purity of blood. And the Jew guards this better than any other people of the earth. Thereby he continues to move farther on his fatal course, until another force opposes him and, in a mighty struggle, once more pitches the stormer of the heavens back to Lucifer.

Germany is today the next great battle aim of bolshevism. It requires all the force of a young missionary idea once again to inspire our nation to break out of the snare of this international snake and internally to check the tainting of our blood, so that the nation's forces can thereby be devoted to the securing of our nationality, which may make it possible to prevent a repetition of the final catastrophe until the end of time. . . .

. . . *Neither western nor eastern orientation should be the future goal of our foreign policy, but an eastern policy signifying the acquisition of the necessary soil for our German people. Since we need strength for this, but the mortal enemy of our nation, France, relentlessly throttles us and robs our strength, we must undertake every sacrifice which may help bring about a nullification of the French drive for European hegemony. Every power which, like us, finds intolerable France's aspiration to dominion over the continent, is today our natural ally. No path to such a power must seem too difficult to us and no renunciation must seem unspeakable if the end result only offers the possibility of subduing our most enraged enemies.* Once we have been able to cauterize and close the biggest, we will calmly be able to leave to the gentle ministrations of time the healing of our little wounds. . . .

. . . I do not believe for a moment that France's intentions with respect to us can ever change; because they have their deepest motive nowhere but in the French nation's sense of self-preservation. Were I a Frenchman myself, and were France's greatness as dear to me as is Germany's sacred, then I could and would not act otherwise than Clemenceau himself did in the end. Only through the obliteration of Germany can a France, which is slowly withering, not only in its population figures, but especially in its racially best elements, maintain its world importance in the long run. French policy may make a thousand detours, but somewhere at the end will always be this goal as the realization of its last desire and deepest yearning. But it is wrong to believe that a purely *passive* will, seeking only self-preservation, can in the long run offer resistance to a not less powerful but *actively* advancing will. *As long as the eternal conflict between Germany and France is carried on only in the form of a German defense against French attack, it will never be decided, but Germany, from century to century, will lose one position after the other. . . .*

Only when this is fully understood in Germany so that the German nation's will to live is no longer allowed to waste itself in purely passive defensiveness, but is drawn together for a decisive, active settlement with France, and is thrown into a final, decisive battle for the vastest German final goals: only then will it be possible to bring to a conclusion our eternal struggle with France, in itself so fruitless; on condition, of course, that Germany really sees in France's destruction a means of subsequently and finally giving our nation a chance to expand elsewhere. Today we are eighty million Germans in Europe! That foreign policy will be acknowledged as correct only if, a bare century from now, two hundred and fifty million Germans are living on this continent, and then not squeezed together as factory coolies for the rest of the world, but as peasants and workers mutually guaranteeing each other's life by their productivity. . . .

Just as in the year 1918 bloody vengeance was taken for the fact that in 1914 and 1915 we did not proceed to crush the head of the Marxist serpent underfoot, so, too, the most tragic vengeance would be taken if in the spring of 1923 the opportunity was not seized to forbid the exercise of their craft to the Marxist traitors and national murderers. . . .

Then did I know in my very heart that the German *bourgeoisie* had reached the end of its mission and is called to no further task. Then did I see how all these parties were squabbling with Marxism only because of competitive jealousy without seriously seeking to annihilate it; they had finally reconciled themselves inwardly with the fatherland's general decline, and what moved them was only a deep concern that they themselves have a place at the wake. It was for that alone that they were still "struggling."

In those days—I admit it openly—I conceived the most profound admiration for that great man south of the Alps who, full of ardent love for his people, would not deal with the internal enemies of Italy, but pushed their annihilation in every way and by all means. What will rank Mussolini among the great of this earth is the determination not to share Italy with Marxism, but to save the fatherland from it by dooming internationalism to annihilation.

How wretchedly dwarfish our German State yes-men appeared in contrast, and how nauseating it is when these nonentities undertake, with boorish conceit, to criticize a man a thousand times as great; and how painful it is to think that this goes on in a country which, barely half a century ago, might still call a Bismarck its leader!

The fate of any active Ruhr resistance in 1923 was decided in advance because of this *bourgeois* attitude and tenderness towards Marxism. To want to fight France with the deadly enemy in one's own ranks would have been pure idiocy. What was then done was shadowboxing at best, undertaken in order to give some satisfaction to the nationalist element in Germany, to calm the "seething national soul", in reality to dupe it. Had there been serious thought about what was being done, it must have been recognized that a nation's strength lies primarily not in its weapons but in its will, and that, before conquering alien foes, the domestic foe must be wiped out; otherwise, should victory not reward the first day of the struggle, beware. . . .

. . . A Germany liberated from Marxism, this deadly enemy of its existence and its future, would have possessed a potency which not even the whole world could longer have strangled. *On the day when Marxism is smashed in Germany, its chains will really be broken forever.* For never in our history have we been conquered by the force of our foes, but always by our own vices and the enemy in our own camp alone.

C. Conclusion

On November 9, 1923, in the fourth year of its existence, the National Socialist German Workers' Party was dissolved and forbidden throughout the entire territory of the Reich. Today, in November, 1926, it stands again before us, free through the whole Reich, stronger and internally more stable than ever before.

Not all the persecutions of the movement and of its individual leaders, not all the defamations and slanders, have been able to do it any harm. The correctness of its ideas, the purity of its purposes, the readiness of its adherents to sacrifice, have thus far enabled it to emerge from all oppressions stronger than ever.

If, in the world of our contemporary parliamentary corruption, it attends more and more to the deepest meaning of its struggle and feels itself and conducts itself as the pure embodiment of the values of race and personality, it will, in consequence of an almost mathematical law, some day bear victory from its struggle. Just as Germany must inevitably win its rightful place on this earth, should it be led and organized on similar principles.

A State which, in the epoch of race poisoning, dedicates itself to the cherishing of its best racial elements, must some day be master of the world.

Let the adherents of our movement never forget this, should ever the greatness of the sacrifice lead them to a fearful comparison with the possible triumph.

35. WOODROW WILSON'S FOURTEEN POINTS

On January 8, 1918, Woodrow Wilson (1856–1924), the twenty-eighth president of the United States, read before a joint session of Congress a declaration defining "the only possible programme" of world peace. The introduction gave a succinct summary of the reasons, as Wilson saw them, for the entrance of the United States into the "Great European War" (April, 1917), which thereby became the (First) World War. The entrance of the United States into the war gained in importance by the fact that it followed by only one month the democratic Russian Revolution of March, 1917.

Except for the first three points, the programme, as developed by Wilson, was eminently sound. As far as changed circumstances beyond the control of the United States and the Allied powers—e.g., the disintegration of the Austrian empire in October, 1917—and the various bitterly competing national claims allowed (especially on the part of the newly liberated European nations), Wilson's programme on the whole served as a basic outline for the Peace Treaty of Versailles (June 28, 1919).

Its main points were the abandonment of German conquests and of German control of non-German subject peoples (Alsace-Lorraine, Poles, and Danes), the emphasis on national autonomy and self-determination for subject peoples, the establishment of collective security through the League of Nations, and special consideration for the interests and rights of colonial populations. To this the Peace Treaty added, in Article XIII, the creation of an International Labor Office, declaring the well-being of the working class everywhere a concern of all mankind. By these principles, above all by the creation and central role of the League of Nations and of the International Labor Office, the peace treaty of 1919 showed definitive progress compared with previous peace settlements and pointed toward a future which did not become generally accepted until forty years later. The Fourteen Points implied also an abandonment of the traditional isolationism of the United States and the recognition of the new interdependence of all mankind.[9]

We entered this war because violations of right had occurred which touched us to the quick and made the life of our own people impossible unless they were corrected and the world secured once for all against their recurrence. What we demand in this war, therefore, is nothing peculiar to ourselves. It is that the world be made fit and safe to live in; and particularly that it be made safe for every peace-loving nation which, like our own, wishes to live its own life, determine its own institutions, be assured of justice and fair dealing by the other peoples of the world as against force and selfish aggression. All the peoples of the world are in effect partners

[9] *The Messages and Papers of Woodrow Wilson* (New York: The Review of Reviews Corporation, 1924), 2 vols., vol. I, pp. 464 ff.

in this interest, and for our own part we see very clearly that unless justice be done to others it will not be done to us. The programme of the world's peace, therefore, is our programme; and that programme, the only possibly programme, as we see it, is this:

I. Open covenants of peace, openly arrived at, after which there shall be no private international understandings of any kind but diplomacy shall proceed always frankly and in the public view.

II. Absolute freedom of navigation upon the seas, outside territorial waters, alike in peace and in war, except as the seas may be closed in whole or in part by international action for the enforcement of international covenants.

III. The removal, so far as possible, of all economic barriers and the establishment of an equality of trade conditions among all the nations consenting to the peace and associating themselves for its maintenance.

IV. Adequate guarantees given and taken that national armaments will be reduced to the lowest point consistent with domestic safety.

V. A free, open-minded, and absolutely impartial adjustment of all colonial claims, based upon a strict observance of the principle that in determining all such questions of sovereignty the interests of the populations concerned must have equal weight with the equitable claims of the government whose title is to be determined.

VI. The evacuation of all Russian territory and such a settlement of all questions affecting Russia as will secure the best and freest cooperation of the other nations of the world in obtaining for her an unhampered and unembarrassed opportunity for the independent determination of her own political development and national policy and assure her of a sincere welcome into the society of free nations under institutions of her own choosing; and, more than a welcome, assistance also of every kind that she may need and may herself desire. The treatment accorded Russia by her sister nations in the months to come will be the acid test of their good will, of their comprehension of her needs as distinguished from their own interests, and of their intelligent and unselfish sympathy.

VII. Belgium, the whole world will agree, must be evacuated and restored, without any attempt to limit the sovereignty which she enjoys in common with all other free nations. No other single act will serve as this will serve to restore confidence among the nations in the laws which they have themselves set and determined for the government of their relations with one another. Without this healing act the whole structure and validity of international law is forever impaired.

VIII. All French territory should be freed and the invaded portions restored, and the wrong done to France by Prussia in 1871 in the matter of Alsace-Lorraine, which has unsettled the peace of the world for nearly fifty years, should be righted, in order that peace may once more be made secure in the interest of all.

IX. A readjustment of the frontiers of Italy should be affected along clearly recognizable lines of nationality.

X. The peoples of Austria-Hungary, whose place among the nations we wish to see safeguarded and assured, should be accorded the freest opportunity of autonomous development.

XI. Rumania, Serbia, and Montenegro should be evacuated; occupied territories restored; Serbia accorded free and secure access to the sea; and the relations of the several Balkan states to one another determined by friendly counsel along historically established lines of allegiance and nationality; and international guarantees of the political and economic independence and territorial integrity of the several Balkan states should be entered into.

XII. The Turkish portions of the present Ottoman Empire should be assured a secure sovereignty, but the other nationalities which are now under Turkish rule should be assured an undoubted security of life and an absolutely unmolested opportunity of autonomous development, and the Dardanelles should be permanently opened as a free passage to the ships and commerce of all nations under international guarantees.

XIII. An independent Polish state should be erected which should include the territories inhabited by indisputably Polish populations, which should be assured a free and secure access to the sea, and whose political and economic independence and territorial integrity should be guaranteed by international covenant.

XIV. A general association of nations must be formed under specific covenants for the purpose of affording mutual guarantees of political independence and territorial integrity to great and small states alike.

In regard to these essential rectifications of wrong and assertions of right we feel ourselves to be intimate partners of all the governments and peoples associated together against the Imperialists. We cannot be separate in interest or divided in purpose. We stand together until the end.

36. J. C. SMUTS: *THE LEAGUE OF NATIONS*

The League of Nations was one of the few encouraging outcomes of the First World War. The British Foreign Office submitted in the autumn of 1916 a memorandum to the prime minister in which they proposed the creation of such a league:

We are under no illusion that such an instrument will become really effective until nations have learned to subordinate their personal and individual ambitions and dreams for the benefit of the community of nations. We have witnessed such a process in individual states with the development of what we call a civilized condition of things, but this process has been of slow growth, and we shall have to exercise considerable patience in watching and promoting a similar development among the nations of the world. This consideration brings up the question of whether it will be possible to secure the adhesion of the United States of America. . . . If America could be persuaded to associate itself to such a League of Nations, a weight and influence might be secured for its decisions that would materially promote the object for which it had been created.

Woodrow Wilson took up and sponsored the idea of a League of Nations in his Fourteen Points. The most thorough analysis of its purpose was written in December, 1918, by J. C. Smuts in the pamphlet *The League of Nations, A Practical Suggestion.*[10]

Jan Christiaan Smuts (1870–1950), a South African statesman, general, and lawyer, fought on the Boer side in the war, but after its conclusion he became a protagonist of Boer-British reconciliation. After the establishment of the Union of South Africa (1910) he became a member of the Cabinet and, from 1917 on, served in the Imperial War Cabinet in London. He was one of the fathers of the concept of the British Commonwealth of Nations. In 1945 he participated as South African delegate in the United Nations conference in San Francisco.

An attempt will be made in this sketch to give an essential extension to the functions of the League; indeed to look upon the League from a very different point of view, to view it not only as a possible means for preventing future wars, but much more as a great organ of the ordinary peaceful life of civilization, as the foundation of the new international system which will be erected on the ruins of this war, and as the starting point from which the peace arrangements of the forthcoming Conference should be made. Such an orientation of the idea seems to me necessary if the League is to become a permanent part of our international machinery. It is not sufficient for the League merely to be a sort of deus ex machina, called in in very grave emergencies when the spectre of war appears;

---

[10] London: Hodder & Stoughton, 1918.

if it is to last, it must be much more. It must become part and parcel of the common international life of States, it must be an ever visible, living, working organ of the polity of civilization. It must function so strongly in the ordinary peaceful intercourse of States that it becomes irresistible in their disputes; its peace activity must be the foundation and guarantee of its war power. How would it be possible to build the League so closely into the fabric of our international system?

I would put the position broadly as follows: The process of civilization has always been towards the League of Nations. The grouping or fusion of tribes into a national State is not a case in point. But the political movement has often gone beyond that. The national State has too often been the exception. Nations in their march to power tend to pass the purely national bounds; hence arise the Empires which embrace various nations, sometimes related in blood and institutions, sometimes again different in race and hostile in temperament. In a rudimentary way such composite Empires of the past were leagues of nations, keeping the peace among the constituent nations, but unfortunately doing so not on the basis of freedom but of repression. Usually one dominant nation in the group overcame, coerced, and kept the rest under. The principle of nationality became over-strained and over-developed, and nourished itself by exploiting other weaker nationalities. Nationality over-grown became Imperialism, and the Empire led a troubled existence on the ruin of the freedom of its constituent nations. That was the evil of the system; but with however much friction and oppression the peace was usually kept among the nations falling within the Empire. These empires have all broken down, and today the British Commonwealth of Nations remains the only embryo league of nations because it is based on the true principles of national freedom and political decentralization. . . .

The attempt to form empires or leagues of nations on the basis of inequality and the bondage and oppression of the smaller national units has failed, and the work has to be done all over again on a new basis and an enormous scale. The vast elemental forces liberated by this war, even more than the war itself, have been responsible for this great change. . . . The creative process in the political movement of humanity cannot be paralysed; the materials lie ready for a new reconstructive task, to which, let us hope, the courage and genius of Western civilization will prove equal. . . . Europe is being liquidated, and the League of Nations must be the heir to this great estate. . . . Surely the only statesmanlike course is to make the League of Nations the reversionary in the broadest sense of these Empires. In this debacle of the old Europe the League of Nations is no longer an outsider or stranger, but the natural master of the house. It becomes naturally and obviously the solvent for a problem which no other means will solve. . . .

The horrors and sufferings of this war have produced a temper in the peoples which must be reckoned with as the fundamental fact of the political situation in Europe today. The feeling of grief, bitterness, disillusion, despair goes very deep; even in the victorious Entente countries that feeling goes much deeper than the more superficial feeling of joy at the final result. How could it be otherwise? The prolonged horror through which all have passed is a far more real, abiding and fundamental experience than the momentary joy at the end. What has reconciled our Entente peoples to the burdens they were enduring? It was their consciousness of right and their vague hope of a better, fairer world to come which would justify their sacrifices. But if that prospect is rudely blotted out; if the peace really comes, not in the settlement of universal human principles and the dawning of a better order, but in a return of the old policy of grab and greed and partitions, then the bitterness of the disillusion would indeed be complete. . . . Let not that faith be shattered at the peace. Let the peace be founded in human ideals, in principles of freedom and equality, and in institutions which will for the future guarantee those principles against wanton assault. Only such a peace would be statesmanlike and assure lasting victory. Any other might open the fountains of the deep and overwhelm victor and vanquished alike in the coming flood. . . .

In fact, I would be prepared to go further, and to submit for consideration that this non-military policy should be applied to all independent States arising from the break-up of the old European system. If we are deliberately deciding in favor of a peaceful regime for the future, it seems to me a fair proposition that all newly-arising States shall conform to the new order of ideas, and shall agree, as a condition of their recognition and admission into the League of Nations to raise no military forces and collect no armaments beyond what the League may lay down as reasonable in their case. The result will be that militarism will be scotched ab initio in the case of all new States, and a vast impetus will be given to the peace movement all over the world. In such case it will also be much easier for the older States and Powers to adopt a policy of disarmament and reduction of military forces, and the new peaceful policy will become identified with the very constitution of the new order of things. Practically all the independent States arising from the decomposition of Russia, Austria, Turkey, and, perhaps, even Germany, will then have to adopt the new policy, and thereby help to entrench peace in the new political system of Europe. It is an idea which seems to me well worthy of our consideration, as more likely to preserve peace than more ambitious measures adopted to keep well-armed and militarily equipped States from coming to blows. . . .

Many of the States which will arise from the break-up of the Empires will be able to look after their own affairs as new independent States, and will not require any administrative assistance or control. Any questions arising out of their origin and existence will be dealt with by the League itself without delegation to individual Powers. A gigantic task will thereby be imposed on the League as the successor of the Empires. The animosities and rivalries among the independent Balkan States in the past, which kept that pot boiling, and occasionally boiling over, will serve to remind us that there is the risk of a similar state of affairs arising on a much larger scale in the new Europe, covered as it will be with small independent States. In the past the Empires kept the peace among their rival nationalities; the League will have to keep the peace among the new States formed from these nationalities. That will impose a task of constant and vigilant supervision on it. The nationalities of Europe are, in many cases, animated by historic hostility to one another, the tendency will be for them to fly at one another's throats on very slight provocation, and we have had sad experience of the danger of a general conflagration which arises from these local outbursts. It is important to bear in mind that but for the active control of the League, the danger of future wars will be actually greater, because of the multitudinous discordant States now arisen or arising. In this and many other respects the League will have a very real role to play as the successor to the Empires. It will have to deal in advance with all the numerous sources of trouble and friction which will continue to exist among the small independent nations. Without unnecessary or undue interference in their internal affairs, it will have to watch over their relations inter se, and any internal conditions or situations which will directly affect those relations. . . .

It is not improbable that this supervision of the new European States will impose the heaviest task of all on the League of Nations, at any rate for this generation. But it will have to be performed efficiently, as there is little doubt that the old historic feuds surviving among the European nationalities may easily become a fruitful source of future danger. If the League is ever to be a reality, it will have to succeed in this great task. And it will succeed, if it takes itself seriously and looks upon itself, not as a merely nominal, but as a real live active heir to the former Empires, and is determined to discharge the duties of the great beneficent position which has devolved upon it as supreme guardian of the peace interests of humanity. . . .

Europe requires a liquidator or trustee of the bankrupt estate, and only a body like the League could adequately perform that gigantic task.

I am very conscious of the grave defects of the programme for a League of Nations here sketched. But my object is not to produce a complete scheme. That would be a vain and impossible task. My object is to sketch a scheme which will be workable in practice and which, while preventing a scramble among the Powers for loot, will not be so far in advance of the existing political practice of Europe as to make cautious statesmen reject it at once. My object further is to base that scheme on the recognition of the principles which I consider vital. A modest beginning on the right basis and on the right principles will enable the future to give full development of form and substance to the whole system. The vital principles are: the principle of nationality involving the ideas of political freedom and equality; the principle of autonomy, which is the principle of nationality extended to peoples not yet capable of complete independent statehood; the principle of political decentralisation, which will prevent the powerful nationality from swallowing the weak autonomy as has so often happened in the now defunct European Empires; and finally an institution like the League of Nations, which will give stability to that decentralisation and thereby guarantee the weak against the strong. The only compromise I make, and make partly to conciliate the great Powers and partly in view of the administrative inexperience of the League at the beginning, is the concession that, subject to the authority and control of the League, which I mean to be real and effective, suitable Powers may be appointed to act as mandataries of the League in the more backward peoples and areas. That compromise will, I hope, prove to be only a temporary expedient. . . .

I have advocated the view that the League should occupy the vacant place left by the disappearance of those Empires. The greatest opportunity in history would be met by the greatest step forward in the government of man. On the debris of the old dead world would be built at once the enduring Temple of future world-government. The new creative peace world would come to us, not as a fleeting visitant from some other clime, but out of the very ruins of our own dead past. . . .

Now in discussing a problem like the Constitution of the League of Nations we must be careful not to set too much store on past precedents. Our problem is gigantic and entirely novel; its solution will depend, not so much on following precedents never meant for such a novel and complex situation, but in boldly facing that situation and, if need be, creating a new precedent to meet it. The grand success of the British Empire depends not on its having followed any constitutional precedent of the past but on having met a new situation in history with a new creation in law; and as a matter of fact the new constitutional system grew empirically and organically out of the practical necessities of the colonial situation. So it will have to be here. And above all let us avoid cut-and-dried schemes meant as a complete, definitive, and final solution of our problem. Let us remember that we are only asked to make a beginning, so long as that beginning is in the right direction; that great works are not made but grow; and that our Constitution should avoid all rigidity, should be elastic and capable of growth, expansion, and adaptation to the needs which the new organ of government will have to meet in the process of the years. Above all it must be practical and be so devised as to be a real working organ of government.

And from this point of view let us proceed at once to discard the idea of a super-State which is in the minds of some people. No new super-sovereign is wanted in the new world now arising. States will here be controlled not by compulsion from above but by consent from below. Government by consent of the governed is our formula. The old Empires were ruined by their theories of sovereignty, which meant centralisation, absorption and denationalisation of the weaker national constituents of the population. The great League of Nations, like the lesser league already existing in the British Empire, will have to avoid the old legal concepts of Imperialism in the new world of Freedom. . . .

The League will never be a great success until there is formed as its main support a powerful international public opinion. With that public opinion behind it, it may go confidently forward with its great tasks; deprived of that support all its power for good will be neutralised and nullified. It is therefore essential that it should create a favourable international atmosphere for its work, that an organized public opinion should be formed in favour of the League and its activities. The enlightened public all over the world will have to be taught to think internationally, to look at public affairs, not merely from the sectional national point of view, but also from a broad human international point of view. And the debates periodically taking place in the General Conference [possibly] might well become of immense importance in this great task of forming and educating a strong body of international opinion behind and in support of the League and its work. For the first time in history people will hear great subjects discussed on an international platform, and the narrow national influence of the local Parliament and still more the local press will gradually be neutralised, and a broader opinion and spirit will be fostered.

Let no one be alarmed at this formidable list of first-class difficulties which I am lavishly scattering in the path of the League. All these matters, and many more, are rapidly, unavoidably becoming subjects for international handling. Questions of industry, trade, finance, labour, transit and communications, and many others, are bursting through the national bounds and are clamouring for international solution. Water-tight compartments and partition walls between the nations and the continents have been knocked through, and the new situation calls for world-government. If the League of Nations refuses to function, some other machinery will have to be created to deal with the new problems which transcend all national limits. The task is there; all that is required is a carefully thought out form of government by which that task could be undertaken. It is a unique problem, both in its magnitude and in the benefits for the world which a successful solution will secure. We can only proceed tentatively and hope for very partial success. In that spirit the above scheme is suggested. . . .

We come now to that part of our subject which has received most consideration and discussion during the war. The stupendous character of this tragedy has forced to the front, as the most important and vital issue before the civilised world, the question whether an end cannot be made to war, whether the resources of civilisation are not adequate to the prevention of similar calamities overwhelming and perhaps finally engulfing mankind in future. . . .

The League must be such as to mean much more than new Councils to provide for Arbitration and Conciliation in future troubles. The new institution of peace must not be something additional, something external, superimposed on the pre-existing structure. It must be an organic change; it must be woven into the very texture of our political system. The new motif of peace must in future operate internally, constantly, inevitably from the very heart of our political organisation, and must, so to speak, flow from the nature of things political. Then, and not till then, will the impulse to war atrophy and shrivel up, and war itself stand stripped in all its horrible nakedness, and lose all the association of romance, all the atmosphere of honour, which has proved so intoxicating and irresistible in the past. That is why I am pleading for a more fundamental conception of the League, for a League whose task will not be to stem the on-coming tide with a broom, but for one which will prevent the tide from flowing at all. I hope I have shown the way to such a conception of the League; and if at this unique juncture in the fortunes of Christendom that conception, or something similar, could be translated into a real living institution, this war, with all its untold miseries for the world, will not have been in vain. I believe this war has ripened public opinion for a far-reaching change. . . .

The need, political and psychological, is imperative; the opportunity is unique; and only the blindness of statesmen could now prevent the coming of the new institution, which will, more than anything else, reconcile the peoples to the sufferings they have endured in this war. It will be the only fitting monument to our heroic dead. . . .

For there is no doubt that mankind is once more on the move. The very foundations have been shaken and loosened, and things are again fluid. The tents have been struck, and the great caravan of humanity is once more on the march. Vast social and industrial changes are coming, perhaps upheavals which may, in their magnitude and effects, be comparable to war itself. A steadying, controlling, regulating influence will be required to give stability to progress, and to remove that wasteful friction which has dissipated so much social force in the past, and in this war more than ever before. These great functions could only be adequately fulfilled by the League of Nations. Responding to such vital needs and coming at such a unique opportunity in history, it may well be destined to mark a new era in the Government of Man, and become to the peoples the guarantee of Peace, to the workers of all races the great International, and to all the embodiment and living expression of the moral and spiritual unity of the human race.

. . . To enable it to do so, the League will have to occupy the great position which has been rendered vacant by the destruction of so many of the old European Empires and the passing away of the old European order. And the League should be put into the very forefront of the programme of the Peace Conference, and be made the point of departure for the solution of many of the grave problems with which it will be confronted.

37. HOBHOUSE: *THE METAPHYSICAL THEORY OF THE STATE*

Leonard Trelawney Hobhouse (1864–1929), a British sociologist, an active liberal, and a supporter of democratic socialism, upheld, in his numerous writings dealing with ethic and political theory, rationalist individualism against the irrational glorification of the state, the nation, the group, or the class. During the First World War, in which Western liberalism confronted the German theory of the state as "Divine Will," Hobhouse wrote *The Metaphysical Theory of the State: A Criticism,* published in 1918, from which the following excerpts are taken.[11]

Several years later, in 1924, reviewing the international situation, Hobhouse wrote:

There are in the world today the elements of a world-polity; there are also the forces making for tyranny, rebellion, confusion, and the ultimate renewal of an ever more destructive war. The opposing tendencies seem nearly balanced, and which shall prevail is perhaps a question of time. In this question lies the issue between an advance to an international order which, by relieving the peoples of the burden of hate and fear, may set free ethical and economic forces great enough to carry the race to a height of civilization hitherto unknown, and on the other hand to a recrudescence of warfare in a form calculated to bring the entire structure of civilization as we have known it to a violent end.

The metaphysical theory of the State is the endeavor to exhibit the fabric of society in a light in which we shall see it, in or through its actual condition, as the incarnation of something very great and glorious indeed, as one expression of that supreme being which some of these thinkers call the Spirit and others the Absolute. There is no question here of realizing an ideal by human effort. We are already living in the ideal. It does not much matter whether we are rich or poor, healthy or enfeebled, personally aware of happiness or misery; nay, it does not seem to matter very much whether we are just or unjust, virtuous or depraved, for we are all integral parts in something much wider and nobler than the individual life, something to which mere human good and evil, happiness or misery, are small matters, mere constituent elements that, whatever they may be for each one of us, play their part right well in the magnificent whole. Evil is indeed necessary to good. It is a part of the Perfection of the Absolute, and anything which would point to its extirpation as an ideal is condemned as an offshoot of popular notions of progress or ridiculed as a piece of humanitarian enthusiasm.

Such, then, is the spirit of the metaphysical theory of society which I propose to examine in the shape given to it by its founder, Hegel. This theory is commonly spoken of as idealism, but it is in point of fact a more subtle and dangerous enemy to the ideal than any brute denial of idealism emanating from a one-sided science. Against every attempt to construe the world as mere fact which cannot modify, there will always spring up the reaction of human

[11] Reprinted by permission of George Allen & Unwin Ltd., London.

hope, of human endeavor, of the deep-seated indignation at injustice, the "rebel passion" of pity. If the scientific man insists that as this world rose out of the whirl of atoms, agitated by mechanical forces, so it will ultimately disappear in the cold and darkness, none the less men will say "Here are we, conscious living beings palpitating with emotion, with feeling, products it may be of your whirl of atoms, yet allowed meanwhile some latitude to shape our lives, to avoid the worst evils, and to cultivate some fleeting happiness; let us at least stand together against this unkindly fate and make the best of life while we can, not only for our short-lived selves, but for our feeble race." Thus mechanical science stimulates at least the ethics of revolt. But when we are taught to think of the world which we know as a good world, to think of its injustices, wrongs, and miseries as necessary elements in a perfect ideal, then, if we accept these arguments, our power of revolt is atrophied, our reason is hypnotized, our efforts to improve life and remedy wrong fade away into a passive acquiescence in things as they are; or, still worse, into a slavish adulation of the Absolute in whose hands we are mere pawns.

The happiness of the State is not to be judged by the happiness of the individual; the happiness of the individual must be judged by the goodness of the State. It is to be valued by the perfection of the whole to which he belongs. In the conception, therefore, of the State as a totality, which is an end in itself, an end to which the lives of men and women are mere means, we have the working model of an Absolute. For the thoroughgoing idealist, all the conscious beings that live under the shadow of the Absolute seem to have just as much or as little title to independent consideration as the cells of the human body. Now, for Hegel, the State is a form of the absolute spirit, which is the essence of all things. "The State is the divine idea as it exists on earth." For "all the worth which the human being possesses—all spiritual reality—he possesses only through the State." "The State is the spirit which stands in the world and realizes itself therein consciously. . . . The existence of the State is God's movement in the world." "The State is the divine will as the present spirit unfolding itself to the actual shape and organization of a world." It is the absolute power upon earth." "It is its own end [*Seibstzweck*]. It is the ultimate end which has the highest right against the individual, whose highest duty is to be a member of the State."

In older days we passed by the Hegelian exaltation of the State as the rhapsodical utterances of a metaphysical dreamer. It was a mistake. The whole conception is deeply interwoven with the most sinister developments in the history of Europe. It is fashionable to conceive German militarism as a product of the reaction against a beautiful sentimental idealism that reigned in the pre-Bismarckian era. Nothing could be more false. The political reaction began with Hegel, whose school has from first to last provided by far the most serious opposition to the democratic and humanitarian conceptions emanating from eighteenth century France, sixteenth century Holland, and seventeenth century England. It was the Hegelian conception of the State which was designed to turn the edge of the principle of freedom by identifying freedom with law; of equality, by substituting the conception of discipline; of personality itself, by merging the individual in the State; of humanity, by erecting the State as the supreme form of human association.

The direct connection between Bismarckian ethics and Hegelian teaching was ably worked out many years ago by a close student of the relations of ideas and facts in the political sphere, Mr. William Clark, but it is not in Germany alone that the Hegelian influence has profoundly affected the course of thought in one form or another. It has permeated the British world, discrediting the principles upon which liberal process has been founded and in particular depreciating all that British and French thinkers have contributed. Perhaps it has been none the less dangerous because it has captivated men of real humanity, genuinely interested in liberal progress, so much so that in the hands of T. H. Green[12] the Hegelian theory was for a time transmuted into a philosophy of social idealism, a variant which has a value of its own and does not lack distinguished living disciples. But as a fashionable academic philosophy genuine Hegelianism has revived, and the doctrine of the State as an incarnation of the Absolute, a super-personality which absorbs the real living personality of men and women, has in many quarters achieved the position of an academic orthodoxy. For academic purposes, it is a convenient doctrine; its bed-rock conservatism is proof against all criticisms of the existing order. It combats the spirit of freedom in the most effective method possible, adopting its banner and waving it from the serried battalions of a disciplined army. It justifies that negation of the individual which the modern practice of government is daily emphasizing. It sets the State above moral criticism, constitutes war a necessary incident in its existence, contemns humanity, and repudiates a Federation or League of Nations. In short, we see in it a theory admirably suited to the period of militancy and regimentation in which we find ourselves. The truth or fallacy of such a theory is a matter of no small interest; indeed, it is not a question of theory alone but of a doctrine whose historical importance is written large in the events of the nineteenth and twentieth centuries. . . .

[12] Thomas Hill Green (1836–1882), professor of philosophy at Oxford

The best and the worst things that men do they do in the name of a religion. Some have supposed that only supernatural religion could mislead. The history of our times shows that if men no longer believe in God they will make themselves gods of Power, of Evolution, of the Race, the Nation, or the State. In the name of gods will they drench a continent with blood, and the youth will offer themselves up as willing martyrs. There is no double dose of original sin which established this worship in Germany. It is the product of a combination of historic causes—the long division of the people, their geographical situation, the national reaction against Napoleon, the achievement of union by military means, the fear of the Czardom, causing the acquiescence of the more pacific elements in militarism, the loss by emigration of those who would not tolerate the governing system. The idealized exaltation of the State supervened to reconcile the thinking classes and give them a creed justifying their dislike of humanitarianism. In Hegel's hands this creed had, as we have seen, its idealistic side, and events had to move before this could be shed, and the naked doctrine of Power be proclaimed by Treitschke. But the elevation of the State above men means at bottom the supremacy of Power. It is the natural creed of an aristocracy or a bureaucracy, as insistence on Personality is the natural creed of the people. Theories of politics or of conduct that live long and retain influence have something more than theory behind them. They appeal to powerful instincts and interests, and the Hegelian philosophy is no exception. It appeals to the instincts and interests of counsellors and kings, of privileged classes, of Property and Order. It plays on the fear of fundamental criticism of the razoredge of thought, of the claim of conscience to scrutinize institutions and ordinances. It appeals to the slavishness which accepts a master if he will give the slave a share of tyranny over others more deeply enslaved. It satisfies national egoism and class ascendancy.

It was by no accident that the Greatest Happiness Principle took root and flourished during and after the last great war that devastated Europe.[13] The spectacle of the massive misery caused by governments had its recoil. Men began to test institutions and ideas of life by their effect on the felt happiness and misery of millions, and they found in the "happy fireside for weans and wife" a truer measure of a nation's greatness than stricken fields and extended territory. To that view in essence we are returning today. Much has been learnt in the interval, and a modern thinker could not regard happiness crudely as a sum of pleasures, or divorce it from the mode of life which is its substance, or judge the well-being of a whole society by the contentment of a numerical majority. But the desire

[13] the Napoleonic Wars

to arrest the misery of mankind will revive in double strength. Europe has undergone its martyrdom, millions in the service of false gods, other millions in resisting them. It will ask itself what is the true God and where the true religion. The answer, whatever it be, must rest on this truth, that the higher ethics and the deeper religion do not come to destroy the simplest rights and duties of neighbor to neighbor, but to fulfill and extend them. Great purposes, vast schemes, haunt the imagination of man, and urge him on to achievements without which life would be relatively poor and stagnant. But too often such purposes are built on foundations of human misery and wrong. It is the rarer insight which sees in the great good the comprehensive unity of all the little things that make up the life of the common man.

The theory of the State is a case in point. The State is a great organization. Its well-being is something of larger and more permanent import than that of any single citizen. Its scope is vast. Its service calls for the extreme of loyalty and self-sacrifice. All this is true. Yet, when the State is set up as an entity superior and indifferent to component individuals it becomes a false god, and its worship the abomination of desolation, as seen at Ypres or on the Somme.[14] When it is conceived as a means to the extension of our duty towards our neighbor, a means whereby we can apply effectively and on the large scale what we know to be good in the simple personal relations of life, no such discord arises. The purposes of political action are no way narrowed, but purified and humanized. We learn to think of our political conduct in terms of the vast reverberation of consequences on thousands and millions of lives, great and lowly, present and to come. We cannot, indeed, ever adequately interpret great general truths in terms of the particulars which they cover. To give to vast social issues all their human meaning is beyond the power of imagination—an imagination which recoils even from the effort to appreciate the daily list of casualties. But the true progress of political thought lies in the cultivation of imaginative power. It insists on going back from the large generality, the sounding abstraction, the imposing institution, to the human factors which it covers. Not that it wishes to dissolve the fabric. Men must continue to build, and on deeper foundations and with larger plans. But there must be no slave buried alive beneath the cornerstone. Or rather, the fabric is no building, but a tissue of living, thinking, feeling beings, of whom every one is "an end and not a means merely," and the value of the whole is marred if it requires the suffering of any single element. There is no lack of vastness in this design. It might rather be accused of vagueness, if it were not that it starts with the simple relations of man and man and bids

14 great battles in World War I

each of us seek to realize in political conduct and through social institutions, on the widest scale and in impersonal relations, what we well understand in our private lives as "our duty towards our neighbor."

Political morality is not super-morality, setting ordinary obligations aside. It is morality extended and defined, stripped of the limitations of class or national prejudice, generalized for application in great impersonal organizations, the only thing that can save such organizations from becoming inhuman. It may be said that institutions and politics generally can do little to make individuals happy. That may be true, but they can do a vast deal to make individuals unhappy, and to cut off this great source of woe is no unworthy aim. That is why a sound political philosophy will always insist on the individual, the freedom which is his basis of self-respect, the equality which is his title to consideration, the happiness whereof "the tiny bowl is so easily split." It is not that our little lives are rounded in ourselves. On the contrary, if we find happiness anywhere, it is only in merging ourselves in some greater object. If all objects worthy of effort may be considered as contributing to the advancement of mankind, this advancement, properly understood, goes not over the bodies and souls of individuals like a Juggernaut's car, but through their heightened activities and larger lives like a quickening spirit. Here precisely lies the issue between two views of the State. In the democratic or humanitarian view it is a means. In the metaphysical view it is an end. In the democratic view it is the servant of humanity in the double sense that it is to be judged by what it does for the lives of its members and by the part that it plays in the society of humankind. In the metaphysical view it is itself the sole guardian of moral worth. In the democratic view the sovereign State is already doomed, destined to subordination in a community of the world. In the metaphysical view it is the supreme achievement of human organization. For the truth let the present condition of Europe be witness.

38. ANDRÉ BRETON:
WHAT IS SURREALISM?

Surrealism was an intellectual, literary, and artistic movement in the wake of World War I. Its immediate precursor was the Dadaist movement, which originated in Zurich during the war as an irrational protest against the traditional moral and esthetic values and institutions. Life seemed meaningless and absurd. Out of Dadaism surrealism, or super-realism, developed, above all in France, under the leadership of André Breton (born 1896). Freud, with his theories of the subconscious, and Lenin's Russian revolution exercised a strong influence upon the movement. Surrealism aimed at "breaking down the barriers, both physical and psychical, between the conscious and the unconscious, between the inner and the outer world, and to create a super-reality in which the real and unreal, meditation and action, meet and mingle and dominate the whole life" (Herbert Read).

The surrealist movement later split into various factions. Some members, such as the poet Paul Eluard (1895–1952) and the writer Louis Aragon (born 1897), joined the communist movement. In a number of manifestos Breton tried to define surrealism. The following essay gives a good survey of the origins, intentions, and claims of the surrealist movement, which had a stimulating influence on all "modern movements" in Europe and America.[15]

At the beginning of the war of 1870 (he was to die four months later, aged twenty-four), the author of the *Chants de Maldoror* and of *Poésies,* Isidore Ducasse, better known by the name of Comte de Lautréamont,[16] whose thought has been of the very greatest help and encouragement to my friends and myself through the fifteen years during which we have succeeded in carrying on a common activity, made the following remark, among many others which were to electrify us fifty years later: "At the hour in which I write, new tremors are running through the intellectual atmosphere; it is only a matter of having the courage to face them." 1868–75: it is impossible, looking back upon the past, to perceive an epoch so *poetically* rich, so victorious, so revolutionary and so charged with distant meaning as that which stretches from the separate publication of the *Premier Chant de Maldoror* to the insertion in a letter to Ernest Delahaye of Rimbaud's[17] last poem, *Rêve,* which has not

[15] Translated by David Gascoyne and published by Faber & Faber (London, 1936).

[16] Isidore-Lucien Ducasse, who was born in Uruguay in 1847 and died in greatest poverty in Paris in 1870, wrote *Les Chants de Maldoror,* published 1890. He, the Marquis de Sade (1740–1814), and Alfred Jarry (1873–1907), author of "Ubu Roi" (1896), a grotesque farce, fascinated the "antibourgeois" French generation after 1918.

[17] Jean Arthur Rimbaud (1854–1891) was a great French poet who wrote his masterpieces before he was twenty. With him, poetry was a revolutionary force to change life and open up new realms of experiences.

so far been included in his Complete Works. It is not an idle hope to wish to see the works of Lautréamont and Rimbaud restored to their correct historical background: the coming and the immediate results of the war of 1870. Other and analogous cataclysms could not have failed to rise out of that military and social cataclysm whose final episode was to be the atrocious crushing of the Paris Commune; the last in date caught many of us at the very age when Lautréamont and Rimbaud found themselves thrown into the preceding one, and by way of revenge has had as its consequence—and this is the new and important fact—the truimph of the Bolshevik Revolution.

I should say that to people socially and politically uneducated as we then were—we who, on the one hand, came for the most part from the petite-bourgeoisie, and on the other, were all by vocation possessed with the desire to intervene upon the artistic plane—the days of October [1917] which only the passing of the years and the subsequent appearance of a large number of works within the reach of all were fully to illumine, could not there and then have appeared to turn so decisive a page in history. We were, I repeat, ill-prepared and ill-informed. Above all, we were exclusively preoccupied with the campaign of systematic refusal, exasperated by the conditions under which in such an age, we were forced to live. But our refusal did not stop there; it was insatiable and knew no bounds. Apart from the incredible stupidity of the arguments which attempted to legitimize our participation in an enterprise such as the war, whose issue left us completely indifferent, this refusal was directed—and having been brought up in such a school, we are not capable of *changing* so much that it is no longer so directed—against the whole series of intellectual, moral and social obligations that continually and from all sides weigh down upon man and crush him. Intellectually, it was vulgar rationalism and choplogic that more than anything else formed the causes of our horror and our destructive impulse; morally, it was all duties: religious, civic and of the family; socially, it was work. . . . The more I think about it, the more certain I become that nothing was to our minds worth saving, unless it was . . . unless it was, at last, "l'amour la poésie," to take the bright and trembling title of one of Paul Eluard's[18] books, "l'amour la poésie," considered as inseparable in their essence and as the sole good. Between the negation of this good, a negation brought to its climax by the war, and its full and total affirmation ("Poetry should be made by all, not one"), the field was not, to our minds, open to anything but a Revolution truly extended into all domains, improbably radical, to the highest degree impractical and tragically destroy-

[18] Paul Eluard (1895–1952), surrealist and later Communist poet, whose "L'Amour la Poésie" appeared in 1929

ing within itself the whole time the feeling that it brought with it both of desirability and of absurdity. Many of you, no doubt, would put this down to a certain youthful exaltation and to the general savagery of the time; I must, however, insist on this attitude, common to particular men and manifesting itself at periods nearly half a century distant from one another. I should affirm that in ignorance of this attitude one could form no idea of what surrealism really stands for. This attitude alone can account, and very sufficiently at that, for all the excesses that may be attributed to us but which cannot be deplored unless one gratuitously supposes that we could have started from any other point. The ill-sounding remarks that are imputed to us, the so-called inconsiderate attacks, the insults, the quarrels, the scandals—all the things that we are so much reproached with—turned up on the same road as the surrealist poems. From the very beginning, the surrealist attitude has had that in common with Lautréamont and Rimbaud which once and for all binds our lot to theirs, and that is wartime *defeatism*.

I am not afraid to say that this *defeatism* seems to me more relevant than ever. "New tremors are running through the intellectual atmosphere: it is only a matter of having the courage to face them." They are, in fact *always* running through the intellectual atmosphere: the problem of their propagation and interpretation remains the same and, as far as we are concerned, remains to be solved. But, paraphrasing Lautréamont, I cannot refrain from adding that at the hour in which I speak, old and mortal shivers are trying to substitute themselves for those which are the very shivers of knowledge and of life. They come to announce a frightful disease, a disease inevitably followed by the deprivation of all rights; it is only a matter of having the courage to face them also. This disease is called fascism.

Let us be careful today not to underestimate the peril: the shadow has greatly advanced over Europe recently. Hitler, Dollfuss, and Mussolini have either drowned in blood or subjected to corporal humiliation everything that formed the effort of generations straining towards a more tolerable and more worthy form of existence. In capitalist society, hypocrisy and cynicism have now lost all sense of proportion and are becoming more outrageous every day. Without making exaggerated sacrifices to humanitarianism, which always involves impossible reconciliations and truces to the advantage of the stronger, I should say that in this atmosphere, thought cannot consider the exterior world without an immediate shudder. . . .

. . . I consider that one can distinguish two epochs in the surrealist movement, of equal duration, from its origins (1919), until today: a purely *intuitive* epoch, and a *reasoning* epoch. The first can summarily be characterized by the belief expressed during this time in the all-powerfulness of thought, considered capable of freeing itself by means of its own resources. This belief witnesses to a prevailing view that I look upon today as being extremely mistaken, the view that *thought is supreme over matter.* The definition of surrealism that has passed into the dictionary, a definition taken from the *Manifesto* of 1924, takes account only of this entirely idealist disposition and (for voluntary reasons of simplification and amplification destined to influence in my mind the future of this definition) does so in terms that suggest that I deceived myself at the time in advocating the use of an automatic thought not only removed from all control exercised by the reason but also disengaged from "*all aesthetic or moral preoccupations.*" It should at least have been said: *conscious* aesthetic or moral preoccupations. During the period under review, in the absence, of course, of all seriously discouraging exterior events, surrealist activity remained strictly confined to its first theoretical premises, continuing all the while to be the vehicle of that total "non-conformism" which, as we have seen, was the binding feature in the coming together of those who took part in it, and the cause, during the first few years after the war, of an uninterrupted series of adhesions. No coherent political or social attitude, however, made its appearance until 1925, that is to say (and it is important to stress this), until the outbreak of the Moroccan war,[19] which, re-arousing in us our particular hostility to the way armed conflicts affect man, abruptly placed before us the necessity of making a public protest. This protest, which, under the title *La Révolution d'Abord et Toujours* (October 1925), joined the names of the surrealists proper to those of thirty other intellectuals, was undoubtedly rather confused ideologically; it none the less marked the breaking away from a whole way of thinking; it none the less created a precedent that was to determine the whole future direction of the movement. Surrealist activity, faced with a brutal, revolting, *unthinkable* fact, was forced to ask itself what were its proper resources and to determine their *limits;* it was forced to adopt a precise attitude, exterior to itself, in order to continue to face whatever exceeded these limits. Surrealist activity at this moment entered into its *reasoning* phase. It suddenly experienced the necessity of crossing over the gap that separates absolute idealism from dialectical materialism. . . .

In 193[6], more than ever before, surrealism owes it to itself to defend the postulate of the necessity of change. It is amusing, in-

[19] Abdel Krim, a Moroccan chieftain, led a victorious campaign against the Spanish and French colonial armies, until he was defeated in 1926 by the French under Maréchal Henri Pétain.

deed, to see how the spiteful and silly of our adversaries affect to triumph whenever they stumble on some old statement we may have made and which now sounds more or less discordantly in the midst of others intended to render comprehensible our present conduct. This insidious manoeuver, which is calculated to cast a doubt on our good faith, or at least on the genuineness of our principles, can easily be defeated. The development of surrealism throughout the decade of its existence is, we take it, a function of the unrolling of historical realities as these may be speeded up between the period of relief which follows the conclusion of a peace and the fresh outbreak of war. It is also a function of the process of seeking after new values in order to confirm or invalidate existing ones. . . .

Strangely enough, it was round a discovery of language that there was seeking to organize itself in 1920 what . . . assumed the name of *surrealism,* a word fallen from the lips of Apollinaire,[20] which we had diverted from the rather general and very confusing connotation he had given it. What was at first no more than a new method of poetic writing broke away after several years from the much too general theses which had come to be expounded in the *Surrealist Manifesto—Soluble Fish,* 1924, the *Second Manifesto* adding others to them, whereby the whole was raised to a vaster ideological plane; and so there had to be revision.

In an article, "Enter the Mediums," published in *Littérature,* 1922, reprinted in *Les Pas Perdus,* 1924, and subsequently in the *Surrealistic Manifesto,* I explained the circumstance that had originally put us, my friends and myself, on the track of the surrealist activity we still follow and for which we are hopeful of gaining ever more numerous new adherents in order to extend it further than we have so far succeeded in doing. It reads:

It was in 1919, in complete solitude and at the approach of sleep, that my attention was arrested by sentences more or less complete, which became perceptible to my mind without my being able to discover (even by very meticulous analysis) any possible previous volitional effort. One evening in particular, as I was about to fall asleep, I became aware of a sentence articulated clearly to a point excluding all possibility of alteration and stripped of all quality of vocal sound; a curious sort of sentence which came to me bearing—in sober truth—not a trace of any relation whatever to any incidents I may at that time have been involved in; an insistent sentence, it seemed to me, a sentence I might say, that *knocked at the window.* I was prepared to pay no further attention to it when the organic character of the sentence detained me. I was really be-

[20] Guillaume Apollinaire (1880–1918), the most important of the young French poets on the eve of World War I

wildered. Unfortunately, I am unable to remember the exact sentence at this distance, but it ran approximately like this: "A man is cut in half by the window." What made it plainer was the fact that it was accompanied by a feeble visual representation of a man in the process of walking, but cloven, at half his height, by a window perpendicular to the axis of his body. Definitely, there was the form, re-erected against space, of a man leaning out of a window. By the window following the man's locomotion, I understood that I was dealing with an image of great rarity. Instantly the idea came to me to use it as material for poetic construction. I had no sooner invested it with that quality, than it had given place to a succession of all but intermittent sentences which left me no less astonished, but in a state, I would say, of extreme detachment.

Preoccupied as I still was at that time with Freud, and familiar with his methods of investigation, which I had practised occasionally upon the sick during the War, I resolved to obtain from myself what one seeks to obtain from patients, namely a monologue poured out as rapidly as possible, over which the subject's critical faculty has no control—the subject himself throwing reticence to the winds—and which as much as possible represents *spoken thought*. It seemed and still seems to me that the speed of thought is no greater than that of words, and hence does not exceed the flow of either tongue or pen. It was in such circumstances that, together with Phillipe Soupault, whom I had told about my first ideas on the subject, I began to cover sheets of paper with writing, feeling a praiseworthy contempt for whatever the literary result might be. Ease of achievement brought about the rest. By the end of the first day of the experiment we were able to read to one another about fifty pages obtained in this manner and to compare the results we had achieved. The likeness was on the whole striking. There were similar faults of construction, the same hesitant manner, and also, in both cases, an illusion of extraordinary verve, much emotion, a considerable assortment of images of a quality such as we should never have been able to obtain in the normal way or writing, a very special sense of the picturesque, and, here and there, a few pieces of out and out buffoonery. The only differences which our two texts presented appeared to me to be due essentially to our respective temperaments, Soupault's being less static than mine, and, if he will allow me to make this slight criticism, to his having scattered about at the top of certain pages—doubtlessly in a spirit of mystification—various words under the guise of titles. I must give him credit, on the other hand, for having always forcibly opposed the least correction of any passage that did not seem to me to be quite the thing. In that he was most certainly right.

It is of course difficult in these cases to appreciate at their just value the various elements in the result obtained; one may even say that it is entirely impossible to appreciate them at a first reading. To you who may be writing them, these elements are, in appearance, *as strange as to anyone else,* and you are yourself naturally distrustful of them. Poetically speaking, they are distinguished chiefly by a very high degree of *immediate absurdity*, the peculiar quality of that absurdity being, on close examination, their yielding to whatever is most admissible and legitimate in the world; divulgation of a given number of facts and properties on the whole not less objectionable than the others. . . .

Surrealism then was securing expression in all its purity and force. The freedom it possesses is a perfect freedom in the sense that it recognizes no limitations exterior to itself. As it was said on the cover of the first issue of *La Révolution Surréaliste,* "it will be necessary to draw up a new declaration of the Rights of Man." The concept of surreality, concerning which quarrels have been sought with us repeatedly and which it was attempted to turn into a metaphysical or mystic rope to be placed afterwards round our necks, lends itself no longer to misconstruction, nowhere does it declare itself opposed to the need of transforming the world which henceforth will more and more definitely yield to it.

And I said in the *Manifesto:*

I believe in the future transmutation of those two seemingly contradictory states, dream and reality, into a sort of absolute reality, of surreality, so to speak. I am looking forward to its consummation, certain that I shall never share in it, but death would matter little to me could I but taste the joy it will yield ultimately. . . .

We were forced to agree with Pierre Naville when he wrote:

Surrealism is at the crossroads of several thought-movements. We assume that it affirms the possibility of a certain steady downward readjustment of the mind's rational (and not simply conscious) activity towards more absolutely *coherent* throught, irrespective of whatever direction that thought may take; that is to say, that it proposes or would at least like to propose a new solution of all problems, but chiefly moral. It is, indeed, in that sense that it is epoch-making. That is why one may express the essential characteristic of surrealism by saying that it seeks to calculate the quotient of the unconscious by the conscious.

It should be pointed out that in a number of declarations in *La Révolution et les Intellectuels: Que peuvent faire les surréalistes?* (1926), this same author demonstrated the utter vanity of intellectual bickerings in the face of the human exploitation which results from the wage-earning system. These declarations gave rise amongst us to considerable anxiety and, attempting for the first time to justify surrealism's social implications, I desired to put an end to it in *Légitime Defense.* This pamphlet set out to demonstrate that there is no fundamental antinomy in the basis of surrealist thought. In reality, we are faced with two problems, one of which is the problem raised, at the beginning of the twentieth century, by the discovery of the relations between the conscious and the unconscious. . . .

This brings us to the eve of the *Second Manifesto*. . . . An important part of the work was devoted to a statement of the reasons which moved surrealism to dispense for the future with certain collaborators. It was attempted, on the same occasion, to complete the specific method of creation proposed six years earlier, and thoroughly to tidy up surrealist ideas. . . .

While surrealism undertakes particularly the critical investigation of the notions of reality and unreality, of reason and unreason, of reflection and impulse, of knowing and "fatal" ignorance, of utility and uselessness, there is nevertheless between it and Historical Materialism this similarity in tendency, that it sets out from the "colossal abortion" of the Hegelian system. I do not see how limits, those for instance of the economic framework, can be assigned to the exercise of a thought which is definitely adapted to negation and the negation of negation. How allow that the dialectical method is only to be applied validly to solving social problems? It is the whole of surrealism's ambition to supply it with nowise conflicting possibilities of application in the most immediate conscious domain. I really cannot see, *pace* a few muddle-headed revolutionaries, why we should abstain from taking up the problems of love, of dreaming, of madness, of art and of religion, so long as we consider these problems from the same angle as they, and we too, consider Revolution. . . .

There is no need to indulge in subtleties: inspiration is familiar enough. And there can be no mistake: it is inspiration which has supplied the supreme need of expression in all times and in all places. A common remark is that inspiration either *is* or is not, and when it is not, nothing summoned to replace it by the human skill which interest obliterates, by the discursive intelligence, or by the talent acquired with labour, can make up in us for the lack of it. We recognize it easily by the way it completely takes possession of the mind, so that for long periods when any problem is set we are momentarily prevented from being the playthings of one rational solution rather than another; and by that kind of short-circuit which it sets up between a given idea and what answers to it (in writing, for example). Just as in the physical world, the short-circuit occurs when the two "poles" of the machine are linked by a conductor having little or no resistance. In poetry and in painting, surrealism has done everything it could to increase the number of the short-circuits. Its dearest aim now and in the future must be the artificial reproduction of that ideal moment in which a man who is a prey to a particular emotion, is suddenly caught up by "the stronger than himself," and thrust, despite his bodily inertia, into immortality. If he were then lucid and awake, he would issue from that predicament in terror. The great thing is that he should not be free to come out, that he should go on talking all the time the mysterious ringing is going on: indeed, it is thanks to that whereby he ceases to belong to himself that he belongs to us. . . .

From 1930 until today the history of surrealism is that of successful efforts to restore it to its proper *becoming* by gradually removing
from it every trace both of political opportunism and of artistic opportunism. The review *La Révolution Surréaliste* (12 issues) has
been succeeded by another, *Le Surréalisme au Service de la Révolution* (6 issues). Owing particularly to influences brought to bear
by new elements, surrealist experimenting, which had for too long
been erratic, has been unreservedly resumed; its perspectives and
its aims have been made perfectly clear; I may say that it has not
ceased to be carried on in a continuous and enthusiastic manner.
This experimenting has regained momentum under the master-
impulse given to it by Salvador Dali, whose exceptional interior
"boiling" has been for surrealism, during the whole of this period, an
invaluable ferment. . . . Dali has endowed surrealism with an
instrument of primary importance, in particular the paranoiac-
critical method, which has immediately shown itself capable of being applied wtih equal success to painting, poetry, the cinema, to
the construction of typical surrealist objects, to fashions, to sculpture
and even, if necessary, to all manner of exegesis.

He first announced his convictions to us in *La Femme Visible*
(1930):

I believe the moment is at hand when, by a paranoiac and active
advance of the mind, it will be possible (simultaneously with automatism
and other passive states) to systematize confusion and thus to help to
discredit completely the world of reality. . . .

. . . Here we find ourselves confronted by a new affirmation, accompanied by formal proofs, of the *omnipotence* of desire, which
has remained, since the beginnings, surrealism's sole act of faith.
At the point where surrealism has taken up the problem, its only
guide has been Rimbaud's sibylline pronouncement: "I say that one
must be a *seer*, one must make oneself a seer." As you know, this was
Rimbaud's only means of reaching "the *unknown*." Surrealism can
flatter itself today that it has discovered and rendered practicable
many other ways leading to the unknown. The abandonment to
verbal or graphic impulses and the resort to paranoiac-critical activity are not the only ones, and one may say that, during the last four
years of surrealist activity, the many others that have made their
appearance allow us to affirm that the automatism from which we
started and to which we have unceasingly returned does in fact
constitute the *crossroads* where these various paths meet. . . .
manner in which it is possible today to make use of the magnificent
. . . By surrealism we intend to account for nothing less than the

and overwhelming *spiritual legacy* that has been handed down to us. We have accepted this legacy from the past, and surrealism can well say that the use to which it has been put has been to turn it to the routing of capitalist society. I consider that for that purpose it was and is still necessary for us to stand where we are, to beware against breaking the thread of our researches and to continue these researches, not as literary men and artists, certainly, but rather as chemists and the various other kinds of technicians. To pass on to the poetry and art called (doubtless in anticipation) *proletarian:* No. The forces we have been able to bring together and which for fifteen years we have never found lacking, have arrived at a particular point of application: the question is not to know whether this point of application is the best, but simply to point out that the application of our forces at this point has given us up to an activity that has proved itself valuable and fruitful on the plane on which it was undertaken, and has also been of a kind to engage us more and more on the revolutionary plane. What it is essential to realize is that no other activity could have produced such rich results, nor could any other similar activity have been so effective in combating the present form of society. On that point we have history on our side.

39. THE PONTIFICATE OF PIUS XI

Pope Pius XI (Achilles Ratti, 1857–1939) ascended the Papal throne in 1922. Amidst the intellectual and moral upheaval in the wake of the First World War, he tried to reaffirm the position of the Church and at the same time to take into account the changing reality of Western society.

On May 15, 1931, the fortieth anniversary of the encyclical *Rerum Novarum*, Pius XI published the encyclical *Quadragesimo Anno* (A), in which he reiterated and elaborated the admonitions of Leo XIII against economic liberalism and for social legislation, but at the same time stressed the opposition of the Church to socialism.

In the preceding year Pius XI had turned his attention to another of the great problems of modern times, which the situation after the war had aggravated: the problem of marriage. In his encyclical *Casti Connubii* (B), on December 31, 1930, he reaffirmed the Catholic attitude toward marriage as a divine institution, and stressed the sacramental dignity and perpetual stability of matrimony.[21]

A. The Church and Socialism

With regard to the civil power, Leo XIII boldly passed beyond the restrictions imposed by Liberalism, and fearlessly proclaimed the doctrine that the civil power is more than the mere guardian of law and order, and that it must strive with all zeal "to make sure that the laws and institutions, the general character and administration of the commonwealth, should be such as of themselves to realize public well being and private prosperity." It is true, indeed, that a just freedom of action should be left to individual citizens and families: but this principle is only valid as long as the common good is secure and no injustice is entailed. The duty of rulers is to protect the community and its various elements; in protecting the rights of individuals they must have special regard for the infirm and needy. "For the richer class have many ways of shielding themselves and stand less in need or help from the state, whereas the mass of the poor have no resources of their own to fall back upon and must chiefly depend upon the assistance of the state. And for this reason wage-earners, since they mostly belong to that class, should be especially cared for and protected by the government."

We do not, of course, deny that even before the Encyclical of Leo, some rulers had provided for the more urgent needs of the working classes, and had checked the more flagrant acts of injustice perpetrated against them. But after the Apostolic Voice had sounded from the Chair of Peter throughout the world, the leaders of the nations became at last more fully conscious of their obligations, and set to work seriously to promote a broader social policy. . . .

This is the aim which Our Predecessor urged as the necessary object of our efforts: the uplifting of the proletariat. It calls for more emphatic assertion and more insistent repetition on the present occasion because these salutary injunctions of the Pontiff have not infrequently been forgotten, deliberately ignored, or deemed impracticable, though they were both feasible and imperative. They have lost none of their force or wisdom for our own age, even though the horrible condition of the days of Leo XIII is less prevalent today. The condition of the workingman has indeed been improved and rendered more equitable in many respects, particularly in the larger and more civilized states, where the laboring class can no longer be said to be universally in misery and want. But

[21] Distributed by the Catholic Truth Society (including A & B), London.

after modern machinery and modern industry had progressed with astonishing speed and taken possession of many newly colonized countries no less than of the ancient civilizations of the Far East, the number of the dispossessed laboring masses, whose groans mount to Heaven from these lands, increased beyond all measure.

Moreover, there is the immense army of hired rural laborers, whose condition is depressed in the extreme, and who have no hope of ever obtaining a share in the land. These too, unless efficacious remedies be applied, will remain perpetually sunk in the proletarian condition. . . .

The capitalist economic regime, with the world-wide diffusion of industry, has penetrated everywhere, particularly since the publication of Leo XIII's Encyclical. It has invaded and pervaded the economic and social sphere even of those who live outside its ambit, influencing them, and as it were, intimately affecting them by its advantages, inconveniences and vices.

When we turn our attention, therefore, to the changes which this capitalistic economic order has undergone since the days of Leo XIII, we have regard to the interests, not of those only who live in countries where "capital" and industry prevail, but of the whole human race.

In the first place, then, it is patent that in our days not alone is wealth accumulated, but immense power and despotic economic domination is concentrated in the hands of a few, and that those few are frequently not the owners, but only the trustees and directors of invested funds, who administer them at their good pleasure.

This power becomes particularly irresistible when exercised by those who, because they hold and control money, are able also to govern credit and determine its allotment, for that reason supplying, so to speak, the life-blood to the entire economic body, and grasping, as it were, in their hands the very soul of production, so that no one dare breathe against their will.

This accumulation of power, the characteristic note of the modern economic order, is a natural result of limitless free competition which permits the survival of those only who are the strongest, which often means those who fight most relentlessly, who pay least heed to the dictates of conscience.

This concentration of power had led to a threefold struggle for domination. First, there is the struggle for dictatorship in the economic sphere, itself; then, the fierce battle to acquire control of the state, so that its resources and authority may be abused in the economic struggles. Finally, the clash between states themselves.

This latter arises from two causes:—because the nations apply their power and political influence, regardless of circumstances, to promote the economic advantages of their citizens; and because, vice versa, economic forces and economic domination are used to decide political controversies between peoples. . . .

Since the days of Leo XIII, Socialism too, the great enemy with which his battles were waged has undergone profound changes, no less than economics. . . . One section of Socialism has undergone approximately the same change; through which, as we have described the capitalistic economic regime has passed; it has degenerated into Communism. . . . The other section, which has retained the name of Socialism, is much less radical in its views. Not only does it condemn recourse to physical force; it even mitigates and moderates to some extent class warfare and the abolition of private property. . . . Class war, provided it abstains from enmities and mutual hatred, is changing gradually to an honest discussion of differences, based upon the desire of social justice. If this is by no means the blessed social peace which we all long for, it can be and must be an approach towards the mutual cooperation of vocational groups. . . . If these changes continue, it may well come about that gradually the tenets of mitigated Socialism will no longer be different from the program of those who seek to reform human society according to Christian principles. . . . If, like all errors, Socialism contains a certain element of truth (and this the Sovereign Pontiffs have never denied), it is nevertheless founded upon a doctrine of human society peculiarly its own, which is opposed to true Christianity. "Religious Socialism," "Christian Socialism" are expressions implying a contradiction in terms. No one can be at the same time a sincere Catholic and a true Socialist. . . .

B. The Catholic Attitude toward Marriage

Therefore the sacred partnership of true marriage is constituted both by the will of God and the will of man. From God comes the very institution of marriage, the ends for which it was instituted, the laws that govern it, the blessings that flow from it; while man, through generous surrender of his own person made to another for the whole span of life, becomes, with the help and the cooperation of God, the author of each particular marriage, with the duties and blessings annexed thereto from divine institution. . . .

Amongst the blessings of marriage, the child holds the first place. And how great a boon of God this is, and how great a blessing of matrimony is clear from a consideration of man's dignity and of his sublime end. For man surpasses all other visible creatures by the superiority of his rational nature alone. Besides, God wishes men to be born not only that they should live and fill the earth, but much more that they may be worshippers of God, that they may know Him and love Him and finally enjoy Him for ever in heaven; and this end, since man is raised by God in a marvellous way to the supernatural order, surpasses all that eye hath seen, and ear heard, and all that hath entered into the heart of man from which it is easily seen how great a gift of divine goodness and how remarkable a fruit of marriage are children born by the omnipotent power of God through the cooperation of those bound in wedlock. . . .

Nor did Christ Our Lord wish only to condemn any form of polygamy or polyandry, as they are called, whether successive or simultaneous, and every other external dishonorable act, but, in order that the sacred bonds of marriage may be guarded absolutely inviolate, He forbade also even wilful thoughts and desires on such like things: "But I say to you, that whosoever shall look on a woman to lust after her hath already committed adultery with her in his heart." Which words of Christ Our Lord cannot be annulled even by the consent of one of the partners of marriage for they express a law of God and of nature which no will of man can break or bend. . . .

In the first place Christ Himself lays stress on the indissolubility and firmness of the marriage bond when He says: "What God hath joined together let no man put asunder," and: "Everyone that putteth away his wife and marrieth another committeth adultery, and he that marrieth her that is put away from her husband committeth adultery.". . .

When we consider the great excellence of chaste wedlock, Venerable Brethren, it appears all the more regrettable that particularly in our day we should witness this divine institution often scorned and on every side degraded.

For now, alas, not secretly nor under cover, but openly, with all sense of shame put aside, now by word, again by writings, by theatrical productions of every kind, by romantic fiction, by amorous and frivolous novels, by cinematographs portraying vivid scenes, in addresses broadcast by radio telephony, in short by all the inventions of modern science, the sanctity of marriage is trampled upon and derided, divorce, adultery, all the basest vices either are extolled or at least are depicted in such colors as to appear to be free of all reproach and infamy. Books are not lacking which dare to pronounce themselves as scientific but which in truth are merely coated with a veneer of science in order that they may the more easily insinuate their ideas. The doctrines defended in these are offered for sale as the productions of modern genius, of that genius namely, which, anxious only for truth, is considered to have emancipated itself from all those old-fashioned and immature opinions of the ancients; and to the number of these antiquated opinions they relegate the traditional doctrine of Christian marriage. . . .

To begin at the very source of these evils, their basic principle lies in this, that matrimony is repeatedly declared to be not instituted by the Author of nature nor raised by Christ the Lord to the dignity of a true statement, but invented by man. . . .

And now, Venerable Brethren, we shall explain in detail the evils opposed to each of the benefits of matrimony. First consideration is due to the offsprings, which many have the boldness to call the disagreeable burden of matrimony, and which they say is to be carefully avoided by married people not through virtuous continence (which Christian law permits in matrimony when both parties consent) but by frustrating the marriage act. Some justify this criminal abuse on the ground that they are weary of children and wish to gratify their desires without their consequent burden. Others say that they cannot on the one hand remain continent nor on the other can they have children because of the difficulties whether on the part of the mother or on the part of family circumstances.

But no reason, however grave, may be put forward by which anything intrinsically against nature may become conformable to nature and morally good. Since, therefore, the conjugal act is destined primarily by nature for the begetting of children, those who in exercising it deliberately frustrate its natural power and purpose sin against nature and commit a deed which is shameful and intrinsically vicious. . . .

The same false teachers who try to dim the lustre of conjugal faith and purity do not scruple to do away with the honorable and trusting obedience which the woman owes to the man. Many of them go even further and assert that such subjection of one party to the other is unworthy of human dignity, that the rights of husband and wife are equal; wherefore, they boldly proclaim, the emancipation of women has been or ought to be effected. This emancipation in their ideas must be threefold, in the ruling of the domestic society, in the administration of family affairs and in the rearing of the children. It must be social, economic, physiological;— physiological, that is to say, the woman is to be freed at her own good pleasure from the burdensome duties properly belonging to a wife as companion and mother. (We have already said that this is not an emancipation but a crime); social, inasmuch as the wife being freed from the care of children and family, should, to the neglect of these, be able to follow her own bent and devote herself to business and even public affairs; finally economic, whereby the woman even without the knowledge and against the wish of her husband may be at liberty to conduct and administer her own affairs, giving her attention chiefly to these rather than to children, husband and family.

This, however, is not the true emancipation of woman, nor that rational and exalted liberty which belongs to the noble office of a Christian woman and wife; it is rather the debasing of the womanly character and the dignity of motherhood, and indeed of the whole family, as a result of which the husband suffers the loss of his wife, the children of their mother, and the home and the whole family of an ever watchful guardian. More than this, this false liberty and unnatural equality with the husband is to the detriment of the woman herself, for if the woman descends from her truly regal throne to which she has been raised within the walls of the home by means of the Gospel, she will soon be reduced to the old state of slavery (if not in appearance, certainly in reality) and become as amongst the pagans the mere instrument of man. . . .

To bring forward a recent and clear example of what is meant, it has happened quite in conscience with right order and entirely according to the law of Christ, that in the solemn Convention happily entered into between the Holy See and the Kingdom of Italy, also in matrimonial affairs a peaceful settlement and friendly cooperation has been obtained, such as befitted the glorious history of the Italian people and its ancient and sacred traditions. These decrees are to be found in the Lateran Pact: "The Italian State, desirous of restoring to the institution of matrimony, which is the basis of the family, that dignity conformable to the traditions of its people, assign as civil effects of the sacrament of matrimony all that is attributed to it in Canon Law." To this fundamental norm are added further clauses in the common pact.

This might well be a striking example to all of how, even in this our own day (in which, sad to say, the absolute separation of the civil power from the Church and indeed from every religion, is so often taught), the one supreme authority can be united and associated with the other without detriment to the rights and supreme power of either thus protecting Christian parents from pernicious evils and menacing ruin. . . .

40. KARL BARTH: *GOD AND MAN*

Sören Kierkegaard (1813–1855), the Danish theologian, was among the first to oppose the optimistic humanism and the easy accommodation of nineteenth-century Christianity. Almost forgotten in the nineteenth century, his influence grew in Central

Europe with the deep shock produced by the war of 1914, which was felt as a great crisis of the human mind and the human condition. It was during the war that Karl Barth, born in 1886 in Basel, Switzerland, and then a pastor in a small Swiss village, began to preach his "theology of crisis," which he first submitted to a wider circle in 1919 in his interpretation of Paul's Epistle to the Romans.

Like Kierkegaard, Barth insisted that God could not be found by starting from man's intellectual life and emotional needs, but that the Biblical revelation was the unique fountainhead and the only measure of all things. Calvin's doctrine, *Deus in sua inscrutabili altitudine non est investigandus* ("God in his inaccessible height must not be investigated"), established for Barth the unbridgeable distance between God and man, unbridgeable except for God's love. Barth restored the faith in the revelation as a miracle, and in the Gospel as something radically new and incomparable. Today Barth is generally recognized as the most influential Protestant theologian of the twentieth century.

From 1921 to 1934 he was professor of theology in German universities, until his resistance to National Socialism forced him to return to his native city. In 1932 he began the publication of the multivolume work *Dogmatics of the Church*. The addresses which he delivered between 1916 and 1923 were published in 1924 under the title *Das Wort Gottes und die Theologie* ("The Word of God and Theology").[22]

We must not for one moment think we can escape being part of the world in which we live, in which we can do no more than demonstrate our existence, and within which the ethical good can not be found—for to find or to be able to find a thing here is to prove that it can not be the good. But at the same time the fact remains that our demonstrated existence in this world is measured upon a standard which is not at all a part of existence as we know it or conceive it. The fact remains that man as man is irresistibly compelled to acknowledge that his life is the business for which he is responsible, that his desires require examination, and that the might-be is sometimes the ought-to-be which is the truth about truth, the ultimate governor of conduct.

[22] They were translated into English under the title *The Word of God and the Word of Man.* by Douglas Horton, copyright 1928, 1956, and 1957 by Douglas Horton. The following excerpts are reprinted by permission of Harper & Row, Publishers, Inc.

The historical and psychological happenings in which man becomes aware of the ethical question, and the particular ideal in
which yesterday, today, or tomorrow he may think he discerns the
answer to it—these may be derivable from existence as we conceive or may conceive it, from contingent, secondary, non-causative
causes, from fate or nature, from caprice or chance, from hunger
or love, but the problem of ethics itself does not stand or fall
with its expressions within the world of existing things, and certainly not with yesterday's, today's, or tomorrow's attempt at solving it. Its roots reach beyond its temporal beginnings and beyond
all its actual and possible temporal solutions; in its origin as in its
goal it stands in its own right, in its own dignity. It is not touched
by the scepticism to which all ethical systems are exposed, for the
reason that long before sceptics arose, it, itself, was the pitiless
crisis which produced all ethical systems.

The problem of the good calls in question all actual and possible
forms of human conduct, all temporal happenings in the history
both of the individual and of society. What ought we to do? is
our question; and this what, infiltrating and entrenching itself everywhere, directs its attack against all that we did yesterday and shall
do tomorrow. It weighs all things in the balance, constantly dividing
our manifold activities into good and bad—in order the next moment to do the same thing over again, as if for the first time since
the world began. It continually breaks out in crisis, causing us to
reexamine what but now we thought to be good, as well as what
but now we thought to be bad.

When the ethical problem arises, we begin to perceive what
the perfect life may mean; but, for us, what can it mean except
death? We begin to build that life, but how can it be completed except by progressive destruction? Perfect timelessness opens up, but
it is a timelessness which might better be defined as the time-limit
of all things. And when men venture to ask themselves the simple
question, What ought we to do? they take their place before this
perfection and put themselves at its disposal, in its service; they
enter into relationship with it—a relationship in comparison to
which all other intercourse with the heavenly or demonic powers
of the supersensual world fades to insignificance. For this question
asks how man ought to live and move and have his being not only
in this but in all possible worlds. When he makes it his own, he not
only acknowledges that he sees an Eye looking at him from beyond
all the worlds, but that he also sees what this eternal Eye sees,
that every act of his life is weighed in the balance, that his conduct
is wholly and constantly in crisis. Not only is he asked but he must
himself ask the question by which, in so far as he understands it,
he annihilates himself. For by the question, he proves his peculiar

connection with the One who regards him from the viewpoint of eternity, and so he bids an unavoidable farewell to all viewpoints peculiarly his own. By the question, he proves his relationship to God, and takes upon himself the immense, the abysmal consequences which that relationship must have for him. For all we could say of a man who gave himself to the ethical question with a seriousness corresponding to its counsel of perfection would be that he was committed to God and lost in God. How could we think of him but as deliberately and willfully dying? And how could a counsel of perfection seriously call upon man (as we know man) deliberately and willfully to die? The problem of ethics contains the secret that man as we know him in this life is an impossibility. This man, in God's sight, can only perish.

We must still be clear upon one fact: we have no choice as to whether or not we will take up the ethical problem, as to whether we will accept or reject the crisis which accompanies all our choices, or as to whether we will approve or disregard our underlying relationship with God. The ethical problem does not wait upon any ethical theorizing we may indulge in, nor the crisis upon our becoming critical—nor our relationship to God upon our so-called religious experiences. The ethical problem dominates; it is fundamental, first, a priori in the situation; it takes us up. We live within this crisis and relationship; and our theory and criticism and so-called experiences are possible only as we bow continually before a truth which stands firm without our aid—only as we face the fact that the problem is given us and that we must accept it. There is no moment in which we may hope to be free from the burden of it.

We live from moment to moment. And living means doing, even when doing means doing nothing. Of living which was not doing we could have no awareness; it would be our kind of living. But all doing, all conduct, since it must be related to its goal, is subject to the question as to its truth, as to its inner meaning and law. And our question is not answered when we perceive the inner meaning and law which relates our conduct to this or that proximate and finite goal. For this or that goal must look toward its own goal, and so on toward the ultimate goal of all goals—and so our question reaches toward a good which lies beyond all existence. Every random and temporal What shall we do? contains a What to which no random and temporal That can give a satisfying answer, because it is a last and eternal What. And with the question, the crisis in our lives continues, and with the crisis, our relationship to God. We live in this relationship. Let us look well to our responsibilities in it!

Further illustrations are hardly necessary. Those I have given are not important taken separately, but common to them all there is evidence that the present problem of ethics is disquieting, perplexing, aggressive. Into the bright circle of our lives it makes its uncanny and disturbing entrance like a strange guest of stone. Whoever wishes seriously to ask and to answer the question, What ought we to do? whether or not he is imbued with Dostoevsky and Kierkegaard, must have remarked something of the difference between today's situation and yesterday's. It is foolish to go on talking with glibness and certainty as if nothing had happened. The era of the old ethics is gone forever. Whoever now desires certainty must first of all become uncertain. And whoever desires to speak must first of all be silent. For something has happened. The world has not been destroyed, to be sure, and the old man has not been put off, in spite of what we may have thought, under the first impact of these devastating times. It is simply that over against man's confidence and belief in himself, there has not been written, in huge proportions and with utmost clearness, a mene, mene, tekel.

We are not of course sceptical of the authority and urgency of the ethical problem, for we think we see better than ever how imperative it is. And neither indeed are we sceptical of the connection between the ethical problem and our relation to God. Quite the opposite. It is the very fact of this relation that frightens us today, and makes us wholly sceptical of ourselves, of man, and of man's ideas as to moral personality and the moral goal.

One may also observe the situation in its relation to the ethical objective. Consider therefore the apparently, but only apparently, remote conception of the millennium. For many of our contemporaries—and I confess that I belong with them—this conception has taken the definite form of the socialistic ideal. . . . It is concerned with the goal of earthly history—and this without prejudice to the hope of eternal life in another world. The ethical question, as we have just seen, though an individual question, is not a question concerning individuals, but is concerned rather with the universally applicable law of humanity. It therefore contains within itself a more or less distinct question as to the historical ideal, as to the goal which lies, and is capable of being realized, not outside of time but within it, and to the order of human society which is to be grounded in what our stammering paraphrases call truth and righteousness, intelligence and love, peace and freedom. This question is manifestly embodied in the "we" of the larger question, "What ought we to do?" When the individual regards himself as the subject of the ethical question, he conceives himself in association with his fellow men, he regards himself as the subject of society; but this means that more or less consciously he regards what he does, his moral objective, as a goal of history. Ethics can no more exist without millenarianism, without at least some minute degree of it, than without the idea of a moral personality.

Keeping this situation in view, let us return to a consideration of the dialectic of the thought of God. I should like to set before you, as far as possible in my own words, the teaching of Paul, Luther, and Calvin—a teaching which is paralleled in many ways, I should say, by that of Plato.

That teaching begins with an unconditioned affirmation of the truth we have now arrived at from two different points of departure: that man condemns himself to death by his question about the good, because the only certain answer is that he, man, is not good, and from the viewpoint of the good, is powerless. But this insight, this all-inclusive critical negation under which we and our world exist, this fear of death into which the insight leads the upright conscience, is the narrow way and the strait gate that lead to truth, to the real, to the redeeming answer. The first demand is that we stand firm to the negative insight, face it squarely, and avoid it, not by making light of the basic seriousness of our question, nor by discounting something of the transcendent quality of the origin and end of truly moral conduct, nor by giving ourselves any illusion, when confronted by Scylla and Charybdis, as to our own ability to escape them. We are to understand the whole unbearable human situation, espouse it, take it upon ourselves. We are to bend before the doom revealed in the problem of ethics.

It is through the unescapable severity of this doom that we come upon the reality of God. It is this that proves that the problem of ethics, when it becomes our own, is the bond that relates us to God. We apply our hearts unto wisdom when we number our days, for by this very act we arrive at a world which is superior both in quality and kind to this in which we live. The impassable frontier of death, the unbridgeable chasm before which we are called to a halt, is the boundary that separates and must separate God from the world, Creator from creation, the Holy One from sinners, the heavenly idea of the good from all its necessarily fragmentary and infinitely imperfect appearances. Would God be God if he met us in any other way? Would he be the Source of all being and Creator of all things, unless, in comparison to him, all being had to be disqualified as not being, and all things recognized as estranged and fallen away from the good and perfect life which belongs to him alone? And can man conceivably enter in to him except through that door of death and hell which is the perception of his remoteness from him, his condemnation by him, and his powerlessness before him? We meet our doom upon the rocks of imperishable truth, but that is the only way we may be saved from the sea of appearance and delusion. The devastating negation under which we live has its positive, obverse side.

The meaning of our situation is that God does not leave us and that we cannot leave God. It is because God himself and God alone lends our life its possibility that it becomes so impossible for us to live. It is because God says Yes to us that the No of existence here is so fundamental and unescapable. It is because the answer to all our questions is God and God's conduct toward us, that the only answers that we can find in terms of our own conduct either change immediately into questions or are otherwise too vast for us. . . . It is when man is most remote from God that God in his mercy seeks out and finds him. In order to let him realize his own relation to him in its positive significance, that is, as love, forgiveness, life, mercy, grace, God waits only—if God may be said to wait—for the submissiveness which gives to him the glory due unto his name, for the penitence in which man makes an unconditional surrender, for the *desperatio fiducialis,* the confident despair in which man joyfully gives himself up for lost—joyfully, because he knows what it means to be lost in this way. The ethical question not only casts a dark shadow upon what we do in life, but lets through, at the very point where it is darkest, a new light. If the primary and positive relation of man to God is brought out by a last wholly negative and annihilating crisis, then evidently the whole conduct of man, since it is determined and disrupted by this valley-of-death crisis, participates in the justification, the promise, and the salutary meaning which are hidden there.

Up to now I have designedly omitted two central conceptions of the dialectic of Paul and the Reformation because, though they belong theoretically to the curve of our circle, they are part of another also: these are the conceptions of "faith" and of "revelation." For a definition of faith I go to that place in the gospel where the words are found, "Lord, I believe, help Thou mine unbelief"; and for a definition of revelation to a sentence of Luther, "I do not know it and do not understand it, but sounding from above and ringing in my ears I hear what is beyond the thought of man." Faith and revelation expressly deny that there is any way from man to God and to God's grace, love, and life. Both words indicate that the only way between God and man is that which leads

from God to man. Between these words—and this is the inner
kernel of the theology of Paul and the Reformation—there are two
other words: Jesus Christ. These two are also dialectical. They
were for Paul himself. A deluge of arguments and counter-argu-
ments has flowed over them in the past; and there is nothing to
indicate any change in the future. By words, we shall never reach
the place where problems cease—not even by these words. We
can only say that by these words Paul and Luther and, finally and
most positively, Calvin—whatever they thought about the moral
conduct of man on his way—meant to point toward another world,
toward that other circle which cuts the circle of our ethical problem, toward that way of God to man which is the channel by which
all reality reaches us.

41. ALBERT CAMUS: *THE MYTH OF SISYPHUS*

Just before, and for some time after, the Second World War,
Existentialism became the fashionable "philosophy" of continental Europe, comparable therein to surrealism after the
First World War. Though there is general agreement about the
influence of Sören Kierkegaard (1813–1855) and Friedrich
Nietzsche (1844–1900) on the various thinkers who call themselves existentialists, they among themselves are sharply divided in their outlook. Among the leading existentialists are
the German philosophers Karl Jaspers (b. 1883) and Martin
Heidegger (b. 1889), the French atheist philosopher Jean-Paul
Sartre (b. 1905), the Catholic theologian Gabriel Marcel (b.
1889), the Protestant theologian Paul Tillich (b. 1886), and
the Jewish religious philosopher Martin Buber (b. 1878).

A younger writer, Albert Camus (1913–1960), enjoyed
through his likable personality and his moral seriousness a
high authority among post-1945 European youth. Born in
Algeria and trained as a philosopher, he became one of the
most successful writers of the Second World War generation
in France. He analyzed the twentieth century dilemmas with
remarkable lucidity. His existentialist chief work was *Le
Mythe de Sisyphe* (1942), which was translated into English
by Justin O'Brien as *The Myth of Sisyphus* (1955). Camus was
awarded the Nobel Prize for literature in 1957.[23]

[23] Albert Camus, *The Myth of Sisyphus and Other Essays*, Vintage Books,
New York, 1959. Reprinted by permission of Alfred A. Knopf, Librairie Gallimard and Hamish Hamilton Ltd. Copyright 1955 by Alfred A. Knopf, Inc.

Of whom and of what indeed can I say: "I know that!" This heart within me I can feel, and I judge that it exists. This world I can touch, and I likewise judge that it exists. There ends all my knowledge, and the rest is construction. For if I try to seize this self of which I feel sure, if I try to define and to summarize it, it is nothing but water slipping through my fingers. I can sketch one by one all the aspects it is able to assume, all those likewise that have been attributed to it, this upbringing, this origin, this ardor or these silences, this nobility or this vileness. But aspects cannot be added up. This very heart which is mine will forever remain indefinable to me. Between the certainty I have of my existence and the content I try to give to that assurance, the gap will never be filled. Forever I shall be a stranger to myself. In psychology as in logic, there are truths but no truth. Socrates' "Know thyself" has as much value as the "Be virtuous" of our confessionals. They reveal a nostalgia at the same time as an ignorance. They are sterile exercises on great subjects. They are legitimate only in precisely so far as they are approximate.

And here are trees and I know their gnarled surface, water and I feel its taste. These scents of grass and stars at night, certain evenings when the heart relaxes—how shall I negate this world whose power and strength I feel? Yet all the knowledge on earth will give me nothing to assure me that this world is mine. You describe it to me and you teach me to classify it. You enumerate its laws and in my thirst for knowledge I admit that they are true. You take apart its mechanism and my hope increases. At the final stage you teach me that this wondrous and multi-colored universe can be reduced to the atom and that the atom itself can be reduced to the electron. All this is good and I wait for you to continue. But you tell me of an invisible planetary system in which electrons gravitate around a nucleus. You explain this world to me with an image. I realize then that you have been reduced to poetry: I shall never know. Have I the time to become indignant? You have already changed theories. So that science that was to teach me everything ends up in a hypothesis, that lucidity founders in metaphor, that uncertainty is resolved in a work of art. What need had I of so many efforts? The soft lines of these hills and the hand of evening on this troubled heart teach me much more. I have returned to my beginning. I realize that if through science I can seize phenomena and enumerate them, I cannot, for all that, apprehend the world. Were I to trace its entire relief with my finger, I should not know any more. And you give me the choice between a description that is sure but that teaches me nothing and hypotheses that claim to teach me but that are not sure. A stranger to myself and to the world, armed solely with a thought that negates itself as soon as it asserts, what is this condition in which I can have peace only by refusing to know and to live, in which the appetite for conquest bumps into walls that defy its assaults? To will is to stir up paradoxes. Everything is ordered in such a way as to bring into being that poisoned peace produced by thoughtlessness, lack of heart, or fatal renunciations.

Hence the intelligence, too, tells me in its way that this world is absurd. Its contrary, blind reason, may well claim that all is clear; I was waiting for proof and longing for it to be right. But despite so many pretentious centuries and over the heads of so many eloquent and persuasive men, I know that is false. On this plane, at least, there is no happiness if I cannot know. That universal reason, practical or ethical, that determinism, those categories that explain everything are enough to make a decent man laugh. They have nothing to do with the mind. They negate its profound truth, which is to be enchained. In this unintelligible and limited universe, man's fate henceforth assumes its meaning. A horde of irrationals has sprung up and surrounds him until his ultimate end. In his recovered and now studied lucidity, the feeling of the absurd becomes clear and definite. I said that the world is absurd, but I was too hasty. This world in itself is not reasonable, that is all that can be said. But what is absurd is the confrontation of this irrational and the wild longing for clarity whose call echoes in the human heart. The absurd depends as much on man as on the world. For the moment it is all that links them together. It binds them one to the other as only hatred can weld two creatures together. This is all I can discern clearly in this measureless universe where my adventure takes place. Let us pause here. If I hold to be true that absurdity that determines my relationship with life, if I become thoroughly imbued with that sentiment that seizes me in face of the world's scenes, with that lucidity imposed on me by the pursuit of a science, I must sacrifice everything to these certainties and I must see them squarely to be able to maintain them. Above all, I must adapt my behavior to them and pursue them in all their consequences. I am speaking here of decency. But I want to know beforehand if thought can live in those deserts....

From the moment absurdity is recognized, it becomes a passion, the most harrowing of all. But whether or not one can live with one's passions, whether or not one can accept their law, which is to burn the heart they simultaneously exalt—that is the whole question. It is not, however, the one we shall ask just yet. It stands at the center of this experience. There will be time to come back to it. Let us recognize rather those themes and those impulses born of the desert. It will suffice to enumerate them. They, too, are known to all today. There have always been men to defend the rights of the irrational. The tradition of what may be called humiliated thought has never ceased to exist. The criticism of rationalism has been made so often that it seems unnecessary to begin again. Yet our epoch is marked by the rebirth of those paradoxical systems that strive to trip up the reason as if truly it had always forged ahead. But that is not so much a proof of the efficacy of the reason as of the intensity of its hopes. On the plane of history, such a constancy of two attitudes illustrates the essential passion of man torn between his urge toward unity and the clear vision he may have of the walls enclosing him.

But never perhaps at any time has the attack on reason been more violent than in ours. Since Zarathustra's great outburst: "By chance it is the oldest nobility in the world. I conferred it upon all things when I proclaimed that above them no eternal will was exercised," since Kierkegaard's fatal illness, "that malady that leads to death with nothing else following it," the significant and tormenting themes of absurd thought have followed one another. Or at least, and this proviso is of capital importance, the themes of irrational and religious thought.

How can one fail to feel the basic relationship of these minds! How can one fail to see that they take their stand around a privileged and bitter moment in which hope has no further place? I want everything to be explained to me or nothing. And the reason is impotent when it hears this cry from the heart. The mind aroused by this insistence seeks and finds nothing but contradictions and nonsense. What I fail to understand is nonsense. The world is peopled with such irrationals. The world itself, whose single meaning I do not understand, is but a vast irrational. If one could only say just once: "This is clear," all would be saved. But these men vie with one another in proclaiming that nothing is clear, all is chaos, that all man has is his lucidity and his definite knowledge of the walls surrounding him.

All these experiences agree and confirm one another. The mind, when it reaches its limits, must make a judgment and choose its conclusions. This is where suicide and the reply stand. But I wish to reverse the order of the inquiry and start out from the intelligent adventure and come back to daily acts. The experiences called to mind here were born in the desert that we must not leave behind. At least it is essential to know how far they went. At this point of his effort man stands face to face with the irrational. He feels within him his longing for happiness and for reason. The absurd is born of this confrontation between the human need and the unreasonable silence of the world. This must not be forgotten. This must be clung to because the whole consequence of a life can depend on it. The irrational, the human nostalgia, and the absurd that is born of their encounter—these are the three characters in the drama that must necessarily end with all the logic of which an existence is capable.

Absurd Creation

PHILOSOPHY AND FICTION

All those lives maintained in the rarefied air of the absurd could not persevere without some profound and constant thought to infuse its strength into them. Right here, it can be only a strange feeling of fidelity. Conscious men have been seen to fulfill their task amid the most stupid of wars without considering themselves in contradiction. This is because it was essential to elude nothing. There is thus a metaphysical honor in enduring the world's absurdity. Conquest or play-acting, multiple loves, absurd revolt are tributes that man pays to his dignity in a campaign in which he is defeated in advance.

It is merely a matter of being faithful to the rule of the battle. That thought may suffice to sustain a mind; it has supported and still supports whole civilizations. War cannot be negated. One must live it or die of it. So it is with the absurd: it is a question of breathing with it, of recognizing its lessons and recovering their flesh. In this regard the absurd joy par excellence is creation. "Art and nothing but art," said Nietzsche; "we have art in order not to die of the truth."

. . .

It would be impossible to insist too much on the arbitrary nature of the former opposition between art and philosophy. If you insist on taking it in too limited a sense, it is certainly false. If you mean merely that these two disciplines each have their peculiar climate, that is probably true but remains vague. The only acceptable argument used to lie in the contradiction brought up between the philosopher enclosed *within* his system and the artist placed *before* his work. But this was pertinent for a certain form of art and of philosophy which we consider secondary here. The idea of an art detached from its creator is not only outmoded; it is false. In opposition to the artist, it is pointed out that no philosopher ever created several systems. But that is true in so far, indeed, as no artist ever expressed more than one thing under different aspects. The instantaneous perfection of art, the necessity for its renewal—this is true only through a preconceived notion. For the work of art likewise is a construction and everyone knows how monotonous the great creators can be. For the same reason as the thinker, the artist commits himself and becomes himself in his work. That osmosis raises the most important of æsthetic problems. Moreover, to anyone who is convinced of the mind's singleness of purpose, nothing is more futile than these distinctions based on methods and objects. There are no frontiers between the disciplines that man sets himself for understanding and loving. They interlock, and the same anxiety merges them.

The Myth of Sisyphus

The gods had condemned Sisyphus to ceaselessly rolling a rock to the top of a mountain, whence the stone would fall back of its own weight. They had thought with some reason that there is no more dreadful punishment than futile and hopeless labor.

If one believes Homer, Sisyphus was the wisest and most prudent of mortals. According to another tradition, however, he was disposed to practice the profession of highwayman. I see no contradiction in this. Opinions differ as to the reasons why he became the futile laborer of the underworld. To begin with, he is accused of a certain levity in regard to the gods. He stole their secrets. Ægina, the daughter of Æsopus, was carried off by Jupiter. The father was shocked by that disappearance and complained to Sisyphus. He, who knew of the abduction, offered to tell about it on condition that Æsopus would give water to the citadel of Corinth. To the celestial thunderbolts he preferred the benediction of water. He was punished for this in the underworld. Homer tells us also that Sisyphus had put Death in chains. Pluto could not endure the sight of his deserted, silent empire. He dispatched the god of war, who liberated Death from the hands of her conqueror.

It is said also that Sisyphus, being near to death, rashly wanted to test his wife's love. He ordered her to cast his unburied body into the middle of the public square. Sisyphus woke up in the underworld. And there, annoyed by an obedience so contrary to human love, he obtained from Pluto permission to return to earth in order to chastise his wife. But when he had seen again the face of this world, enjoyed water and sun, warm stones and the sea, he no longer wanted to go back to the infernal darkness. Recalls, signs of anger, warnings were of no avail. Many years more he lived facing the curve of the gulf, the sparkling sea, and the smiles of earth. A decree of the gods was necessary. Mercury came and seized the impudent man by the collar and, snatching him from his joys, led him forcibly back to the underworld, where his rock was ready for him.

You have already grasped that Sisyphus is the absurd hero. He *is*, as much through his passions as through his torture. His scorn of the gods, his hatred of death, and his passion for life won him that unspeakable penalty in which the whole being is exerted toward accomplishing nothing. This is the price that must be paid for the passions of this earth. Nothing is told us about Sisyphus in the underworld. Myths are made for the imagination to breathe life into them. As for this myth, one sees merely the whole effort of a body straining to raise the huge stone, to roll it and push it up a slope a hundred times over; one sees the face screwed up, the cheek tight against the stone, the shoulder bracing the clay-covered mass, the foot wedging it, the fresh start with arms outstretched, the wholly human security of two earth-clotted hands. At the very end of his long effort measured by skyless space and time without depth, the purpose is achieved. Then Sisyphus watches the stone rush down in a few moments toward that lower world whence he will have to push it up again toward the summit. He goes back down to the plain.

It is during that return, that pause, that Sisyphus interests me. A face that toils so close to stones is already stone itself! I see that man going back down with a heavy yet measured step toward the torment of which he will never know the end. That hour like a breathing-space which returns as surely as his suffering, that is the hour of consciousness. At each of those moments when he leaves the heights and gradually sinks toward the lairs of the gods, he is superior to his fate. He is stronger than his rock.

If this myth is tragic, that is because its hero is conscious. Where would his torture be, indeed, if at every step the hope of succeeding upheld him? The workman of today works every day in his life at the same tasks, and this fate is no less absurd. But it is tragic only at the rare moments when it becomes conscious. Sisyphus, proletarian of the gods, powerless and rebellious, knows the whole extent of his wretched condition: it is what he thinks of during his descent. The lucidity that was to constitute his torture at the same time crowns his victory. There is no fate that cannot be surmounted by scorn.

If the descent is thus sometimes performed in sorrow, it can also take place in joy. This word is not too much. Again I fancy Sisyphus returning toward his rock, and the sorrow was in the beginning. When the images of earth cling too tightly to memory, when the call of happiness becomes too insistent, it happens that melancholy rises in man's heart: this is the rock's victory, this is the rock itself. The boundless grief is too heavy to bear. These are our nights of Gethsemane. But crushing truths perish from being acknowledged. Thus, Œdipus at the outset obeys fate without knowing it. But from the moment he knows, his tragedy begins. Yet at the same moment, blind and desperate, he realizes that the only bond linking him to the world is the cool hand of a girl. Then a tremendous remark rings out: "Despite so many ordeals, my advanced age and the nobility of my soul make me conclude that all is well." Sophocles' Œdipus, like Dostoevsky's Kirilov, thus gives the recipe for the absurd victory. Ancient wisdom confirms modern heroism.

One does not discover the absurd without being tempted to write a manual of happiness. "What! by such narrow ways—?" There is but one world, however. Happiness and the absurd are two sons of the same earth. They are inseparable. It would be a mistake to say that happiness necessarily springs from the absurd discovery. It happens as well that the feeling of the absurd springs from happiness. "I conclude that all is well," says Œdipus, and that remark is sacred. It echoes in the wild and limited universe of man. It teaches that all is not, has not been, exhausted. It drives out of this world a god who had come into it with dissatisfaction and a preference for futile sufferings. It makes of fate a human matter, which must be settled among men.

All Sisyphus' silent joy is contained therein. His fate belongs to him. His rock is his thing. Likewise, the absurd man, when he contemplates his torment, silences all the idols. In the universe suddenly restored to its silence, the myriad wondering little voices of the earth rise up. Unconscious, secret calls, invitations from all the faces, they are the necessary reverse and price of victory. There is no sun without shadow, and it is essential to know the night. The absurd man says yes and his effort will henceforth be unceasing. If there is a personal fate, there is no higher destiny, or at least there is but one which he concludes is inevitable and despicable. For the rest, he knows himself to be the master of his days. At that subtle moment when man glances backward over his life, Sisyphus returning toward his rock, in that slight pivoting he contemplates that series of unrelated actions which becomes his fate, created by him, combined under his memory's eye and soon sealed by his death. Thus, convinced of the wholly human origin of all that is human, a blind man eager to see who knows that the night has no end, he is still on the go. The rock is still rolling.

I leave Sisyphus at the foot of the mountain! One always finds one's burden again. But Sisyphus teaches the higher fidelity that negates the gods and raises rocks. He too concludes that all is well. This universe henceforth without a master seems to him neither sterile nor futile. Each atom of that stone, each mineral flake of that night-filled mountain, in itself forms a world. The struggle itself toward the heights is enough to fill a man's heart. One must imagine Sisyphus happy.

42. ORTEGA y GASSET: *THE HISTORICAL SIGNIFICANCE OF EINSTEIN'S THEORY*

The twentieth century will be distinguished in history by its great and revolutionary scientific discoveries. Among them the theory of relativity of Albert Einstein (1879–1955) ranks very high. Born in Germany but brought up in Switzerland, where he taught until 1913, Einstein became in that year director of the Kaiser Wilhelm Institute for Physics in Berlin. The Hitler regime deprived him of this post in 1933, and Einstein joined the Institute for Advanced Study in Princeton, New Jersey.

He began his work on the theory of relativity with the publication of the restricted principle with its consequences in 1905. In 1923, in one chapter of his *El tema de nuestro tiempo,* the Spanish philosopher José Ortega y Gasset (1883–1955) discussed the historical significance of Einstein's theory. The book was translated into English under the title *The Modern Theme* by James Cleugh and published in 1933. Ortega has become well known through two of his other books which are characteristic of the contemporary mood: *The Revolt of the Masses* (Spanish original, 1930; English translation, 1932) and *The Dehumanization of Art* (Spanish original, 1925; English translation, 1948).[24]

The theory of relativity, the most important intellectual fact that the present time can show, inasmuch as it is a theory, admits of discussion whether it is true or false. But, apart from its truth or falsity, a theory is a collection of thoughts which is born in a mind, in a spirit or in a conscience in the same way as a fruit is born upon a tree. Now, a new fruit indicates that a new species is making its appearance in the flora of the world. Accordingly, we can study the theory of relativity with the same design as a botanist has in describing a plant: we can put aside the question whether the fruit is beneficial or harmful, whether the theory is true or erroneous, and attend solely to the problem of classifying the new species. Such an analysis will enable us to discover the historical significance of the theory, viz., its nature as an historical phenomenon.

[24] José Ortega y Gasset. *The Modern Theme,* translated by James Cleugh (London, 1933)

The peculiarities of the theory of relativity point to certain specific tendencies in the mind which has created it. And as a scientific edifice of this magnitude is not the work of one man but the result of the inadvertent collaboration of many, of all the best contemporary minds, in fact, the orientation which these tendencies reveal will indicate the course of western history.

I do not merely mean by this that the triumph of the theory will influence the spirit of mankind by imposing on it the adoption of a definite route. That is an obvious banality. What is really interesting is the inverse proposition: the spirit of man has set out, of its own accord, upon a definite route, and it has therefore been possible for the theory of relativity to be born and to triumph. The more subtle and technical ideas are, the more remote they seem from the ordinary preoccupations of men, the more authentically they denote the profound variations produced in the historical mind of humanity.

It will be enough to lay some little emphasis upon the general tendencies operative in the invention of the theory, and to prolong their lines somewhat beyond the precincts of physics, for the pattern of a new sensibility to shape itself before our eyes, a sensibility antagonistic to that which has prevailed in recent centuries.

1. Absolutism

The whole system centres, organically, in the idea of relativity. Everything depends, therefore, on the physiognomy assumed by this conception in Einstein's work of genius. It would not be lacking in all sense of proportion to assert that it is at this point that genius has applied its inspired vigour, its thrust of adventurous energy, its sublime archangelic audacity. Once this point was admitted, the rest of the theory could have been worked out with no more than ordinary care.

Classical mechanics recognizes the common relativity of all our conclusions on the question of movement and, therefore, the relativity of every position in space and time which the human mind can observe. How is it, then, that the theory of Einstein which, we are told, has destroyed the entire edifice of classical mechanics, throws into relief in its very name, as its principal characteristic, relativity itself? This is the multiform equivocation which we are bound, above all, to expose. *The relativism of Einstein is strictly inverse to that of Galileo and Newton.* For the latter the empirical conclusions we come to concerning duration, location and movement are relative because they believe in the existence of absolute space, time and movement. We cannot perceive them immediately; at most we possess indirect indications of them (centrifugal forces are an example). But if their existence is believed in all, the effective conclusions we come to will be disqualified as mere appearances, values relative to the standpoint of comparison occupied by the observer. Consequently, relativism here connotes failure. The physical science of Galileo and Newton is relative in this sense.

Let us suppose that, for one reason or another, a man considers it incumbent upon him to deny the existence of those unattainable absolutes in space, time and transference. At once those concrete conclusions, which formerly appeared relative in the sinister sense of the word, being freed from comparison with the absolute, become the only conclusions that express reality. Absolute (unattainable) reality and a further reality, which is relative in comparison with the former, will not now exist. There will only be one single reality, and this will be what positive physics approximately describes. Now, this reality is what the observer perceives from the place he occupies; it is therefore a relative reality. But as this relative reality, in the suppositious case we have taken, is the only one there is, it must, as well as being relative, be true or, what comes to the same thing, absolute reality. Relativism is not here opposed to absolutism; on the contrary, it merges with it and, so far from suggesting a failure in our knowledge, endows the latter with an absolute validity.

This is the case with the mechanics of Einstein. His physical science is not relative, but relativist, and achieves, thanks to its relativism, an absolute significance.

The most absurd misrepresentation which can be applied to the new mechanics is to interpret it as one more offspring of the old philosophic relativism, of which it is in fact the executioner. In the old relativism our knowledge is relative because what we aspire to know, viz., space-time reality, is absolute and we cannot attain to it. In the physics of Einstein our knowledge is absolute; it is reality that is relative.

Consequently, we are above all bound to note as one of the most genuine features of the new theory its absolutist tendency in the sphere of knowledge. It is inexplicable that this point should not have been emphasized as a matter of course by those who interpret the philosophic significance of this innovation of genius. The tendency is perfectly clear, however, in the capital formula of the whole theory: physical laws are true whatever may be the system of reference used, that is to say, whatever the point of observation may be. Fifty years ago thinkers were preoccupied with the question whether "from the point of view of Sirius" human truths would be valid. This is equivalent to a degradation of the science practised by man by an attribution to it of a purely domestic value. The mechanics of Einstein permit our physical laws to harmonise with those which may be conjectured to prevail in minds inhabiting Sirius.

But this new absolutism differs radically from that which animated rationalist doctrine during the last few centuries. Such rationalists believed that it was man's privilege to unveil the secrets of nature without doing more than exploring the recesses of his own soul for the eternal truths which it contained. In this belief Descartes creates physics, not from experience, but from what he calls the *trésor de mon esprit*. The value of such truths, which do not proceed from observation, but from pure reason, is universal in character, and instead of learning them from nature we actually, in a certain sense, impose them on nature. They are *à priori* truths. In the works of Newton himself are to be found phrases which reveal the rationalist spirit. "In natural philosophy," he says, "we must abstract our senses." In other words, in order to verify the nature of anything we must turn our backs on it. An example of these magical truths is the law of inertia: according to this law, a moving body, free from all influence, will go on moving indefinitely in a rectilineal and uniform way. Now, such a body, exempt from all influence, is unknown to us. Why make such an affirmation? Simply because space has a rectilineal or euclidian structure and consequently all "spontaneous" movement, which is not diverted by some force, will accommodate itself to the law of space.

But what guarantees this euclidian nature of space? Experience? In a way it does; the nature of pure reason is to resolve, previously to all experience, on the absolute necessity of the space in which physical bodies move being euclidian. Man cannot *see* except in euclidian space. This peculiarity of the inhabitants of the earth is promoted by rationalism to the dignity of a law of the whole cosmos. The old absolutists perpetrated a similar naiveté in every sphere of thought. They begin with an excessive estimate of man. They make him a centre of the universe, though he is only a corner of it. This is the cardinal error that the theory of Einstein now corrects.

2. Perspectivism

The provincial spirit has always, and with good reason, been accused of stupidity. Its nature involves an optical illusion. The provincial does not realise that he is looking at the world from a decentralised position. He supposes, on the contrary, that he is at the centre of the whole earth, and accordingly passes judgment on all things as if his vision were directed from that centre. This is the cause of the deplorable complacency which produces such comic effects. All his opinions are falsified as soon as they are formulated because they originate from a pseudo-centre. On the other hand, the dweller in the capital knows that his city, however large it may be, is only one point of the cosmos, a decentralised corner of it. He knows, further, that the world has no centre, and that it is therefore necessary, in all our judgments, to discount the peculiar perspective that reality offers when it is looked at from our own point of view. This is the reason why the provincial always thinks his neighbor of the great city a sceptic, though the fact is that the latter is only better informed.

The theory of Einstein has shown modern science, with its exemplary discipline—the *nuova scienza* of Galileo, the proud physical philosophy of the West—to have been labouring under an acute form of provincialism. Euclidian geometry, which is only applicable to what is close at hand, had been extended to the whole universe. In Germany today the system of Euclid is beginning to be called "proximate geometry" in contradistinction to other collections of axioms which, like those of Riemann,[25] are long-range geometries.

The refutation of this provincial geometry, like that of all provincialism, has been accomplished by means of an apparent limitation, an exercise of modesty in the claims of its conqueror. Einstein is convinced that to talk of Space is a kind of megalomania which inevitably introduces error. We are not aware of any more extensions than those we measure, and we cannot measure more than our instruments can deal with. These are our organs of scientific vision; they determine the spatial structure of the world we know. But as every other being desirous of constructing a system of physics from some other place in the earth is in the same case, the result is that there is no real limitation involved at all.

There is no question, then, of our relapsing into a subjectivist interpretation of knowledge, according to which the truth is only true for a pre-determined subjective personality. According to the theory of relativity, the event A, which from the terrestrial point of view precedes the event B in time, will, from another place in the universe—Sirius, for example—seem to succeed B. There cannot be a more complete inversion of reality. Does it mean that either our own imagination or else that of the mind resident in Sirius is at fault? Not at all. Neither the human mind nor that in Sirius alters the conformation of reality. The fact of the matter is that one of the qualities proper to reality is that of possessing perspective, that is, of organising itself in different ways so as to

25 Georg Friedrich Bernhard Riemann (1826–1866), German mathematician who originated a noneuclidian system of geometry.

be visible from different points. Space and time are the objective ingredients of physical perspective, and it is natural that they should vary according to the point of view.

What surprises me more is that no one has yet noticed this cardinal feature in the work of Einstein. Without a single exception —so far as I know—all that has been written on the matter interprets his great discovery as one step more on the road of subjectivism. In all languages and in all centres of culture we continue to hear that Einstein has confirmed the Kantian doctrine in at least one point, viz., the subjectivity of space and time. It is important for my purpose to declare circumstantially that this belief seems to me the most complete misconception of the significance that the theory of relativity implies.

Let us define the question in a few words, but in the clearest way we can. Perspective is the order and form that reality takes for him who contemplates it. If the place that he occupies varies, the perspective also varies. On the other hand, if another observer is substituted for him in the same place, the perspective remains identical. It is true that if there is no contemplating personality by whom reality is observed there is no perspective. Does this mean that the latter is subjective? Here we have the equivocation which has for centuries, to say the least, misled all philosophy and consequently the attitude of man to the universe. To avoid this difficulty all we have to do is to make a simple distinction.

When we see a stationary and solitary billiard ball we only perceive its qualities of colour and form. But suppose another ball collides with the first. The latter is then driven forward with a speed proportionate to the shock of the collision. Thereupon we note a new quality of the ball, which was previously latent, viz., its resilience. But, someone may say, resilience is not a quality of the first ball, for the quality in question only appears when the second ball collides with it. We shall answer at once that it is not so. Resilience is a quality of the first ball no less than its colour and form, but it is a reactive quality, i.e., one responsive to the action of another object. Thus, in a man, what we usually call his character is his way of reacting to externality—things, persons or events.

Well, now: when some reality collides with another object which we denominate "conscious subject," the reality responds to the subject by *appearing to it*. Appearance is an objective quality of the real, its response to a subject. This response is, moreover, different according to the condition of the observer; for example, according to his standpoint of contemplation. It is to be noted that perspective and point of view now acquire an objective value, though they were previously considered to be deformations imposed by the subject upon reality. Time and space are once more, in defiance of the Kantian thesis, forms of the real.

If there had been among the infinite number of points of view an exceptional one to which it might have been possible to assign a superior correspondence with nature, we could have considered the rest as deforming agents or as "purely subjective." Galileo and Newton believed that this was the case when they spoke of absolute space, that is to say, of a space contemplated from a point of view which is in no way concrete. Newton calls absolute space *sensorium Dei*, the visual organ of God; or, we might say, divine perspective. But we have scarcely thought out in all its implications this idea of a perspective which is not seen from any determined and exclusive place when we discover its contradictory and absurd nature. There is no absolute space because there is no absolute perspective. To be absolute, space has to cease being real—a space full of phenomena—and become an abstraction.

The theory of Einstein is a marvellous proof of the harmonious multiplicity of all possible points of view. If the idea is extended to morals and aesthetics, we shall come to experience history and life in a new way.

The individual who desires to master the maximum amount possible of truth will not now be compelled, as he was for centuries enjoined, to replace his spontaneous point of view with another of an exemplary and standardised character, which used to be called the "vision of things *sub specie aeternitatis*." The point of view of eternity is blind: it sees nothing and does not exist. Man will henceforth endeavor, instead, to be loyal to the unipersonal imperative which represents his individuality.

It is the same with nations. Instead of regarding non-European cultures as barbarous, we shall now begin to respect them, as methods of confronting the cosmos which are equivalent to our own. There is a Chinese perspective which is fully as justified as the Western.

3. Antiutopianism or antirationalism

The same tendency which in its positive form leads to perspectivism signifies in its negative form hostility to utopianism.

The utopian conception is one which, while believing itself to arise from "nowhere," yet claims to be valid for everyone. To a sensibility of the type evident in the theory of relativity this obstinate refusal to be localised necessarily appears over-confident. There is no spectator of the cosmic spectacle who does not occupy a definite position. To want to see something and not to want to see it from some particular place is an absurdity. Such puerile insubordination to the conditions imposed on us by reality, such incapacity for the cheerful acceptance of destiny, so ingenuous an assumption that it is easy to substitute our own sterile desires, are features of a spirit which is today nearing its end and on the verge of giving place to another completely antagonistic to it.

The utopian creed has dominated the European mind during the whole of the modern epoch in science, in morals, in religion and in art. The whole weight of the intensely earnest desire to master reality—a specifically European characteristic—had to be thrown into the scales to prevent Western civilisation from perishing in a gigantic fiasco. For the most troublesome feature of utopianism is not that it gives us false solutions to problems—scientific or political —but something worse: the difficulty is that it does not accept the problem of the real as it is presented, but immediately, viz., *à priori,* imposes a form on it which is capricious.

If we compare Western life with that of Asia—Indian or Chinese —we are at once struck by the spiritual instability of the European as opposed to the profound equilibrium of the Oriental mind. This equilibrium reveals the fact that, at any rate in the greatest problems of life, the Easterner has discovered formulae more perfectly adjusted to reality. The European, on the other hand, has been frivolous in his appreciation of the elemental factors of life and has contrived capricious interpretations of them which have periodically to be replaced.

The utopist aberration of human intelligence begins in Greece and occurs wherever rationalism reaches the point of exacerbation. Pure reason constructs an exemplary world—a physical or political cosmos—in the belief that it is the true reality and must therefore supplant the actually existent one. The divergence between phenomena and pure ideas is such that the conflict is inevitable. But the rationalist is sure that the struggle will result in the defeat of reality. *This conviction is the main characteristic of the rationalist temperament.*

Reality, naturally, possesses more than sufficient toughness to resist the assaults of ideas. Rationalism then looks for a way out: it recognises that, *for the moment,* the idea cannot be realised, but believes that success will be achieved in an "infinite process" (Leibnitz, Kant). Utopianism [no-where] takes the form of "uchronianism," [no-time]. During the last two centuries and a half every difficulty was resolved by an appeal to the infinite, or at least to periods of indeterminate length. In Darwinism, for instance, one species is born of another without the intervention of more than a few millennia between the two. It is assumed that time, that ghostly river, by merely elapsing, can be an efficient cause and make what is actually inconceivable a probability.

We do not realise that science, whose sole pleasure is to obtain a reliable image of nature, can be nourished on illusion. I remember one detail that has exercised a very great deal of influence over my thought. Many years ago I was reading a lecture of the physiologist Loeb[26] on tropism, a concept by means of which it was thought possible to describe and explain the law which regulates the elemental movements of infusoria. This concept, with certain corrections and additions, serves as a basis for understanding some of these phenomena. But at the end of his lecture Loeb adds: "The time will come when what we call today the moral acts of man will be explained simply as tropisms." This piece of audacity shocked me extremely, for it opened my eyes to many other opinions of modern science which makes, with less ostentation, the same mistake. So then, I thought, such a concept as tropism, which is scarcely capable of penetrating the secret of phenomena so simple as the transference of infusoria, can be thought sufficient, in some vague future, to explain so mysterious and complex a thing as the ethical acts of man. What sense can there be in this? Science has to solve its problems today, not put us off to the Greek kalends. If its actual methods are not enough at present to master the riddle of the universe the proper thing to do is to replace them with others which may be more efficacious. Current science, however, is full of problems which are left intact because they are incompatible with the methods employed. It is, apparently, the former which are to overcome the latter, and not *vice versa*. Science is full of uchronianism, of Greek kalends.

When we emerge from this scientific beatitude, with its cult of idolatrous worship of pre-established methods, and turn to the thought of Einstein we feel, as it were, a fresh morning breeze. The attitude of Einstein is completely distinct from the traditional one. We see him advancing directly upon problems with the gesture of a young athlete and, by employing the method readiest to hand, catching them by the horns. He makes a virtue and an effiicacious system of tactics out of what appeared to be a defect and a limitation in science.

A short digression will enable us to see this question in a clearer light.

One part of the work of Kant will remain imperishable, viz., his

[26] Jacques Loeb (1859–1924), German biologist, famous for his tropism theory which he published before he was thirty, emigrated in 1891 to the United States, where he was professor of biophysiology and member of the Rockefeller Institute for Medical Research.

great discovery that experience is not only the aggregate of data transmitted by the senses, but also a product of two factors. The sensible datum has to be received, given its correct affiliation and organised in a system of disposition. This order is supplied by the subjective personality and is *à priori*. In other words, physical experience is a compound of observation and geometry. Geometry is a pentagraph elaborated by pure reason: observation is the work of the senses. All science which is explanatory of material phenomena has contained, contains and will contain these two ingredients.

This identity of composition, invariably exhibited by modern physics throughout its entire history, does not, however, exclude the most profound variations in its spirit. The mutual relation maintained between its two ingredients leaves room, in fact, for very diverse interpretations. Which of the two is to supplant the other? Ought observation to yield to the demands of geometry, or geometry to observation? To decide one way or the other will mean our adherence to one of two antagonistic types of intellectual tendency. There is room for two opposed castes of opinion in one and the same system of physics.

It is common knowledge that the experiment of Michelson[27] is crucial in the hierarchy of such tests: physical theory is there placed between the devil and the deep sea. The geometrical law which proclaims the unalterable homogeneity of space, whatever may be the processes which occur in it, enters into uncompromising conflict with observation, with fact, with matter. One of two things must happen: either matter is to yield to geometry or the latter to the former.

In this acute dilemma two intellectual temperaments come before us, and we are able to observe their reaction. Lorentz[28] and Einstein, confronted by the same experiment, take opposite resolutions. Lorentz, in this particular representing the old rationalism, believes himself obliged to conclude that it is matter which yields and contracts. The celebrated "contradiction of Lorentz" is an admirable example of utopianism. It is the Oath of the Tennis Court[29] transferred to physics. Einstein adopts the contrary solution. Geometry must yield, pure space is to bow to observation, to curve, in fact.

[27] Albert Abraham Michelson (1852–1931), American physicist, received the Nobel prize in 1907. His demonstration that the absolute motion of the earth through the ether is not measurable was the starting point of the theory of relativity.

[28] Hendrik Anton Lorentz (1853–1928), Dutch physicist, received the Nobel Prize in 1902. He did work on phenomena of moving bodies that led to the theory of relativity.

[29] Oath taken on the tennis court of the Tuilleries Palace in Paris on June 20, 1789, by the National Assembly

In the political sphere, supposing the analogy to be a perfect one, Lorentz would say: Nations may perish, provided we keep our principles. Einstein, on the other hand, would maintain: We must look for such principles as will preserve nations, because that is what principles are for.

It is not easy to exaggerate the importance of the change of course imposed by Einstein upon physical science. Hitherto the *rôle* of geometry, of pure reason, has been to exercise an undisputed dictatorship. Common speech retains a trace of the sublime function which used to be attributed to reason: people talk of the "dictates of reason." For Einstein the *rôle* of reason is a much more modest one: it descends from dictatorship to the status of a humble instrument, which has, in every case, first to prove its efficiency.

Galileo and Newton made the universe euclidian simply because reason dictated it so. But pure reason cannot do anything but invent systems of methodical arrangement. These may be very numerous and various. Euclidian geometry is one, Riemann's another, Lobachevsky's[30] another, and so on. But it is clearly not these systems, not pure reason, which resolve the nature of the real. On the contrary, reality selects from among these possible orders or schemes the one which has more affinity with itself. This is what the theory of relativity means. The rationalist past of four centuries is confronted by the genius of Einstein, who inverts the time-honoured relation which used to exist between reason and observation. Reason ceases to be an imperative standard and is converted into an arsenal of instruments; observation tests these and decides which is the most convenient to use. The result is the creation of the science of mutual selection between pure ideas and pure facts.

This is one of the features which it is most important to emphasize in the thought of Einstein, for here we discover the initiation of an entirely new attitude to life. Culture ceases to be, as hitherto, an imperative standard to which our existence has to conform. We can now see a more delicate and more just relation between the two factors. Certain phenomena of life are selected as possible forms of culture; but of these possible forms of culture life, in its turn, selects the only ones which are suitable for future realisation.

4. Finitism

I should not like to conclude this genealogical sketch of the profound tendencies rife in the theory of relativity without alluding

[30] Nikolai Ivanovich Lobachevsky (1793–1853), Russian mathematician, pioneer in noneuclidian, "imaginary" geometry

to the most clear and patent of them. While the utopist past used to settle all disputes by the expedient of recourse to the infinite in space and time, the physics of Einstein annotates the universe. The world of Einstein is curved, and therefore closed and finite.

For anyone who believes that scientific doctrines are born by means of spontaneous generation and need do no more than open our eyes and minds to facts the innovation under discussion has no real importance. It merely amounts to a modification of the form which used to be attributed to the world. But the original supposition is false: a scientific doctrine is not born, however obvious the facts upon which it is based may appear, without a well-defined spiritual orientation. It is necessary to understand the genesis of our thoughts in all their delicate duplicity. No more truths are discovered than those we are already in search of. To the rest, however evident they may be, the spirit is blind.

This gives an enormous range of reference to the fact that physics and mathematics are suddenly beginning to have a marked preference for the finite and a great distaste for the infinite. Can there be a more radical difference between two minds than that one should tend to the idea that the universe is unlimited and that the other should feel its environment to be circumscribed? The infinity of the cosmos was one of the great intoxicating ideas produced by the Renaissance. It flooded the hearts of men with tides of pathetic emotion, and Giordano Bruno suffered a cruel death on its behalf. During the whole of the modern epoch the most earnest desires of Western man have concealed, as though it were a magical foundation for them, this idea of the infinity of the cosmic scene.

And now, all at once, the world has become limited, a garden surrounded by confining walls, an apartment, an interior. Does not this new setting suggest an entirely different style of living, altogether opposed to that at present in use? Our grandsons will enter existence armed with this notion, and their attitude to space will have a meaning contrary to that of our own. There is evident in this propensity to finitism a definite urge towards limitation, towards beauty of serene type, towards antipathy to vague superlatives, towards antiromanticism. The Greek, the "classical" man, also lived in a limited universe. All Greek culture has a horror of the infinite and seeks the *metron*, the mean.

It would be superficial, however, to believe that the human mind is being directed towards a new classicism. The classical man sought the limit, but it was because he had never lived in an unlimited world. Our case is inverse: the limit signifies an amputation for us, and the closed and finite world in which we are now to draw breath will be, irremediably, a truncated universe.

43. WHITEHEAD:
REQUISITES OF SOCIAL PROGRESS

Alfred North Whitehead (1861–1947), an English mathematician and philosopher, was for many years professor at the Imperial College of Science and Technology at the University of London, until he became professor of philosophy at Harvard (1924–1936). In 1910 he published, together with Bertrand Russell (born 1872), *Principia Mathematica*.

The following text is from chapter XIII, "Requisites of Social Progress," from his book *Science and the Modern World*.[31] The text deals with one of the central problems of our time: the impact of science on society and civilization. Against a prevailing cultural pessimism in the middle of the twentieth century, which so sharply contrasts with the prevailing easy optimism of the middle of the nineteenth century, it is good to recall Whitehead's last sentence in the essay reproduced here—that throughout history "the great ages have been unstable ages."

Another great fact confronting the modern world is the discovery of the method of training professionals, who specialise in particular regions of thought and thereby progressively add to the sum of knowledge with their respective limitations of subject. In consequence of the success of this professionalising of knowledge, there are two points to be kept in mind, which differentiate our present age from the past. In the first place, the rate of progress is such that an individual human being, of ordinary length of life, will be called upon to face novel situations which find no parallel in his past. The fixed person for the fixed duties, who in older societies was such a godsend, in the future will be a public danger. In the second place, the modern professionalism in knowledge works in the opposite direction so far as the intellectual sphere is concerned. The modern chemist is likely to be weak in zoology, weaker still in his general knowledge of the Elizabethan drama, and completely ignorant of the principles of rhythm in English versification. It is probably safe to ignore his knowledge of ancient history. Of course I am speaking of general tendencies; for chemists are no

[31] Reprinted with permission of the publisher from *Science and the Modern World* by Alfred North Whitehead. Copyright 1925 by the Macmillan Company. Copyright 1953 by Evelyn Whitehead.

worse than engineers, or mathematicians, or classical scholars. Effective knowledge is professionalised knowledge, supported by a restricted acquaintance with useful subjects subservient to it.

This situation has its dangers. It produces minds in a groove. Each profession makes progress, but it is progress in its own groove. Now to be mentally in a groove is to live in contemplating a given set of abstractions. The groove prevents straying across country, and the abstraction abstracts from something to which no further attention is paid. But there is no groove of abstractions which is adequate for the comprehension of human life. Thus in the modern world, the celibacy of the medieval learned class has been replaced by a celibacy of the intellect which is divorced from the concrete contemplation of the complete facts. Of course, no one is merely a mathematician, or merely a lawyer. People have lives outside their professions or their businesses. But the point is the restraint of serious thought within a groove. The remainder of life is treated superficially, with the imperfect categories of thought derived from one profession.

The dangers arising from this aspect of professionalism are great, particularly in our democratic societies. The directive force of reason is weakened. The leading intellects lack balance. They see this set of circumstances, or that set; but not both sets together. The task of coordination is left to those who lack either the force or the character to succeed in some definite career. In short, the specialised functions of the community are performed better and more progressively, but the generalised direction lacks vision. The progressiveness in detail only adds to the danger produced by the feebleness of coordination.

This criticism of modern life applies throughout, in whatever sense you construe the meaning of a community. It holds if you apply it to a nation, a city, a district, an institution, a family, or even to an individual. There is a development of particular abstractions, and a contraction of concrete appreciation. The whole is lost in one of its aspects. It is not necessary for my point that I should maintain that our directive wisdom, either as individuals or as communities, is less now than in the past. Perhaps it has slightly improved. But the novel pace of progress requires a greater force of direction if disasters are to be avoided. The point is that the discoveries of the nineteenth century were in the direction of professionalism, so that we are left with no expansion of wisdom and with greater need of it.

Wisdom is the fruit of a balanced development. It is this balanced growth of individuality which it should be the aim of education to secure. The most useful discoveries for the immediate future would concern the furtherance of this aim without detriment to the necessary intellectual professionalism. . . .

There is no easy single solution of the practical difficulties of education. We can, however, guide ourselves by a certain simplicity in its general theory. The student should concentrate within a limited field. Such concentration should include all practical and intellectual acquirements requisite for that concentration. This is the ordinary procedure; and, in respect to it, I should be inclined even to increase the facilities for concentration rather than to diminish them. With the concentration there are associated certain subsidiary studies, such as languages for science. Such a scheme of professional training should be directed to a clear end congenial to the student. It is not necessary to elaborate the qualifications of these statements. Such a training must, of course, have the width requisite for its end. But its design should not be complicated by the consideration of other ends. This professional training can only touch one side of education. Its centre of gravity lies in the intellect, and its chief tool is the printed book. The centre of gravity of the other side of training should lie in intuition without an analytical divorce from the total environment. Its object is immediate apprehension with the minimum of eviscerating analysis. The type of generality, which above all is wanted, is the appreciation of variety of value. I mean an aesthetic growth. There is something between the gross specialised values of the mere practical man, and the thin specialised values of the mere scholar. Both types have missed something; and if you add together the two sets of values, you do not obtain the missing elements. What is wanted is an appreciation of the infinite variety of vivid values achieved by an organism in its proper environment. When you understand all about the sun and all about the atmosphere and all about the rotation of the earth, you may still miss the radiance of the sunset. There is no substitute for the direct perception of the concrete achievement of a thing in its actuality. We want concrete fact with a highlight thrown on what is relevant to its preciousness.

What I mean is art and aesthetic education. It is, however, art in such a general sense of the term that I hardly like to call it by that name. Art is a special example. What we want is to draw out habits of aesthetic apprehension. According to the metaphysical doctrine which I have been developing, to do so is to increase the depth of individuality. The analysis of reality indicates the two factors, activity emerging into individualised aesthetic value. Also the emergent value is the measure of the individualisation of the activity. We must foster the creative initiative towards the maintenance of objective values. You will not obtain the apprehension without the initiative, or the initiative without the apprehension. As soon as you get towards the concrete, you cannot exclude action. Sensitiveness without impulse spells decadence, and impulse without sensitiveness spells brutality. I am using the word "sensitiveness" in its most general signification, so as to include apprehension of what lies beyond oneself; that is to say, sensitiveness to all the facts of the case. Thus "art" in the general sense which I require is any selection by which the concrete facts are so arranged as to elicit attention to particular values which are realisable by them. For example, the mere disposing of the human body and the eyesight so as to get a good view of a sunset is a simple form of artistic selection. The habit of art is the habit of enjoying vivid values. . . .

In regard to the aesthetic needs of civilised society the reactions of science have so far been unfortunate. Its materialistic basis has directed attention to *things* as opposed to values. The antithesis is a false one, if taken in a concrete sense. But it is valid at the abstract level of ordinary thought. This misplaced emphasis coalesced with the abstractions of political economy, which are in fact the abstractions in terms of which commercial affairs are carried on. Thus all thought concerned with social organisation expressed itself in terms of material things and of capital. Ultimate values were excluded. They were politely bowed to, and then handed over to the clergy to be kept for Sundays. A creed of competitive business morality was evolved, in some respects curiously high; but entirely devoid of consideration for the value of human life. The workmen were conceived as mere hands, drawn from the pool of labour. To God's question, men gave the answer of Cain—"Am I my brother's keeper?"; and they incurred Cain's guilt. This was the atmosphere in which the industrial revolution was accomplished in England, and to a large extent elsewere. The internal history of England during the last half century has been an endeavour slowly and painfully to undo the evils wrought in the first stage of the new epoch. It may be that civilisation will never recover from the bad climate which enveloped the introduction of machinery. This climate pervaded the whole commercial system of the progressive northern European races. It was partly the result of aesthetic errors of Protestantism and partly the result of scientific materialism, and partly the result of the natural greed of mankind, and partly the result of the abstractions of political economy. An illustration of my point is to be found in Macaulay's Essay criticising Southey's *Colloquies on Society*. It was written in 1830. Now Macaulay was a very favourable example of men living at that date, or at any date. He had genius; he was kind-hearted, honourable, and a reformer. This is the extract:—"We are told, that our age has invented atrocities beyond the imagination of our fathers; that society has been brought into a state compared with which extermination would be a blessing; and all because the dwellings of cotton-spinners are naked and rectangular. Mr. Southey has found out a way he tells us, in which the effects of manufacturers and agriculture may be compared. And what is this way? To stand on a hill, to look at a cottage and a factory, and to see which is the prettier."

Southey seems to have said many silly things in his book; but so far as this extract is concerned, he could make a good case for himself if he returned to earth after the lapse of nearly a century. The evils of the early industrial system are now a commonplace of knowledge. The point which I am insisting on is the stone-blind eye with which even the best men of that time regarded the importance of aesthetics in a nation's life. I do not believe that we have as yet nearly achieved the right estimate. A contributory cause, of substantial efficacy to produce this disastrous error, was the scientific creed that matter in motion is the one concrete reality in nature; so that aesthetic values form an adventitious, irrelevant addition.

There is another side to this picture of the possibilities of decadence. At the present moment a discussion is raging as to the future of civilisation in the novel circumstance of rapid scientific and technological advance. The evils of the future have been diagnosed in various ways, the loss of religious faith, the malignant use of material power, the degradation attending a differential birth rate favouring the lower types of humanity, the suppression of aesthetic creativeness. Without doubt, these are all evils, dangerous and threatening. But they are not new. From the dawn of history, mankind has always been losing its religious faith, has always suffered from the malignant use of material power, has always suffered from the infertility of its best intellectual types, has always witnessed the periodical decadence of art. In the reign of the Egyptian king, Tutankhamen, there was raging a desperate religious struggle between Modernists and Fundamentalists; the cave pictures exhibit a phase of delicate aesthetic achievement as superseded by a period of comparative vulgarity; the religious leaders, the great thinkers, the great poets and authors, the whole clerical caste in the Middle Ages, have been notably infertile; finally, if we attend to what actually has happened in the past, and disregard romantic visions of democracies, aristocracies, kings, generals, armies, and merchants, material power has generally been wielded with blindness, obstinacy and selfishness, often with brutal malignancy. And yet, mankind has progressed. Even if you take a tiny oasis of peculiar excellence, the type of modern man who would have most chance of happiness in ancient Greece at its best period is probably (as now) an average professional heavy-weight boxer, and not an average Greek scholar from Oxford or Germany. Indeed, the main use of the Oxford scholar would have been his capability of writing an ode in glorification of the boxer. Nothing does more harm in unnerving men for their duties in the present, than the attention devoted to the points of excellence in the past as compared with the average failure of the present day.

But after all, there have been real periods of decadence; and at the present time, as at other epochs, society is decaying, and there is need for preservative action. Professionals are not new to the world. But in the past, professionals have formed unprogressive castes. The point is that professionalism has now been mated with progress. The world is now faced with a self-evolving system, which it cannot stop. There are dangers and advantages in this situation. It is obvious that the gain in material power affords opportunity for social betterment. If mankind can rise to the occasion, there lies in front a golden age of beneficent creativeness. But material power in itself is ethically neutral. It can equally well work in the wrong direction. The problem is not how to produce great men, but how to produce great societies. The great society will put up the men for the occasions. The materialistic philosophy emphasised the given quantity of material, and thence derivatively the given nature of the environment. It thus operated most unfortunately upon the social conscience of mankind. For it directed almost exclusive attention to the aspect of struggle for existence. It is folly to look at the universe through rose-tinted spectacles. We must admit the struggle. The question is, who is to be eliminated. In so far as we are educators, we have clear ideas upon that point; for it settles the type to be produced and the practical ethics to be inculcated.

But during the last three generations, the exclusive direction of attention to this aspect of things has been a disaster of the first magnitude. The watchwords of the nineteenth century have been, struggle for existence, competition, class warfare, commercial antagonism between nations, military warfare. The struggle for existence has been construed into the gospel of hate. The full conclusion to be drawn from a philosophy of evolution is fortunately of a more balanced character. Successful organisms modify their environment. Those organisms are successful which modify their environments so as to assist each other. This law is exemplified in nature on a vast scale. For example, the North American Indians accepted their environment, with the result that a scanty population barely succeeded in maintaining themselves over the whole continent. The European races when they arrived in the same con-

tinent pursued an opposite policy. They at once cooperated in modifying their environment. The result is that a population more than
twenty times that of the Indian population now occupies the same
territory, and the continent is not yet full. Again, there are associations of different species which mutually cooperate. This differentiation of species is exhibited in the simplest physical entities, such
as the association between electrons and positive nuclei, and in the
whole realm of animate nature. The trees in a Brazilian forest depend upon the association of various species of organisms, each of
which is mutually dependent on the other species. A single tree by
itself is dependent upon all the adverse chances of shifting circumstances. The wind stunts it: the variations in temperature check
its foliage: the rains denude its soil: its leaves are blown away and
are lost for the purpose of fertilisation. You may obtain individual
specimens of fine trees either in exceptional circumstances, or where
human cultivation has intervened. But in nature the normal way in
which trees flourish is by their association in a forest. Each tree may
lose something of its individual perfection of growth, but they mutually assist each other in preserving the conditions for survival. The
soil is preserved and shaded; and the microbes necessary for its
fertility are neither scorched, nor frozen, nor washed away. A forest
is the triumph of the organisation of mutually dependent species.
Further a species of microbes which kills the forest, also exterminates
itself. Again the two sexes exhibit the same advantage of differentiation. In the history of the world, the prize has not gone to those
species which specialised in methods of violence, or even in defensive armour. In fact, nature began with producing animals en-
cased in hard shells for defense against the ills of life. It also
experimented in size. But smaller animals, without external armour,
warm-blooded, sensitive, and alert, have cleared these monsters off
the face of the earth. Also, the lions and tigers are not the successful
species. There is something in the ready use of force which defeats
its own object. Its main defect is that it bars cooperation. Every
organism requires an environment of friends, partly to shield it from
violent changes, and partly to supply it with its wants. The Gospel of
Force is incompatible with a social life. By *force*, I mean *antagonism* in its most general sense.

Almost equally dangerous is the Gospel of Uniformity. The differences between the nations and races of mankind are required to
preserve the conditions under which higher development is possible. One main factor in the upward trend of animal life has been
the power of wandering. Perhaps this is why the armour-plated
monsters fared badly. They could not wander. Animals wander into
new conditions. They have to adapt themselves or die. Mankind has

wandered from the trees to the plains, from the plains to the sea-coast, from climate to climate, from continent to continent, and from habit of life to habit of life. When man ceases to wander, he will cease to ascend in the scale of being. Physical wandering is still important, but greater still is the power of man's spiritual adventures— adventures of thought, adventures of passionate feeling, adventures of aesthetic experience. A diversification among human communities is essential for the provision of the incentive and material for the Odyssey of the human spirit. Other nations of different habits are not enemies: they are godsends. Men require of their neighbours something sufficiently akin to be understood, something sufficiently different to provoke attention, and something great enough to command admiration. We must not expect, however, all the virtues. We should even be satisfied if there is something odd enough to be interesting.

Modern science has imposed on humanity the necessity of wandering. Its progressive thought and its progressive technology make the transition through time, from generation to generation, a true migration into uncharted seas of adventure. The very benefit of wandering is that it is dangerous and needs skill to avert evils. We must expect, therefore, that the future will disclose dangers. It is the business of the future to be dangerous; and it is among the merits of science that it equips the future for its duties. The prosperous middle classes, who ruled the nineteenth century, placed an excessive value upon placidity of existence. They refused to face the necessities for social reform imposed by the new industrial system, and they are now refusing to face the necessities for intellectual reform imposed by the new knowledge. The middle class pessimism over the future of the world comes from a confusion between civilisation and security. In the immediate future there will be less security than in the immediate past, less stability. It must be admitted that there is a degree of instability which is inconsistent with civilisation. But, on the whole, the great ages have been unstable ages.

44. BERTRAND RUSSELL:
SCIENCE AND VALUES

Bertrand Russell, Third Earl Russell, was born in 1872 of one of Britain's leading aristocratic families. He was a grandson of the First Earl (Lord John Russell, 1792–1878), British statesman and advocate of liberal parliamentary reforms, who was a son of the Duke of Bedford and himself twice prime minister (1846–1852, 1865–1866). Bertrand Russell became in his younger years a leading mathematician and logician.

In the First World War he was active in the pacifist movement, dismissed as a Fellow of Trinity College in Cambridge University and imprisoned for his support of conscientious objectors. Since then, Bertrand Russell has continued in his double role as a propagandist for political-ethical causes and as a scientist and philosopher.

In the following essay on "Science and Values" Russell clearly envisages the hopes and dangers of the scientific age into which mankind has entered by the middle of the twentieth century. To counter the dangers, Russell insists, "a new moral outlook is called for in which submission to the powers of nature is replaced by respect for what is best in man. The dangers exist, but they are not inevitable, and hope for the future is at least as rational as fear."[32]

The impulse towards scientific construction is admirable when it does not thwart any of the major impulses that give value to human life, but when it is allowed to forbid all outlet to everything but itself it becomes a form of cruel tyranny. There is, I think, a real danger lest the world should become subject to a tyranny of this sort, and it is on this account that I have not shrunk from depicting the darker features of the world that scientific manipulation unchecked might wish to create.

Science in the course of the few centuries of its history has undergone an internal development which appears to be not yet completed. One may sum up this development as the passage from contemplation to manipulation. The love of knowledge to which the growth of science is due is itself the product of a twofold impulse. We may seek knowledge of an object because we love the object or because we wish to have power over it. The former impulse leads to the kind of knowledge that is contemplative, the latter to the kind that is practical. In the development of science the power impulse has increasingly prevailed over the love impulse. The power impulse is embodied in industrialism and in governmental technique. It is embodied also in the philosophies known as pragmatism and instrumentalism. Each of these philosophies holds, broadly

[32] Reprinted from *The Scientific Outlook* by Bertrand Russell by permission of W. W. Norton & Company, Inc. Copyright 1931, 1959 by Bertrand Russell.

speaking, that our beliefs about any object are true in so far as they enable us to manipulate it with advantage to ourselves. This is what may be called a governmental view of truth. Of truth so conceived science offers us a great deal; indeed there seems no limit to its possible triumphs. To the man who wishes to change his environment science offers astonishingly powerful tools, and if knowledge consists in the power to produce intended changes, then science gives knowledge in abundance.

But the desire for knowledge has another form, belonging to an entirely different set of emotions. The mystic, the lover, and the poet are also seekers after knowledge—not perhaps very successful seekers, but none the less worthy of respect on that account. In all forms of love we wish to have knowledge of what is loved, not for purposes of power, but for the ecstasy of contemplation. "In knowledge of God standeth our eternal life," but not because knowledge of God gives us power over Him. Wherever there is ecstasy or joy or delight derived from an object there is the desire to know that object—to know it not in the manipulative fashion that consists in turning it into something else, but to know it in the fashion of the beatific vision, because in itself and for itself it sheds happiness upon the lover. In sex love as in other forms of love the impulse to this kind of knowledge exists, unless the love is purely physical or practical. This may indeed be made the touchstone of any love that is valuable. Love which has value contains an impulse towards that kind of knowledge out of which the mystic union springs.

Science in its beginnings was due to men who were in love with the world. They perceived the beauty of the stars and the sea, of the winds and the mountains. Because they loved them their thoughts dwelt upon them, and they wished to understand them more intimately than a mere outward contemplation made possible. "The world," said Heraclitus, "is an ever-living fire, with measures kindling and measures going out." Heraclitus and the other Ionian philosophers, from whom came the first impulse to scientific knowledge, felt the strange beauty of the world almost like a madness in the blood. They were men of Titanic passionate intellect, and from the intensity of their intellectual passion the whole movement of the modern world has sprung. But step by step, as science has developed, the impulse of love which gave it birth has been increasingly thwarted, while the impulse of power, which was at first a mere camp-follower, has gradually usurped command in virtue of its unforeseen success. The lover of nature has been baffled, the tyrant over nature has been rewarded. As physics has developed, it has deprived us step by step of what we thought we knew concerning the intimate nature of the physical world. Colour and sound, light and shade, form and texture, belong no longer to that external nature that the Ionians sought as the bride of their devotion. All these things have been transferred from the beloved to the lover, and the beloved has become a skeleton of rattling bones, cold and dreadful, but perhaps a mere phantasm. The poor physicists, appalled at the desert that their formulae have revealed, call upon God to give them comfort, but God must share the ghostliness of His creation, and the answer that the physicists think they hear to their cry is only the frightened beating of their own hearts. Disappointed as the lover of nature, the man of science is becoming its tyrant. What matters it, says the practical man, whether the outer world exists or is a dream, provided I can make it behave as I wish? Thus science has more and more substituted power-knowledge for love-knowledge, and as this substitution becomes completed science tends more and more to become sadistic. The scientific society of the future as we have been imagining it is one in which the power impulse has completely overwhelmed the impulse of love, and this is the psychological source of the cruelties which it is in danger of exhibiting.

Science, which began as the pursuit of truth, is becoming incompatible with veracity, since complete veracity tends more and more to complete scientific scepticism. When science is considered contemplatively, not practically, we find that what we believe, we believe owing to animal faith, and it is only our disbeliefs that are due to science. When, on the other hand, science is considered as a technique for the transformation of ourselves and our environment, it is found to give us a power quite independent of its metaphysical validity. But we can only wield this power by ceasing to ask ourselves metaphysical questions as to the nature of reality. Yet these questions are the evidence of a lover's attitude towards the world. Thus it is only in so far as we renounce the world as its lovers that we can conquer it as its technicians. But this division in the soul is fatal to what is best in man. As soon as the failure of science considered as metaphysics is realized, the power conferred by science as a technique is only obtainable by something analogous to the worship of Satan, that is to say, by the renunciation of love.

This is the fundamental reason why the prospect of a scientific society must be viewed with apprehension. The scientific society in its pure form, which is what we have been trying to depict, is incompatible with the pursuit of truth, with love, with art, with spontaneous delight, with every ideal that men have hitherto cherished, with the sole exception of ascetic renunciation. It is not knowledge that is the source of these dangers. Knowledge is good and ignorance is evil: to this principle the lover of the world can admit no exception. Nor is it power in and for itself that is the source of danger. What is dangerous is power wielded for the sake of power, not power wielded for the sake of genuine good. The leaders of the modern world are drunk with power: the fact that they can do something that no one previously thought it possible to do is to them a sufficient reason for doing it. Power is not one of the ends of life, but merely a means to other ends, and until men remember the ends that power should subserve, science will not do what it might to minister to the good life. But what then are the ends of life, the reader will say. I do not think that one man has a right to legislate for another on this matter. For each individual the ends of life are those things which he deeply desires, and which if they existed would give him peace. Or, if it be thought that peace is too much to ask this side of the grave, let us say that the end of life should give delight or joy or ecstasy. In the conscious desires of the man who seeks power for its own sake there is something dusty: when he has it he wants only more power, and does not find rest in contemplation of what he has. The lover, the poet and the mystic find a fuller satisfaction than the seeker after power can ever know, since they can rest in the object of their love, whereas the seeker after power must be perpetually engaged in some fresh manipulation if he is not to suffer from a sense of emptiness. I think therefore that the satisfactions of the lover, using that word in its broadest sense, exceed the satisfactions of the tyrant, and deserve a higher place among the ends of life. When I come to die I shall not feel that I have lived in vain. I have seen the earth turn red at evening, the dew sparkling in the morning, and the snow shining under a frosty sun; I have smelt rain after drought, and have heard the stormy Atlantic beat upon the granite shores of Cornwall. Science may bestow these and other joys upon more people than could otherwise enjoy them. If so, its power will be wisely used. But when it takes out of life the moments to which life owes its value, science will not deserve admiration, however cleverly and however elaborately it may lead men along the road to despair. The sphere of values lies outside science, except in so far as science consists in the pursuit of knowledge. Science as the pursuit of power must not obtrude upon the sphere of values, and scientific technique, if it is to enrich human life, must not outweigh the ends which it should serve.

The number of men who determine the character of an age is small. Columbus, Luther and Charles V dominated the sixteenth century; Galileo and Descartes governed the seventeenth. The important men in the age that is just ended are Edison, Rockefeller, Lenin, and Sun Yat-sen. With the exception of Sun Yat-sen these were men devoid of culture, contemptuous of the past, self-confident and ruthless. Traditional wisdom had no place in their thoughts and feelings; mechanism and organisation were what interested them. A different education might have made all these men quite different. Edison might in his youth have acquired a knowledge of history and poetry and art; Rockefeller might have been taught how he had been anticipated by Crœsus and Crassus; Lenin, instead of having hatred implanted in him by the execution of his brother during his student days, might have made himself acquainted with the rise of Islam and the development of Puritanism from piety to plutocracy. By means of such an education some little leaven of doubt might have entered the souls of these great men. Given a little doubt their achievement would perhaps have been less in volume, but much greater in value.

Our world has a heritage of culture and beauty, but unfortunately we have been handing on this heritage only to the less active and important members of each generation. The government of the world, by which I do not mean its ministerial posts but its key positions of power, has been allowed to fall into the hands of men ignorant of the past, without tenderness towards what is traditional, without understanding what they are destroying. There is no essential reason why this should be the case. To prevent it is an educational problem, and not a very difficult one. Men in the past were often parochial in space, but the dominant men of our age are parochial in time. They feel for the past a contempt that it does not deserve, and for the present a respect that it deserves still less. The copy book maxims of a former age have become outworn, but a new set of copy book maxims is required. First among these I should put: "It is better to do a little good than much harm." To give content to this maxim it would of course be necessary to instil some sense of what is good. Few men in the present day, for example, can be induced to believe that there is no inherent excellence in rapid locomotion. To climb from Hell to Heaven is good, though it be a slow, a laborious process; to fall from Heaven to Hell is bad, even though it be done with the speed of Milton's Satan. Nor can it be said that a mere increase in the production of material commodities is in itself a thing of great value. To prevent extreme poverty is important, but to add to the possessions of those who already have too much is a worthless waste of effort. To prevent crime may be necessary, but to invent new crimes in order that the police may show skill in preventing them is less admirable. The new powers that science has given to man can only be wielded safely by those who, whether through the study of history or through their own experience of life, have acquired some reverence for human feelings and some tenderness towards the emotions that give colour to the daily existence of men and women. I do not mean to deny that scientific technique may in time build an artificial world in every way preferable to that in which men have hitherto lived, but I do say that if this is to be done it must be done tentatively and with a realization that the purpose of government is not merely to afford pleasure to those who govern, but to make life tolerable for those who are governed. Scientific technique must no longer be allowed to form the whole culture of the holders of power, and it must become an essential part of men's ethical outlook to realize that the will alone cannot make a good life. Knowing and feeling are equally essential ingredients both in the life of the individual and in that of the community. Knowledge, if it is wide and intimate, brings with it a realization of distant times and places, an awareness that the individual is not omnipotent or all-important, and a perspective in which values are seen more clearly than by those to whom a distant view is impossible. Even more important than knowledge is the life of the emotions. A world without delight and without affection is a world destitute of value. These things the scientific manipulator must remember and if he does his manipulation may be wholly beneficial. All that is needed is that men should not be so intoxicated by new power as to forget the truths that were familiar to every previous generation. Not all wisdom is new, nor is all folly out of date.

Man has been disciplined hitherto by his subjection to nature. Having emancipated himself from this subjection, he is showing something of the defects of a slave-turned-master. A new moral outlook is called for in which submission to the powers of nature is replaced by respect for what is best in man. It is where this respect is lacking that scientific technique is dangerous. So long as it is present, science, having delivered man from bondage to nature, can proceed to deliver him from bondage to the slavish part of himself. The dangers exist, but they are not inevitable, and hope for the future is at least as rational as fear.

45. *THE UNIVERSAL DECLARATION OF THE RIGHTS OF MAN*

This *declaration* was accepted by the General Assembly of the United Nations on December 10, 1948 by unanimous vote, the six members of the Soviet bloc, Saudi Arabia and the Union of South Africa abstained. The declaration expresses the Western liberal, not the totalitarian or Leninist, point of view. It is a direct descendant of the Bill of Rights, an English parliamentary enactment of 1689 which marked the Glorious Revolution of that year and has been ranked as one of the fundamental documents in the growth of English and (indirectly) human liberty which began with the Magna Charta and the Petition of Rights. The Bill of Rights protected, above all, the individual from governmental encroachments and established the freedom of discussion in Parliament. It became the model for similar bills of rights in the former Anglo-American colonies, first in 1776 in Virginia and finally in the first ten amendments to the Constitution of the United States in 1789. These bills of rights in turn furnished the model for the French Declaration of the Rights of Man and the Citizen (August 27, 1789), which in turn influenced similar declarations in later European constitutions. The theory underlying these declarations was set forth by the English philosopher John Locke (1632–1704) in his *Second Treatise of Government* (1690). His theory forms the foundation of the political thought and traditions common to the British and North American peoples. The Universal Declaration adopted in 1948 corresponds to the new universal concept of the United Nations. It follows here in its entirety.[33]

PREAMBLE. Whereas recognition of the inherent dignity and of the equal and inalienable rights of all members of the human family is the foundation of freedom, justice and peace in the world,

Whereas disregard and contempt for human rights have resulted in barbarous acts which have outraged the conscience of mankind, and the advent of a world in which human beings shall enjoy freedom of speech and belief and freedom from fear and want has been proclaimed as the highest aspiration of the common people,

Whereas it is essential, if man is not compelled to have recourse, as a last resort, to rebellion against tyranny and oppression, that human rights should be protected by the rule of law,

Whereas it is essential to promote the development of friendly relations between nations,

Whereas the people of the United Nations have in the Charter reaffirmed their faith in fundamental human rights, in the dignity and worth of the human person and in the equal rights of men and women and have determined to promote social progress and better standards of life in larger freedom,

Whereas Member States have pledged themselves to achieve, in cooperation with the United Nations, the promotion of universal

[33] United Nations, General Assembly, *Official Records of the Third Session.*

respect for and observance of human rights and fundamental freedoms,

Whereas a common understanding of these rights and freedoms is of the greatest importance for the full realization of this pledge,

Now, therefore,

The General Assembly

Proclaims this Universal Declaration of Human Rights, as a common standard of achievement for all peoples and all nations, to the end that every individual and every organ of society, keeping this Declaration constantly in mind, shall strive by teaching and education to promote respect for these rights and freedoms and by progressive measures, national and international, to secure their universal and effective recognition and observance, both among the peoples of Member States themselves and among the peoples of territories under their jurisdiction.

ARTICLE 1.   All human beings are born free and equal in dignity and rights. They are endowed with reason and conscience and should act towards one another in a spirit of brotherhood.

ARTICLE 2.   Everyone is entitled to all the rights and freedoms set forth in this Declaration, without distinction of any kind, such as race, colour, sex, language, religion, political or other opinion, national or social origin, property, birth or other status.

Furthermore, no distinction shall be made on the basis of the political, jurisdictional or international status of the country or territory to which a person belongs, whether it be independent, trust, non-self-governing or under any other limitation of sovereignty.

ARTICLE 3.   Everyone has the right to life, liberty and the security of person.

ARTICLE 4.   No one shall be held in slavery or servitude; slavery and the slave trade shall be prohibited in all their forms.

ARTICLE 5.   No one shall be subjected to torture or to cruel, inhuman or degrading treatment or punishment.

ARTICLE 6.   Everyone has the right to recognition everywhere as a person before the law.

ARTICLE 7.   All are equal before the law and are entitled without any discrimination to equal protection of the law. All are entitled to equal protection against any discrimination in violation of this Declaration and against any incitement to such discrimination.

ARTICLE 8.   Everyone has the right to an effective remedy by the competent national tribunals for acts violating the fundamental rights granted him by the constitution or by law.

ARTICLE 9.   No one shall be subjected to arbitrary arrest, detention or exile.

ARTICLE 10.   Everyone is entitled in full equality to a fair and public hearing by an independent and impartial tribunal, in the determination of his rights and obligations and of any criminal charge against him.

ARTICLE 11. 1. Everyone charged with a penal offense has the right to be presumed innocent until proved guilty according to law in a public trial at which he has had all the guarantees necessary for his defence.

2. No one shall be held guilty of any penal offence on account of any act or omission which did not constitute a penal offence, under national or international law, at the time when it was committed. Nor shall a heavier penalty be imposed than the one that was applicable at the time the penal offence was committed.

ARTICLE 12. No one shall be subjected to arbitrary interference with his privacy, family, home or correspondence, nor to attacks upon his honour and reputation. Everyone has the right to the protection of the law against such interference or attacks.

ARTICLE 13. 1. Everyone has the right to freedom of movement and residence within the borders of each State.

2. Everyone has the right to leave any country including his own, and to return to his country.

ARTICLE 14. 1. Everyone has the right to seek and to enjoy in other countries asylum from persecution.

2. This right may not be invoked in the case of prosecutions genuinely arising from non-political crimes or from acts contrary to the purposes and principles of the United Nations.

ARTICLE 15. 1. Everyone has the right to a nationality.

2. No one shall be arbitrarily deprived of his nationality nor denied the right to change his nationality.

ARTICLE 16. 1. Men and women of full age, without any limitation due to race, nationality or religion, have the right to marry and to found a family. They are entitled to equal rights as to marriage, during marriage and at its dissolution.

2. Marriage shall be entered into only with the free and full consent of the intending spouses.

3. The family is the natural and fundamental group unit of society and is entitled to protection by society and the State.

ARTICLE 17. 1. Everyone has the right to own property alone as well as in association with others.

2. No one shall be arbitrarily deprived of his property.

ARTICLE 18. Everyone has the right to freedom of thought, conscience and religion; this right includes freedom to change his religion or belief, and freedom, either alone or in community with others and in public or private, to manifest his religion or belief in teaching, practice, worship and observance.

ARTICLE 19. Everyone has the right to freedom of opinion and expression; this right includes freedom to hold opinions without interference and to seek, receive and impart information and ideas through any media and regardless of frontiers.

ARTICLE 20. 1. Everyone has the right to freedom of peaceful assembly and association.

2. No one may be compelled to belong to an association.

ARTICLE 21. 1. Everyone has the right to take part in the government of his country, directly or through freely chosen representatives.

2. Everyone has the right to equal access to public service in his country.

3. The will of the people shall be the basis of the authority of government; this will shall be expressed in periodic and genuine elections which shall be by universal and equal suffrage and shall be held by secret vote or by equivalent free voting procedures.

ARTICLE 22. Everyone, as a member of society, has the right to social security and is entitled to realization, through national effort and international cooperation and in accordance with the organization and resources of each State, of the economic, social and cultural rights indispensable for his dignity and the free development of his personality.

ARTICLE 23. 1. Everyone has the right to work, to free choice of employment, to just and favourable conditions of work and to protection against unemployment.

2. Everyone, without any discrimination, has the right to equal pay for equal work.

3. Everyone who works has the right to just and favourable remuneration ensuring for himself and his family an existence worthy of human dignity, and supplemented, if necessary, by other means of social protection.

4. Everyone has the right to form and to join trade unions for the protection of his interests.

ARTICLE 24. Everyone has the right to rest and leisure, including reasonable limitation of working hours and periodic holidays with pay.

ARTICLE 25. 1. Everyone has the right to a standard of living adequate for the health and well-being of himself and of his family, including food, clothing, housing and medical care and necessary social services, and the right to security in the event of unemployment, sickness, disability, widowhood, old age or other lack of livelihood in circumstances beyond his control.

2. Motherhood and childhood are entitled to special care and assistance. All children, whether born in or out of wedlock, shall enjoy the same social protection.

ARTICLE 26. 1. Everyone has the right to education. Education shall be free, at least in the elementary and fundamental stages.

Elementary education shall be compulsory. Technical and professional education shall be made generally available and higher education shall be equally accessible to all on the basis of merit.

2. Education shall be directed to the full development of the human personality and to the strengthening of respect for human rights and fundamental freedoms. It shall promote understanding, tolerance and friendship among all nations, racial or religious groups, and shall further the activities of the United Nations for the maintenance of peace.

3. Parents have a prior right to choose the kind of education that shall be given to their children.

ARTICLE 27. 1. Everyone has the right freely to participate in the cultural life of the community, to enjoy the arts and to share in scientific advancement and its benefits.

2. Everyone has the right to the protection of the moral and material interests resulting from any scientific, literary or artistic production of which he is the author.

ARTICLE 28. Everyone is entitled to a social and international order in which the rights and freedoms set forth in this Declaration can be fully realized.

ARTICLE 29. 1. Everyone has duties to the community in which alone the free and full development of his personality is possible.

2. In the exercise of his rights and freedoms, everyone shall be subject only to such limitations as are determined by law solely for the purpose of securing due recognition and respect for the rights and freedoms of others and of meeting the just requirements of morality, public order and the general welfare in a democratic society.

3. These rights and freedoms may in no case be exercised contrary to the purposes and principles of the United Nations.

ARTICLE 30. Nothing in this Declaration may be interpreted as implying for any State, group or person any right to engage in any activity or to perform any act aimed at the destruction of any of the rights and freedoms set forth herein.

46. ARNOLD J. TOYNBEE: *WORLD ORDER AND WORLD CIVILIZATION*

In 1848 Marx recognized that the industrial civilization of the Western middle classes was destined to draw all, even the most remote and backward peoples, into its orbit, and to create a world-wide civilization after its own image. Though most of

Marx's confident predictions about the capitalist-democratic society, such as that of the growing impoverishment of the people and the concentration of wealth into fewer and fewer hands, proved wrong, his prediction about the growth of a world community of interdependent and communicating peoples came true in the 1960's. With this development came the problems of an intelligible pattern of world history, of the establishment of a world order, and of the validity of modern Western civilization. Spengler tried to answer the questions involved in a strictly deterministic "closed" way and with a pessimistic rejection of modern civilization. He believed in the inevitability of great class and racial wars. Twenty years later the English scholar Arnold J. Toynbee (born 1889) gave his answer. He rejected a strict determinism and accepted history as an open road. He viewed the future of the modern West with cautious and reasonable confidence and believed in the possibility of a peaceful world order.

Toynbee, originally a student of ancient Greece, was from 1925 to 1955 Director of Studies at the Royal Institute of International Affairs in London. His *A Study of History* appeared in ten volumes between 1934 and 1954. Its great merit rests on its universal, or ecumenical, approach to history. It is the first major work abandoning a Western-centered view in accordance with the first global era of history, which is being realized in the 1960's as a result of the spread of modern Western civilization.

In a supplementary volume called *Reconsiderations* (1961) Toynbee reviewed and revised his theories in the light of comments and criticisms made by a number of scholars since the first publication of his work. He has clarified his conclusions about the probable future course of mankind and the character and role of modern Western civilization in influencing this course. The following excerpts are reprinted from chapters XVI, "The History and Prospects of the West," and XIX, "The Next Ledge," of *"Reconsiderations."*[34]

Unlike the histories of a majority of the civilizations known to us, the history of the West is today still an unfinished story. It is

[34] *A Study of History,* vol. XII, *Reconsiderations,* by Arnold J. Toynbee. © 1961 by Oxford University Press, and reprinted by permission.

therefore hazardous to try to forecast its prospects, even in the form of suggesting a number of alternative possibilities. . . .

It is true that I think that a pattern of breakdown and disintegration, common to the histories of a number of past civilizations, can be detected when we make a comparative study of them. But I do not believe that this pattern was predetermined or inevitable in any single past case; and therefore, *à fortiori*, I do not believe that it can be projected into a prediction about the future of a civilization that is still a going concern. I do not believe, as Spengler believes, that there is a fixed pattern to which the history of every civilization is bound to conform. My unwillingness to predict that the Western Civilization will go the way that a number of its predecessors have gone is a consistent application of my conviction that the course of human affairs is not predetermined. It is not a sentimental refusal to apply to the prospects of my own civilization some pattern of breakdown and disintegration that I unavowedly believe to be every civilization's inevitable fate. I have no such cast-iron pattern in my bag of intellectual tools. . . .

By the end of the Second World War the expansion of the Western World had gone to extremes on the technological planes of communications and warfare. On these planes the Western system had become, by then, coextensive with the whole habitable and traversable surface of the planet. By the same date a new weapon had been invented that, for the first time in Western history, made it possible for a Western power to unite by force even a Western World that had now become coextensive with the World itself. Since, however, this new weapon was the annihilating atomic one, the condition for its possible use for the old-fashioned purpose of eliminating all competing powers but one was that the user should not merely possess the new weapon but should have a monopoly of it. This condition was fulfilled during the years 1945–9. During those years the atomic weapon was possessed by the United States, and by it alone. If either Germany or Japan had emerged from the Second World War victorious, with the atomic weapon in her hands and with a monopoly of it, we may guess that she would have taken advantage of this unique military opportunity and would have established, by the traditional military method, a universal state that, this time, would have been literally world-wide. The people and administration of the United States did not do this and were not tempted to do it. They would have been horrified if the project had been suggested to them by some American Themistocles. The possibility passed away when the Soviet Union, in its turn, acquired the atomic weapon in 1949. Since then, this weapon has ceased to be a practicable means of imposing political unity on mankind; it has become, instead, a threat to the survival of civilization, of the human race, and of life itself.

Thus the apparent elimination of the possibility of imposing unity by force has made it a matter of life and death for mankind to achieve unity by agreement. The year 1949 opened a new era in human history. Before that date the survival of the human race had been assured ever since the time, part way through the Paleolithic Age, when mankind had won a decisive and unchallengeable ascendancy over all other forms of life on this planet as well as over inanimate nature. Between that time and the year 1949 Man's crimes and follies could and did wreck civilizations and bring unnecessary and undeserved sufferings upon countless numbers of men, women, and children. But the worst that Man could do with his pre-atomic technology was not enough to enable him to destroy his own race. Genocide, at least, was beyond his power until the atomic weapon had been invented and had been acquired by more states than one in a society that was still partitioned politically among a number of local states and in an age in which states were still in the habit of going to war with each other.

The unprecedented situation arising from the acquisition of the atomic weapon by the Soviet Union as well as by the United States does seem to have made an impression on the minds and imaginations of governments as well as peoples. Between 1949 and 1961 a number of international incidents and crises that, in the past, would have been likely to lead to war were surmounted without a breach of the peace; and the local wars that did flare up in Korea and Vietnam were brought to an end by negotiated settlements on terms that were distasteful to both parties. This indicates that, under the threat of atomic warfare, both the governments and the peoples had become more prudent in their conduct of their relations with their adversaries, and had schooled themselves to exercise an unaccustomed self-restraint. This, in turn, made the continuance of "co-existence" seem more probable; and mere coexistence, accepted sullenly on both sides as being the less bad of two bad alternatives, was a boon that was not to be despised. It promised to give mankind at least a temporary reprieve; and, in a bad situation, the mere passage of time may bring relief, since human affairs are always on the move and can never be frozen into fixity.

Time could bring relief by altering the balance of power and by shifting people's attention and emotions into new channels. A continuing increase in China's power, for instance, might one day make the Soviet Union and the United States huddle together for mutual protection. (In the recent past they had been drawn together by the menace, to both of them, of the lesser power of

Japan.) A continuing rise in West Germany's power might make Czechoslovakia and Poland come to feel that Russia's hegemony was not too high a premium to pay for insurance against the risk of a German *revanche*. West Germany's recovery might also make Russia's existence seem a welcome political and military asset to West European countries that, within living memory, had been victims of German aggression in two world wars. In fact, it seemed probable that, under a continuing regime of coexistence, old feuds would gradually have their edge taken off them by new anxieties, new quarrels, and new enthusiasms. There were encouraging precedents in the history of the coexistence of Protestantism with Catholicism and of Islam with Christianity since the dates at which the Catholic-Protestant and the Christian-Muslim Wars of Religion had petered out. These wars had come to an end because it had become evident to both belligerent parties simultaneously that it was beyond the power of either of them to wipe its adversary off the map. After this recognition, on both sides, of the inevitability of coexistence, the old quarrel between them had gradually become less acrimonious and less absorbing. . . .

By the middle decades of the twentieth century the Western Society had passed through a number of revolutions on a number of different planes since it had emerged out of the social and cultural interregnum that had followed the preceding Hellenic Civilization's dissolution. Among all these successive Western revolutions the spiritual revolution during the closing decades of the seventeenth century had been perhaps the most decisive and the most significant up to date. At any rate, this was certainly the revolution that, in the twentieth century, was exerting the greatest continuing influence, not only on the West itself, but on the rest of the World as well. The seventeenth-century revolution had given the Western Civilization a new form, and, above all, a new spirit, which for the first time in history, had made the heirs of non-Western civilizations willing to embrace the Western Civilization in exchange for their ancestral heritages. The seventeenth-century Western Revolution had thus opened the way for a cultural development of world-wide importance: the Westernization of the World. This, in turn, had opened the way for the transformation of the post-seventeenth-century Western Civilization into a common civilization for the whole human race. . . .

As against my emphasis on the original negativeness of the seventeenth-century Western revolution, Hans Kohn emphasizes the positiveness of the virtues that it developed. On this point I agree with Kohn. I ought to have done more justice to this revolution's positive side. In the light of Kohn's critique I will try to make amends now. Toleration spelled freedom of conscience, and the new respect for this spelled a respect for the rights and dignity of human beings. This brought with it a new standard of social responsibility, social justice, and humane feeling. Noble monuments of this new ideal of human fraternity have been the abolition of the slave-trade and of slavery itself and the legislation for the protection of the poor and weak that has eventually been consolidated in "the welfare state." This has had the beneficent positive effect of spreading the amenities of civilization more widely, and that has been made practically possible by the increase in wealth resulting from progress in technology. But Kohn is maintaining that there is something more in the modern Western Civilization than just its technological prowess. The West's technological triumphs have been "a by-product of the Western freedom of inquiry and the Western sense of personal initiative. They are unthinkable without respect for individual liberty and tolerance of diversity." Non-Westerners have not always been alive to the spiritual causes of the West's technological success.

Moreover, this success has had an intellectual as well as a moral cause. Intellectually, the progress of Western technology has been due to the application of science to it. And the modern Western cultivation of science, which had started negatively as a diversion from the cult of theology, bred a heightened sense of curiosity and a new spirit of critical inquiry. Neither the Renaissance nor the Reformation had liberated Western minds from their medieval subservience to external authority. The Renaissance had abrogated the intellectual authority of the Christian religion in favour of that of the Greek and Latin classics. The Reformation had substituted the intellectual authority of the text of the Bible and the ecclesiastical authority of the local secular governments (*cuius regio, eius religio*) for the authority of the Catholic Church. Perhaps the most fundamental and radical feature of the seventeenth-century Western revolution was that now, for the first time, Western minds dared consciously and deliberately to think for themselves. In the Battle of the Ancients and Moderns, Westerners made a declaration of their independence from their Hellenic cultural heritage; and this time they did not exchange one mental servitude for another, as their forefathers had done in the Renaissance. Truly "there is in modern Western Civilization a vital spiritual force which, in the nineteenth and twentieth centuries, has helped to revitalise other civilizations and to enhance their self-awareness." . . .

It is true that, even in the religious field, the achievement of the modern phase of the Western Civilization has been respectable. It can truly be said that Westerners have never before come so near to acting up to Christian standards of moral conduct as they have in this modern age in which the official tenets of Christianity have been progressively losing their hold on the intellectual allegiance of an ever-growing minority of educated Western men and women. All the same, a quarter of a millennium of religious toleration has, after all, not availed to rehabilitate the West's ancestral religion from the moral discredit brought upon it by the Wars of Religion; and the corrosive effects of this moral discredit have been reinforced by the intellectual scepticism that the triumph of the scientific outlook has brought with it. The tenets of Christianity, and those of other living higher religions too, are incompatible, in their traditional form, with the scientific vision of the nature of the Universe. It seems improbable that, in this traditional form, they can ever recapture their former hold on hearts and minds; and, if this were possible, surely it would not be desirable.

The rising gale of scientific discovery has blown away the chaff of traditional religion, and in doing this it has done mankind a service; but it has blown so hard that it has blown away the grain with the husk; and this has been a disservice, since neither science nor the ideologies have grain of their own to offer as a substitute. Their horizons, unlike those of the higher religions, fall far short of the bounds (if there are bounds) of the Universe, and what lies hidden beyond these restricted horizons is the heart of this mysterious and formidable Universe—the very part of it that is of the greatest moment to human beings. Science's horizon is limited by the bounds of Nature, the ideologies' horizon by the bounds of human social life, but the human soul's range cannot be confined within either of these limits. Man is a bread-eating (and rice-eating) social animal; but he is also something more. He is a person, endowed with a conscience and a will, as well as with a self-conscious intellect. This spiritual endowment of his condemns him to a life-long struggle to reconcile himself with the Universe into which he has been born. His inborn instinct is to try to make the Universe revolve round himself; his spiritual task in life is to overcome his self-centredness in order to put himself in harmony with the absolute spiritual Reality that is the true centre of everything in the phenomenal world. This "flight of the alone to the alone" is the goal of Man's endeavours. His yearning to reach this goal is the only motive strong enough to break through the barrier of self-centredness that stands in the way. Neither science nor the ideologies have anything to say about this spiritual crux. On the other hand, all the higher religions and philosophies are concerned with it. Their visions may be partly delusions; their counsels may be partly misguided; their very concern with the soul's ultimate problem and task may be almost smothered under a heap of irrelevant accretions: ritual, observances, social regulations, astronomical theories, and what not. Yet in spite of all their manifest weaknesses the higher religions are the only ways of life, known to Man so far, that do recognise what is the soul's true problem and true quest, and do offer Man some guidance for reaching his spiritual goal.

This means that, however grievously the trustees of the historic higher religions may have abused these religions' mandate, the mandate itself has not been forfeited. It cannot be forfeited unless and until mankind is presented with some new ways of life that offer to human souls more effective spiritual help than the historic higher religions can give them. Kohn is unwilling to concede that the Western Civilization is now in decline and that a return to religion is the remedy for this. On this my comment would be that these two theses, both of which Kohn rejects, are not interdependent. The Western Civilization may or may not be in decline in our time; contemporary Westerners are not in a position to diagnose their own civilization's prospects. But, whatever this particular civilization's present prospects may be, a recovery of the essence of religion, if this has been lost, is needed at all times and in all social situations. It is needed because human beings cannot live without it. In order to recover the essence we have to distinguish it and to disengage it from non-essential accretions. This is a task that we undertake at our peril. It is also a task that we dare not shirk on that account. To shirk it is the one course that is undoubtedly more dangerous than to attempt to carry it out. This sifting is a task that can never be accomplished once for all. Each successive generation has to repeat the attempt on its own account. In setting our hand to this perennial human task in our day, we can find some light in modern science; but this glimmer is faint, and may be misleading. Like our predecessors, we have to work in the twilight. We should be fortunate if our groupings were to lead us to the Buddha's approach to Nirvana or to Deutero-Isaiah's vision of the One True God. . . .

One of the first steps on the road is to acquire some sense of responsibility and to act on this by restraining one's own self-centered impulses. All sane adult human beings are responsible-minded to some minimum degree. Indeed, this is one of the definitions of what sanity means. One field in which ordinary human beings in the mass have managed to behave more or less responsibly is the handling of tools. In making his tools progressively more effective, Man has also made the misuse of them progressively more dangerous. In harnessing atomic energy he has now acquired a tool which is so potent that, if used as a weapon, it might destroy, not merely a hostile army or people or merely the users themselves, but the whole human race. This new powers has challenged the holders of it not to misuse it; and, since the dropping of the bombs on Japan in 1945, there have been indications that the holders of atomic power have been conscious of the new and awful responsibility that their possession of this power entails. The invention of the atomic weapon has made future resort to war a crime against the human race. And it is noteworthy that, since the end of the Second World War, the World's most powerful nations and governments have shown an uncustomary self-restraint on some critical occasions. They have given priority to their sense of responsibility for avoiding a world-war that would be fought, this time, with atomic weapons, and they have subordinated, to this paramount concern, their national *amour propre* and ambitions and even their ideological convictions. . . .

If the first step on Man's road towards sainthood is the renunciation of Man's traditional role of being his brother's murderer, the second step would be an acceptance of Man's new role of being his brother's keeper; and, happily, this sense of responsibility for the positive welfare of Man's fellow human beings has already declared itself. It is, indeed, one of the fruits of the seventeenth-century Western spiritual revolution. We have noticed, in another context, that, in the post-seventeenth-century Western World, the progressive recession of belief in Christianity's traditional doctrines has been accompanied by a progressive advance in the practice of Christianity's moral precepts; and that, although this advance has been opposed, in the West itself, by the reactionary ideologies that have raised their heads there in our generation, the ideals of Howard and Wilberforce have, so far, not been driven off the field by the counter-ideals of Mussolini and Hitler, but have, on the contrary, been disseminated, in company with other elements of the modern Western Civilization, among the non-Western majority of the human race. As landmarks in the advance of this modern humanitarianism, we may single out the abolition of the slave-trade and of slavery itself, the abolition of barbarous forms of punishment, the humanization of the treatment of prisoners and lunatics, the establishment of old-age pensions and national health services, and, in general, the narrowing of the gulf between a poor majority's and a rich minority's conditions of life. This advance towards greater social justice through an increase in human kindness has been taking place in two fields simultaneously: as between different classes in a single country and also as between different countries in a world that is now in process of being unified morally and socially as well as technologically and militarily. The relatively rich minority of the human race has now recognized that it has an obligation to make material sacrifices in order to assist the relatively poor majority to raise its standard of living on both the material and the spiritual plane. Peoples that are still exercising political control over other peoples have now come, thanks to an American lead, to expect to pay for this political privilege instead of any longer expecting to draw the traditional profits of empire.

These practical steps towards the vindication of fundamental and universal human rights leave us still far away from the achievement of a communion of saints. Yet this conscious and deliberate advance towards brotherhood in a community embracing the whole human race is surely even farther removed from the involuntary sociality of the bee-hive and the ant-heap.